THE TOWNSEND LECTURES

The Department of Classics at Cornell University is fortunate to have at its disposal the Prescott W. Townsend Fund – established by Mr. Townsend's widow, Daphne Townsend, in 1982. Since 1985, income from the fund has been used to support the annual visit of a distinguished scholar in the field of classics. Each visiting scholar delivers a series of lectures, which, revised for book publication, are published by Cornell University Press in Cornell Studies in Classical Philology.

During the semester of their residence, Townsend lecturers effectively become members of the Cornell Department of Classics and teach a course to Cornell students as well as deliver the lectures.

The Townsend Lectures bring to Cornell University, and to Cornell University Press, scholars of international reputation who are in the forefront of current classical research and whose work represents the kind of close reading of texts that has become associated with current literary discourse, or reflects broad interdisciplinary concerns, or both.

SOCRATES,
Ironist and Moral Philosopher

SOCRATES,

Ironist and Moral Philosopher

GREGORY VLASTOS

CORNELL UNIVERSITY PRESS

Ithaca, New York

First published 1991 by Cornell University Press.
Second printing 1991.
First printing, Cornell Paperbacks, 1991.
Third printing 1992.

Library of Congress Cataloging-in-Publication Data
Vlastos, Gregory.
Socrates, ironist and moral philosopher / Gregory Vlastos.
p.   cm.–(Cornell studies in classical philology: v. 50.
The Townsend lectures)
Includes bibliographical references and indexes.
ISBN 0-8014-2551-4 (cloth).–ISBN 0-8014-9787-6 (paper)
1. Socrates. I. Title. II. Title: Socrates, ironist and moral philosopher.
III. Series: Cornell studies in classical philology: v. 50. IV. Series: Cornell
studies in classical philology. Townsend lectures.
B317. V56 1991b
183'. 2–dc20   90-37095

Printed in the United States of America

I dedicate this book to colleagues and students whose partnership has shaped my search:

Berkeley (1979–87)
Cambridge (1983–4)
Cornell (1986)
St. Andrews (1981)
Toronto (1978)

CONTENTS

ADDITIONAL NOTES

SOCRATES,
Ironist and Moral Philosopher

INTRODUCTION:
HOW THIS BOOK CAME TO BE

Socrates' "strangeness"[1] is the keynote of Alcibiades' speech about him in the *Symposium*. The talk starts on that note (215A); and reverts to it near the end:

Such is his strangeness that you will search and search among those living now and among men of the past, and never come close to what he is himself and to the things he says. (221D)

This book is for readers of Plato's earlier dialogues[2] who have felt this strangeness, have asked themselves what to make of it, have pondered answers to its enigmas, and are willing to work their way through yet another. What I offer should not distract them from their encounter with the Socrates who lives in Plato's text. It should take them back there for a closer look.

The book has been a long time in the making. It started with a non-start. A stroke of luck in 1953 had assured me of a year entirely free from teaching. I had gone to the Institute for Advanced Study at Princeton to work on Plato's philosophy, uncommitted as to how I would proceed. Harold Cherniss, the great scholar in my field there, declined to give advice – how like Socrates he was in this. Left to my own devices, I cut the project in half, allocating the whole of that year to a study of Plato's Socratic dialogues. This much at least I was determined to finish, for a somewhat ridiculous reason: so I could win at last (I was then in mid-career) that *sine qua non* of

---

1 ἀτοπία. The Greek is stronger; "strangeness" picks it up at the lower end of its intensity-range. At the higher end "outrageousness" or even "absurdity" would be required to match its force: when Callicles in the *Gorgias* (494D) exclaims "how ἄτοπος you are, Socrates," "how outrageous you are" ("absurd" in Woodhead and in Irwin) is just what he means. (Translations of Plato's dialogues to which I refer throughout the book are listed in the Bibliography at the end.)

2 Their protagonist is, for all practical purposes, the only "Socrates" I shall be talking about throughout this book. Is this the real Socrates, the Socrates of history? Yes. But isn't it Plato? Yes. Can it be both? Yes, How so? Readers will get an answer in chapter 2, if they can bear the suspense. If they can't, they may skip to chapter 2 at once.

respectability in American academia, a book-length work between
hard covers. So I toiled and moiled and, sure enough, by that year's
end a MS of the desired length sat finished on my desk. But when I
was about to package it and send it off I paused to take a cool,
critical look at it. I went through it from start to finish as I would if
it had been written by someone else and I was reading it for a
publisher. By the time I had got to the end a feeling in the pit of my
stomach told me that the MS was a lemon. It did give, I was
satisfied, correct answers to the questions I had asked – much the
same questions as those which specialists in the field had been
addressing in the preceding half-century. And still it was wrong.
Why? If I could have given then my present verdict on it, it would
have been that the strangeness of Socrates had been missed. A vague
sense of this, more instinct than reasoned judgement, left me with the
conviction that the best thing I could do with that MS was to junk
it. And so I did.

Looking back on that decision now, decades later, I see it as one
of the wisest I have ever made. If I had put that book into print and
moved into position to defend it, I would have gone further and
further into the morass. Having cut my losses, what was the result?
A wasted year? Hardly. Putting into black and white that wrong
account of Socrates enabled me to glimpse some of the things needed
to put it right. The first of these was that his paradoxes, pushed to
the margins in that book, had to be brought into dead center.[3] Even
if I did not succeed in cracking them, the anguished sense of their
presence would have to be my companion in any writing on Socrates
I would ever do.

The chance of a new start on a smaller scale came immediately.
I was asked to do the Introduction to the *Protagoras* for the Liberal
Arts Press. Its series of classics was aimed at the college audience –
the one I had been addressing with relish in my undergraduate
classes for over twenty years, first at Queen's in Canada, then at
Cornell and then again at Princeton. Greekless, rebuffed by techni-
calities, turned off by the paraphernalia of research, but respectful of
its aims, they were eagerly responsive if one caught them where they
lived. I tried this voice in that Introduction[4] and I felt that it
succeeded where the book had failed.[5] This Socrates was alive.

3 That Socrates' strangeness is the key to his personality has been occasionally noticed in the
   scholarly literature (e.g. Robin, 1928: 186; cf. also Barabas, 1986: 89ff.). The present book
   is written with the conviction that it is also the key to his philosophy.
4 Vlastos, 1956: vii–lvi.
5 It elicited a handwritten one-sentence note from Robert Oppenheimer, then Director of the
   Institute, that warmed my heart more than anything anyone had ever said to me about my

I kept that voice the following year in an address to the Humanities Association of Canada, entitled, in private recollection of the aborted book, "The paradox of Socrates".[6] Here again I was not talking to fellow-specialists. Addressing scholars hailing from widely different bands of the academic spectrum I acknowledged the perils of *docta ignorantia*, never greater than in our own day of professionalized, dispersed, fragmented, minutely specialized research. Lamenting the scholar's alienation from humanity, I said (1958: 497) that what I would offer in my address would not be scholarship but "humanism" on a jokey definition of the "humanist" as "a scholar making a strenuous effort to be human, trying, first, to find the relevance of his individual work to our common humanity; secondly to state his findings in common speech – not folksy talk, just the Queen's English, unassisted by a suitcaseful of technical glossaries." Is it really possible to do scholarship *and* that sort of "humanism," both at once? I cannot be sure. But that is what I was trying for in that address. And I am not giving up in the present book, though it will be more difficult now, for this work will have to be weighted more heavily on the side of scholarship.

There were errors in that early work which I have never tried to dig up and recant. It is boringly self-important to excavate the archaeology of one's mistakes.[7] But one of them is too big – a real whopper – and too noxious to be allowed a place in the limbo of forgettable mishaps.[8] It concerns what I had made of Socrates' central paradox, his profession of ignorance. He *asserts* that he has no knowledge, none whatever, not a smidgin of it, "no wisdom, great or small" (*Ap.* 21B–D). But he speaks and lives, serenely confident that he has a goodly stock of it – sufficient for the quotidian pursuit of virtue. And he *implies* as much in what he says.[9] To keep faith with Socrates' strangeness some way has to be found to save both the assertion of his ignorance and the implied negation. My mistake – explicit in the Introduction to the *Protagoras*, implicit in "The

work: "Thank you, Gregory, for the pure gold of your Socrates." Is it not rank boastfulness to make this public? It would be if it had come from a fellow-specialist.

6 Vlastos, 1958: 496–516.

7 But I am gratified to see Donald Morrison (1987: 9–22) taking seriously enough things I had said in a semi-popular essay thirty years ago to think them worth rebutting now in a technical journal. Should I be reproached for having misled Santas and Kraut in the way he thinks I did? I think not. If either of these fine scholars did swallow an erroneous view of Xenophon on the strength of nothing better than my say-so (which I gravely doubt), they would have only themselves to blame.

8 Since that work is still being read by college students there is some point in correcting its major error.

9 In Vlastos, 1985: 1ff., at 3–11 I assemble seven texts in which the implication is unambiguous; I shall be citing more of them in the present volume in due course.

paradox of Socrates" – had been to accept the assertion and ignore the balancing reservation. I had maintained: "he has seen [1] that his investigative method's aim cannot be final demonstrative certainty, and [2] that its practice is quite compatible with suspended judgment as to the material truth of any of its conclusions" (Vlastos, 1956: xxxi). [1] is exactly right and it goes to the heart of what is ground-breakingly new in Socrates. What I had said to this effect – placing Socrates' renunciation of epistemic certainty at the core of his philosophizing – was one of the best things in that Introduction. But it was wrong to conjoin with it claim [2]. There is no necessary connection. John Dewey was not giving up the search for knowledge when making the quest for certainty his *bête noire*.[10] Neither was Socrates in *his* disclaimer of certainty – he least of all philosophers, maintaining as he did that knowledge *is* virtue. My error had been to saddle Socrates with [2] on the strength of nothing better than [1].

Others beside myself had fallen into that trap. This is how George Grote, prince of Victorian Platonists, represents the position he thinks Socrates is holding throughout his elenctic searches: "I have not made up my mind... I give you the reasons for and against... You must decide for yourself."[11] Invoking Cicero's authority, Grote associated Socrates with the leaders of the "New Academy," Arcesilaus and Carneades, those out-and-out skeptics, who maintained suspended judgement (ἐποχή) about everything in the belief that they were following in Socrates' footsteps.[12] Cicero, who finds this position attractive,[13] speaks of it as "propounded by Socrates, reaffirmed by Arcesilaus and confirmed by Carneades."[14]

It should not have taken me twenty years to discover that this is badly out of line with what we see of Socrates in Plato's earlier dialogues, the most reliable of our sources. When told in the *Gorgias* (473B) that it would not be difficult to refute his thesis, Socrates retorts: "not difficult, Polus, but impossible; for what is true is never refuted." A little later (479E) he asks: "Has it not been proved that what I said was true?" By no stretch of the imagination could Plato have put such words into the mouth of someone who is maintaining "suspended judgement," has "not made up his mind," "argues against everything and makes no positive assertions."[15] No moral

10 "The Quest for Certainty" had been the title of his Gifford Lectures.
11 Grote, 1865: 1 239.
12 See Glucker, 1978: 32ff.; cf. also Long, 1986: 431ff. at 440–1.
13 He too falls into the trap, associating principled abstention from either assent or dissent (*neque adfirmare quemquam, neque adsensione approbare*) with the renunciation of certainty (*de omnibus quaeritur, nihil certi dicitur*) (*Acad.* 1.45–6), as though the latter required the former.
14 *De Natura Deorum* 1.11.
15 The last of these quotations is Cicero's description of the position of the New Academy: *contra omnia disserendi nullamque rem aperte iudicandi* (*Acad.* 1.44–6.)

philosopher has ever avowed more positive conviction of the truth of a risky thesis than does Socrates when he argues, for example, that he who wrongs another person always damages his own happiness more than his victim's.[16] How Arcesilaus and Carneades could have associated their systematic adherence to ἐποχή with Socrates' ringing affirmations we shall never know: our information about them is all too scant. But in Grote's case we do have his three-volume work on Plato (1865). When we scan it and find it ignoring texts scattered throughout Plato's earlier dialogues which repel that description of Socrates' epistemic stance, we have no choice but to say that, fine Platonist though Grote was, in this he had missed his bus and jumped on another going the opposite way. *A fortiori* so had I in those early essays.

The wonder of it is that criticism was so slow in coming. While bucketfuls of it were being poured on a paper I had published a little earlier on Plato's metaphysics[17] (it was to prove the most relentlessly rebutted monograph of the fifties in its field),[18] not a word was raised against my skeptical Socrates until late in the sixties, except for an aside in a footnote in E. R. Dodds' commentary on the *Gorgias*.[19] Extended critique was to come only nine years after that, in Norman Gulley's *The Philosophy of Socrates*,[20] the first book-length work on Socrates to appear in English since A. E. Taylor's *Socrates* (1933). Gulley put his finger on various defects in my agnostic Socrates, so unlike Aristotle's and Xenophon's. I discounted that critique because it was based on the traditional view which emasculates Socrates' profession of ignorance by reducing it to a pedagogical feint.[21] Anyhow, by that time I was too deep in other concerns. All I managed to write about Socrates in the sixties was a short paper, "Was Polus Refuted?",[22] which was on the right lines but did not get to the bottom of the problem it raised (this would await Irwin and Santas in the seventies),[23] a breezy essay in the *Yale Review* (1974) "Socrates on Political Obedience and Disobedience," which provoked (and probably deserved) the withering irony in the title of Dybikowski's rebuttal in the same journal (1975), "Was Socrates as Rational as Professor Vlastos?"; and a longer not entirely successful, paper entitled "Socrates on Acrasia" (1969). In none of

16 *G.* 473Aff.; see especially chapter 5, section III below. (References to Plato's dialogues will be made by abbreviations, listed at pp. 83–5 below, adapted from those in Irwin, 1977a.)
17 Vlastos, 1954: 319ff.
18 Twenty-one papers by other scholars on the Third Man Argument followed (most of them are listed in Vlastos, 1981: 361–2); almost all of them contain criticism of mine.
19 1959: 16, n. 2.   20 1968: 68ff.
21 I had not yet got it through my head that a critic who is dead wrong on one point may be dead right on several others.   22 1967: 454ff.
23 See section III of chapter 5 below.

these did I undertake to remedy, or even so much as acknowledge, the major fault in the account of Socrates' philosophy I had put into those two essays in the fifties. Those I was now dismissing as the juvenilia of my middle age.

The stimulus for fresh thinking on Socrates came in a stunning new book, *Plato's Moral Theory*, by Terry Irwin.[24] At Princeton I had been *pro forma* the supervisor of the vast thesis (the longest and also the best ever written under my supervision, all of it lean, close-packed argument) of which the book was a partial result. To read it in its final form, now organized into an outrageously bold argument, proved one of the outstanding learning experiences of my life. It did more to invigorate and deepen my understanding of its topic than anything I had yet read. Everything in Irwin's bibliography, extending to hundreds of items (books and journal articles), was well known to me, as was only to be expected: by this time I had been teaching Plato for nearly fifty years. I had read virtually all of them; some of them I had studied in depth. But none of them had made anything like the same impact on me. For none had cut so brutally to the bone of the fundamental questions.

The biggest of these is whether or not the moral philosophy in Plato's dialogues is broadly *utilitarian*. This, certainly, is how it strikes one on first encounter, since the claim persistently made there is that "justice pays" – pays off in happiness for the agent. This looks like saying that one's final reason for moral conduct should be that this is one's safest guide to a non-moral end. Highly reputable books have taken this line when expounding the earlier, Socratic, part of Plato's corpus. Others merely dodged the problem. In W. K. C. Guthrie's *History of Greek Philosophy* (certified by its Cambridge imprint as an authoritative reference work and widely used as such throughout the world) we read that "Socrates was famous for this utilitarian approach to goodness and virtue."[25] The author assumes that *of course* we all know what "utilitarianism" would mean when lifted out of the works of nineteenth-century British moralists and made to categorize the very different kind of theorizing assayed by the Greek pioneers.

Read the first four chapters of Irwin's book if you have the stomach for them and you may see why, when I went through them,

---

24 Irwin, 1977a.
25 Guthrie, 1969: 462. He would not have been wrong if he had said this only with reference to certain passages in Xenophon (as in the conversations with Aristippus, *Mem.* 2.1 and Euthydemus 4.5.1–11; he attributes the same view to his other hero, Cyrus: *Cyr.* 1.5.8–12. But neither does Xenophon make Socrates a consistent utilitarian; see e.g. *Mem.* 4.8.6 to the contrary.

I was so often reminded of the saying *malheur au vague, mieux vaut le faux*. Irwin discards "utilitarianism," finding it hopeless as the precision tool he needs to analyze what Socrates has to say about virtue and happiness. He replaces it with "instrumentalism", the view that virtue is only an "instrumental means" to happiness – "entirely distinct" from happiness, only causally connected with it.[26] The question then becomes crystal-clear: Does the relation of virtue to happiness in Socrates' moral philosophy satisfy this specification? In his investigation of the works of Plato's middle period Irwin's answer to this precise question is, precisely, "No." But when discussing the Socratic dialogues of Plato's earlier years Irwin's answer in that book is a no less precise "Yes."

Agreeing with the "No" in Irwin's book – certainly, Plato is no "instrumentalist" – I dissented sharply from its "Yes": there was even less of that, I felt, in Socrates than in Plato. I said so in no uncertain terms in reviewing the book for the *Times Literary Supplement*,[27] recognizing Irwin's extraordinary talent[28] but arguing hard against his view of Socrates, insisting on a diametrically opposite view which hails Socrates as the founder of that long line of theorizing first expounded in the Platonic corpus, reaffirmed more cautiously in Aristotle, in recklessly extreme terms by Antisthenes and his Cynic progeny and also by the Stoics,[29] which makes virtue no mere external means to happiness but its inmost core, its sole or major component. Irwin replied, rebutting my critique in a letter to the *T.L.S.* I replied to the reply, and so did he again and again. The merry-go-round went on for nearly six months[30] – the longest philosophical exchange on record in the correspondence columns of *T.L.S.*

What was it that I found unacceptable in the view that for Socrates virtue is only an "instrumental" means to happiness? It was the claim that for Socrates happiness and virtue are "entirely distinct,"[31] so much so that the happiness desired by all human beings as the final end of all their actions is *the same for all of them,*

26 Irwin, 1977a: 300, n. 52.   27 Vlastos, 1978a.

28 My judgment was to be amply vindicated by his subsequent work on Aristotle. No more fundamental contribution to Aristotelian studies has been made in my lifetime than his *Aristotle's First Principles* (1988).

29 But *not* by another member of the Socratic circle, Aristippus, founder of the hedonist line of moral theory, in which the end is pleasure and virtue is valued only as a means to pleasure (D.L. 2.87).

30 Irwin's first letter was in March, my last was in September. It ended when I announced in my September letter that this would be my last and Irwin then, by courtesy, allowed me the last word.

31 See the description of "instrumental means" in Irwin, 1977a: 300, n. 53.

regardless of differences in their moral character: all of them, the noblest and the most depraved, have the same "determinate" final end; they differ only in their choice of means.[32] Is such a view ever stated by Socrates in our texts? Obviously not. But every philosophical interpretation of his philosophy has to go, to some degree, beyond what is said in so many words in our texts. Irwin's is no exception. It is a brilliant feat of the constructive imagination. To decide whether or not it is true we have to ask: Is it a credible account of what is taught by Socrates in the text of Plato's earlier dialogues?

Here the first question has to be: Does it allow the Socrates of Plato's *Apology*, *Crito*, and *Gorgias* an internally consistent theory? In my July letter to *T.L.S.* I argued that it does not.[33] Let me try to make the same point more simply now. Here is what Plato's Socrates says when explaining himself to the court that was to sentence him to death. Addressing an imaginary fellow-citizen who is reproaching him for having lived in a way that now puts him in peril of execution as a criminal, he retorts:

Ap. 28B5–9: "You don't speak well, O man, if you believe that someone worth anything at all would give countervailing weight to danger of life or death or *give consideration to anything but this* when he acts: whether his action is just or unjust, the action of a good or evil man."[34]

And this is how Irwin himself glosses a text in the *Gorgias* (512D–E): "it is living well that matters, *however bad the consequences* for the future welfare may be" (1977a: 240). Could Socrates be saying *this* if the instrumentalist construction of his view were correct? On that construction what must determine the choice between just and unjust action would have to be *only the consequences* for something distinct from virtue. But what Socrates in fact believes is that the choice should be determined by adherence to virtue *regardless of the consequence for anything distinct from virtue*. The ultimate choice would be for happiness in either case, since Socrates holds that this is everyone's ultimate end. But the motivation would be radically different in the two cases, as I emphasize in my last letter.[35]

---

32 A brief quote from the second paragraph in my review of his book: "Socrates is supposed to hold that the virtuous and the vicious are pursuing the same end, differing only in their choice of means, and that the moralist's task is simply to enlighten that choice... The programme is reductionist. Moral knowledge is only 'technical' knowledge – knowledge of means."

33 But in such a labored way that I have only myself to blame if the point did not get across.

34 I shall be quoting this text again and discussing its implications in chapter 8, and then again in the Epilogue.   35 *T.L.S.*, Sept. 3, 1978.

However, the brunt of my critique does not fall on the inconsistency between

(1) Virtue should be pursued "however bad the consequences" for anything distinct from virtue,

and

(2) Virtue should be pursued only for its consequences for happiness, which is something distinct from virtue.[36]

I argue that even if Socratic instrumentalism were internally consistent it would be sadly deficient in good sense.[37] Consider Socrates' claim that the just man is always happier than his unjust oppressor. In the example in my first letter (March) Socrates makes the claim that the tyrant who breaks an innocent man and prospers as a result has damaged his own happiness more than his victim's. Allow those two men sufficiently different conceptions of happiness and the claim, thought still very hard to believe, could be *sanely* held within the limits of Socrates' strangeness. Not so on the instrumentalist hypothesis that the tyrant and his victim both want the same thing and the victim gets more of that same thing than does the tyrant.[38] Socrates would be lacking in the most rudimentary good sense if he had really believed such a thing. Did I get *this* point across to Irwin? In his May letter he retorts that "philosophers [sometimes] believe implausible things." True enough. But has any philosopher ever believed anything *that* implausible?

Had the debate been judged by an impartial referee the decision would have undoubtedly gone to Irwin on "points": he made the

---

36 Though this would suffice to discredit the interpretation in the absence of direct evidence for it in Plato's text: a well established "principle of charity" (on which see additional note 0.1 below) makes a construction of a writer's words which preserves consistency preferable to any which does not.

37 Cf. the belief that a scratch on my finger would cause the destruction of the universe. Suppose that, as Hume thought, this belief were internally consistent. Who but a madman would entertain it seriously?

38 Quoting from my letter to *T.L.S.* of April 21: "the tyrant would have got more of what he wants if he had changed places with his victim." The absurdity of this hypothesis did not faze Irwin: he retorted that it is no more implausible than is J. S. Mill's version of utilitarianism. But the latter is no more absurd than is any respectable philosophical view which we consider mistaken. Conversely that Plato's tyrant should elect to suffer the wreck of his wordly fortunes and excruciating suffering for the sake of justice is a flat psychological impossibility: in Plato's characterization of him he gives expediency–power–pleasure top place in his established preference-ranking, justice bottom place. Someone with these preference-rankings would have to jump out of his psychological skin to elect the most extreme suffering for the sake of preserving justice. The trouble with the position Irwin gives Socrates in 1977a: ch. 3 is that it postulates in all human beings a uniform desire for an identical undescribed happiness which has no relation to their psychological differences. Its people have no psychological skin to jump out of.

best case for the weaker thesis. He thereby confirmed himself in his adherence to the instrumentalist view of Socrates.[39] So the controversy in *T.L.S.* did not do much for him. But it did wonders for me. It marked a milestone in my own understanding of Socrates. I could now see, more clearly than ever before, Socrates' true place in the development of Greek thought:[40] he is the first to establish the eudaemonist foundation of ethical theory which becomes common ground for all of the schools that spring up around him, and more; he is the founder of the non-instrumentalist form of eudaemonism held in common by Platonists, Aristotelians, Cynics, and Stoics, i.e. of all Greek moral philosophers *except* the Epicureans. For this enhanced understanding I was indebted to Irwin, and also for something else: for his deportment in the debate. He argued his case with cool composure, without the least hostility, thereby evoking from me too argument free from acrimony. So the debate put no strain on our personal relations, and did not impede the development of what was to become one of the cherished friendships of my life and one of the most productive. In subsequent exchanges by correspondence Irwin has given me positive help in clarifying my own view. The first essay I published after that debate, "Socrates' Contribution to the Greek Sense of Justice,"[41] had swung too far to the other extreme, taking Socrates' view of the relation of virtue to happiness to be identity, no less. As I shall be explaining in chapter 8 below, this was wrong – not so wrong as to degrade it to a mere instrumentality, but still wrong, and it had to be put right. Irwin had pointed out to me a mistake in logic which had facilitated that conclusion.[42]

An unexpected sequel to the controversy in *T.L.S.* (perhaps even a by-product of it: it had advertised the fact that my retirement from Princeton had not proved a sentence of civil death) was the invitation to give the Gifford Lectures at St. Andrews in 1981. Considering that the roster of earlier Gifford lecturers had included awe-inspiring names – Josiah Royce, William James, John Dewey – the invitation was intimidating. But I resisted the impulse to chicken

---

39 A subsequent development of his view (1986: 85–112) seeks to take the madness out of it by allowing Socrates an "adaptive conception of happiness," namely that once we understand that some desire of ours is unrealizable, it vanishes, and then its frustration is no blot on our happiness (97 *et passim*). This looks like making sour grapes a highest-level principle of moral choice. Nothing remotely like this is ever said or implied in our Socratic texts. And any suggestion of an affinity between Socratic and Epicurean thought could only be made in defiance of the historical facts: In the writings of the Epicureans "Socrates was portrayed as the complete anti-Epicurean" (Long, 1988; 155); for detailed documentation see Kleve, 1981.   40 Cf. section III, chapter 8.   41 1980: 301ff.
42 I acknowledge his help when making the correction in 1984: see chapter 8, n. 46.

out and the result has been the work behind this book and more: all the intellectual effort I have mustered since 1978 was elicited by the challenge of that invitation. For this I could never be grateful enough to the Gifford Trust. Years which might have slid into vacuous tranquillity were galvanized. Nothing I had ever done before – neither my struggles with the Presocratics in the late forties nor with Plato's ontology in the fifties and with his moral psychology and social philosophy in the sixties and seventies – had engaged me so totally. For a time I even dropped my research on Plato's ontology. I returned to it[43] only when I realized that the contrast between the metaphysical entities which Plato called "Forms" or "Ideas" and the foci of Socratic definitional inquiry which could also be called "forms" or "ideas"[44] was crucial for the right understanding of the relation of the "Socrates" of Plato's earlier dialogues to his namesake who expounds thereafter the Platonic two-world view.[45]

Though I knew that a highly finished performance was expected at St. Andrews, the three years allowed me to prepare were used up just in the preliminary task of clarifying my understanding of their theme. I pursued this by means of hand-outs on various subtopics presented for discussion in graduate and post-graduate seminars. There was one at Toronto, attended by faculty and students in philosophy or classics, where I ventured, with enormous benefit, a trial run of the material I was working up for the St. Andrews Lectures.[46] I did the same, with equally helpful results, in seminars on Socrates at Berkeley, both regular ones for the University[47] and a Summer Seminar for College Teachers in Philosophy under the auspices of the National Endowment of the Humanities. In the latter I was privileged to share my thoughts on Socrates with younger scholars whose teaching in their own institutions abutted on Greek philosophy, and they did more for me than I for them.[48] Helpful to

---

43 See chapter 2, sections II and III.
44 The shift in typography from "Forms" in Plato to "forms" in Socrates will be reminding the reader of that difference throughout the book.
45 This will be a major theme in chapter 2.
46 I record with gratitude the benefit to me of contributions to the discussions in that seminar whose membership included the late Leonard Woodbury, and David Gauthier, Ronnie de Sousa, Hans Herzberger, Kenneth Henwood, and Edward Halper.
47 I acknowledge with warmest thanks clarification of my thought through comments made in those seminars at Berkeley, or later ones on the same campus, by Alan Code, A. A. Long, Benson Mates, Alan Silverman, and Stephen White.
48 I derived particular benefit from contributions by Hugh Benson, John Beversluis, Tom Brickhouse, Daniel Graham, David Halperin, Grant Luckhardt, Mark McPherran, William Prior, Nicholas Smith, Roslyn Weiss, and Donald Zeyl.

me in a different way had been special presentations I had the chance to make at the National Center for the Humanities in North Carolina which I attended as a Senior Fellow in the Fall of 1980 and 1981,[49] working there under ideal conditions of interaction with scholars in other humanistic fields.

I reached St. Andrews quaking in my shoes, my preparation of the lectures I was to give there nowhere near the point they would have had to reach before being entitled to publication. They could take my audience no further than I had yet managed to come myself. Their audience was town no less than gown, so once again I was challenged to speak in a voice that reached non-specialists. At the same time I had the benefit of expert criticism from scholars in the University which had enjoyed a highly distinguished tradition of Socratic scholarship. That fine Hellenist, John Burnet, with whose Oxford text of Plato's works (1900) and commentaries on the *Euthyphro, Apology, Crito* (1924), and on the *Phaedo* I had lived for decades, had been the Professor of Greek there in the first part of the present century. Third in succession to him had been Kenneth Dover, whose masterly essay on Socrates in the Introduction to his edition of the *Clouds* (1968) I had reprinted in my collection, *The Philosophy of Socrates* (1971). His successor was Ian Kidd, the learned editor of the definitive *Posidonius*[50] to whose article on Socrates in the *Encyclopedia of Philosophy* (1954) I had been referring my students as the best available essay-length introduction to Socrates' character and philosophy.

It was very fortunate, I feel, that the terms of the appointment, though inviting publication, did not require it. Because of this I had the chance to pursue my own understanding of Socrates' thought while expounding it at St. Andrews and continuing to reflect on it critically thereafter. The lectures were written out, and could have been published immediately. But their thought was far from complete. To print them in that form would have been almost as much of a disaster as the publication of the aborted MS I had produced twenty-five years earlier at Princeton. Missing from the material I had brought to St. Andrews was what I would be learning there from audience-response. A good example concerns the topic to which I have alluded already: the view that the relation of virtue to happiness in Socrates' thought was identity. This interpretation had

49 Two of them contained much of the material I was to publish under the titles of "The Socratic Elenchus" (1983a: 27–58 and 71–4) and "Socrates' Disavowal of Knowledge" (1985: 1–31).
50 His edition of vol. I of Posidonius' Fragments had appeared in 1972 (second edition in 1989). The Commentary in Volume II of the work appeared in 1988.

not been made without considerable textual support. What else but this, I had thought, could Socrates have meant in saying that virtue is "the mark (σκοπός) to which one should look in living, *all* actions, one's own or those of one's city, directed to the end that justice and *sōphrosynē* shall be present in one who is to be blessed" (*G.* 507D)? But it was strongly contested in the seminar which followed the lecture where I argued for that claim. Ian Kidd pointed out that to give Socrates this view would be to collapse the difference between his position and that of the Stoics, which sound historical judgment could hardly allow. I recognized the justice of his criticism and said so in one of the later lectures in the series. But to find the right terms in which the true relation of virtue to happiness is understood in Plato's account of Socrates' view was a much longer job. It was not to be until more than two years later that I would hit on my solution to this extremely difficult problem.[51]

And this is only one of several things that needed to be put right before the picture of Socratic philosophizing I had presented in those lectures would be ready for print. One of them was the irony of Socrates. Nothing about him, I felt, had been less well understood than this in the preceding literature. In a misinterpretation that was virtually canonical – it was even ensconced in the dictionaries – Socratic irony had been taken to mean Socratic *deception*, be it malicious, as Thrasymachus is made to see it in the *Republic*,[52] or benign, as Alcibiades has often been understood to represent it in the *Symposium*.[53] It would be a long time before I could put my finger on *why* this was wrong. I did so in a lecture on "Socratic Irony" in Cambridge,[54] three years after I had delivered the one on the same theme at St. Andrews which I could now see was hopelessly inadequate: it got no further than identifying the ironical component in Socrates' character (which I described, correctly enough, as "a collage of ironies"), failing to see how irony served as the vehicle of his profession of ignorance, intelligible only if understood to disclaim one sort of knowledge, while claiming another in the same breath. I consider this proposal so fundamental that I am putting it into the first chapter in the present book. But I am not suggesting that it can stand alone. Its indispensable support is in the essay I published shortly after, "Socrates' Disavowal of Knowledge" (1985), in which I argue systematically for the claim that the disavowal is a "complex irony," a figure of speech in which what is said both is and isn't what

---

51 In a lecture in Cambridge in 1984, now chapter 8 of this book.
52 T1 in chapter 1 below.   53 T8, T9 in the same chapter.
54 Vlastos, 1987b: 79–96, now reprinted as chapter 1.

is meant. I give a brief version of that argument in additional note
1.1 on "Socrates' complex philosophical ironies."

The other lecture at St. Andrews where the thought had failed to
touch bottom was the one on the Socratic Elenchus. Not that there
was anything there I would want to take back. Its claim that the
elenchus is a method of philosophical investigation – no mere device
for exposing confusions in his interlocutors, which is what Richard
Robinson had made of it in his book, *Plato's Earlier Dialectic*[55] – was
dead right. In my lecture I maintained *contra* Robinson that while
the elenchus was adversative, pervasively negative in form, its aim
was strongly positive: to discover and defend true moral doctrine.[56]
This emphasis, I believe, was right, and so too the claim[57] that what
Socrates aimed to discover by this means was knowledge, not just
true belief. So too was the restricted scope I allowed it, insisting, with
Woodruff,[58] that in the earlier dialogues it is used to test only moral,
never metaphysical or epistemological theses: contrary to what he
will be doing in the dialogues of Plato's middle period, this earlier
Socrates uses the elenchus exclusively in the pursuit of moral truth,
remaining from first to last a single-minded moralist, never venturing
into meta-elenctic argument intended to probe the validity of his
investigative method or the truth of its ontological presuppositions.
And so finally was my insistence on the importance of Socrates'
frequent injunction "Say only what you believe." Richard Robinson
had been well aware of the presence of this rule in Socratic
argument.[59] But neither he nor anyone else had realized the
methodological implication of this rule – that its operative force was
to exclude debate on unasserted premises, thereby distinguishing Socratic
from Zenonian and, indeed (so far as we know), from all earlier
dialectic.

On all these aspects of the elenchus I was entirely clear in that
lecture on it in my Gifford series at St. Andrews. But I was still
stumped on what I had been calling in seminars throughout

55 Though differing from Robinson on this score my debt to him on other grounds is
   immense. The appreciation of the elenchus as a fundamental and distinctive feature of
   Socrates' method of investigation is something for which Robinson had fought single-
   handed in mid-century. How far ahead of his time he was on this is best seen by comparing
   his treatment of the elenchus with what other scholars say or, rather, fail to say, about it
   in important work anteceding the publication of Robinson's book (Maier, 1913: 367ff.; A.
   E. Taylor, 1929: *passim*; Cornford, 1932: 29ff.; Shorey, 1933: *passim*; Hardie, 1936: *passim*)
   or even decades after its publication (Kneale & Kneale, 1962: 1ff.; Crombie, 1963: 517ff.;
   Guthrie, 1969: 417ff.; von Fritz, 1971: 250ff.).
56 As Gulley had argued before me (1968: 22ff.) and Irwin (1977a: 36–8 *et passim*).
57 See Vlastos, 1985: 1ff. at 5, n. 12.
58 Woodruff, 1982: 137–8. I acknowledge the debt in Vlastos, 1983a: 33, n. 22.
59 Robinson, 1953: 15ff.

preceding years "the puzzle of the elenchus," namely, how it is that Socrates expects to reach truth by an argumentative method which of its very nature could only test consistency. On Donald Davidson's theory of knowledge, consistency should suffice for truth.[60] But no one, least of all Davidson himself, would suggest that Socrates could be regarded as a preternaturally prescient Davidsonian, two and a half millennia ahead of his time. In fidelity to our texts no *epistemological theory* at all can be ascribed to Socrates.[61] How else then could we reasonably account for his conviction that moral truth is what he did reach by means of his elenctic arguments? Light on this point broke when it occurred to me to ask: Is it not just possible that Socrates was making certain assumptions, without any philosophical theory to support them, which would have made it seem reasonable to believe that the elenchus did more than show the inconsistency of his interlocutors' false belief with those other beliefs of theirs from which Socrates deduced its negation? Suppose he had believed that the moral truth for which he was searching was already *in* each of his interlocutors in the form of true beliefs, accessible to him in his elenctic encounters with them, and that he could *always* count on the presence of these beliefs in their mind and could use them as the premises from which the negation of their false thesis could be derived. *Then* it seemed to me Socrates' conviction that he could discover moral truth by means of his elenctic arguments would not seem so unreasonable after all. This is the new approach to the problem I was to take in "The Socratic Elenchus" (Vlastos, 1983a)[62] and this I reached only after I had delivered that lecture on the elenchus in my Giffords in 1981.

Less than two years after my return to Berkeley, Dame Fortune unexpectedly smiled again. I received an invitation to go to Cambridge on a visiting appointment as Distinguished Professorial Fellow at Christ's College and Lecturer in the University's Faculty of Classics. To Cambridge I had a long-standing personal debt, dating back to pre-war years. I had gone there in 1938 while still uncertain of my future, still in search of a vocation. I had come, as a private scholar, unharnessed to any research project, unattached to any College, without standing in the University, my only tie to it a library card. What had drawn me there was Cornford. His writings

---

60 Davidson, 1986: 307–19.   61 Cf. n. 5 to additional note 1.1, and n. 12 to ch. 2.
62 I was pleased to find support for it from Davidson: "As Vlastos explains, the elenchus would make for truth simply by ensuring coherence in a set of beliefs if one could assume that in each of us there are always true beliefs inconsistent with the false...I think there is good reason to believe the assumption is true – true enough, anyway, to ensure that when our beliefs are consistent they will in most large matters be true" (1985: 16).

had inspired and guided my study of Plato and I had longed for closer contact with him. Though I had no institutional claim on him, and though he had just suffered a traumatic loss, the death of his son in Spain, he graciously afforded me the opportunity to meet him. In the course of our discussion I voiced objection to his view of the creation story in the *Timaeus*. He encouraged me to write up my position and when I did he said: "You still haven't convinced me. But we must get this into the *C.Q.*" There it appeared in due course to mark a new turn in my life – the end of my vocational doldrums, admission into the company of working scholars in the field of classical philosophy. It was the gift of the foremost Platonist of his day to a young unknown.

My residence in Cambridge in 1983 was under the happiest of auspices. As visiting Fellow at Christ's, voting member of its governing board during that year, I had the rare privilege of an inside view of something still unknown in the United States and Canada: a distinguished institution of higher learning which was completely self-governing. Aside from a formal lecture, my statutory duties called only for one seminar – but what a seminar it proved to be! Its like I had never experienced in my life. Almost all of the people in it were dons, and they included some of the world's best scholars in the field of ancient philosophy. The opportunity to place before them week by week the conclusions I had so far reached on Socrates was as rewarding a challenge as I had ever had in my life. What I had put into my St. Andrews lectures and also the highly controversial points at which my thinking now pushed further on had the benefit of critical discussions in that seminar and of spin-offs from it in private discussions.

The most fruitful of these were with Myles Burnyeat, now Laurence Professor, fourth in succession to the Chair which had been established for Cornford. By the time I reached Cambridge studies of Burnyeat's had appeared which I had recognized as the best work on the *Theaetetus* produced in my lifetime – better than Cornford's, fully as sensitive to Plato's text but distinctly stronger on the philosophical side. And I had found it entirely congenial to my own approach. Thus, to give one example, his paper on "Socratic Midwifery" had established conclusively that the metaphor is a Platonic invention, foreign to the Socrates of Plato's earlier dialogues – a thesis I had expounded myself at Princeton and at Berkeley, albeit without the subtlety of textual analysis and power of critical argument now deployed in this paper. In discussion Burnyeat has that rare gift of seeing what you are driving at before you have got there yourself and helping you complete your own thought without butting in. My proposed solution to the "puzzle of the elenchus" had been produced with his help.[63] But I still don't know whether or not he agrees with it. I have learned the most about Plato *through* Irwin, but *from* Burnyeat.

While I was still in Cambridge came Dame Fortune's third big smile on my post-retirement years: the invitation to give the second in the newly established series of Townsend Lectures at Cornell. This university had been a philosophical *alma mater* to me. Here is where I had started teaching Greek philosophy at the graduate level – and concurrently had started learning modern analytical philosophy myself. I had got precious little of this in my graduate days at Harvard, where A. N. Whitehead, my supervisor, had befriended and inspired me, but taught me little of contemporary philosophy except his own along with a powerfully Whiteheadianized Plato[64] – a heady brew from whose high I luckily sobered up soon after leaving Harvard to start learning Plato for myself while teaching philosophy to undergraduates at Queen's in Canada. At Cornell I ingested great gobs of analytical epistemology in our philosophical discussion club from Norman Malcolm, Max Black, Arthur Murphy, and their students. Most of what I know of contemporary philosophy I learned at Cornell, as a superannuated graduate student masquerading as a professor. So the invitation to give the Townsends evoked a sentiment not unlike that which pulls the aging alumnus back to the haunts of his youth. And there was more than affection-laced nostalgia to make that invitation compellingly attractive. I have seldom been able to resist an opportunity to try out *viva voce* on a new audience any substantial piece of work I have written out. What made it even less resistible in this case was the chance to resume personal contact with Irwin, now on the Cornell faculty and a member of the Townsend Committee, and also to make contact with Gail Fine, the other distinguished Platonist on the Cornell faculty,[65] and with their graduate students,[66] presenting my thoughts

---

63 I acknowledge the indebtedness in Vlastos, 1983a: 57, n. 65.
64 At this stage of his life Whitehead had come under Plato's spell. His enthusiasm for Plato took the form of allowing him large gifts from his own philosophy. In this he was abetted by some contemporary Platonists. In A. E. Taylor's interpretation of the cosmology of the *Timaeus* (1929) there is as much of Whitehead as of Plato, and sometimes more. Fortunately for me, a powerful antidote was being produced by Cornford: see Cornford, 1937: Preface.
65 My paper on Platonic ontology (Vlastos, 1987a) was produced in response to a challenging contribution she had made to my Cornell seminar, which both she and Irwin were attending.
66 The most valuable critique of my paper on "Socratic Irony" I have yet received from anyone came from Don Adams, then a graduate student at Cornell, who attended my seminar. I acknowledge his help in n. 64 of chapter 1.

on Socrates in a setting where my audience, as at St. Andrews, would include both classicists and philosophers, with an attractive sprinkling of non-specialists as well.

Here in this book are the lectures I gave there. Chapters 1, 2, 3, 4, 5, 6, and 7 are revisions of the seven lectures I delivered at Cornell. Chapter 8 is my Cambridge paper on Socrates' ethical theory. It gives the positive side of my interpretation of Socrates' moral philosophy to round out my side of the 1978 controversy in *T.L.S.* My understanding of Socrates has now achieved considerably greater maturity than in my Gifford Lectures. But it has reached neither fixity nor completeness. I am now working on additional essays, rewrites of Giffords. They are to go into a later volume of Socratic Studies which should also include revised versions of the previously published essays on "The Socratic Elenchus," on "Socrates' Disavowal of Knowledge," and also the paper entitled "The Historical Socrates and Athenian Democracy" which I would pit against the picture of Socrates as a crypto-oligarchic ideologue lately given currency in Stone's popular book.[67] Denying that Socrates' attitude is anti-populist, I argue in the third of these papers that it is *demophilic*, though not strictly *democratic*: we should not credit Socrates with a democratic political theory, for he has no political *theory* at all.[68] But he does have political sentiments and loyalties, strong ones. How profoundly democratic in the broader sense of the term[69] *these* are we can see by comparing him on this point with Plato in the *Republic*. To confine, as Plato does in books IV to VII of that work, moral inquiry to a tiny elite,[70] is to obliterate the Socratic vision which opens up the philosophic life to all. If "the unexamined life is not worth living by a human being" (*Ap.* 38A), Plato's restriction of the examined life to an elite Socrates would have been seen as making life not worth living for the mass of human beings.

Thirty years ago work on Socrates was a rarity in the scholarly

---

67 Stone, 1988. For what is wrong with that book see my letter to *T.L.S.*, November 4–10, 1988. For the view that the motive for Socrates' condemnation was essentially political one could hardly do better than consult the pioneering essays by two eighteenth-century *savants*, Fréret and Dresig, now edited by Mario Montuori (1981b) and the review of scholarship sympathetic to this approach by the same author (1981a).

68 On this latter point I differ from my friend Richard Kraut: see my review of his *Socrates and the State* (Vlastos, 1984a).

69 The late Eric Havelock remarked that the Greeks "democratized literacy" (1976: 45). In that sense of the term Socrates democratized moral philosophy: he brought it within the reach of "the many."

70 This is not made explicit until book VII (537D–539D: quoted, in part, in T4 in chapter 4). But the ground for it is prepared already in book IV, in the class-structure of the "perfectly good" (427E), state, all of it made "wise" exclusively by the wisdom of its philosopher-rulers.

literature in English. Today it is appearing in abundance.[71] I feel privileged to have had a share in this greening of Socratic studies whose beginning can be dated to the sixties, with the publication of the late Laszlo Versenyi's *Socratic Humanism* (1963), Michael O'Brien's *The Socratic Paradoxes and the Greek Mind* (1967), Norman Gulley's *The Philosophy of Socrates* (1968), and W. K. C. Guthrie, part 2 of vol. III of his *History of Greek Philosophy* (1969). For me the turnaround began with Santas' paper on "The Socratic Paradox" in 1964,[72] which first shed light on one of the thickets of Socratic strangeness, making good sense of a thesis which Socrates had long seemed to me to be asserting in mulish defiance of common sense.[73] In this book I am toiling in the same vineyard. Many of my proposals are controversial, some of them highly so. Well aware of this, I have chosen not to present them in a controversial context, for then I would have had to write a very different kind of book, addressing the expert instead of the "common reader" of Plato's work.

As I said at the start, what I offer in this book is not meant to distract attention from Plato's story but to invite closer scrutiny of it. If it does not strike my readers, on due consideration, as the most reasonable interpretation of our Socratic texts, they should junk it. If it has any worth at all, it is to make Plato's words more understandable than they would be without it. Anything written about them that fails in this is worthless. Readers who find enough good sense in my suggestions to engage their critical attention I trust will not deny me their reasoned censure.[74] I have made mistakes in the past and will doubtless make more in the future. Anyone who points them out to me is my friend.

PERSONAL ACKNOWLEDGEMENTS

To my colleagues in the Berkeley Department of Philosophy: for giving me an academic home upon my retirement from Princeton in 1976; for affording me, with incredible generosity, optimal conditions for teaching and research; for keeping me as Professor

---

71 More work on Socrates is appearing now in a single year than in a decade during the thirties, forties or fifties.

72 1964: 147–64. Curiously ignored by other scholars at the time: it is not listed in Guthrie's (1969) extensive bibliography nor yet subsequently in the one in Guthrie, 1975.

73 See section IV of chapter 5.

74 I shall expect to read it with profit, though I may be unable to compose replies. Contingencies of advancing age and precarious health now constrain me to conserve my time and energy with penurious frugality for my own creative work. First priority in its agenda goes to the Socratic studies which are to follow the present volume.

Emeritus in their midst upon my second retirement in 1987, an honour I had scarcely earned, since my appointment here during my working years had only been that of a Visiting Professor.

To Terry Irwin: as if all the help he has given me in the past were not enough, he offered, entirely of his own accord, out of the goodness of his heart, to read through the whole of the present MS, and offer me numerous critical comments, some of which have led to improvements.

To my instructors in the Mackintosh, principally Alan Code, but also Steve White and Henry Mendel: for their patience with a backward pupil and their forbearance at being importuned by telephoned S.O.S. at all hours of the day or night when I was stuck. Without a mastery of this gadget I doubt if I would have been capable of the production of the MS, now or ever.

I

SOCRATIC IRONY[1]

"Irony," says Quintilian, is that figure of speech or trope "in which something contrary to what is said is to be understood" (*contrarium ei quod dicitur intelligendum est*).[2] His formula has stood the test of time. It passes intact in Dr Johnson's dictionary ("mode of speech in which the meaning is contrary to the words" [1755]), and survives virtually intact in ours: "Irony is the use of words to express something other than, and especially the opposite of, [their] literal meaning" (*Webster's*). Here is an example, as simple and banal as I can make it: a British visitor, landing in Los Angeles in the midst of a downpour, is heard to remark, "What fine weather you are having here." The weather is foul, he calls it "fine," and has no trouble making himself understood to mean the contrary of what he says.

Why should we want to put such twists on words, making them mean something so different from their "literal" – i.e. their established, commonly understood – sense that it could even be its opposite? For one thing, humour. For another, mockery. Or, perhaps both at once, as when Mae West explains why she is declining President Gerald Ford's invitation to a state dinner at the White House: "It's an awful long way to go for just one meal." The joke is *on* someone, a put-down made socially acceptable by being wreathed in a cerebral smile.

A third possible use of irony has been so little noticed[3] that there is no name for it. Let me identify it by ostension. Paul, normally a

---

1 Originally written for the B Club of the Classics Faculty of Cambridge University, this essay has been presented and discussed at Cornell (as a Townsend Lecture) and Columbia (at a Trilling Seminar). I thank those whose comments have influenced the essay's present form.
2 *Institutio Oratorica* 9.22.44. Much the same definition occurs at 6.2.15 and 8.6.54.
3 The samples in Muecke, 1969: 15–19, several of them perfect gems, include no pure specimen of this variety. Neither in this nor in that other excellent book, Booth, 1974, is this dimension of irony noticed, far less explored.

good student, is not doing well today. He stumbles through a tutorial, exasperating his tutor, who finally lets fly with, "Paul, you are positively brilliant today." Paul feels he is being consigned to the outer darkness. But what for? What has he done that is so bad? Has he been rambling and disorganized, loose and sloppy in his diction, ungrammatical, unsyntactical, ill-prepared, uninformed, confused, inconsistent, incoherent? For which sub-class of these failings is he being faulted? He hasn't been told. He has been handed a riddle and left to solve it for himself. Though certainly not universal, this form of irony is not as rare as one might think. Only from its most artless forms, as in my first example, is it entirely absent. There is a touch of it in the second. Mae West puts us off teasingly from her reasons for declining that gilt-edged invitation. She is implying: "If you are not an utter fool you'll know this isn't my real reason. Try guessing what that might be."

When irony riddles it risks being misunderstood. At the extreme the hearer might even miss the irony altogether. If Paul had been fatuously vain, sadly deficient in self-criticism, he could have seized on that remark to preen himself on the thought that he must have said *something* brilliant after all. If so, we would want to say that the deception occurred contrary to the speaker's intent. For if the tutor had meant to speak ironically he could not have meant to deceive. Those two intentions are at odds; in so far as the first is realized the second cannot be. That in fact there was no intention to deceive should be obvious in all three of my examples. And that this is not a contingent feature of these cases can be seen by referring back to the definition at the start. Just from that we can deduce that if the visitor had meant to deceive someone – say, his wife back in London – into thinking that the weather just then was fine in L.A., he could not have done it by saying to her *ironically* over the phone, "The weather is fine over here." For to say this ironically is to say it intending that by "fine" she should understand the contrary; if she did, she would not be deceived: the weather in L.A. *was* the contrary of "fine" just then.

This is so basic that a further example may not be amiss. A crook comes by a ring whose stone he knows to be a fake and goes round saying to people he is trying to dupe, "Can I interest you in a diamond ring?" To call this "irony" would be to confess being all at sea about the meaning of the word. Our definition tells us why: to serve his fraud the literal sense of "diamond" has to be the one he intends to convey. To see him using the word ironically we would have to conjure up a case in which he did not have this intention –

say, by his saying to his ten-year-old daughter with a tell-tale glint in his eye, "Luv, can I interest you in a diamond ring?" Now suppose he had said this to her without that signal. Might we still call it "irony"? We might, provided we were convinced he was not trying to fool her: she is ten, not five, old enough to know that if that trinket were a diamond ring it would be worth thousands and her father would not let it out of his sight. If we thought this is what he was about – testing her intelligence and good sense – we could still count it irony: a pure specimen of the riddling variety. It would not be disqualified as such if the little girl were to fail the test, for the remark was not made with the intention to deceive. Similarly, the tutor might have said "brilliant" well aware there was a chance Paul might miss the irony and mistake censure for praise – knowing this and for good reasons of his own willing to take the chance.

Once this has sunk in we are in for a surprise when we go back to the Greeks and discover that the intention to deceive, so alien to our word for irony, is normal in its Greek ancestor *eirōneia, eirōn, eirōneuomai.*[4] The difference is apparent in the first three occurrences of the word in the surviving corpus of Attic texts, all three of them in Aristophanes. In *Wasps* 174, ὡς εἰρωνικῶς refers to Philocleon's lying to get his donkey out of the family compound to make a dicast out of him. In *Birds* 1211, it is applied to Iris for lying her way into the city of the birds. In *Clouds* 449, εἴρων, sandwiched in between two words for "slippery," figures in "a catalogue of abusive terms against a man who is a tricky opponent in a lawsuit."[5] We meet more of the same in fourth-century usage. Demosthenes (*1 Phil.* 7) uses it of citizens who prevaricate to evade irksome civic duty. Plato uses it in the *Laws* (901E) when prescribing penalties for heretics. The hypocritical ones he calls the *eirōnikon* species of the class: for them he legislates death or worse; those equally wrong-headed but honestly outspoken are let off with confinement and admonition. In the *Sophist*, pronouncing Socrates' dialectic a superior form of *sophistikē,*[6] Plato contrasts it with the run-of-the-mill *sophistikē* practiced by ordinary sophists: these are the people he puts into the *eirōnikon* species of the art. Not Socrates, but his arch-rivals, whom Plato thinks imposters, are the ones he calls *eirōnes* (268A–B).

---

4 On εἴρων as a term of abuse (*Schimpfwort*) in the classical period see the groundbreaking paper by Ribbeck, 1876: 381ff.: it has not been superseded by the later studies, which I shall not be undertaking to review.
5 Dover (1968) *ad loc.* in his invaluable edition of the *Clouds*.
6 ἡ γένει γενναία σοφιστική ("the sophistry of noble lineage"), 321B.

How entrenched in disingenuousness is the most ordinary use of *eirōn* we can see in the picture of the *eirōn* in Aristotle and Theophrastus. Strikingly different though he is in each – odious in Theophrastus, amiable in Aristotle[7] – in one respect he is the same in both[8]: he willfully prevaricates in what he says about himself. Aristotle takes a lenient view of such dissembling in the case of Socrates. Casting him as an *eirōn* Aristotle contrasts him with his opposite, the braggart (*alazōn*), and finds him incomparably more attractive because the qualities he disclaims are the prestigious ones and his reason for disclaiming them – "to avoid pompousness" – is commendable (*N.E.* 1127b23–6), though still, it should be noted, not admirable in Aristotle's view. When he expresses admiration for Socrates' personal character he shifts to an entirely different trait: it is for indifference to the contingencies of fate (*apatheia*), not at all for εἰρωνεία, that he reckons Socrates "great-souled" (*megalopsuchos*, *Po. An.* 98a16–24; cf. D.L. 6.2). In Theophrastus the *eirōn* is flayed mercilessly,[9] portrayed as systematically deceitful,[10] venomously double-faced,[11] adept at self-serving camouflage.[12]

This is how Thrasymachus views Socrates in that famous passage in which he refers to Socrates' "customary" *eirōneia*:

T1 *R.* 337A: "Heracles!" he said. "This is Socrates' habitual shamming (εἰωθυῖα εἰρωνεία). I had predicted to these people that you would refuse to answer and would sham (εἰρωνεύσοιο) and would do anything but answer if the question were put to you."

Thrasymachus is charging that Socrates lies in saying that he has no answer of his own to the question he is putting to others: he most certainly has. Thrasymachus is protesting, but pretends he hasn't to keep it under wraps so he can have a field-day pouncing on ours and tearing it to shreds while his is shielded from attack. So there is no

---

7 In the references to Socrates in the *N.E.*, *E.E.*, and *M.M.*, but perhaps not in the *Rhet.*, where εἰρωνεία is reckoned a "disdainful" trait (καταφρονητικόν, 1379b31–2).

8 The same at the core: προσποίησις ἐπὶ τὸ ἔλαττον in Aristotle (*N.E.* 1108a22), προσποίησις ἐπὶ τὸ χεῖρον in Theophrastus (1.1): affectation (or pretense) in either case.

9 "Such men are more to be avoided than adders" (1, *sub fin.*).

10 "He pretends not to have heard what he heard, not to have seen what he saw, to have no recollection of the thing to which he agreed" (1.5).

11 "He will praise to their faces those he attacks behind their backs" (1.2). I find it astonishing that Friedländer (1958: 138) should say that Theophrastus portrays, but "does not evaluate," εἰρωνεία. Could there be a more emphatic devaluation than the remark quoted here and in the preceding notes? By leaving Socrates out of it, Theophrastus feels free to vent on the εἴρων the scorn he deserves in the common view.

12 Aristotle too observes that your most dangerous enemies are "the quiet, dissembling, and unscrupulous" (οἱ πρᾶοι καὶ εἴρωνες καὶ πανοῦργοι), hiding their evil intent under a cool exterior (*Rhet.* 1382b21).

excuse for rendering *eirōneia* here by "irony" (Bloom, Grube, Shorey);[13] if that translation were correct, lying would be a standard form of irony.[14]

From the behavior of εἰρωνεία in all of the above Attic texts from Aristophanes to Theophrastus one could easily jump to a wrong conclusion: *because* it is so commonly used to denote sly, intentionally deceptive speech or conduct throughout this period, *must* it be always so used of Socrates by Plato? This is what many noted Hellenists have assumed: Burnet,[15] Wilamowitz,[16] Guthrie,[17] among them. Let me point out how unsafe this kind of inference would be. From the fact that a word is used in a given sense in a multitude of cases it does not follow that it cannot be used in a sharply different sense in others. Such statistical inferences are always risky. This one is certainly wrong. Consider the following:

T2 *G.* 489D–E: [a] Socrates: "Since by 'better' you don't mean 'stronger,' tell me again what you mean. And teach me more gently, admirable man, so that I won't run away from your school." Callicles: "You are mocking me (εἰρωνεύῃ)."

[b] Socrates: "No, by Zethus, whom you used earlier to do a lot of mocking (πολλὰ εἰρωνεύου) of me."[18]

---

13 Bloom (1968) and Grube (1974) take this to be the sense of εἰρωνεία and εἰρωνεύσοιο. Shorey too (1930) takes "irony" to be the sense of εἰρωνεία (referring to *Smp.* 216E, to be discussed below); but he shifts, without explanation, to "dissemble" for the latter. I suspect he is confused about the meaning of the English word "irony," taking *it* to mean "dissembling."

14 For acceptable translations consult Lindsay, 1935 ("slyness"), Cornford, 1945 ("shamming ignorance"), Robin, 1956 ("feinte ignorance"). That "shamming," "feigning" is the sense should be completely clear from the context.

15 In his note on Plato, *Ap.* 38A1: "The words εἴρων, εἰρωνεία, εἰρωνεύομαι (in Plato) are only used of Socrates by his opponents, and have always an unfavourable meaning." He is not overlooking εἰρωνευομένῳ at *Ap.* 38A1; the same sense in Allen's translation (1984): "You will think that I am being sly and dishonest." But Burnet is ignoring (or "misunderstanding"?) both of the notable uses of the word in Alcibiades' speech in the *Symposium* (to be discussed below).

16 1948: 451, n. 1: "Wo [die Ironie] dem Sokrates beigelegt wird [im Platon] geschieht es immer als Vorwurf, auch von Alkibiades, *Smp.* 216E." Neither he nor Burnet (preceding note) takes any notice of Ribbeck's discussion of *R.* 337A, which captures exactly the sense of εἰωθυῖα εἰρωνεία here.

17 "In Plato it retains its bad sense, in the mouth of a bitter opponent like Thrasymachus or of one pretending to be angry at the way in which Socrates deceives everyone as to his real character (Alcibiades at *Smp.* 216E, 218D)" (Guthrie, 1969: 446). Guthrie could have added *Ap.* 38A1, οὐ πείσεσθέ μοι ὡς εἰρωνευομένῳ. Socrates expects the "command" he gets from the oracle story, and the story itself, to be taken as a dishonest fiction. But Guthrie is taking no notice of *G.* 489D–E (to be discussed directly in the text above); and he assumes that in *R.* 337A εἴρων- has the same sense as at *Smp.* 216E and 218D.

18 My translation follows Croiset & Bodin, 1955. Woodhead's "you are ironical" is acceptable in [a] where the mockery *is* ironical (it takes the form of saying something contrary to what the speaker believes to be true), but not at [b], where this is not the case.

In part [a] Callicles is protesting Socrates' casting himself as a pupil of his – a transparent irony, since Callicles no doubt feels that, on the contrary, it is Socrates who has been playing the schoolmaster right along. In [b] Socrates is retorting that Callicles had used the figure of Zethus to mock him earlier on, associating him with the latter's brother, the pathetic Amphion, who "despite a noble nature, puts on the semblance of a silly juvenile" (485E–486A). In both cases mockery is being protested without the slightest imputation of intentional deceit. In neither case is there any question of shamming, slyness, or evasiveness – no more so than if they had resorted to crude abuse, like calling each other "pig" or "jack-ass."

No less instructive for my purpose is the following from the *Rhetorica ad Alexandrum* (a treatise of uncertain authorship, probably of the fourth century):[19]

T3 *Eirōneia* is [a] saying something while pretending not to say it or [b] calling things by contrary names. (21)

At [a] we get nothing new: *eirōneuein* is one of the many tricks of the trade this handbook offers the rhetorician.[20] Not so at [b], as becomes even clearer in his example:

T4 Evidently, those good people (οὗτοι μὲν οἱ χρηστοί) have done much evil to the allies, while we, the bad ones, have caused them many benefits (*loc. cit.*).

The way χρηστοί is used here reminds us of the line Aristophanes gives Strepsiades in the opening monologue of the *Clouds*: "this good youth" (ὁ χρηστὸς οὗτος νεανίας), says the old man of his good-for-

Irwin's "sly" will not do: there is nothing particularly "cunning, wily or hypocritical" (*O.E.D.* for "sly") in the tone or content. We must also reject Ribbeck's understanding of the sense in [a]: inexplicably, he reads "chicanery" into εἰρωνεύη. But there is nothing wrong with his gloss on εἰρωνεύου at [b] ("a form of mockery through false, insincere, praise"), rightly connecting the use of εἰρωνεύειν here with Pollux 2.78, καὶ τὸν εἴρωνα ἔνιοι μυκτῆρα καλοῦσι, and the sillographer Timon's reference to Socrates (fr. 25D, *ap.* D.L. 2.19), μυκτὴρ ῥητορόμυκτος ὑπαττικὸς εἰρωνευτής. Ribbeck remarks apropos of [b]: "hence the current conception of εἰρωνεύεσθαι must have been broader than is usually assumed" (*loc. cit.*). He should have specified more definitely this "wider" use. That εἰρωνεύεσθαι can be used to express mockery pure and simple without any insinuation of deceit Ribbeck does not seem to have grasped, else why "chicanery" as the sense at [a]?

19 Long attributed to Aristotle (included in the Berlin edition of Aristotle's works), it then came to be ascribed to Anaximenes of Lampsacus, a contemporary of Theophrastus (see the introduction by H. Rackham in his translation of it in the Loeb Classical Library, 1973: 258ff.). The ascription is far from certain, but its date cannot be much later. Its linguistic and political ambience is that of fourth-century Athens, echoing Isocrates' *Technē Rhetorikē*. Eight fragments of it turn up in a papyrus dated by its editors in the first half of the third century (Grenfell & Hunt, *Hibeh Papyri* pt. 1, no. 26, pp. 113ff.).

20 Cope, 1967: 401ff., describes the form of persuasion recommended by the treatise as "a system of tricks, shifts and evasions, showing an utter indifference to right and wrong, truth and falsehood."

nothing son.[21] This is irony of the purest water: mockery without the least intention of deceit.

Can we make sense of this state of affairs? In a mass of Attic texts (eight of those to which I have referred; I could have added many more of the same kind) we find εἰρωνεία implying willful misrepresentation; yet in the ninth (T2) we see it standing for mockery entirely devoid of any such connotation and so too in part [b] of the tenth (T3), where a rhetorician who is thoroughly at home in fourth-century Attic usage gives a definition of εἰρωνεία which anticipates Quintilian so perfectly that the two definitions are precisely equivalent: each is a description of the same speech-act, viewed from the speaker's point of view in T3[b], from the hearer's in Quintilian. Is this linguistic phenomenon understandable? Yes, perfectly, if we remind ourselves of the parallel behavior of our word "pretending." To say that a malingerer is "pretending" to be sick and a con man "pretending" to have high connections is to say that these people are deceivers: "to allege falsely" is the basic use of to pretend. But there are contexts where "to pretend" by-passes false allegation because it by-passes falsehood, as when we say that the children are "pretending" that their coloured chips are money ("pretend-money" they call them) or that their dolls are sick or die or go to school. In just the same way we could say that the crook in the example is "pretending" that the stone on the trinket is a diamond when he offers it to his daughter, which is as far as anything from his pretending it is a diamond when putting it up to the people he is trying to hook. That the latter should be the most common (and, in point of logic, the primary) use of "pretending" does nothing to block a secondary use of the word, tangential to the first – a subsidiary use which is altogether innocent of intentional deceit, predicated on that "willing suspension of disbelief" by which we enter the world of imaginative fiction in art or play. This is the sense of "pretending" we could invoke to elucidate ironical diction, as in Mae West's remark: we could say she is "pretending" that the length of the journey is her reason for declining, which would be patently absurd if "pretending" were being used in its primary sense. There is no false allegation, because there is no allegation: she is pulling our leg.

---

21 Should the reader be reminded that the occurrence of ironical speech-acts is independent of the availability of a description of them as such in the speaker's language? The use of irony, as distinct from reflection on it, is as old as the hills. We can imagine a caveman offering a tough piece of steak to his mate with the remark, "Try this tender morsel." No lack of examples in Homer (Eumaeus to the "beggar": "good repute and virtue I would have among men, if I were to kill you," *Od.* 14.402: he means just the opposite).

This, I suggest, gives a good explanation of the fact that though *eirōn*, *eirōneia*, *eirōneuomai* are commonly used to imply disingenuousness, even so, they are capable of an alternative use which is completely free of such evocation and, *pace* Burnet, Wilamowitz, Guthrie,[22] Dover[23] are so used at times by Socrates in Plato. What happened, I suggest, is this: when εἰρωνεία gained currency in Attic use (by the last third of the fifth century at the latest), its semantic field was as wide as is that of "pretending" in present-day English, and *eirōn* had strongly unfavorable connotations – was used as a term of denigration or abuse – because the first of those two uses predominated heavily over the second; to be called an *eirōn* would be uncomplimentary at best, insulting at the worst. But turn the pages of history some three hundred years – go from Greece in the fourth century B.C. to Rome in the first – and you will find a change which would be startling if long familiarity had not inured us to it. The word has now lost its disagreeable overtones. When Cicero, who loves to make transliterated Greek enrich his mother tongue, produces in this fashion the new Latin word, *ironia*, the import has an altogether different tone. Laundered and deodorized, it now betokens the height of urbanity, elegance, and good taste:

T5 Cicero, *De Oratore* 2.67: Urbana etiam dissimulatio est, cum alia dicuntur ac sentias... Socratem opinor in hac *ironia* dissimulantiaque longe lepore et humanitate omnibus praestitisse. Genus est perelegans et cum gravitate salsum...[24]

And when Quintilian, two generations later, consolidating Cicero's use of the term, encapsulates its meaning in the definition cited above, we are no longer in any doubt that *ironia* has shed completely its disreputable past, has already become what it will come to be in the languages and sensibility of modern Europe: speech used to express a meaning that runs contrary to what is said – the perfect medium for mockery innocent of deceit. Subsidiary in the use of the parent word in classical Greece, this now becomes the standard use. *Eirōneia* has metastasized into irony.

22 See nn. 15, 16, 17 above.
23 Cf. his gloss on *Smp.* 216E4: "εἰρωνεία (unlike 'irony') is 'mock-modesty', 'pretended ignorance'; in *Rep.* 337A Thrasymachus speaks (in no friendly tone) of 'Socrates' accustomed εἰρωνεία'." Dover is assuming that εἰρωνεία is used in the same sense in both passages.
24 "Urbane is the dissimulation when what you say is quite other than what you understand... In this irony and dissimulation Socrates, in my opinion, far excelled all others in charm and humanity. Most elegant is this form and seasoned in seriousness." Translating *dissimulatio* here by "dissembling" (as we may, with good warrant from the dictionaries), we should bear in mind that *deceitful* concealment, normally conveyed by the English word, is absent from the figure of speech Cicero has in view. Deceitful speech would not be what he calls *urbane* dissimulation, "where the whole tenor of your speech shows that you are gravely jesting (*severe ludens*) in speaking differently from what you think" (*loc. cit.*).

Exactly what made this happen we cannot say: we lack the massive linguistic data to track the upward mobility of the word. What, I submit, we can say is *who* made it happen: Socrates. Not that he ever made an assault upon the word. There is no reason to believe he ever did. In none of our sources does he ever make *eirōneia* the *F* in his "What is the *F*?" question or bring it by some other means under his elenctic hammer. He changes the word not by theorizing about it but by creating something new for it to mean: a new form of life realized in himself which was the very incarnation of εἰρωνεία in that second of its contemporary uses, as innocent of intentional deceit as is a child's feigning that the play chips are money, as free from shamming as are honest games, though, unlike games, serious in its mockery (*cum gravitate salsum*), dead earnest in its playfulness (*severe ludens*), a previously unknown, unimagined type of personality, so arresting to his contemporaries and so memorable for ever after, that the time would come, centuries after his death, when educated people would hardly be able to think of *ironia* without its bringing Socrates to mind. And as this happened the meaning of the word altered. The image of Socrates as the paradeigmatic *eirōn* effected a change in the previous connotation of the word.[25] Through the eventual influence of the after-image of its Socratic incarnation, the use which had been marginal in the classical period became its central, its normal and normative use: *eirōneia* became *ironia*.

I have made a large claim. What is there in our sources to show that Socrates really was the arch-ironist Cicero and Quintilian thought him?

Nothing in Aristophanes. The anti-hero of the *Clouds* is many things to many men, but an ironist to none: too solemn by half as natural philosopher, sage or hierophant, too knavish[26] as a preceptor of the young. Nor is he represented as an ironist in the sideswipe at him in the *Frogs* (1491–9). The portrait is now appreciably different. Outside the thinkery – else the question of an ordinary Athenian

---

25 A change so drastic as to eclipse the original meaning of the word from Cicero's and Quintilian's view. The occultation seems total: from what they say about *ironia* we would never guess that in texts they knew well its Greek original had been a *Schimpfwort*. The authority of the Socratic paradigm becomes so definitive for Cicero that he is content to understand the word simply "that *ironia*... found in Socrates, which he deploys in the dialogues of Plato, Xenophon, and Aeschines" (*Brutus* 292). And when Quintilian remarks that "ironia may characterize a man's whole life" he refers to Socrates and only to him (*Inst. Or.* 9.2.46).

26 Though he does not himself inculcate crooked argument, he panders to the demand for it. He keeps both this and its opposite (the δίκαιος and the ἄδικος λόγος) on the premises and the customer can have his choice. Cf. Nussbaum, 1980: 48: "Throughout the play Socrates makes no attempt to teach justice and to urge the just use of rhetorical skill. His attitude is at best neutral; at worst he condones deceit."

picking a seat next to him would not arise – he is no longer a sinister figure. But he is still a quibbler, whose hair-splitting solemnities (ἐπὶ σεμνοῖσιν λόγοισι καὶ σκαριφησμοῖσι λήρων, 1496–7), engulf his interlocutors in tasteless triviality. No hint of irony in this pretentious idler's chatter.

We turn to Xenophon. At first it looks as though neither here shall we find what we are looking for. Through most of the *Memorabilia* this tirelessly didactic, monotonously earnest, Socrates appears to have no more jesting, mocking, or riddling in his soul than the atheistic natural philosopher and "highpriest of subtlest poppy-cock"[27] of the Aristophanic caricature. But once in a while we get a flash of something different,[28] and then, in chapter 11 of book III, we get a big break. Here Socrates turns skittish and goes to pay a visit to the beautiful Theodote.[29] He offers her suggestions to enlarge her clientele and she invites him to become her partner in the pursuit of *philoi*. He demurs, pleading much business, both private and public, and adding:

T6 Xenophon, *Mem.* 3.11.16: "I have my own girlfriends (*philai*) who won't leave me day or night, learning from me philters and enchantments."

Since she is meant to see, and does see, that these "girlfriends" are philosophers,[30] depressingly male and middle-aged, there is no question of her being misled into thinking that her visitor has a stable of pretty girls to whom he teaches love-potions. So here at last we do get something Cicero and Quintilian would recognize as *ironia*, though hardly a gem of the genre: its humor is too arch and strained.

After the visit to Theodote, Socrates in the *Memorabilia* resumes his platitudinously wholesome moralizing. But he snaps out of it for good in Xenophon's *Symposium*.[31] There we see what he might have been in the *Memorabilia* if the severely apologetic aims of that work had not toned down the hues of its Socratic portrait to shades of gray. The convivial *mise-en-scène* of the drinking-party prompts Xenophon to paint bright, even garish, colours into the picture. Asked what is that art of his in which he takes great pride he says it is the art of the procurer (*mastropos*, 4.56). Challenged to a beauty-contest by the handsome Critobulus (5.1ff.), he pleads the superior

---

27 *Clouds*, 359, in Arrowsmith's (1962) translation.
28 Kierkegaard, 1965, notes (58–9 and 64) flashes of irony in the dialogue with Charicles (1.2.36ff.) and Hippias (4.4.6).
29 Here Kierkegaard's taste, usually faultless, deserts him. He finds the episode "disgusting" (1965: 61–2).
30 He names Apollodorus and Antisthenes, his inseparables, and also his frequent visitors from Thebes, Cebes and Simmias (3.9.17).
31 For shrewd appreciation of irony in this work see the comments on the goings-on at the drinking party in Higgins, 1977: 15–20. Full discussion of the same material also in Edelstein, 1935: 11–12, though curiously enough she does not perceive it as irony.

beauty of his own ugliest features – his snub nose, his oversized flaring nostrils – on the ground that useful is beautiful (5.6). Here we see a new form of irony, unprecedented in Greek literature to my knowledge, which is peculiarly Socratic. For want of a better name, I shall call it "complex irony"[32] to contrast it with the simple ironies I have been dealing with in this chapter heretofore. In "simple" irony what is said just isn't what is meant: taken in its ordinary, commonly understood, sense the statement is simply false. In "complex" irony what is said both is and isn't what is meant: its surface content is meant to be true in one sense, false in another. Thus when Socrates says he is a "procurer" he does not, and yet does, mean what he says. He obviously does not in the common, vulgar, sense of the word. But nonetheless he does in another sense he gives the word *ad hoc*, making it mean someone "who makes the procured attractive to those whose company he is to keep" (4.57). Xenophon's Socrates can claim he does exactly that. Again, when he says that his flat, pushed-in nose, his protruding eyes, and his large, flaring nostrils are beautiful, he does not, and yet does, mean what he says. In the ordinary sense of the word he would be the first to deny that they are. But if by "beautiful" he were allowed to mean "well made for their required function" (5.4), then he would have us know that his particular sort of eyes and nose are superlatively beautiful: unlike the deep-set ones of fashion-models, his can see sideways, not merely straight ahead; his nose is a more efficient vent than that of the currently admired profile (5.5–6).

Undoubtedly then there is an authentic streak of irony in Xenophon's depiction of Socrates.[33] But for the purpose of assuring us that it was really Socrates who played the critical role in the mutation of *eirōneia* into irony, what Xenophon tells us about Socrates would still be defective in important ways.

In the first place, the ironies Xenophon puts into the portrait have little doctrinal significance. They contribute nothing to the elucidation of Socrates' philosophy because Xenophon system-atically ignores those very features of it which Socrates wants to be understood as "complex ironies" of the sort he illustrates in making his hero say he is a procurer and has a charming nose. I mean the

32 I shall be employing this term here and hereafter throughout the book as a quasi-technical term, harking back to my introduction of it in Vlastos, 1985: 1ff. at 30.

33 So it is understandable that Cicero (*Brutus* 292: cf. n. 25 above) should speak of Socratic *ironia* in the dialogues of Xenophon (as well as Aeschines) along with those of Plato. But it is only to the latter that he turns to illustrate it and in doing so it is clear that the Socrates he has in view ("ignorant of everything," *omnium rerum inscium*) could not be the Xenophontic figure, though it could be the Aeschinean: see fr. 11 (translated in additional note 1.4 below, and quoted again as T21 in chapter 3), "I had no knowledge through which I could benefit him by teaching it to him."

great philosophical paradoxes of which we hear in Plato's earlier dialogues, like Socrates' disavowal of knowledge and of teaching.[34] Each of these is intelligible only as a complex irony. When he professes to have no knowledge he both does and does not mean what he says. He wants it to assure his hearers that in the moral domain there is not a single proposition he claims to know with certainty. But in another sense of "knowledge," where the word refers to justified true belief – justifiable through the peculiarly Socratic method of elenctic argument – there are many propositions he does claim to know.[35] So too, I would argue, Socrates' parallel disavowal of teaching should be understood as a complex irony. In the conventional sense, where to "teach" is simply to transfer knowledge from a teacher's to a learner's mind, Socrates means what he says: that sort of teaching he does not do. But in the sense which *he* would give to "teaching" – engaging would-be learners in elenctic argument to make them aware of their own ignorance and enable them to discover for themselves the truth the teacher had held back – in that sense of "teaching" Socrates would want to say that he *is* a teacher, the only true teacher; his dialogue with his fellows is meant to have, and does have, the effect of evoking and assisting their own effort at moral self-improvement.[36]

In the second place, the words *eirōneia*, *eirōn*, *eirōneuomai* are never applied to Socrates in Xenophon's Socratic writings either by Xenophon himself or by anyone else. If we had only Xenophon's picture of Socrates we would have no reason to think that Socrates' contemporaries had thought of *eirōneia* as a distinctively Socratic trait. That noun and its cognate verb, so conspicuous in Thrasymachus' attack on Socrates in T1 above, drop out when the identical reproach is ventilated by Hippias in the *Memorabilia*. This is how the complaint is now made to read:

T7 Xen. *Mem.* 4.4.9:[37] "We've had enough of your ridiculing others, questioning and refuting everyone, while never willing to render an account yourself to anyone or state your own opinion about anything."

The reference in T1 to Socrates' "habitual *eirōneia*" has been washed out.[38]

---

34 On these complex ironies and a third, closely associated with them, see additional note 1.1.
35 The textual basis for this claim is set forth in considerable detail in Vlastos, 1985 (at pp. 6–11).
36 He says he is "one of the few Athenians, not to say the only one, to undertake (ἐπιχειρεῖν: cf. additional note 1.1, n. 21) the true political art" (*G.* 521D) in a context in which the criterion for the practice of this art is one's effect on the moral character of one's fellow-townsmen (*G.* 515A). Both texts are discussed in additional note 1.1.
37 Quoted more fully as T25 in chapter 3.
38 Nor does any other of Socrates' interlocutors ever say or imply in Xenophon that Socrates is an εἴρων. He is never represented there as producing on friend or foe the impression he

Fortunately, we have Plato's Socratic dialogues where what Xenophon denies us is supplied in such abundance that to go through all of it would be work for a whole book. Forced to be selective,[39] I shall concentrate on one piece of it – the half dozen pages or so that make up the speech of Alcibiades in Plato's *Symposium*. Despite the provenance of this composition from a dialogue of Plato's middle period, its Socrates is unmistakably the philosopher of the earlier one:[40] he is portrayed as voicing that total disavowal of knowledge[41] which is so striking a feature of the Socrates of the earlier period who, as I shall be arguing in chapter 2, is Plato's re-creation of the historical figure. The discourse of Diotima which Socrates professes to report in his own speech in the *Symposium* is as strong an affirmation of Plato's *un*Socratic doctrine of transcendent Forms[42] as is anything he ever wrote. But Alcibiades has not heard what Socrates says he learned from Diotima. He joins the drinking-party after Socrates has finished. In the speech about Socrates Alcibiades now proceeds to deliver, the last in the *Symposium*, Plato brings back to life the earlier *un*Platonic Socrates as surely as he does also in book I of the *Republic*.[43] He ushers us into the *Republic* through a Socratic portico and escorts us out of the *Symposium* through a Socratic back-porch.[44]

The key sentence in Alcibiades' speech is

T8 *Smp.* 216E4: "He spends his entire life *eirōneuomenos* and jesting with people."

How shall we read *eirōneuomenos*? When Quintilian (*Inst. Or.* 9.2.46) remarks that *ironia* may characterize not just a text or a speech but "an entire life" (*vita universa*) Socrates is his only example. So we know how *he* would have read *eirōneuomenos* in the text. But time and again it is read differently by scholars. Guthrie[45] takes it to refer to "the way in which Socrates deceives everyone as to his real character." Dover,[46] assimilating it to T1 above, denying that the word means "irony" here, takes it to refer to Socrates' "pretended ignorance." Suzy Groden translates,

makes on Alcibiades in Plato of being *habitually* and *characteristically* ironical (the sense of εἰρωνικῶς at T9 below, as I shall be arguing in glossing that text). The people to whom he says in Xenophon's *Symposium* that he is a procurer and has lovely facial features do understand, of course, that he is speaking ironically; but they give no indication of recognizing this as a habitual Socratic trait.   39 But see also section II of chapter 5.

40 The multiple differences between these two periods of Plato's literary output in its portrayal of Socrates will be discussed in chapter 2.

41 216D (= T15 below): "he knows nothing and is ignorant of everything."

42 To be discussed in section III of chapter 2. See especially the gloss on T22 there.

43 See additional note 2.1 ("The composition of *Rep.* I").

44 Similarly in the *Phaedo* authentic Socratic material is used to introduce (57A–64a) and cap (115A to the end) the no less authentically Platonic philosophical argument of the dialogue.   45 Guthrie, 1969: 446.   46 See n. 23 above.

He *pretends* [my emphasis] to be ignorant and spends his whole life putting people on.

and W. Hamilton,

He spends his whole life *pretending* [my emphasis] and playing with people.

If we follow Quintilian we shall understand Alcibiades to be saying that Socrates is a lifelong ironist. If we follow Guthrie & Co. we shall understand him to be saying that Socrates is a lifelong deceiver. Since, as I explained above, the latter was the most common of the current uses of the word, the presumption should indeed be that these scholars are right. So if one believes that, on the contrary, Quintilian's reading is the right one, one must assume the burden of proof. I gladly assume it.

But I must start with another sentence in Alcibiades' speech which is equally important for my thesis, for here again the critical word is applied not to what Socrates says in this or that passage but to his usual, characteristic, way of speaking:

T9 *Smp.* 218D6–7: "He heard me out. Then, most *eirōnikōs*, in his extremely characteristic and habitual[47] manner, he said..."

Here Groden and Hamilton translate, respectively,

"He answered in that extremely *ironical* way he always uses [my emphasis], very characteristically."

"He made a thoroughly characteristic reply in his usual *ironical* style [my emphasis]."

Thus of their own accord both of them give me all I want. Do they realize what they are doing? Do they see that they are welshing on their previous translation of *eirōneuomenos* in T8? I don't know and I don't need to know. It suffices that here Plato's text allows no other choice.

Let us recall the context. T9 comes at the climax of the *pièce de résistance* of Alcibiades' speech: his narration of an episode from his distant youth, when he was still in his "bloom" – that final phase in a boy's transition to manhood, which in that culture marked the peak of his physical attractiveness to males older than himself. The story begins as follows:

T10 *Smp.* 217A: "Believing that he was seriously smitten by my bloom, I thought it a windfall, a wonderful piece of luck, since by allowing him my favors I would be able to learn from him all he knew."

---

47 εἰωθότως, with which cf. εἰωθυῖα εἰρωνεία in T1 above.

The project of swapping sex for moral wisdom may seem incredible today. It would not have seemed so *in the least* to someone in Alcibiades' circumstances at the time. Let me enumerate them:

(1)   As we know from Pausanias' speech in the *Symposium* (218D6–219A), this is the norm (*nomos*) in the higher form of pederastic love: the boy gives "favors," the man gives intellectual and moral improvement.

(2)   Alcibiades already had (and knew he had):[48] that asset to which he was to owe throughout his life so much of his unprincipled success: stunning beauty and grace.[49]

(3)   We know from other Platonic dialogues[50] and from Xenophon too[51] that Socrates has a high susceptibility to male beauty to which a sexy teenager could hardly have failed to resonate.[52]

(4)   Socrates does not answer questions, does not expound his "wisdom." Pieces of it spill out in elenctic arguments, leaving the interlocutor wondering how much is being held back.

(5)   We know that the speaker is a highly acratic character. He starts his whole speech with a confession:

T11 *Smp.* 216B3–5:   "I know that I cannot contradict him and I should do as he bids, but when I am away from him I am defeated by the adulation of the crowd."

There is no reason to think that he was different as a teenager.

Put those five things together and it should not seem strange if a boy who longs to become a "good and noble man" (*kalos kagathos*) should get it into his head that the key to what he wanted was hidden away in the vast, undisclosed store of wisdom in Socrates, who might be induced to slip him the key were he to offer as a *quid pro quo* something as irresistibly attractive to all the men of his acquaintance as was his own superlative "bloom." He pursues the project methodically, going through all the ploys in the current repertoire of

48 217A5–6, "I had a wonderful opinion of my bloom."
49 Cf. W. Ferguson in the *Cambridge Ancient History* v (Cambridge, 1935), 263: "Arrestingly handsome, he received from men in Athens the recognition and privileges ordinarily given in other societies to extraordinary beauty in women; and his insolence he draped in such charm of manner that, when he showed respect for neither gods nor men, age nor authority, guardian nor wife, the outrageousness of the act was often forgotten and only the air of the actor remembered."
50 *Prt.* 309A; *G.* 481D; *Chrm.* 155C–E; *Men.* 76C1–2.   51 Xen. *Smp.* 8.2.
52 Xenophon (*Mem.* 3.11.3) adds the precious information (which we never get from Plato) that Socrates is also susceptible to female beauty. The sight of the scantily clad Theodote makes Socrates (speaking for himself and his companions) "long to touch what we saw; we shall go away excited (ὑποκνιζόμενοι) and with longing (ποθήσομεν)."

homosexual seduction.[53] But nothing works. Socrates remains
friendly but distant. When Alcibiades wants to hear the sweet
nothings of love all he gets is elenctic argument, more of the same old
thing. Finally he sets Socrates up and blurts out his proposition.
Here is the response he gets:

T12 *Smp.* 218D6–219A1: "He heard me out. Then, most *eirōnikōs*, in his
extremely characteristic and habitual manner,[54] he said: 'Dear Alcibiades,
it looks as though you are not stupid (*phaulos*), if what you say about me is
true and there really is in me some power which could make you a better
man: you must be seeing something inconceivably beautiful in me,
enormously superior to your good looks. If that is what you see and you
want to exchange beauty for beauty, you mean to take a huge advantage
of me: you are trying to get true beauty in exchange for seeming beauty
– "gold for brass".'"

Here, I submit, it is incontestably clear that "ironically" *has* to be
the sense of *eirōnikōs*, for the context gives no foothold to the notion
of pretence or deceit. Socrates is turning down flat the proposed
exchange, saying it is a swindle. He starts off with a simple irony,
saying to Alcibiades, "you are not stupid," when he clearly means:
"you *are* stupid, very stupid: what could be more stupid than to
think I would fall for a barter of gold for brass?" When such a thing
happens in those verses of the *Iliad* he echoes here – Glaucus
exchanges his golden armour for one of brass – the poet explains:
"Zeus had taken away his wits."[55] Socrates is saying to Alcibiades:
"I would have to be out of my head to buy your proposal; what a
fool you must think me, a complete ass, to think that I would let you
pull it off."
　　He winds up with a "complex"[56] irony:

T13 *Smp.* 219A1–3: "But look more closely, blessed boy, lest you have
missed that I am nothing. The mind's vision grows sharp only when the
eyesight has passed its peak, and you are still far from that."

Alcibiades is told that the "gold" he has been looking for isn't there
after all. If moral wisdom is to be understood – as Alcibiades
understands it – as the sort of thing which can be handed over in a
swap, Socrates will insist that he has absolutely none: *qua* repository
of such wisdom he is "nothing." To say this is not to deny that he
does have wisdom of another sort which Alcibiades could have for
free if he would seek it himself, looking to Socrates not as a guru but

53 Though here the roles are reversed: the boy is chasing, not chased.
54 This first part of T12 was cited as T9 above.   55 *Il.* 6.234.
56 Pp. 31–2 above and additional note. 1.1.

as a partner in the search.[57] To find deception anywhere in this speech we would have to plant it there ourselves: there is not a shadow of the will to mislead in what Socrates has said to Alcibiades most *eirōnikōs*.

Does that settle the sense of *eirōneuomenos* at T8? No. But it does create a presumption that there too the sense is the same: it would be unlikely that *eirōnikōs* would be used as we have now seen it used in T9 if just two Stephanus pages earlier "he spends his entire life *eirōneuomenos*" had carried the thought that Socrates went through life "deceiving everyone as to his real character."[58] So let us look as closely into the context there – the paragraphs in Alcibiades' speech which precede immediately the seduction story. They are pursuing the famous simile with which the whole speech had begun:

T14 *Smp.* 215A7–B3: "I maintain that he is very like those Sileni that sit in the workshops of the statuaries... who, when opened into two,[59] turn out to have images of gods inside."

This is the picture of a man who lives behind a mask – a mysterious, enigmatic figure, a man nobody knows: "You should know that none of you know him" (216C–D), says Alcibiades to Socrates' friends. To say this is not at all to imply that Socrates has been deceiving them: to be reserved and to be deceitful are not the same thing. All we can get from the simile is concealment,[60] not deceit. Even so, we have to ask if Alcibiades does not insinuate deceit in his own explication of the simile:

T15 *Smp.* 216D2–5: "You see that [a] Socrates is erotically disposed towards beautiful youths, always hanging round them, smitten by them; and again [b] that he knows nothing and is ignorant of everything... Isn't this like Silenus? Enormously so."

---

57 Cf. Socrates' behavior in the *Laches*. The moral wisdom he is asked to supply on demand he disclaims strenuously: "he has no knowledge of that thing, nor the ability to judge which of you speaks truly [of it]; he has not been discoverer or learner of anything of the kind" (186D–E). But when Laches offers himself to Socrates for instruction (189C) he is welcomed – not to have knowledge poured into him by someone else, but to join with Socrates in "common counsel and search" (συμβουλεύειν καὶ συσκοπεῖν· the prefix conveys twice over the cooperative nature of the relation). 58 So Guthrie, 1975.

59 The image of "opening up" to disclose something infinitely precious, which is concealed from the vulgar view, recurs at 216D6, 216E6, 222A. I see no foundation in any of these texts for Martha Nussbaum's notion that the image, as used by Plato, is "essentially sexual" (1986: 189). There is profound truth in her thought that in sexual intimacy a unique form of knowledge of the beloved person is acquired; in our desire for it, she remarks, "sexual and epistemological [epistemic] need are joined and, apparently, inseparable" (1986: 190). But Plato's text gives no warrant for reading this thought into it; Alcibiades is not suggesting to his fellow-drinkers at 216D–E that the real Socrates would be revealed ("opened up") to him or to them through sexual intimacy.

60 Cf. my gloss in n. 24 above on *dissimulantia* in Cicero's description of Socratic *ironia*.

The allusion to Socrates' eroticism in part [a] of this text is amply corroborated elsewhere in Plato and in Xenophon as well.[61] But here, after putting Socrates' bloom-chasing into the centre of the picture, Alcibiades seems to take it all back:

T16 *Smp.* 216D7–E1: "You should know he does not care at all if someone is beautiful: you wouldn't believe how he scorns that sort of thing."

He says the same thing no less than four times at the climax of the attempted seduction:

T17 *Smp.* 219C3–5: "He was so superior, so scornful and derisive of my bloom, so insulting of it."

So on one hand we are told that Socrates is "smitten" by male beauty, on the other, that he is utterly scornful of it. Isn't this what Guthrie might have cited as good reason for reading deceit into *eirōneuomenos* at T8? If Socrates is so contemptuous of such beauty, how could his pursuit of it be anything but a sham?

This is a highly pertinent question. I must meet it head-on. To do so I must say something about Socratic *erōs* to distinguish it from Platonic *erōs*, with which it is so often conflated – most recently in Dover's *Greek Homosexuality* (1978) and again in volume II of Foucault's *Histoire de la Sexualité* (1985). There are four differences.

1. In Platonic *erōs* what is loved in a beautiful boy is the transcendent Form of Beauty whose image[62] he is. Socrates' ontology has no transcendent Forms. So what he loves in a beautiful boy is a beautiful boy, and that is all.

2. In Platonic *erōs* passionate body-contact[63] is normal: the lovers in the *Phaedrus* touch, kiss, "lie down together," and "sleep together" (255E).[64] In the Socratic counterpart erotic intimacy is limited to mind- and eye-contact.[65]

---

61 Cf. the references in nn. 50 and 51 above and in Dover, 1978: 154–5.
62 Or "namesake" (ἐπωνυμίαν, *Phdr.* 250E3) or "likeness" (μεμιμημένον, *ibid.* 251A).
63 Which is described as powerfully arousing, making the "intemperate horse" clamor for gratification (255E–256A).
64 This physical intimacy, so explicit in the text of the *Phaedrus* (cf. Vlastos, 1974 and 1981: 39) is seldom noticed in accounts of Platonic *erōs*. It is ignored in Wilamowitz, 1948: 368–9 (cf. n. 16 above); Gould, 1963: 119; Guthrie, 1975: 405. Earlier translations blunt the force of Plato's words and conceal their intent: in Jowett συγκατακεῖσθαι becomes "embrace," ἐν τῇ συγκοιμήσει, "when they meet together."
65 In Xenophon, Socrates' fear of physical contact with an attractive youth is obsessive (to kiss a pretty face is "to become forthwith a slave instead of a free man," *Mem.* 1.3.11; a momentary contact of his nude shoulder with that of the beautiful Critobulus affects Socrates like "the bite of a wild beast": his shoulder stings for days, Xen. *Smp.* 4.27–8). In Plato Socrates shows no terror of skin-contact with a beautiful boy: wrestling in the

3. While both Plato and Socrates interdict terminal gratification, they do so for different reasons. In Plato's case these are strongly metaphysical, for he regards the soul's conjunction with the body as a doom calling for a life-long discipline whose aim is to detach soul from body, so far as possible, in the present life and liberate it from the wheel of reincarnation after death; sexual bliss defeats this endeavour, "nails" the soul to the body and distorts its sense of what is real (*Phd.* 83D).[66] This doctrine is utterly foreign to Socrates. In none of our sources does Socrates object to orgasmic pleasure as such – only to that form of it which is pursued in pederastic coupling,[67] and there for moral, not metaphysical, reasons: he thinks it bad for the boy,[68] viewing it as a form of predation in which a younger male is exploited ("devoured"[69]) by his lover, used for the latter's one-sided gratification.[70]

4. Platonic *erōs* generates an emotion that has torrential force, matching that imputed by the poets to all forms of sexual passion: pederastic, lesbian, or heterosexual. Like the poets, Plato calls *erōs* "madness" and so describes it:

T18 *Phdr.* 251D–252B: "And so between joy and anguish [the lover] is distraught at being in such a strange condition: perplexed and frenzied, with madness upon him, he can neither sleep by night nor sit still by day...mother, brother, friends, he forgets them all, not caring if his property is being ruined by neglect; those rules and graces in which he previously took pride he now scorns, welcoming a slave's estate, sleeping anywhere at all, if only it can be as close as possible to his darling."

For such amiable insanity Socratic *erōs* has no place. It is even-keeled, light-hearted, jocular, cheerfully and obstinately sane.[71] Not

nude with Alcibiades happens "often," though only on the latter's initiative (*Smp.* 217c) and there is nothing in Plato to suggest that Socrates would encourage physical endearment with any of the youths he "loves."

66 See nn. 42 and 43 in ch. 2 below.
67 Cf. Xen. *Mem.* 2.6.22: Socrates counsels "those who delight in the sexual charms of boys in bloom" to resist the attraction "in order to cause no distress to those who should be spared it."   68 Cf. additional note 1.3 on ἔρως καλός.
69 *Chrm.* 155D–E: "And I thought how well Cydias understood the ways of *erōs*; giving advice to someone about a beautiful boy, he warned: 'Don't bring the fawn too close to the lion that would devour his flesh'"; and *Phdr.* 241D1: "As wolves are fond of lambs, so lovers love a boy."
70 Xen. *Smp.* 8.19: the man "reserves the pleasure for himself, the most shameful things for the boy." *Ibid.* 21 (translation, in part, after E. C. Marchant): "the boy does not share, like a woman, the delight of sex with the man, but looks on sober at another in love's intoxication."
71 It is so pictured in both Plato's and Xenophon's Socratic dialogues. Nor does the reference to Socrates' ἔρως for Alcibiades in the eponymous dialogue by Aeschines Socraticus (fr. 11 Dittmar: to be cited in full and discussed in additional note 1.4) tell a different tale.

that Socrates is sexually anorexic (I stressed the contrary above) or that he anticipates the Cynic and Christian determination to expunge the joy of sex from the economy of happiness. The sliver of it he allows himself he pursues openly, without the least embarrassment, and in any case without fear that it could get out of hand, for in the dynamics of his psyche it is held in the field of force of an incomparably mightier drive. When Alcibiades comes to speak of the glimpse he once got of the "images of gods" concealed by the satyr's bestial exterior, his language becomes ecstatic. It dissolves in a shimmer of glittering, evocative adjectives:

T19 *Smp.* 216E–217A: "I saw them once and they seemed so divine, golden, altogether beautiful, wonderful."

What is this dazzling, enchanting thing Socrates keeps hidden inside his own soul? His *sōphrosynē*, says Alcibiades:

T20 *Smp.* 216D7–8: "But, O my fellow-drinkers, how full of *sōphrosynē* [he would be seen to be] inside, if he were opened up."

But it could hardly be only that, for this is in the public view. What no one but Socrates himself can see is, I suggest, the happiness he finds in that *sōphrosynē*, which is so much more alluring for him than anything he could hope to get from physical beauty or any other mundane good – health, wealth, honour, life itself – that he can enjoy each of these for what each is worth, savoring in each its own sweet little quota of contentment or delight – that, and no more, thumbing his nose at it ("scorning" it) when it promises more. A maxipassion keeps all the minipassions effortlessly under control. It has been recently said,[72] following Foucault, that "sex is a hard knot of anxiety" in all Western discourse about love. If this is true, then Socrates is an exception. From what we learn about Socratic *erōs* from Plato,[73] in it there is no *inquiétude* at all.[74]

---

72 Michael Ignatieff, in his review of M. Foucault, *Histoire de la Sexualité*, in the *Times Literary Supplement*, 28 Sept., 1984, p. 1071.

73 Though not from Xenophon: that obsessive fear of physical contact (cf. n. 64 above) would certainly be symptomatic of anxiety. On this, as on other points, when Xenophon's testimony conflicts with Plato's we would be wiser to prefer the latter's: there is good reason to believe that his personal acquaintance with Socrates had been far more intimate than Xenophon's.

74 This fundamental feature of Socratic ἔρως has been missed in all accounts of it known to me, from Kierkegaard, whose romantic fancy reads "passionate turmoil into it" (1965: 88), to Foucault, whose highly discerning discussion of "le véritable amour" in Plato reveals its residual blind-spot in the hyphenated expression, "l'Erotique socratico-platonicienne" (vol. II of *Histoire de la Sexualité*, 1985). *Inquiétude* in Platonic *erōs* pulses in the *Phaedrus*: the charioteer and the good horse are "sorely troubled" lest the bad horse "force them to a monstrous and forbidden act" (254A, Hackforth's tr.); they are saved only by the timely return of the vision of the Form of beauty "throned on her chaste seat" (254B).

Once we take this into account it becomes arbitrary to read deceit or pretence into Socrates' dalliance with youthful "bloom." We can understand Socratic *erōs* as a complex irony of the same sort Alcibiades allows him in part [b] of T15 above – that of "knowing nothing and being ignorant of everything." Just as when maintaining "he knows nothing" Socrates does and does not mean what he says, so too when he says he is erotically attracted to beautiful young men he both does and does not mean what he says. In the currently understood sense of pederastic love Socrates does *not* love Alcibiades[75] or any of the other youths he pursues. But in the other sense which *eran* has in the doctrine and practice of Socratic *erōs*, he does love them: their physical beauty gives special relish to his affectionate encounters with their mind. So there is no pretence and no deceit in saying to others that he is Alcibiades' lover (*G.* 581D) and saying the same thing, as he no doubt did, to Alcibiades himself.

"But surely," it will be said, "to court those giddy young things, whose head is swimming with the compliments being paid to them by powerful Athenians, will deceive them. So isn't Socrates guilty of intentional deceit after all?" On how it was in other cases we have no positive information. But in the case of Alcibiades we do have the data for a confident reply. Yes, Alcibiades was deceived, for otherwise he would not have hatched that crazy scheme of swapping bloom for wisdom and would not have stuck to it for who knows how long, while Socrates kept refusing to take the bait. Deceived he was, but by whom? Not by Socrates, but by himself. He believed what he did because he wanted to believe it. We might have guessed as much. But we don't need to guess. Just from his own story we can tell that this is what happened. At T12 Socrates is saying "No" to the offer, doing so as emphatically as would a Zen Roshi responding to a foolish question by bringing down his staff full strength on the questioner's head. Alcibiades could not but see that his proposition is being refused. And still he refuses to believe it. He moves into Socrates' couch as though he had been told "Yes" or, at least, "Maybe." And if this is what happened then, there is no reason to believe that Socrates had ever said or done anything intended to deceive Alcibiades into thinking that skin-love was what he wanted from the youth.

But I may be asked: "Even so, can we not gather from the account that long before that night Socrates was aware of what was going on

---

75 Cf. *Pr.* 309A1–D2: admitting that he has been "chasing" Alcibiades' bloom (standard metaphor for pederastic courting), Socrates proceeds to smother it in irony.

in the boy's head, and yet was willing to let his young friend wallow in self-deception without taking any decisive action to dispel it?" To this we surely have to answer: Yes. Over and over again before that night Socrates would have had ample opportunity to explain that Alcibiades was making a fool of himself, duped by his own wishful thinking. Yet Socrates said nothing. Day after day he watched and kept still. Why so? The only reasonable answer is that he wanted Alcibiades to find out the truth for himself by himself. The irony in his love for Alcibiades, riddling from the start, persisted until the boy found the answer the hard way, in a long night of anguished humiliation, naked next to Socrates, and Socrates a block of ice.

This chapter has been an investigation of the meaning of two words, "irony" and *eirōneia*, a good part of it devoted to the meaning of just two tokens of the latter occurring in Alcibiades' speech: *eirōneuomenos* at T8, *eirōnikōs* at T9. It does, however, have wider implications. A word about these by way of conclusion.

A question always hanging over our head as we work in Plato's Socratic dialogues is whether or not their protagonist allows himself deceit as a debating tactic.[76] Some of Socrates' most devoted students have taken it for granted that he does. For Kierkegaard Socrates is the anti-sophist who by ironies of sophistry tricks sophists into truth.[77] For Paul Friedländer, whose three-volume work on Plato is as learned a work of scholarship as any produced in his time, Socrates is "the living witness to the fact that he who knows the truth can deceive better than he who does not, and that he who deceives voluntarily is better than he who deceives involuntarily" (1964: 145). This point of view has been widely influential. One sees it at the center of Michael O'Brien's brilliant book,[78] and at the edges of much distinguished work on Plato.[79] The obvious objection is in what Plato makes Socrates say:

76 This will be discussed more fully in ch. 5.
77 "Socrates tricks Protagoras out of every concrete virtue; by reducing each virtue to unity, he completely dissolves it; while the sophistry lies in the power through which he is able to accomplish this. Hence we have at once an irony borne by a sophistic dialectic and a sophistic dialectic reposing in irony" (1965: 96).
78 O'Brien, 1967, whose contribution to our understanding of Socrates is sidetracked because the author, misapplying the use of irony in the Socratic dialogues, is prepared to jettison some of Socrates' most fundamental doctrines. Thus, if καλῶς at *Pr.* 352D4 means the contrary of what it says, the whole Socratic doctrine of the impossibility of *akrasia* goes down the drain; to cite its Aristotelian attestation would be useless: it would be met by the retort that he too missed the irony.
79 Most recently in Charles Kahn (1983: 75ff.). He speaks of the "trickery" by which Socrates rebuts Polus (90). I would not accept his description of my own analysis of the argument (Vlastos, 1967: 454ff.) as "Socrates tricks Polus" (90); I argued *against* the suggestion that Socrates' argument is intentionally fallacious. I return to this issue in section III of chapter 5.

T21 *G.* 458A–B: "As for me, I would be pleased to cross-question you, provided you are the same sort of human being as I; if not I would let you go. Of what sort is that? One of those who would be pleased to be refuted if I say something untrue, and pleased to refute another if *he* says something untrue, but more pleased to be refuted than to refute – as much more as being rid oneself of the greatest evil is better than ridding another of it; for I do not believe that anything could be as evil for a human being as to harbor false beliefs about the things we are now discussing."

These words are familiar to those scholars. We ask them if they doubt their sincerity and they assure us that they don't. Well then, we ask, if Socrates would rather lose than win the argument when the truth is on the other side, what could he stand to gain by slipping in a false premise or a sophistical inference? But this argument, which ought to be conclusive, falls flat on scholars who tell us that just in making it we are revealing that we have been reading Plato's text with a tin ear for irony. It should be obvious, they say, that what would be out of the question in the usual mode of philosophical discourse may be normal in the ironical one: that Socrates should outsophist the sophists is no paradox if the sophistries with which he plies them are ironical.[80]

In this essay I have tried to nail down the mistake in the conception of irony which underlies this point of view. For this purpose I have gone back to the primary, down-to-earth, meaning of the living word which "irony" has been in all the languages of the Western world, beginning with Cicero's Latin. In this primary use from which all philosophically invented ones are derived (including the one Kierkegaard fished out of Hegel: "infinite absolute negativity"),[81] what irony means is simply expressing what we mean by saying something contrary to it. This is something we do all the time – even children do it – and if we choose to do it we forfeit in that very choice the option of speaking deceitfully. To think otherwise is to mistake *ironia* for *eirōneia*, thereby reversing the process by which the former evolved out of the latter, denying Socrates one of his chief titles to fame: his contribution to the sensibility of Western Europe, no less memorable an achievement than is his contribution to our moral philosophy.

But in the course of this inquiry I stumbled upon something I had

---

80 Cf. Kierkegaard in n. 77 above.

81 Kierkegaard, 1965: 276 *et passim.* His treatment of Socratic irony is hopelessly perplexed by this dazzling mystification. It seduces him into finding in the Platonic texts he purports to be glossing the vagaries of a romantic novella: "the disguise and mysteriousness which it [irony] entails... the infinite sympathy it assumes, the elusive and ineffable moment of understanding immediately displaced by the anxiety of misunderstanding" etc. (85).

not reckoned on at the start: that in the persona of Socrates depicted by Plato there is something which helps explain what Kierkegaard's genius and Friedländer's learning have read into Socrates. In that small segment of the evidence I have scrutinized we can see how Socrates could have deceived without intending to deceive. If you are young Alcibiades courted by Socrates you are left to your own devices to decide what to make of his riddling ironies. If you go wrong and he sees you have gone wrong, he may not lift a finger to dispel your error, far less feel the obligation to knock it out of your head. If this were happening over trivia no great harm would be done. But what if it concerned the most important matters – whether or not he loves you? He says he does in that riddling way which leaves you free to take it one way though you are meant to take it in another, and when he sees you have gone wrong he lets it go. What would you say? Not, surely, that he does not care that you should know the truth, but that he cares more for something else:[82] that if you are to come to the truth, it must be by yourself for yourself.

The concept of moral autonomy never surfaces in Plato's Socratic dialogues[83] – which does not keep it from being the deepest thing in their Socrates, the strongest of his moral concerns. What he is building on is the fact that in almost everything we say we put a burden of interpretation on our hearer. When we speak a sentence we do not add a gloss on how it should be read. We could not thus relieve the hearer of that burden, for this would be an endless business: each gloss would raise the same problem and there would have to be gloss upon gloss *ad infinitum*. Socratic irony is not unique in accepting the burden of freedom which is inherent in all significant communication. It is unique in playing that game for bigger stakes than anyone else ever has in the philosophy of the West. Socrates doesn't say that the knowledge by which he and we must live is utterly different from what anyone has ever understood or even imagined moral knowledge could be. He just says he has no knowledge, though without it he is damned, and lets us puzzle out for ourselves what that could mean.

82 In an earlier version of this essay I had offered "failure of love" in explanation. Don Adams, then a member of my seminar at Cornell, convinced me that this line of explanation was wrong: that Socrates should want Alcibiades to find out the truth for himself the hard way is perfectly compatible with Socratic love for the youth.

83 αὐτονομία is never given a moral (or political) application in any of our Socratic sources.

2

SOCRATES *CONTRA* SOCRATES
IN PLATO[1]

I

That excellent book Gerasimos Santas contributed to the "Arguments of the Philosophers" series in 1979 is entitled *Socrates*. But once inside it you discover that what it is really about is a "Socrates" in Plato. More than once since I first started working on this book I asked myself: "Why not follow that example? Why not bypass, as he did, that bugbear of Platonic studies, the so-called 'Socratic Problem'? Why not let the historians have the Socrates of history all to themselves, keeping for myself that enchanting figure whose challenge to philosophers would be the same were he historic fact or Platonic fiction?" If my interests had been as purely philosophical as are those of Santas this, certainly, is the way I would have gone. But it so happens that my philosophical interests are impure. I cannot pass the buck to the historians without passing it to myself. All my life I have been one of their tribe and once in it no easy exit is allowed. The question "Who are you talking about – Socrates *or* a 'Socrates' in Plato?" will dog your steps, barking at you, forcing you to turn and face it in self-defense. If you do mean the former, you must argue for it. You must give reasons for the claim that through a "Socrates" in Plato we can come to know the Socrates of history – the Socrates who made history, taught Plato and others, changed their thinking and their lives, and through them changed the course of Western thought.

I have been speaking of *a* "Socrates" in Plato. There are two of

---

1 Much of the material in this chapter and the next was presented in Gifford Lectures at St. Andrews (1981), more of it in Townsend Lectures at Cornell (1986); most of it was discussed in seminars at Berkeley, Cambridge, and Toronto (1978–87). The answer to the so-called "Socratic problem" presented in this chapter and continued throughout the book is set forth summarily in a lecture to the British Academy entitled "Socrates" (appearing in vol. 85 of its *Proceedings* [London, 1989]).

them. In different segments of Plato's corpus two philosophers bear that name. The individual remains the same. But in different sets of dialogues he pursues philosophies so different that they could not have been depicted as cohabiting the same brain throughout unless it had been the brain of a schizophrenic. They are so diverse in content and method that they contrast as sharply with one another as with any third philosophy you care to mention, beginning with Aristotle's. This is a large claim. I shall be arguing for it in this chapter and the next.

Those two groups of dialogues fall arguably into the earlier and middle periods of Plato's literary production.[2] Since I shall have frequent need to refer separately to what Plato puts into the mouth of "Socrates" in each, I shall spare the reader tedious repetition by allowing myself a bit of shorthand. To the "Socrates" of the earlier compositions I shall refer as "Socrates$_E$," or "S_E" for short ("E" for "earlier"). To the "Socrates" of the works of Plato's middle period I shall refer as "Socrates$_M$" or "S_M" for short ("M" for "middle"). I itemize the dialogues which, in my judgment, make up these two groups, and also a third, intermediate group, transitional from the Elenctic[3] Dialogues in Group I to the dialogues in Group II:

Group I.   The dialogues of Plato's earlier period:

(a)   The Elenctic Dialogues, listed in alphabetical order:[4] *Apology, Charmides, Crito, Euthyphro, Gorgias, Hippias Minor, Ion, Laches, Protagoras, Republic* I[5] (abbreviating:[6] *Ap., Ch., Cr., Eu., G., HMi., Ion., La., Pr., R.* I).
(b)   Transitional Dialogues (written after all the Elenctic Dialogues and before all of the dialogues in Group II), listed in alphabetical

---

2 For the near-consensus on this point among Platonic scholars in the present century and for some of the reasons for it see Ross, 1951: ch. I ("The order of the Dialogues"); greater detail in Constantin Ritter, 1910a: 190–272 ("Untersuchung der zeitlichen Folge [der Dialogen]"); best of all in Brandwood, 1958. Particularly significant I regard the fact that when the dialogues are ordered only by stylistic criteria, as in Brandwood, the results (summarized in Brandwood, 1976: xiiiff. at xvii) are broadly in agreement with those I reach *by ordering these dialogues solely by their philosophical content*: see n. 8 below.

3 I so name them because throughout these dialogues Socrates' method of philosophical investigation is elenctic, which it abruptly ceases to be in the Transitionals: see Vlastos, 1983a: 27ff. at 57–8, Appendix on "Demise of the Elenchus in *Eud., Ly., HMa.*". More on this in chapter 4.

4 Because chronological order within the Group is unimportant at the immediate stage of my argument. But most present-day Platonists would agree that the *G.* is the last dialogue in this Group (see e.g. Dodds, 1959: 20 and Irwin, 1979: 5–8).

5 See additional note 2.1 "The composition of Republic I."

6 I follow for the most part the abbreviations employed by Irwin, 1977a.

order:[7] *Euthydemus, Hippias Major, Lysis, Menexenus, Meno* (abbreviating: *Eud., HMa., Ly., Mx., M.*).[8]

Group II. The dialogues of Plato's middle period, listed in probable chronological sequence: *Cratylus, Phaedo, Symposium, Republic* II–X, *Phaedrus, Parmenides, Theaetetus* (abbreviating: *Cra., Phd., Smp., R.* II–X, *Phdr., Prm., Tht.*).

For the sake of completeness I should add

Group III. The dialogues of Plato's latest period, listed in probable chronological sequence: *Timaeus,*[9] *Critias, Sophist, Politicus, Philebus, Laws* (abbreviating: *Ti., Crit., Sph., Pltc., Phlb., Lg.*).

How pronounced and profound are the differences between the philosophy Plato puts into the mouth of Socrates$_E$, upon the one hand, from the philosophy he expounds through Socrates$_M$, upon the other, will be a principal topic of inquiry through much of this book. I list programmatically ten Theses,[10] each of which specifies in its part A a trait of Socrates$_E$ exhibited *only* in (one or more) dialogues in Group I, and in its part B a trait of Socrates$_M$ exhibited *only* in (one or more) dialogues in Group II[11]

IA. Socrates$_E$ is exclusively a moral philosopher.[12]

7 Because here too the chronological order within the set is highly controversial. For the *Mx.* we have a firm *terminus post quem* (the reference at 245C–E to the end of the war with Corinth, 387), which gives no clue to its order relative to the other four dialogues in its Group.

8 Brandwood, 1976: xvii (cf. n. 2 above) places all of *Ap., Ch., Cr., Eu., HMi., Ion, La., Pr.* (his "IA Group") before all of *G., Eud., HMa., Ly., M., Mx., Cra., Phd., Smp.* (his "IB Group"). I differ from him in keeping the *Gorgias* ahead of all the dialogues in his IB Group on the strength of a criterion – use of the elenctic method, deployed with great panache in the *Gorgias* and in no other dialogue of his Group IB – which Brandwood ignores (understandably so: he uses *only* stylistic criteria). But the resulting difference in chronology is not great, since he too holds (1976: xviii) that the three dialogues in his IB Group that fall within my Group II (i.e. *Cra., Phd., Smp.*) "were probably the last to be written" in his IB Group; so if the *Gorgias* were transferred to his IA Group, his IB Group would split up into earlier and later segments, and the earlier (which would then consist of *Eud., HMa., Ly., M., Mx.* would coincide with my Transitionals and we would get complete agreement on the order
   Ap., Ch., Cr., Eu., G., HMi., Ion, La., Pr., followed by
   Eud., HMa., Ly., M., Mx, followed by
   Cra., Phd., Smp., R., Phdr., Prm., Tht.
   The residual difference – my splitting off the first book of the *Republic* from its other nine books to place it with the Elenctic Dialogues – is unimportant (see additional note 2.1).

9 For the *Timaeus* see additional note 2.6.

10 I shall be referring to them as "The Ten Theses" throughout the rest of the book.

11 With the exception of (a) the speech of Alcibiades in the *Smp.* which, as I explained in chapter 1, portrays the Socrates of the earlier dialogues, who "knows nothing and is ignorant of everything" (216D) and (b) the two biographical passages in the *Phaedo* (57A–61C and 115C–118) which also portray Socrates$_E$. The one at 96E–99E I take to be Platonic, not Socratic, biography, since its stated purpose is to introduce the theory of Forms (100Aff.).

12 Cf. n. 5 to additional note 1.1. His arguments sometimes trench on other topics, but the only theses he investigates elenctically are propositions in the moral domain. Thus the

IB.   Socrates$_M$ is moral philosopher *and* metaphysician *and* epistemologist *and* philosopher of science *and* philosopher of language *and* philosopher of religion *and* philosopher of education *and* philosopher of art. The whole encyclopedia of philosophical science is his domain.

IIB.   Socrates$_M$ had a grandiose metaphysical theory of "separately existing" Forms and of a separable soul which learns by "recollecting" pieces of its pre-natal fund of knowledge.
IIA.   Socrates$_E$ has no such theory.

IIIA.   Socrates$_E$, seeking knowledge elenctically, keeps avowing that he has none.
IIIB.   Socrates$_M$ seeks demonstrative knowledge and is confident that he finds it.

IVB.   Socrates$_M$ has a complex, tripartite model of the soul.
IVA.   Socrates$_E$ knows nothing of this model, which would have unsettled his conception of moral virtue and undercut his doctrine of the impossibility of incontinence (*akrasia*).

VB.   Socrates$_M$ has mastered the mathematical sciences of his time.
VA.   Socrates$_E$ professes no interest in these sciences and gives no evidence of expertise in any of them throughout the Elenctic dialogues.

VIA.   Socrates$_E$'s conception of philosophy is populist.
VIB.   Socrates$_M$'s is elitist.

VIIB.   Socrates$_M$ has an elaborate political theory whose ranking order of constitutions places democracy with the worst of contemporary forms of government, lower than timocracy and oligarchy, preferable only to lawless tyranny.
VIIA.   Socrates$_E$ has no such theory. Though harshly critical of political goings-on in Athens, he says that he prefers the city with her laws to any contemporary state. But he leaves the rationale of the preference unexplained.

VIIA & B.   Homoerotic attachments figure prominently in the conception of *erōs* in both Socrates$_E$ and Socrates$_M$. But in the latter they have a metaphysical grounding in love for the transcendent Form of beauty which is wholly lacking in the former.[13]

claim that there is such a thing as "knowledge of knowledge and not-knowledge" he investigates only because it was proposed as (an unacceptable) definiens of *sōphrosynē*; and he gives up the search when he becomes convinced that it is not likely to get anywhere, confessing that he has no confidence "in his ability to clear up these things" (*Ch.* 169A).
13 Cf. the analysis of the difference between Socratic and Platonic *erōs* in chapter 1.

IXA. For Socrates$_E$ piety consists in service to a deity which, though fully supernatural, is rigorously ethical in its own character and in the demands it makes on men. His personal religion is practical, realized in action.

IXB. Socrates$_M$'s personal religion centers in communion with divine, but impersonal, Forms. It is mystical, realized in contemplation.

XA. In the Elenctic Dialogues Socrates$_E$'s method of philosophical investigation is adversative: he pursues moral truth by refuting theses defended by dissenting interlocutors. This ceases in the Transitionals: there he argues against theses proposed and opposed by himself.

XB. In the sequence of dialogues from the *Meno* through the *Phaedrus* Socrates$_M$ is a didactic philosopher, expounding truth to consenting interlocutors. Thereafter the metaphysical theory of the preceding dialogues of the middle period is subjected to searching criticism by "Parmenides" and then Socrates, assaying a fresh start, shifts to a new, "maieutic," mode of investigation in the *Theaetetus*.

I shall present a two-part argument. Its first part, to be presented in the present chapter and in section I of the next, will stay completely inside the Platonic corpus, developing the claim that in Group I dialogues Plato's Socrates exhibits distinctive traits which, in the Ten Theses listed above, set his philosophy in opposition to that of his namesake in the dialogues in Group II. In the second part of my argument, to be laid out in section II of chapter 3, I shall call on evidence external to the Platonic corpus to support the claim that *in those essential respects in which S_E's philosophy differs from that of S_M it is that of the historical Socrates*, recreated by Plato in invented conversations which explore its content and exhibit its method. I say "invented," not "reported." It is Xenophon who professes to be recalling Socratic conversations he had witnessed personally.[14] Plato does no such thing. Except for the *Apology*, where he goes out of his way (twice: 34A, 38B) to call attention to his presence at the trial,[15]

---

14 1.3 of the *Memorabilia* begins: "To support my opinion that he benefited his companions both by actions which showed what sort of man he was and by his discussions with them, I shall set forth as much as I can recollect of these" (*Mem.* 1.3.1). Early in 1.4 he declares: "First of all I shall state what I once heard him say about the divine realm in conversing with Aristodemus..." For more references to such assurances by Xenophon and for how little they are worth see Robin, 1910: 32 and 35–7, who documents in detail their factual unreliability; cf. also Momigliano, 1971: 46–57, who locates Xenophon's work, like that of other Socratics, in "that zone between truth and fiction which is so bewildering to the professional historian" (46).

15 The *Apology* may be credited with the same kind of historical veracity as the speeches in Thucydides (an obvious parallel): recognizing that "it was impossible for him or his

he leaves himself out of the Socratic dramas he creates and rigs some of them so as positively to exclude his presence: in the *Pr.* he dramatizes a scene in which he could not have assisted because he had not yet been born;[16] in the *Cr.*, *Eu.*, *Ion*, *HMa.* he leaves Socrates alone with his interlocutor.[17] This is only to be expected on my hypothesis that those earlier works of Plato, no less than all those he was to produce thereafter, are meant as contributions to *philosophy* – not to biography as such. Socratic personalia Plato brings into his dramatic creations incidentally and, for the most part, only in so far as he considers them relevant to the philosophical content.[18]

On my hypothesis, Plato's overriding concern, in stark contrast to Xenophon's professed aim in his Socratic writings,[19] is not to preserve memories of Socratic philosophizing but to create it anew – to bring it alive in dramas whose protagonist philosophizes *more Socratico*. That remembered material should be used copiously is only to be expected. But my hypothesis does not bank on that. For what it proposes is that Plato in those early works of his, sharing Socrates' basic philosophical convictions, sets out to think through for himself their central affirmations, denials, and reasoned suspensions of belief by pitting them in elenctic encounter against the views voiced by a variety of interlocutors. In doing this Plato is producing, not reproducing, Socratic philosophizing. Employing a literary medium which allows Socrates to speak for himself, Plato makes him say whatever *he* – Plato – thinks *at the time of writing* would be the most reasonable thing for Socrates to be saying just then in expounding and defending his own philosophy.[20]

informants to memorize exactly what had been said" (τὴν ἀκρίβειαν αὐτὴν τῶν λεχθέντων διαμνημονεῦσαι, as paraphrased by A. Andrews, whose defense of the natural meaning of the text [1962: 64ff. at 65–71] I find entirely convincing), Thucydides assures us "they represent what I thought (ὡς ἂν ἐδόκουν ἐμοί) would be most fittingly said by each speaker on their particular topic, coming as close as possible to the general sense of what had been truly said (ἐχομένῳ ὅτι ἐγγύτατα τῆς ξυμπάσης γνώμης τῶν ἀληθῶς λεχθέντων)" (Thuc. 1.22.1).

16 In the year of Plato's birth (427 B.C.) Socrates was 42, well past his youth, to which there are repeated references in the *Pr.*: 314B, 317C, 320C, 361E.

17 To maintain the hypothesis that in these dialogues Plato is "imaginatively recalling, in form and substance, the conversations of his master" (Guthrie, 1975: 67) one would have to suppose, on no evidence whatever, that Plato (or a third party who had insured the transmission to him) had been given a play-by-play report of the arguments in each of these dialogues by Socrates himself or by his interlocutor.

18 See below, additional note 2.2 "Socratic personalia in the Platonic corpus."

19 Cf. n. 14 above and the opening sentence of Xenophon's *Oeconomicus*, "I once heard [Socrates] discuss household management as follows."

20 This part of the hypothesis alerts us to the possibility of shifts within the philosophical position allowed Socrates in Group I dialogues (e.g. it allows him to refute in the *Laches* the definition of "courage" he had propounded in the *Protagoras*, and to make explicit in the *Gorgias* a presupposition of Socratic argument – that the interlocutor always carries in his

Accordingly I can ignore the question which has bullied and befuddled many historians in the past: "Could Plato have heard what he makes Socrates say in this or that scene? If not, could he have had it on good authority?" For want of such authority the great Eduard Zeller lets fall out of his hands a crucial passage in the *Crito* (47cff.)[21] because it comes from a scene where Socrates speaks with his friend in the privacy of the prison cell and there is no indication of a line of transmission to Plato thereafter. Such scruples are obliterated by my hypothesis. Everything Plato puts into the mouth of Socrates is grist to my mill. To be sure, since the depicted character was, above any philosopher of the West, a man who lived his philosophy, the writer, deeply conscious of that fact, has reason to tell us much about the man's life, including his inner life, allowing us a fuller, more intimate, view of the man than is given us of any character, real or fictional, in the whole of ancient Greek literature. Even so, the writer's overriding concern is always the philosophy – the truths affirmed by Socrates, defended by his arguments, realized in his life, propositions which if true for Socrates are true for every human being.[22]

If that is Plato's primary interest, is it surprising that he should have pursued it in the form of dialogues instead of straightforward expository prose? It would have been more surprising if he had done the latter. For generations before him – from the first philosophers of Miletus, down to Socrates' contemporaries, Anaxagoras, Diogenes of Apollonia, and Democritus – expository prose had been the favored medium of natural investigation,[23] while for moral and political reflection Greek writers had regularly turned to dialogue.[24] So Herodotus, for example, in passages where he focuses on moral

own system of beliefs premises entailing the negation of each of his false theses – which had remained purely implicit in the preceding dialogues: cf. Vlastos, 1983a: 27ff. at 71ff. ("Afterthoughts on the Socratic Elenchus," which I now feel is in need of revision).

21 Crucial for the interpretation of Socrates' moral theory (as I shall be pointing out below in chapter 8, n. 38, and in comment on texts quoted there as T12, T13, T14, T15). Zeller discerns the conflict between the instrumentalist ethics in Xenophon's *Memorabilia* and the sovereign claim of justice in Plato's *Apology*; and he believes that the conflict could be resolved through Socrates' teaching in the *Crito* (47D) that injustice is to the soul what a fatal disease would be to the body and hence *ipso facto* detrimental to the agent. But Zeller denies himself the resolution because, he says, "we cannot vouch for it that everything in the *Crito* comes from Socrates, its author not having been present at the conversation therein described" (1885: 151).   22 *G.* 505E, *Ch.* 166D.

23 As also in the parallel case of the Hippocratic treatises. .

24 As the late Eric Havelock had observed, "Acted drama, or dramatized conversations, was the traditional Greek method of discussing and analyzing moral ideas" (1934: 283). This is true, notwithstanding declarative and protreptic sayings in gnomic prose (the dicta of the "Seven Wise Men," the Theognidea, the Hippocratic *Precepts* (παραγγελίαι), the fragments of Heracleitus and of Democritus, if we bear in mind that for the confrontation of opposing views Greek moralizing naturally turns to dialogue.

issues. When Xerxes declines "through highmindedness" to retaliate for Sparta's outrage against his ambassadors the morality tale takes the form of a mini-dialogue.[25] So too when Herodotus ponders the conflicting claims of monarchy, oligarchy, and democracy: he presents his meditation as a Debate on Constitutions (3.80–3). So too Prodicus switches from declamatory prose to dialogue to depict the choice between a life of easy gratification and one of hard, abstemious self-discipline: he stages a dialogue in which Vice and Virtue make opposing offers to Herakles (*ap.* Xen. *Mem.* 2.21–33). And so too Thucydides' reflections on the issue between power and justice produce the Melian Dialogue (5.85–112).

Moreover, just as Plato was about to start his work, prose dialogue had come into its own in that curious spin-off of Socrates' own refusal to write: the emergence of a new genre, the *Sōkratikoi logoi*, which had suddenly become a fashion, almost a craze. Beside Plato and Xenophon each of the following is credited by one or another of our sources with having produced such compositions: Aeschines of Sphettus, Antisthenes, Aristippus, Bryson, Cebes, Crito, Euclid of Megara, Phaedo.[26] That Plato was not the first in the field may be inferred from two reports, both of them well attested: Aristotle names a certain Alexamenus as the first writer of philosophical dialogues;[27] and Theopompus[28] (the historian, contemporary of Demosthenes and Aristotle) charges that most of Plato's had been plagiarized from dialogues by Aristippus, Antisthenes, and Bryson.

Mastery of the resources of a new literary medium which suits so well Plato's dramatic flair challenges his artistic gifts. He tries his hand at it, produces little masterpieces, and delight in successful creation keeps him at it year by year.[29] But the artist in Plato could not have displaced the philosopher. We must assume that philosophical inquiry was the *primum mobile* in the composition of those

---

25 Hdt. 7.136. A similar one on the same theme at 9.78–9. (Both dialogues are quoted in part in section III of chapter 7.) Cf. also the conversation between Solon and Croesus at 1.130–2.

26 For references see Grote, 1865: III, 465ff.

27 Aristotle *ap.* Athenaeus 505B–C (fr. 3 of *On Poets*, Ross). In quoting the fragment Athenaeus notes that Nicias of Nicaea and Sotion of Alexandria (authors of histories of "successions of philosophers," used by Diogenes Laertius as a source) corroborate Aristotle's testimony.

28 *Ap.* Athenaeus 500C (= *Fr. gr. Hist.* II B 115, F 259 Jacoby). The authenticity of the report is accepted by Glucker (1978: 163), defended by Döring, 1988: 69 and Tsouna (1988: 64–5).

29 That several others were exploiting the genre would be no deterrent – quite the opposite: the superiority of his work to theirs would be scarcely less apparent to him than it has been to posterity. The difference is as palpable when his dialogues are compared with Xenophon's Socratic writings as when they are compared with surviving fragments of such work by another Socratic, Aeschines of Sphettus, whose dialogues were highly regarded in antiquity.

earlier dialogues no less than of any he was to write thereafter,[30] and that throughout this first phase of his writing Plato remains convinced of the substantial truth of Socrates' teaching and of the soundness of its method. But the continuing harmony of the two minds, though vital, is not rigid: the father image inspires, guides, and dominates, but does not shackle Plato's philosophical quest. So when he finds compelling reason to strike out along new paths, he feels no need to sever the personal bond with Socrates. And when these lead him to new, unSocratic and antiSocratic conclusions, as they visibly do by the time he comes to write the *Meno*, the dramatist's attachment to his protagonist, replicating the man's love for the friend and teacher of his youth,[31] survives the ideological separation. And so, as Plato changes, the philosophical persona of his Socrates is made to change, absorbing the writer's new convictions, arguing for them with the same zest with which the Socrates of the previous dialogues had argued for the views the writer had shared with the original of that figure earlier on.

Such is the scenario I shall be fleshing out in this chapter and the next two. That it is offered as hypothesis, not dogma or reported fact, should be plain. Such it will remain as I pursue it step by step. Of its truth the reader must be the judge.

II

On the first of those Ten Theses listed above I do not need to linger. Its story will unfold as I tell that of the rest. So I move directly to Thesis II, the most powerful of the ten: as I shall try to show in the balance of the present chapter, *the irreconcilable difference between Socrates$_E$ and Socrates$_M$ could have been established by this criterion even if it had stood alone.*

In the dialogues of his middle period Plato constructs a boldly speculative metaphysical system whose twin foundations are the transmigrating soul and its ontological correlate, the transcendent Form. We can pinpoint the entry of the former into the corpus:

---

30 A subsidiary one would be the very fact that the market was being flooded with rival accounts of Socrates' philosophizing. Plato would be as eager to defend Socratic philosophy against the well-meaning half-truths propagated by Socratics as was Xenophon to defend it against the slanders in Polycrates' *Accusation of Socrates*.

31 Plato's close contact with Socrates early in Plato's youth is attested in Xen. *Mem.* 3.6.11: Plato's elder brother, Glaucon, is aspiring to political leadership at the age of twenty and Socrates restrains him, "taking a friendly interest in him for the sake of Glaucon's [uncle] Charmides *and of Plato.*"

T1 *M.* 81A–B: "...I have heard men and women who are wise in things divine." – "Saying *what*?" – "Something true, I believe, and glorious." – "*What* were they saying? *Who* were they?" – "Priests and priestesses who make it their business to give the reason for the rites they perform... This is what they declare: man's soul is deathless; at times it comes to an ending called 'death', at times it is reborn. It is never destroyed."

Here for the first time in Plato's work we meet this strange, visionary, doctrine that the soul has had many births and many deaths, and also its epistemological pendant, that *all* knowledge is innate, all learning in our present life being but the recovery of what our soul carries along from its primordial past:

T2 *M.* 81C: "As the soul is deathless and has been born many times and has seen all things both here and in Hades, there is nothing it has not learned... As all nature is akin and the soul has learned everything, nothing prevents us once we have recollected one thing – which is what men call 'learning' – to rediscover everything else ourselves, if we are valiant and do not give up inquiring. *For all inquiring and learning is recollecting.*"

Nothing remotely of this sort is stated or implied or even hinted at in any dialogue which precedes the *Meno*.[32] And once it comes in, it comes to stay: it saturates the *Phaedo*,[33] persists in the *Phaedrus* (245C–246A; 249B–D), and is displayed in great style in Plato's late dialogue,[34] the *Timaeus* (42B).[35] How alien this new story is to Socrates$_E$'s[36] whole way of thinking we can judge from the way he refers to the soul in the *Crito*:

32 It has been thought that there are anticipations of it in the myth of the *G.*, but only by tenuous inference (as in Dodds, 1959: 375; for a sounder analysis see Annas, 1982: 117). The central components of the new conception of the soul in the *Meno* (more fully in the *Phaedo*) are [a] its prenatal existence and successive incarnations in mortal lives (T1); (b) its extraordinary prenatal cognitive powers, these being the source of all learning during any of its mortal lives (T2). There is *no trace of either (a) or (b)* in the eschatology of the *G.*, whose myth is a purely moral fable, an embroidery on the popular belief (to which Socrates$_E$ is very hospitable: *Ap.* 41A) in a retributive post-mortem trial by Minos and other divinities of the nether world – a belief with rich moral content and no epistemic import.   33 69E–72D; 72E–77A; 78B–80C; 100B–109A.
34 On the *Timaeus* see additional note 2.6.
35 Since the protagonist of this dialogue impersonates Plato in idealized projection (Timaeus has achieved the highest eminence in philosophy [20A], cosmology, and astronomy [28A], and has also attained the political success [19E–20A] to which Plato had aspired in vain at various times in his life: cf. the antepenultimate paragraph in chapter 4) we are in a position to ascribe to Plato himself this fundamental doctrine which he had put into Socrates' mouth at the very point which marks the transition from Socrates$_E$ to Socrates$_M$.
36 The views and associations of the historical Socrates are perversely misrepresented when the difference between Socrates$_E$ and Socrates$_M$ is ignored and Socrates is then pictured as having lived in close association with Orphics (Taylor, 1949: 147), which gets some semblance of plausibility from the *Phaedo* (though even so would have to be reckoned a misleading exaggeration) but travesties grotesquely the Socrates of Plato's earlier dialogues and of Xenophon.

T3 *Cr.* 47E: " Is life then worth living for us once we have suffered the ruin of that in us which is damaged by injustice and benefited by justice? Or should we think inferior to the body *that in us, whatever it be* (ἐκεῖνο, ὅτι ποτ' ἔστι τῶν ἡμετέρων), that has to do with justice and injustice?"

That phrase, "that in us whatever it be," is symptomatic of the metaphysically reticent temper of the speaker's conception of the soul. For Socrates$_E$ our soul is our self – whatever that might turn out to be. It is the "I" of psychological function and moral imputation – the "I" in "I feel, I think, I know, I choose, I act." For "I believe" he says "my soul believes" (*G.* 486E). When he says that someone's soul is wicked we know this much of what he means: that person is wicked.[37] How much more he means we do not know: he doesn't say; to that question he never speaks. The queries, "Is the soul material or immaterial, mortal or immortal? Will it be annihilated when the body rots?" are never on his elenctic agenda. The first question he never addresses at all. He does allude to the second at the close of the *Apology* but only to suggest that it is rationally undecidable: both options – total annihilation or survival in Hades – are left open. In the *Crito* he reveals his faith in the soul's survival.[38] In the *Gorgias* he declares it.[39] Nowhere does he try to prove it in the earlier dialogues.[40]

For Socrates$_M$, on the other hand, the immateriality of the soul is a formal theorem[41] and its prenatal and post-mortem existence a target for demonstrative overkill. He runs through a string of arguments in the *Phaedo*,[42] adds a new one in the *Republic* (608D–611C), then still another, along quite different lines, in the *Phaedrus* (245C–246A). The entity whose imperishableness S$_M$ is so eager to prove is an immigrant from another world conjoined

37 Burnet's famous and highly misleading essay, "The Socratic Doctrine of the Soul" (1916: 126ff.) has fostered the misapprehension, now surfacing occasionally in the literature (e.g. Havelock, 1963: 204), that this conception of the soul as the psychological personality is a creation of Socrates and/or Plato. For a corrective see e.g. Vlastos, 1945–6: 381ff. and 53ff.; and, better, Solmsen, 1983: 355ff. Solmsen (356) calls attention to references to a person as "a *psuchē*": a "mighty *psuchē*," a "strong-minded *psuchē*," a "sweet *psuchē*" (Soph. *Ajax* 154, 1361, *Philoct.* 1013ff., Eur. *Medea* 110 and so forth).

38 54B–C.

39 Affirming that his eschatological myth is "true" (523A) and that Callicles is grievously mistaken in thinking it an old wives' tale (527A), but saying nothing to indicate that his belief in the soul's survival after death is elenctically defensible or otherwise retracting his declaration in the *Apology* (29B) that he has no knowledge of things in Hades. In particular, he does not offer argument for the truth of that belief. What he can and does argue for is the moral truth conveyed through the myth which he believes *can* be, and has been, proved true (ἀποδέδεικται, 479E), while its contrary cannot (οὐκ ἔχετε ἀποδεῖξαι, 527B).

40 I.e. nowhere prior to the introduction of the belief in reincarnation in the *Meno*, where Plato offers an argument for its corollary, the theory of recollection: in the *Phaedo* (73A–B) he refers to this argument as establishing "very clearly" (σαφέστατα) the truth of that corollary.   41 *Phd.* 79A–B.   42 69E–72D; 72E–77A; 100B–109A.

precariously to a piece of matter in this one. This conjunction is its great misfortune: corruption, exile, incarceration, entombment, defilement.[43] The imagery is Pythagorean.[44] In the *Phaedo* we see that S_M has taken it over. He is now convinced that both intellectually and morally we would be incomparably better off if we had been spared incarnation, and that now, stuck inside an animal, our fondest hope should be to break away, to fly off never to return. Only in Pythagoreanism[45] do we hear of any such view in contemporary or earlier Greek thought.

That as stark a contrast between S_E and S_M marks their conception of what each calls *eidos*, *idea* ("form," "character")[46] is not nearly so obvious. I must argue for it at length, devoting to it all the rest of this chapter. Our best clue to what Socrates$_E$ understands by *eidos* (or, synonymously, by *idea*) is in the work he makes it do. This is strictly definitional work. He mentions forms only when on the track of the answer to a "What is the *F*?" question. In the *Euthyphro* he lays down two conditions the right answer to that question will have to meet:

[1]   The definiens must be true of all cases falling under the definiendum.

43 For the imagery see especially *Phd.* 67D, 81E, 82A, 82E. The incarnate soul is "chained to a body," *Phd.* 81E; "entombed as it were, in its present body," *Cra.* 400C; "disfigured" by its association with the body, *R.* 611C–E; "encased in the body as in an oyster-shell," *Phdr.* 250C. "Defilement" or "pollution" is implied in speaking of the soul as "purified" in so far as it is separated from the body, "polluted" so far as it remains attached to it (*Phd.* 67A–C; 80E). The least gloomy of the images is the soul's "slipping into" the body allotted to it in each of its incarnations, *Phd.* 81E.
44 The soul "slips into" (ἐνδύεται) the body in the "Pythagorean myths" to which Aristotle alludes in *De Anima* 407B20ff.; ἐνδύνειν also in the account of the circuit of rebirths which Herodotus (2.123.2–3) says was Pythagorean in origin and "Greeks, some earlier, some later" made it their own. That the soul is "joined to the body as a penalty, as if entombed" is ascribed by Clement of Alexandria (*Strom.* 3.17) to "the Pythagorean" Philolaus, whom Clement represents as saying that the doctrine is attested by "ancient theologians and seers." Plato ascribes to "those about Orpheus" the doctrine that the body is a "prison and guard-house" of the soul (*Cra. 400C*). This is the doctrine to which Socrates$_M$ refers with approval and which Cebes associates with Philolaus (*Phd.* 61E–62C). The peripatetic philosopher Clearchus of Soli (fr. 2, *ap.* Athenaeus 157C) ascribes it to Euxitheus "the Pythagorean."
45 The belief in reincarnation is the best attested of Pythagoras' doctrines: Xenophanes B7 (*ap.* D.L. 8.36); Empedocles B129 (*ap.* Porphyry, *Vita Pyth.*); Dicaearchus, fr. 29 (*ap.* Porphyry, *Vita Pyth.*). And see Burkert, 1962: 98ff.; Barnes, 1982: 100ff.
46 Though either of these English words translates either of the Greek ones (cf. LSJ *s.v.* εἶδος, ἰδέα), "form" (in the sense of 'kind.' as in "imprisonment is a form of punishment"), is as good an English counterpart of ἰδέα as of εἶδος. But I shall keep "form" for εἶδος, "character" for ἰδέα, so that the reader will know to which word in Plato's text I am referring in translated text. And I shall follow the (fairly common) practice of capitalizing "Form" and "Character" (only) in contexts in which they are being used to refer to the non-sensible, immutable, incorporeal, "separate" entities which enter the Platonic corpus in the middle dialogues (cf. section III of this chapter).

Socrates brings this home by asking if the F "is not the same" in everything which is F (i.e. everything which has the property named "F"):

T4 *Eu.* 5D: "Is not the pious the same as itself in every [pious] action? And the impious, in turn, is it not opposite to all that is pious but similar to itself, everything which is to be impious having a certain single character (*idean*)[47] with respect to impiety?"[48]

[2] The definiens must disclose the reason why anything is an instance of the definiendum.

Socrates$_E$ formulates this condition by saying that the right answer to "What is the F?" must state what is that "because of which" (or "by which" or "through which" or "in virtue of which")[49] anything is F:

T5 *Eu.* 6D–E: "Recall that I did not ask you to teach me one or two of the many pious [actions] but that form itself because of which all the pious [actions] are pious. For you said that it is because of a single character that impious [actions] are impious and pious ones are pious. Or don't you remember?"

In assuming that these two conditions can be met S_E is making a substantial ontological commitment. He is implying that what there

---

47 Cf. the preceding note.
48 The last clause, καὶ ἔχον μίαν τινὰ ἰδέαν κατὰ τὴν ἀνοσιότητα ὅτιπερ ἂν μέλλῃ ἀνόσιον εἶναι, is translated, "and [the impious] possessing one single form in respect of its impiety. Does not this apply to everything that can be characterized as impious?" in Guthrie, 1975: 114–15. Here a separate question is produced by construing its terminal clause as "a conversational afterthought, syntactically detached from the rest of the sentence, which can only be read as applying the predicates to τὸ ἀνόσιον." That Plato's Greek can "only" be so read is false. It has been read as in the above translation by Robinson, 1941 (first edition of Robinson, 1953); Ross, 1951; Allen, 1970. This translation is more faithful to the text (it preserves its original segmentation) and takes it to be predicating impiety not of impiety but of its instances: "everything which is to be impious" (i.e. every possible instance of impiety) is to have the "single character" of impiety.
49 It takes a prepositional phrase (any of those four will do) to put into English what Plato expresses more economically by putting the neuter relative pronoun into the (instrumental) dative case. Alternatively he expresses the same thing by "that which makes (ποιεῖ) F things to be F," employing the non-causal, constitutive, sense of "makes" (cf. O.E.D. *s.v.* "make," sense 13: "constitute," as in "one swallow does not make a summer"). At 11A6–8 Socrates rejects "god-loved" as an answer to "What is pious?" because it is only a πάθος of "pious" (a property which all pious things might just happen to have) instead of being its οὐσία (the property which each of them must have to qualify as pious). When thus contrasted with πάθος, οὐσία clearly stands for the essential nature of the F and thus may be properly translated "essence." If x is F, and P is a πάθος of F, while E is the essence of F, then x is F not *qua* P, but *qua* E; it is E, not P, that "makes" it F.

is contains not only spatio-temporal items, like individuals and events, but also entities of another sort whose identity conditions are strikingly different since they are "the same" in persons and in actions which are not the same: justice here and justice there and again elsewhere, the same in different individuals and occurrences, real in each of them, but real in a way that is different from that in which they are real, its own reality evidenced just in the fact that it can be instantiated self-identically in happenings scattered widely over space and time, so that if justice has been correctly defined for even a single instance, the definiens will be true of every instance of justice that ever was or ever will be anywhere – in Greece or Persia, on earth or on Olympus or in Hades.

That there are things which meet this strong condition is a piece of ontology firmly fixed in Socrates$_E$'s speech and thought. He *has* this ontology. Can he have it, without falsifying the claim I made in Thesis IA above, that he is a moralist and nothing more – no metaphysician, no ontologist? Can one *have* an ontology without being an ontologist?[50] Why not? The belief in the existence of a physical world independent of our own mind, stocked with material objects retaining substantial identity and qualitative continuity over long or short stretches of time, is a solid piece of ontology, as entrenched in the mind of the average Athenian then as in that of the average New Yorker now. Does this make an ontologist of either of them? Why should it? Can't one have a language without being a linguist? One qualifies as a linguist when one makes language an object of reflective investigation. One would qualify as an ontologist if one made ontology an object of reflective investigation. And this is what S$_E$ never does. He never asks what sort of things forms must be if their identity conditions can be so different from those of spatio-temporal individuals and events that the identical form can be "in"[51] non-identical individuals and events. The search for those general properties of forms which distinguish them systematically from non-forms is never on his elenctic agenda. He asks: What is the form piety? What is the form beauty? And so forth. What is form? he never asks. He is perplexed about many things, but never about the fact that what there is contains forms. He is never touched with

---

50 Thirty years ago (Vlastos, 1956: liii, n. 10) I assumed that the answer has to be "No." Woodruff, 1982: 163 *et passim*, now takes that view and argues for it better than I did then. Even so, as I explain above, I am of a different opinion now. Woodruff says that "those who would enlarge ontology to cover every question about what there is would make ontologists of us all." So they would, if all it takes to be an ontologist is to have some belief or other about what there is; not so, if strenuous reflection on such beliefs is also required.
51 Cf. T4 above: "...the same as itself *in* every [pious] action."

wonder that such things as forms should be. He banks on their reality with the same unreflective, unexamined, unargued, undefended assurance with which the man in the street banks on the reality of trees and stones.

That is why it is gratuitous to credit him, as has so often been done in the scholarly literature, with a theory of forms.[52] His belief in their reality is no more evidence of his having such a *theory* than is the man in the street's belief in the reality of physical objects evidence of his having a theory of physical objects. A belief is not a theory if everyone's agreement with it can be presumed as a matter of course – if it is unproblematic for everyone, in need of explanation and justification for no one. This is the vein in which S_E believes in the reality of forms. He asks Euthyphro if piety is not the same character in every pious act, and gets instant assent. He presents Laches with a large variety of courageous acts – brave encounters with danger in war, at sea, in politics, and so forth[53] – and asks:

T6 *La.* 191E: "Try again to say about courage, first of all, what is that which is the same in all of these?"

and Laches offers not the least resistance to the assumption that in that motley collection there *is* something which is "the same in all." Neither Euthyphro nor Laches is a philosopher: one is a soothsayer, the other a military man, a general. But their responses are a fair sample of the one Socrates would have elicited from anyone on the street picked at random.

The same would be true if he had asked whether or not the form he is seeking to define *exists*. Consider this exchange with Hippias:

T7 *HMa.* 287C–D: "He will ask you, 'O stranger from Elis, is it not because of justice that just men are just?' Answer, Hippias, as if the question were being put to you." – "I shall answer that it is because of justice." – "Then this [thing], justice, exists?"[54] – "Very much so." – "And is it not because of wisdom that the wise are wise and because of goodness that all good things are good?" – "How else?" – "Then these [wisdom, goodness] exist: that could not be the case if these did not exist."

52 For an attractive version of this view, which allows S_E to have a piece of S_M's ontology – though only a modest one, still a far cry from S_M's two-world theory of reality – see Allen, 1970: 67ff. *et passim.*   53 *La.* 191A–E.

54 οὐκοῦν ἔστι τι τοῦτο, ἡ δικαιοσύνη; Literally translated (as in Fowler, 1926; Woodruff, 1982), ἔστι τι = "is justice something?", i.e. "is there such a thing as justice?" (in logician's language: "is there some x such that x = justice?"), in fewer words, "does justice exist?" I shall so translate the ἔστι τι phrase throughout its important occurrences, including T11, T12 in the *Phd.* (below in the present chapter); T22 in the *Smp.*; T1, T5 (in additional note 2.5) *et passim* in the *Prm.* (cf. n. 126 below), and *Ti.* 51B–D (quoted in additional note 2.5). Cf. nn. 55 and 66 below.

– "They do exist, indeed." – "Then aren't all beautiful things, too, beautiful because of beauty?" – "Quite so, because of beauty." – "Because this beauty exists?" – "It does exist – what is the worry?" – "'Say then, stranger,' he will say, 'What *is* this beauty?'"

Unlike Euthyphro and Laches, Hippias is an intellectual, a renowned one. He is an accomplished mathematician and astronomer, a historian too, a polymath. But there is no indication that his manifold accomplishments had ever given him occasion to investigate whether or not the justice of just persons *exists*. So there is no reason to believe that on these questions Socrates expects, or gets, from Hippias anything but the simple, unreflective, answers he would have got from anyone he might have fished out of the market. And we can see how they run. The existence of those entities strikes Hippias as so obvious that he grows impatient at being plied with such self-answering questions.[55] Only at the end of T7 is the point of eliciting agreement on the existence of justice, goodness, and finally beauty made clear: Socrates has been working up to a springboard for his great "What is the *F*?" question. From the admission that there is such a thing as beauty – that beauty exists – he moves directly to "What is beauty?", and to this question he hangs on like a bull-dog through the rest of the dialogue, lamenting at the end his failure to find the answer to it.

Now consider the exchange with Protagoras. The same question is put in equivalent[56] terms:

T8 *Pr.* 330c1–2: "Is justice a thing, or is it nothing? To me it seems a thing. How about you?" – "To me too," he said.

Socrates' interlocutor is once again a renowned intellectual, but renowned for something which has no parallel in Hippias' manysided accomplishments. Protagoras is famous for his dictum "Man is the measure of all things," a manifesto of extreme relativism.[57] It is so understood by Plato in the *Cratylus*:

55 Agreeing heartily to the first question, drily to the second, he finally wants to know what is the point of the persistent questioning: ἀλλὰ τί γὰρ μέλλει – "What's the problem? Why are you asking?"

56 The question in T8, πρᾶγμά τί ἐστιν; is no different from the one in T7, ἔστι τι; It could have been asked as well in the latter form as in the former. Socrates is asking, "Is there such a thing as beauty? Is there such a thing as justice?" Cf. n. 66 below, and additional note 2.3.

57 Many years ago (1956: xiiff.) I called the view "subjectivism." I stand by the substance of the account of it I gave there. But I would now agree with Burnyeat, 1976: 44ff., that "relativism" would be a more accurate term for the view that if *a* appears to be *F* to a given subject S at t1, then *a is F* in relation to S at t1, provided it is borne in mind that this is *a highly subjectivized* form of relativism.

T9 *Cra.* 385E: "Come, Hermogenes, let us see: in your opinion is the essence of things[58] private to each of us, as Protagoras used to say, declaring "Man is the measure of all things" – that such as things appear to me, such they are for me; while such as they appear to you, such they are for you? Or do you believe that they have some stability of essence of their own?"

If Protagoras maintains that what any given person believes about, say, justice is true only for the person to whom it appears to be such-and-such, how can he be expected to agree that justice is "the same" throughout the great diversity of actions which diverse persons call "just"? He couldn't and he doesn't. He is never asked the "What is the *F*?" question.[59] And for good reason: for then the metaphysical issue would have surfaced, the rival ontological commitments would have clashed, and Socrates would have been called upon to defend his own, pushed into the role of ontologist which he prefers to avoid, and consistently does avoid in the earlier dialogues.[60] Plato manages things so that the conflict can be ignored. To the "Man is the measure" dictum no direct allusion is made throughout the whole of the *Protagoras*.[61] The first reference by Socrates_E to the Protagorean ontology comes in a Transitional Dialogue, the *Euthydemus* (286B–C). There the Protagorean doctrine that contradiction is impossible is brought into the dialogue not by Socrates but by his interlocutor, Dionysidorus, who parrots it, without acknowledgement of its source, and Socrates does no more than call attention to the plagiarism.[62] He does so to make it clear that the doctrine was old hat and he implies that it was nothing to be excited about, for both it and its corollary, that false statement is impossible, are self-refuting.[63] Those strident paradoxes are not

58 οὐσία τῶν ὄντων. That "essence" is right, against "existence" (cf. additional note 2.3) for οὐσία here is clear from the context in T9 and again at 386E: maintaining that things "have their own essence by themselves according to their own nature (ἥπερ πέφυκεν, 386E4), Socrates is opposing the Protagorean doctrine which destabilizes not the existence of things, but their "nature," as is indicated by πέφυκεν here and repeatedly in the sequel (cf. φύσιν at 387D1).

59 Plato gives Socrates no opportunity to put that question in the *Pr.* There is no definitional inquiry in this dialogue which would have given Socrates the occasion to ask questions such as those he asks Euthyphro at T4 and T5 and Laches at T6 and thus makes explicit the assumption that the *F* denotes a character which is "the same" in all the multiplicity of instances to which its name applies. 60 Cf. Thesis IA at p. 47 above.

61 Though Socrates would be expected to know all about it (he is not depicted as a philosophical illiterate).

62 He remarks that he has heard it "often, from many" and that "it was employed by those about Protagoras and still older thinkers" (he means, but does not name, Parmenides).

63 This "vulgar" (286E10: φορτικώτερόν τι) refutation he thinks is all these claims deserve. There is not the least anticipation here of the sustained critique Plato will be devoting to them many years later in the *Sophist*. Taking no notice of their challenge to the ontologist, Socrates_E treats them as fake paradoxes, pseudological firecrackers that explode harmlessly once their intolerable consequences, intellectual (286D–E) and moral (287A), are perceived.

allowed so much as a whisper in any Elenctic Dialogue and when
they do find a voice in a Transitional one all they elicit is a snub.
Their exclusion from the very work which bears Protagoras' name is
remarkable when so much is to be made of them in dialogues of
Plato's middle[64] and late periods.[65]

Returning to T7, let us note that there is a sense of "thing" so
innocuous that everyone who is willing to discuss justice, piety, and
the rest can be expected to agree that they are "things." This is the
sense we give the word in everyday talk, using it in the quantifiers of
English speech,[66] "everything," "something," "nothing"[67] and in
all-purpose referential phrases like "I haven't understood a thing
you are saying." In this sense of the word Protagoras would have to
agree that justice is a "thing," i.e. something he and Socrates are
arguing over, else the discussion could not proceed at all. But *could*
he agree to even this, consistently with his doctrinaire relativism?
Plato makes Socrates$_E$ decline to raise that question,[68] asking
Protagoras to agree that justice is a "thing" with a determinate
relation to each of the virtues,[69] so that they may proceed to disagree
on just that relation – on whether it is or is not tied to each of four
others in that strictly *moral*[70] bond which is at issue throughout all the

---

64 The rejection of the Protagorean "Man is the measure" doctrine in the *Cra.* is the point
at which the first intimation of the ontology of the middle dialogues shows up at T9 above
(reiterated at 386E). To the "Man is the measure" dictum Plato returns over and over
again in the *Tht.* (152A, 160D, 170D–E, 171C, 178B).

65 The impossibility of false statement becomes the central target of the Eleatic Stranger's
critique of Parmenides in the *Sophist*.   66 Cf. Vlastos, 1956: iiii, n. 10.

67 The third of these is nicely paralleled in Greek: the normal way of saying "nothing" is
οὐδέν, a contraction for οὐδὲν πρᾶγμα, "no thing" = "nothing" (I have so translated at
T8 above). The second is matched by the use of πρᾶγμα for the *x* of the existential
quantifier; cf. n. 56 above.

68 Understandably so, if Socrates is to be kept down to the role of single-minded moralist,
whose elenctic investigations are restricted to moral topics (cf. n. 5 in additional note 1.1,
and n. 12 in the present chapter): he may have views on all sorts of other things, including
ontology, but he declines to debate them. If Protagoras had been allowed to challenge the
assumption that "justice is a thing" the fat would be in the fire: the debate would have
been diverted from a moral to an ontological inquiry.

69 If Protagoras believes that his relativist ontology allows him to challenge Socrates' views
about the virtues, Socrates is perfectly justified in ignoring Protagoras' ontology to focus
his critique on the moral content of the sophist's views.

70 I italicize "moral," for this is the only aspect of Socrates' theses which is consistently
challenged by Protagoras throughout the debate. Their ontological import is left
surprisingly imprecise in the expressions used by Socrates to identify the relation of the
virtues *inter se* which he is defending throughout the argument. At 331B he says that the
virtues in question are "either the same or as similar as they could possibly be"; at 331B
he says they are "one [thing]" and then shifts to "nearly the same." Neither he nor his
adversary assay any specification of the relation other than the very precise one stated in
the simplest possible terms by Socrates at 329E2–4 (whoever has any of them must have
all of them). No further identification of it is necessary for the purposes of their debate;
whatever might be the logic or ontology of the Socratic view Protagoras might wish to
controvert, his substantive disagreement with its moral doctrine is made clear enough at

subsequent twists and turns of dialogue, as he insists and Protagoras denies, that each of the virtues is interentailing with each of the other virtues or, more simply,[71] that a person who has any virtue will "of necessity" have all the virtues. Plato could hardly have made it clearer that the interests of Socrates in this dialogue are exclusively ethical.[72] Brought up face to face with the premier relativist of the day, the chance to debate ontology virtually thrust upon him, Socrates$_E$ turns it down.

Now consider Socrates$_M$. To the existence of the *F*, which had been regularly conceded to Socrates$_E$ by all of his interlocutors without contest, Socrates$_M$ refers as a highly contestable thesis. In the *Republic* he calls it a "posit":

T10 *R.* 596A: "We are accustomed to *posit*[73] a certain single Form for each plurality to which we apply the same name."

In the *Phaedo* he calls it a *hypothesis*:

T11 *Phd.* 100B: "I return to those [things] that are always on our lips and make them my starting-point, *hypothesizing*[74] that Beauty exists itself by itself,[75] and so too Goodness and Greatness and the rest. If you grant me these and concede that they exist I expect that from these I shall be able to discover and expound to you the reason (αἰτία) for the soul's immortality."

329E, where he confronts the thesis asserted by Socrates at 329E2–4 and flatly denied by himself there (at 329E5–6) and then once again at the climax of the debate (349D5–8). Cf. Vlastos, 1981: 221ff., especially at 264, and the notes at 428–33.

71 As he puts it himself at 329E2–4: cf. the preceding note.

72 From which we cannot infer that his own lack of interest in metaphysical and epistemological topics would be shared by his closest adherents. Thus we know from Aristotle that Antisthenes had important logico-metaphysical doctrines (see Caizzi, 1964: 48ff. at 49–65; Giannantoni, 1983: II 319–407 and III 177–370), as did also Euclid of Megara with his Eleaticizing logic (Giannantoni, 1983: I 37–48 and III 31–58), and as would also Aristippus have done *if* (as is possible, though improbable) he had been the originator of that remarkable epistemological doctrine which is ascribed to "the Cyrenaic sect" *ap.* Sextus Empiricus, *Adv. Math.* 7.190–200 (on which see Tsouna, 1988: part 2, ch. 1). One of the most impressive things about Socrates is his ability to attract and hold devoted followers, warmly attached to him and profoundly influenced by him, who felt free to go their separate ways in developing ethical and meta-ethical doctrines in sharp disagreement with one another and no doubt with him as well.

73 τίθεσθαι. Note the difference from Socrates$_E$, who had not asked Hippias to "posit" that justice, beauty, wisdom, exist: he had asked if they do, and got full agreement. (I capitalize "Form" here [cf. n. 46 above], since εἶδος is now being used as a *terminus technicus* to refer to entities unknown to the man in the street whose categorial properties will be laid out in section III below.)   74 ὑποθέμενος.

75 εἶναί τι αὐτὸ καθ' αὑτό. The rendering of εἶναί τι as "is something" = "exists" was explained in n. 54 above. And there is no mystery about the meaning of the first occurrence of the reflexive pronoun: it is used in the sense of αὐτός = *solus* (examples in Riddell, 1867: 134; and cf. Burnet, 1911: "in this technical sense αὐτό is a development of αὐτός, 'alone,'" pointing out that at *Phd.* 67D1 μόνην καθ' αὑτήν is used synonymously with αὑτὴν καθ' αὑτήν just before). But what on earth is the import of καθ' αὑτήν in this context? This will be puzzled out in section III below and further in additional note 2.5.

To speak of a proposition as a *hypothesis* in this context is to treat it as an unasserted premise throughout the ensuing argument whose purpose will not be to probe the truth of that premise but only to demonstrate what would follow *if* that premise were true.[76] When so using that proposition one is not expressing uncertainty about its truth. Absolutely none was voiced earlier on in this dialogue when the existence of the Forms was introduced soon after its start by a question which had anticipated and received instant, enthusiastic, agreement:

T12 *Phd.* 65D. "Do we assert that Justice exists itself by itself or that it does not?[77] – "We assert it, by Zeus."

So far from there being any uncertainty on this score in the mind of Socrates or of his companions, it was presented as itself the ground on which uncertainty about other things could be resolved. To prove the prenatal existence of the soul Socrates thought it sufficient to demonstrate that "it has the same necessity"[78] as the existence of the Forms; and his arguments had produced full conviction. Simmias, to whom it was addressed, had replied:

T13 *Phd.* 76E–77A: "...the argument rightly reduces to this:[79] the existence of our soul before our birth is on a par with that of the reality[80] of which you speak. For nothing is so clear to me as that all those things – Beauty and Goodness and all the other things of which you speak – are as real as anything could possibly be."[81]

Why then should Socrates, upon returning to the Forms later on at T11 above, speak of their existence as a "hypothesis" and ask his interlocutor *if* he would grant it? Because he now wants to make it clear that this is not a proposition which can be simply taken for granted. Assent to it cannot be expected from everyone. Those who do assert it, so readily at T12, with such conviction at T13, are "the philosophers," the "true philosophers," those "who philosophize correctly," "who have the right grip on philosophy"[82] – a select

---

76 He is pursuing a method of investigation he calls ἐξ ὑποθέσεως σκοπεῖσθαι ("investigating from a *hypothesis*") to be discussed in ch. 4) which first enters Plato's corpus in *M.* 86Dff., ostentatiously borrowed from the mathematicians and illustrated by an elaborate geometrical example.

77 φαμέν τι εἶναι δίκαιον αὐτὸ καθ᾽ αὑτὸ ἢ οὐδέν; The import of τι εἶναι αὐτὸ καθ᾽ αὑτό, a *terminus technicus* of crucial importance in the ontology of Plato's middle dialogues, will be discussed later in the present chapter and further in additonal note 2.5.

78 ἴση ἀνάγκη, 76E5.   79 Literally, "escapes (καταφεύγει) to this."

80 So Hackforth, 1955 and Bluck, 1955, without explanation, for οὐσίαν. For explanation see additional note 2.3 below.

81 εἶναι ὡς οἷόν τε μάλιστα. Argument for the above translation in additional note 2.3.

82 οἱ φιλοσοφοῦντες, 64B4–5; οἱ ὡς ἀληθῶς φιλόσοφοι, 64B9; οἱ φιλοσοφοῦντες ὀρθῶς, 67D8, E4; ὅσοι τυγχάνουσι ὀρθῶς ἁπτόμενοι φιλοσοφίας, 64A4–5.

band of true believers, set off from the common mass,[83] the thoughtless, uncomprehending multitudes who

T14 *R.* v, 476D: "believe in beautiful things, but do not believe in Beauty itself, and if one tries to lead them to knowledge of it are unable to follow,"

and so are doomed to spend their lives in ontological bewilderment, "living in a dream instead of waking reality" (*R.* 476D3).

This metaphor should not be pressed. Socrates$_M$ is not saying that while Forms exist their spatio-temporal instances do not – that beautiful objects in the everyday world are dream-images, illusions of mortal mind. He goes on to argue that the objects of sense and opinion "lie between the perfectly real and the utterly unreal."[84] There is no question of his going so far as to deny the existence of the world of the senses. But he goes far enough. He wants to say that those who assert the reality of sensible things while denying that of Forms suffer from a kind of paranoia: "they are not in their right mind."[85] When "we," the philosophers, try to heal them, "they get angry at us,"[86] they protest that "what we are saying is not true."[87]

Both in the earlier and the middle dialogues Plato depicts Socrates *contra mundum*. But in the former the opposition to "the many" is exclusively moral.[88] Socrates$_E$ never says a word to indicate that he has any metaphysical beliefs which clash with theirs. Outside the moral domain his intellectual outlook is by and large no different from theirs. He shares their skepticism of the speculations of the natural philosophers, their suspicion of the claims of the sophists.[89] He does not expect and *never gets* from them objection to the existence of the entities he denominates *eidos*, *idea* while this is the crux of Socrates$_M$'s differences with "the many," the one from which he believes the moral differences follow.[90] Since Plato is not suggesting

83 "The many," *Phd.* 64B2 *et passim.*
84 Following Cornford's (1945) translation of *R.* 486D6–7, μεταξὺ κεῖσθαι τοῦ εἰλικρινοῦς ὄντος τε καὶ τοῦ πάντως μὴ ὄντος. Here ὄντος cannot mean "existent": The existence of sensible instances of Forms on a par with that of Forms is taken for granted. In the *Phaedo* (79A) Socrates$_M$ recognizes two classes of existent (δύο εἴδη τῶν ὄντων), "visible and invisible."   85 So Cornford, 1945 and Grube, 1974 for οὐχ ὑγιαίνει at *R.* 476E2.
86 χαλεπαίνει, 476D.   87 *Loc. cit.*
88 See *Cr.* 48D for Socrates$_E$'s view of the crux of the opposition (his rejection of the *lex talionis*: to be discussed in chapter 7); and *G.* 481C for Callicles' view of it: the doctrine that to suffer injustice is better than to do it "turns our human life upside down."
89 *Ap.* 19C, 20C.
90 Their ignorance of the Forms invalidates their moral beliefs *en bloc*: "the many traditional beliefs of the many about Beauty and the rest [e.g. 'Justice and Goodness,' 479D] are adrift in a sort of twilight zone between pure reality and complete unreality" (*R.* 479D; translation partly after Cornford, 1945). In the *Phaedo* even the best behaved of non-philosophers (οἱ κόσμιοι αὐτῶν, 68E) only achieve "an illusionary facade of virtue": "they are "brave through a sort of fear and cowardice" (68E), "temperate through a sort of intemperance" (69A). Their morality is "slavish, there is no health or truth in it" (69B).

that the ontological beliefs of "the many" have now changed, he must be packing a very different content into the proposition that Forms exist. What this new content is we come to see when he goes to work explaining systematically what Socrates$_E$ never tried to do at all: *how* Forms are real – what sort of reality they have.

III

He is deep in this new project from the moment he mentions Forms in the *Phaedo*, the first dialogue in which Socrates$_M$ expounds systematically his theory of Forms.[91] The first thing he notices about them is their *inaccessibility to the senses*:

T15 *Phd.* 65D4–12: "And again that Beauty and Goodness exist? [continuing T12 above]... Well, then, have you ever seen anything of that sort with your eyes?... Or grasped it through any other bodily sense?"

Here the assertion that Forms exist is not made in the context of a definitional inquiry,[92] as in the *Hippias Major*,[93] where the point of getting Hippias to agree that beauty exists is to spring on him the question, "Say, then, *what* is it?" In the *Phaedo* it becomes the prelude to a different kind of question, never raised in the earlier dialogues: Are Justice, Beauty, etc. the sort of thing we can perceive with any of our senses? If this question had been put to Socrates$_E$ he would have undoubtedly agreed that they are not. This is implicit in the whole of his investigative procedure – elenctic argument, an intellectual exercise in whose procedure appeal to sensible evidence would be a manifest irrelevance: the very idea that headway could be made in a search for a "What is the *F*?" question by referring to what has been seen, heard, smelled, tasted, touched would be absurd. So on this point we could count on ready agreement between S$_E$ and S$_M$. The difference lies precisely in the fact that those questions, which never arise at all for S$_E$, become matters of vital concern for S$_M$. The difference is symptomatic of the fact that S$_E$'s

Cf. Weiss, 1987: 57ff. at 62: "The genuine *agathos* is the philosopher." (But Weiss fails to note that what is said here about the illusory nature of the virtue of non-philosophers is radically qualified in books III–IV of the *Republic*: cf. Vlastos, 1981: 137, n. 79 and Irwin, 1977a: 198–203; also nn. 30–2 in chapter 3.)

91 A first intimation of the new theory had come in the *Cratylus*, though here only one of the categorial properties of forms is argued for – their invariance (439D–E, with which cf. *Ti.* 50B3–5). But this is done in such a masterful, definitive, fashion as to give convincing evidence that Plato is well on the way to his new ontology.

92 There are pointed references in the *Phaedo* (75d, 78D) to such inquiries, but no such inquiry is mounted *in* the dialogue. Neither in this or any other dialogue of the middle period is the existence of Forms used to introduce the "What is the *F*?" question and control answers to it – which is the *only* use made of their existence in earlier dialogues.

93 T7 in section II above.

interests are exclusively ethical. There is no spill-over into epistemology in his pursuit of them to take him even so far as the elementary observation that Form-apprehension eludes the senses.

And this is only the start of it. S_M is not making just that very modest claim, that Forms like Justice, Goodness, etc. cannot be seen, heard, touched – a claim which would be readily granted by anyone who understands the question. He goes far beyond this to *reject the senses as an avenue to knowledge about anything whatever*, maintaining that nothing worthy of the name of "knowledge" can be reached by their means and that our only hope of acquiring any knowledge at all is *via* the purely intellectual activity to which he refers as "reasoning" or "thinking."[94] He had said as much just a few lines before T15:

T16 *Phd.* 65B–C: "So when does the soul grasp truth? For whenever she undertakes to investigate anything with the body it is clear that she will be thoroughly deceived by the body... Therefore it is in reasoning, if anywhere, that any reality becomes clearly revealed to the soul (κατάδηλον αὐτῇ γίνεταί τι τῶν ὄντων)."

Here and in the immediate sequel, as well as in a shorter, but equally forceful, reiteration of its thought later on (82E–83B), the senses are viewed with distrust and hostility, pilloried as causes of perturbation and disorientation to the mind.[95] If this were being said only concerning mathematical knowledge, the interdict on sensory evidence would be unobjectionable; it could be taken as a salutary guide to sound thinking in geometry.[96] But S_M is not referring to the investigation of some restricted class of Forms:

T17 *Phd.* 65D12–13: "I am speaking about all of them, e.g. greatness, health, strength – in a word about the reality which each happens to be (τῆς οὐσίας ὃ τυγχάνει ἕκαστον ὄν)."

Having thus stressed that he is speaking of our knowledge of Forms generally, he declares,

94 λογίζεσθαι, διανοεῖσθαι. διανοεῖσθαι (which I translate, somewhat lamely, "thinking") is the term S_M takes to be the intellectual activity conspicuously (but not exclusively) exercised in mathematics. διάνοια is his term for cognition in the second segment of the Divided Line (*R.* 511D–E, 533D) within which mathematical investigation falls. λογίζεσθαι, Plato's favourite term for moral reasoning, both in earlier and middle dialogues, is also associated with mathematical reasoning. As Burnet, 1924 observes on *Phd.* 65C2, "the primary sense of the word is arithmetical calculation"; cf. λογισάμενος εἰπέ, *M.* 82D4, requesting a simple arithmetical computation.

95 "Eyes, ears, in a word, the whole of the body, disturbs (ταράττοντος [cf. θόρυβον παρέχει καὶ ταραχὴν καὶ ἐκπλήττει, 66D] the soul and does not let her come to possess truth and wisdom when she associates with the body" (65A). "Philosophy, demonstrating that inquiry through the eyes is full of deceit, and so too inquiry through the ears and the other senses, persuades us to withdraw from these, except in so far as their use is unavoidable" (83A).   96 See additional note 2.4.

T18 *Phd.* 65E–66A: "And would not one do this [i.e. come closest to having knowledge of what one is thinking about][97] if one approached it so far as possible by thought alone, and, not admitting sight into one's thinking nor dragging in any other sense alongside one's reasoning, but employing pure thought itself by itself, sought to track each pure reality[98] itself by itself (αὐτὸ καθ᾽ αὐτό)?"

It boggles the mind that S_M should want his warning against the evidential use of sensory data to extend even to the investigation of things like health and strength (T17 above), falling squarely in the domain of the physiological and medical sciences of the day, where sense-experience was firmly ensconced as the primary source of the data for knowledge.[99] But there is no doubt that this is what he means. He is convinced that if knowledge is what we are after, our only hope of reaching it is by "thinking" and "reasoning." There the mind, made safe from illusion-breeding sense-experience, can no more go wrong than it can in Descartes when inspecting "clear and distinct ideas."[100]

Closely related to their inaccessibility to sense-perception is a second categorial property of S_M's Forms: their *absolute exemption from change*. He holds that while all parts of the sensible world are constantly changing, no part of the world of Forms can change at all: in their case immutability is of the very essence of their being. So much S_E could have been expected to grant. He might well have thought it a strict consequence of the assumption that every form is self-identical in each of the distinct temporal occurrences which instantiate it. This seems to be the plain implication of such a question, "Is not the pious the same as itself in every [pious] action?": if piety in pious action *a* is "the same" as in pious action *b*, must it not be unaltered throughout the interval that separates *a* from *b* or from any other instance of piety no matter how remote

---

97 The referent of τοῦτο at 65E6 is γνῶναι ἕκαστον [περὶ οὗ σκοπεῖ], 65E4–5.

98 αὐτῇ καθ᾽ αὑτὴν εἰλικρινεῖ τῇ διανοίᾳ χρώμενος αὐτὸ καθ᾽ αὑτὸ εἰλικρινὲς ἕκαστον ἐπιχειροῖ θηρεύειν τῶν ὄντων. "Realities" for ὄντα: cf. additional note 2.3.

99 From the earliest methodological Greek reflection in these sciences sense-perception had been conceived as the proper source of knowledge in their own domain: so Alcmaeon, early in the fifth century, thinks of the senses as "ducts" through which information is conveyed to the brain (Theophrastus, *De Sens.* 26); so too, soon after, for Empedocles (Diels–Kranz, DK B310) each of the senses is a "duct of understanding." We see this point of view expressed in the (late) Hippocratic treatise *Precepts*, which declares in its opening paragraph: "In medical practice one should pay the greatest attention not to plausible reasoning but to experience combined with reason. For rational reflection is a systematizing of what has been received through the senses."

100 The possibility of purely intellectual error is not allowed in either case. Decartes blames all error on the will, S_M on the senses. The thought that λογισμός may go wrong and needs sense-experience to keep it on the rails, which seems so obvious to the medical man who wrote the *Precepts*, has not occurred to S_M.

from either? The connection of "the same in every F" with "the F always F" is explicit in

T19 *HMa.* 299E6–7: "I was asking him about that which is beautiful for all and always... For beautiful, surely, is always beautiful."[101]

But to what purpose was S_E expressing this conviction? It was to control the definitional search in which he was engaged – to forestall (or refute) a definiens which holds true in the particular case the interlocutor has in view but is falsified in others. S_E did not stop to reflect that if a form is to be self-identical in cases spread over time it must be itself exempt from the change in which each of its temporal instances is enmeshed. The failure parallels the one noticed in the foregoing: that while S_E's elenctic procedures takes it for granted that forms are inaccessible to the senses, he never takes notice of this, never reflects on it, never makes the assumption explicit. Both failures evidence his one-track interest in moral questions, his indifference to the epistemological and metaphysical issues which are precisely the ones S_M finds exciting. The excitement infects his style:

T20 *Phd.* 78D1–7: "That reality of whose essence we give account[102] in asking and answering our questions, is it always invariantly constant or is it different at different times?[103] Equality itself, Beauty itself, each real thing itself, the reality,[104] does it ever admit of any change at all? Or does each of those things which are real,[105] existing always itself by itself,[106] unique in form, remaining invariantly constant,[107] never admitting of any alteration whatever in any respect in any way?"

As a piece of philosophical prose by a fastidious writer who never repeats himself without good reason[108] these lines are remarkable for

---

101 Reading this sentence in the same way as the terminal clause in T4 (*Eu.* 5D3–5) above, I take the predicate to apply to each instance of the Form, not to the Form itself: whatever is an instance of the beautiful is always beautiful.

102 αὐτὴ ἡ οὐσία ἧς λόγον δίδομεν τοῦ εἶναι. The λόγος which answers the "What is the F?" question is an account of the reality (οὐσία) named "the F" which states its essence. See additional note 2.3.

103 πότερον ὡσαύτως ἀεὶ ἔχει κατὰ ταὐτὰ ἢ ἄλλοτ' ἄλλως; The phrase ὡσαύτως ἀεὶ ἔχει κατὰ ταὐτά sounds pleonastic at first blush. Why shouldn't ἀεὶ ἔχει κατὰ ταὐτά suffice to tell the tale of the invariant constancy of S_M's Forms? Why need he add that adverb? Because he wants to specify the full range of invariance he has in view. For suppose F entails G and H. Then F will be not only constantly F but also constantly G and H – *not* constantly F but inconstantly G or H. We need to be assured that the F will be always invariant in all the ways in which it is possible for it to be invariant.

104 αὐτὸ ἕκαστον ὃ ἔστιν, τὸ ὄν.   105 ἢ ἀεὶ αὐτῶν ἕκαστον ὃ ἔστι.

106 ὂν αὐτὸ καθ' αὑτό. The import of the underlined phrase will be discussed below.

107 ὡσαύτως κατὰ ταὐτὰ ἔχει.

108 But has no objection to repeating himself for emphasis upon occasion. Elenctic argument in the earlier dialogues also licenses motivated repetition: "admirable it is, they say, to say twice and even thrice what is admirable," *G.* 498E.

saying the same thing two and three times over with only verbal variations: they "never admit of any change at all" – they "never admit of any alteration whatever"; they "are always invariantly constant" – they "remain invariantly constant." The emphasis produced by such reiterative assertion could hardly be stronger.

Now consider the complementary assertion of the instability of the temporal instances of the Forms:

T21   *Phd.* 78D18–E4:   "What then of the many beautiful [things] – men or horses or anything else whatever of this sort – or of the many equal [things] or of any other namesakes of theirs.[109] Are *they* always in the same state? Or, just the opposite, are they not, so to speak,[110] never in any way in the same state?"

The force of the qualification in "so to speak" should not be missed. Without that scaling-down of the assertion, the denial of stability to sensibles in T21 would be as sweeping as is its assertion in the case of Forms in T20: it would mean absolute, total instability, perpetual change in every possible respect. And this would be not at all what Plato wants to say. For if a sensible instance of a given Form were involved in such all-pervasive, total, change how could we think of it as a *bona fide* instance of that Form? And if we could not, how could we identify *it* at all so that we can refer to *it* as the changing thing?[111] The hypothesis that *everything* is in total change self-destructs: if the hypothesis were true it would be impossible to assert its truth about *anything* in particular. Moreover, no sense could then be given to Plato's doctrine that sensible things are "namesakes" of Forms, each of them "participating"[112] in the particular Form whose "name-

109 πάντων τῶν ἐκείνοις ὁμωνύμων: since an instance of beauty is "a beauty" it is a "namesake" of the Form which it instantiates. Plato resorts to this metaphor to help fill the gap in his philosophical vocabulary left by the absence of a term for "instance" or for "particular." Aristotle's technical term for the latter, τὰ καθ' ἕκαστα has not yet been coined.

110 ὡς ἔπος εἰπεῖν. Plato often uses this phrase (or its shorter variant, ὡς εἰπεῖν: for examples see Ast, 1835: *s.v.* εἶπον) to scale down the force of an assertion, as e.g. at *Lg.* 656E, "I mean really ten thousand – not in a manner of speaking." In T21 he is warning us that the inconstancy of instances of the Forms is by no means as extreme as is the converse invariance of the Forms they instantiate: Forms are absolutely immutable but their instances are not absolutely mutable.

111 It is along such lines that S$_M$ refutes the hypothesis that everything is in total flux: "If something is always slipping away would it be possible to say truly of it, first, 'it is *that*,' secondly, 'it is *such-and-such*,' when, while we are still speaking, it must straightway become different and slip away and no longer be in that state?" (*Cra.* 439D; cf. *Tht.* 182D).

112 "It seems to me that if anything is beautiful other than Beauty itself, it is beautiful just because it participates in *that* Beauty," *Phd.* 100C. The doctrine is spelled out more fully in *Prm.* 128E: "Don't you hold that there is a form of Similarity and the opposite of such a thing, i.e. Dissimilarity? And given these two things, you and I and the other things which we call 'the many' participate in them – and those which participate in Similarity

sake" it is. Nothing contrary to this doctrine is being asserted in T21 once the qualifying phrase is taken into account: we can understand S_M to be asserting that no sensible thing is ever the same in *all* of its properties and relations during any stretch of time, no matter how small.[113] This will allow sensible things to change in some ways while remaining constant in others – innumerable changes, subliminally minute, proceeding within every object of our perceptual experience while its gross perceptible properties remain recognizably the same. "But if this is how Plato wants to be understood couldn't he have said so more explicitly?" Certainly. But why suppose he would want to? Has he any interest in making his doctrine more palatable to the "soundlovers and sightlovers"?[114] He has no desire to conciliate these worldlings. Just the opposite. He wants to startle them, shock them out of the dogmatic certainties of their false ontology. His message to them: "If absolute stability is what you want, you will never find it in the world of sights and sounds. You must look for it in that other world in whose existence you do not believe."[115]

We can now consider a third categorial feature of S_M's Forms: their *incorporeality*. How fundamental this feature of theirs really is Plato comes to see best in retrospect when he views the ontology of his middle dialogues from the perspective of his latest period. In the *Sophist* he sees the great issue in metaphysics[116] as that which divides materialists, for whom body *defines* reality,[117] and immaterialists,[118]

become similar in that respect and in so far as (ταύτῃ τε καὶ κατὰ τοσοῦτον ὅσον ἄν) they participate, while those which participate in Dissimilarity become dissimilar, and those which participate in both become both [similar and dissimilar]?" (*Prm.* 129A).

113 Plato never asserts anything stronger. In the *Philebus* (59B1–2) he declares that nothing in this world "ever was or will be or now is constant." Cherniss, 1957a: 243, took this to mean that "all γιγνόμενα are in perpetual change *in every respect* [my emphasis]." But (as Irwin, 1977b: 3, n. 5, has pointed out) Cherniss's paraphrase misstates what Plato wrote by overstating it: his text contains nothing corresponding to the words I have italicized; read strictly, the text asserts no more than that everything in this world is always changing *in some respect* – a perfectly intelligible claim, which might even be true.

114 S_M's label in *R.* 475ff. for the unphilosophical "many," the people who believe that there is nothing better than the half-real world of the senses: cf. the next note.

115 *R.* 479A1–3: "that fine fellow [the 'sightlover'], who does not believe in Beauty itself – a certain Form of beauty which is always invariantly constant."

116 He likens it to the γιγαντομαχία – the battle of the earthborn giants against the Olympians.

117 ταὐτὸν σῶμα καὶ οὐσίαν ὁριζόμενοι. This categorial property of sensibles has now become so much more salient in his retrospective view of the ontology of his middle period, so definitive of their difference from Forms, that he feels no great need to set forth formally their other categorial properties. The material world's accessibility to the senses he takes for granted (that body is "visible and tangible" comes out in the immediate sequel, at *Sph.* 247B); its perpetual flux appears only in the charge of the immaterialists that their opponents reduce reality to pure process (γένεσιν ἀντ' οὐσίας φερομένην τινα, 246C1–2).

118 I resist the temptation to say "idealists" instead: against all varieties of modern metaphysical idealism, Berkeleyan or Hegelian, Plato's ontology remains solidly realistic.

the "Friends of Forms," who would "force on us the view that true reality[119] consists of certain intelligible and incorporeal Forms" (246c).[120] In the middle dialogues this dimension of the Forms had been taken for granted, needing only to be noticed, not argued for. In the *Phaedo* (79A–B) it was brought up in a lemma in one of the arguments for immortality: the soul must be immortal *because*, as between "the two kinds of existent,"[121] one of which is invisible and immutable, while the other is visible and ceaselessly mutable, the soul is "more alike and akin" to the former, than to the latter. That the latter is material is not mentioned as such, but it is implied in the statement that "it is more akin and more similar"[122] to our body than to our soul. In the *Republic* the corporeality of sensible things gets no formal recognition, but shows up incidentally when S_M contrasts the Form of Unity ("the One itself") with sensible instances of it, describing the latter as "numbers having visible and tangible[123] bodies" (525D). In the *Symposium*[124] the Form of Beauty is set off against "a beautiful face or hands or any other thing in which body partakes." Thus in dialogues of the middle period the incorporeality of Form is taken for granted as one of its standard features, as well it might since it is structurally essential to those two other categorial properties of theirs which get the lion's share of attention: it is because they have no body that Forms *cannot* be accessible to our senses (which are parts of our body and can only record its interactions with other bodies) and that they *can* be immutable (for if they were corporeal they would be caught in the flux that engulfs the material world).

I have left till last the aspect of S_M's Forms expressed by that strange phrase which may have caught the reader's eye in two of the texts cited from the *Phaedo* above: Form *exists itself by itself* (T11, T12 [= T15]).[125] What can S_M mean by the "itself-by-itself existence" of

---

119 τὴν ἀληθινὴν οὐσίαν. Why "true" reality (i.e. its highest degree: cf. Vlastos, 1981: 62, n. 16)? To safeguard the existential status of the material world in contrasting γένεσιν φερομένην with οὐσία Plato does not deny γένεσις *some* degree of reality: cf. *Ti.* 50D, "being and...becoming *exist*" (ὄν τε καὶ...γένεσιν εἶναι).

120 This division between materialists and immaterialists Plato now sees as so far-reaching that useful dialogue between the two parties becomes hopeless: if you tell the materialists that you acknowledge immaterial reality they will have "utter contempt for you, they will not want to hear anything further" (*Sph.* 246B).

121 δύο εἴδη τῶν ὄντων. Cf. n. 75 above.   122 ὁμοιότερον...καὶ συγγενέστερον, 79B–E.

123 The tangibility of body was to be given pride of place in Plato's retrospective view of the ontology of his middle period: in identifying the bodily with the real the "giants" allow reality only to "that which has impact and can be touched." In the *Phaedo* the most conspicuous feature of body is its visibility: so at T18 above and again at 79A–B where the "two kinds of being" are distinguished as "visible" and "invisible" respectively.

124 211A–B (= T22 below).   125 On the literal sense of the phrase see n. 75 above.

the entities he calls εἶδος, ἰδέα?[126] Since he never speaks to this question directly we must ferret out an answer from its use in context. So let us concentrate on the most informative of the many passages[127] in which it occurs in dialogues of Plato's middle period. This is that passage in the *Symposium* where Diotima[128] reveals to Socrates the vision awaiting the lover of the Form of Beauty at the terminus of his quest when he finally comes to "see"[129] face to face the Form he has previously viewed only in its manifestations in beautiful bodies, minds, institutions, or sciences:

T22 *Smp.* 211A5–B6:[130]   "[a] Beauty will not be manifest to him [at that moment] as a face or as hands or as any other corporeal thing nor yet as some discourse or science, [b] nor as existing somewhere in something else as, for example, in a living creature either on earth or in the sky or in anything else, but [c] as *existing itself by itself with itself*, always unique in form, [d] all other beautiful things participating in it in some such manner as this: while those other things arise and perish, it is neither enhanced nor diminished in any way, is not affected at all."

At [a] Diotima says that at the moment of climactic insight into the nature of Beauty the Form will not be seen as existing *in* any beautiful corporeal thing (hands, or face) nor yet *in* any beautiful process or product of thought (discourse or science). Since the disjunction "corporeal/mental" is exhaustive of things and happenings in the world of time, she has said that the Form of beauty will not be seen as existing *in* anything whatever in this world. But still

---

126 This question has been curiously neglected in the vast literature on Plato's Theory of Forms. Though scholars had been well aware that the leaner phrase, "the *F* itself" (αὐτὸ τὸ Φ), had been fully anticipated in Plato's earlier compositions (Riddell, 1857: 134; Campbell, 1894: 305–6; Burnet, 1924 on *Phd.* 64C6, 65D5, 65E3; Ross, 1951: 16–17; Allen, 1970: 74–5), they had apparently failed to notice that the "itself-by-itself existence" of Form is first asserted in the *Phaedo*, never in the earlier dialogues. *A fortiori* inquiry into the distinctive import of αὐτὸ καθ' αὐτὸ τὸ Φ was never put on their agenda. Most surprising is its neglect in the most laborious piece of research ever published on Plato's technical terminology, Constantin Ritter's *Neue Untersuchungen über Platon* (1910b): his investigation, containing a 100-page chapter on "*Eidos, Idea* und verwändte Wörter," makes no allusion to the role of the "itself by itself" phrase in the evolution of Plato's idiolect. The fault is not remedied in his massive two-volume work, *Platon* (1910a, 1923).
127 But also informative is its occurrence in the *Parmenides* (128Eff.) where, as I shall argue in additional note 2.5, we can see Plato using the sentence "the Forms exist themselves by themselves" (128E–129A, 130B7–9, 133A, 133C, 135A–B) to express the same metaphysical claim as that expressed by "the Forms exist separately" (130B3–5, 130C1–2, 130C5–D2).
128 σοφωτάτη Διοτίμα (208B), a fictional figure, whose name, "she who has honour from Zeus," suggests "the possession of highest wisdom and authority" (Bury, 1932: xxxix). The only other passage in the Platonic corpus in which Socrates is represented as incorporating into his own philosophy a higher truth derived from a religious source is in the *Meno* (81A–B = T1 above): it is from priests and priestesses σοφῶν περὶ τὰ θεῖα πράγματα that he had "heard" the doctrine of reincarnation.
129 "Suddenly he will come to see a wonderful sort of beauty" (210E).
130 For comment on the immediate antecedent of this passage see Vlastos, 1981: 67–9.

not satisfied that she has done enough to impress her point on her hearer, Diotima proceeds to say it again at [b]: the Form of beauty will not be seen as existing somewhere[131] *in* something else, such as a soul, incarnate ("on the earth") or discarnate ("in the sky" or beyond it).[132] But surely this was made clear already at [a]? Why harp on it again at [b]? Why such repetitive emphasis?[133]

We can best see why if we recall that to speak of an attribute as being "in" something is current usage for saying that it is instantiated there; this would be ordinary Greek for saying that the thing *has* the property associated with the Form. This is how Socrates$_E$ speaks and thinks: he says "temperance is in you" for "you are temperate,"[134] "piety is in those actions" for "those actions are pious."[135] S_E takes it for granted that if temperance or piety or beauty exist they exist *in* something in the world of time. So if S_E were asked, "Where, in what, does beauty exist?" he would point to beautiful bodies, minds, actions, institutions, thoughts in the world of common experience and say "There – it exists in them." This would be the only possible locus of its existence for him, as for all his interlocutors. And this is just what S_M would want to deny. He declares in T22 that when the Form of Beauty is confronted at the moment of its lover's deepest, most complete, discernment of its nature, it will be seen as *existing beyond all actual or possible*[136] *instantiations of it*. Even if there were superlatively beautiful bodies, minds, actions, institutions in our world, the Form of Beauty would not exist *in* them. The Form would not need any of them in order to exist. To be the very quality which it is suffices for its existence.[137]

What is implied in the sequence of negations in [a] and [b] is

131 που, literally "in some place." Cf. *Ti.* 52B: In the "dreaming" view of reality (that of the ordinary man [cf. ὀνειροπολοῦμεν here with ὀνειρώττειν at *R.* 476c] which denies the existence of Forms) "whatever exists is of necessity somewhere, in some place (που...ἔν τινι τόπῳ)...that which is neither on earth nor in the heavens, is nothing." (Cf. Aristotle, *Phys.* 208A29: "everyone supposes that [all] things which exist are somewhere.")

132 That even purely spiritual beings – discarnate souls and gods – are also "somewhere" ("the super-celestial place", *Phdr.* 247C) is an awkward but unavoidable feature of Plato's transmigration story.

133 As I noted earlier (n. 108 above) Plato is not averse to repetition to produce an intended effect.

134 *Ch.* 159A1–2: ἐνοῦσαν αὐτήν, εἴπερ ἔνεστιν. Or, equivalently, "is present in you," σοὶ πάρεστιν, 158E7 (cf. *Eud.* 301A4, πάρεστιν μέντοι ἑκάστῳ αὐτῶν κάλλος τι).

135 *Eu.* 5D (= T4): ταὐτόν ἐστιν ἐν πάσῃ πράξει τὸ ὅσιον αὐτὸ αὑτῷ. So too in the *Laches* (191E–192A): courage is the same *in* all those actions Socrates asks Laches to consider.

136 The negations in [a] and [b] are perfectly general, unrestricted to actual instances of beauty: they would hold for possible no less than actual ones.

137 If Greek had separate words for "existence" and "essence" (which it does not: cf. additional note 2.3 on οὐσία) Plato would want to say that the essence of Beauty entails its own existence – the only sort of existence which anything in this ontological category *could* have: to exist the Form of Beauty need only *be* what it eternally is.

asserted directly at [c]: beauty *exists itself by itself with itself*; "with itself" is added here to "by itself"[138] to reinforce the Form's capacity for isolated, self-sufficient, existence. Existing "with itself," it does not need to exist in conjunction with anything in the world of time.[139] And we can see why this thought should lead to the one in [d]: the independent existence of the Form must be sustained in the face of the fact that multitudes of other things "participate" in it. So it is at [d], where we are assured that the existence of those "participants" does not affect its own in the slightest. "Unique in form" (μονοειδές), exempt from their endlessly variable diversity, it is untouched by the vicissitudes of their births and deaths: when they "arise and pass away" it is neither enhanced nor diminished, "is not affected at all." If every beautiful object in this world were to perish in a cosmic holocaust;[140] if all souls in the world were to perish with it; even if – blasphemous thought – the Divine Creator himself were obliterated, the Form of Beauty would remain what it always was and will always be, "itself by itself with itself," world or no world.

If this is what the "by itself" existence of Forms means for Plato in the dialogues of his middle period and still in the *Timaeus*,[141] we have good reason to believe that it is meant to express what his greatest pupil and severest critic was to call the "separation" (χωρισμός) of the Platonic Form:[142] *its existential independence of any actual or possible instantiation* of it in the world of time.[143] Aristotle's exact phraseology is not anticipated in Plato's corpus:[144] Plato never writes that his Forms are "separate" (χωριστά).[145] He does not need

---

138 And only here in the Platonic corpus. Plato's application of the "by itself" phrase to the Form is flexible; he usually fills it out by adding the initial reflexive pronoun, "itself by itself," but he does so only for emphasis, for he can use that phrase also without such increment (so at *Cra.* 386E, *R.* 476A11). In our present passage in the *Smp.* he gives it maximal verbal weight by adding "with itself" to "of itself."

139 We should notice that the self-sufficiency of its own existence is asserted *only* with reference to its disjunction from temporal instantiations, *not* from other Forms. The "communion of the Forms with one another" (*R.* 476A) (i.e. the entailment-linkages of each Form with multitudes of other Forms) is integral to the nature of each.

140 A purely notional possibility: Plato's universe, made by "the best of makers," is made to last for ever (*Ti.* 37C–D).

141 Cf. additional note 2.6 below ("Forms in the *Timaeus*").

142 For the meaning of χωρισμός in Aristotle and Plato see additional note 2.7.

143 That (a) this is the right interpretation of what Aristotle means by ascribing "separate" Forms to Plato and that (b) in doing so he is completely faithful to Plato's intentions was powerfully argued against influential views to the contrary by Cherniss (1942: 31ff.). Fine, 1984: 131ff., confirms Cherniss on (a) but dissents on (b). In additional note 2.5 "'Separation' in Plato," section 2, below, I give reasons why we should agree with Cherniss on (b) no less than (a).

144 Though it may have been in oral discussion in the Academy, as I suggest in additional note 2.5, section 2, below.

145 But he comes so close to this in what he does write – that the Forms "exist separately (εἶναι χωρίς)" – with a dependent genitive (*Prm.* 130B4 and C1) or even without one

to: he can, and does, express the same substantive doctrine by
writing that they "exist separately" or, equivalently,[146] that they
"exist themselves by themselves." He plants the latter phrase in the
center of his great "hypothesis" in the *Phaedo* (T11) that beauty
exists itself by itself, feeling no need to offer a separate argument for
it, since the existence of his Forms independent of any other
constituent of reality – sensible bodies or incorporeal souls – is the
immediate consequence of their essence.[147] This is the heart of Plato's
metaphysics: the postulation of an eternal self-existent world,
transcending everything in ours, exempt from the vagaries and
vicissitudes which afflict all creatures in the world of time, containing
the Form of everything valuable or knowable, purged of all sensory
content.[148] We meet this theory in some guise or other wherever
Platonism lives in the philosophy or theology, the poetics, erotics, or
even the mathematical philosophy of the Western world. So to
continue interposing my exegetical mechanics between the "Socrates" who expounds this philosophy in Plato's middle dialogues and
Plato himself would be a vexing affectation. Hereafter I shall not say
"Socrates$_M$" in contexts where Plato is transparently what I
mean.[149]

We can now consider how Plato's non-sensible, eternal, incorporeal, transcendent Forms connect with that extraordinary
conception of the soul which breaks into his corpus in the *Meno* (T1
above). The transmigrating soul necessitates a two-world top-
ography for the diachronic tale of the soul's existence: "this"
world,[150] which is the soul's present habitat, and that other world,
whose location remains mysterious,[151] identifiable only by evocative

---

(130D1), that excellent translators (Cornford, 1939; Diès 1956; Allen, 1980b) regularly
disregard the difference. Thus τούτων ἑκάστου εἶδος εἶναι χωρίς, "a Form of each of these
exists separately," comes through Cornford's translation as "each of these has a separate
Form," in Allen's as "there is a separate character for each of them" as if Plato had
written χωριστὸν εἶδος εἶναι ἑκάστου.

146 As I shall argue in some detail in additional note 2.5.   147 Cf. n. 137 above.

148 Hence S$_M$ refers to it as εἰλικρινές, καθαρόν, using one or the other or both of these epithets
along with the "itself by itself" phrase: αὐτὸ καθ᾽ αὐτὸ εἰλικρινές, *Phd.* 66A (= T18 above)
or even without that phrase: *Phd.* 67B, πᾶν τὸ εἰλικρινές and *Smp.* 211E, αὐτὸ τὸ
καλὸν...εἰλικρινές, καθαρόν, ἄμεικτον. The realm of Form is "pure being" (ὄντος
εἰλικρινῶς, *R.* 478D, 479D); it is the "pure region" (τόπον...καθαρόν, at *Phd.* 80D [quoted
in n. 152 below]).

149 By the same token I shall not say "Socrates$_E$" when it is clear that Plato's recreation of
Socrates in the earlier dialogues is what I mean.

150 Literally, "this place" (τόνδε τὸν τόπον, *Tht.* 176B). The demonstrative is replaceable by
descriptive predications which identify its categorical status: the "corporeal and visible
region" (ἐν τῷ σωματοειδεῖ καὶ ὁρατῷ τόπῳ, *R.* 532C–D).

151 It is that "supercelestial region (τὸν ὑπερουράνιον τόπον) which no earthly poet has yet
hymned worthily or ever will" (*Phdr.* 247C).

epithets,[152] or by traditional locatives,[153] but indispensable for the transmigration tale, since it is the world in which the soul exists before each of its successive incarnations and to which it returns upon its liberation from each. The transcendent Forms are the bridge between our present, incarnate, existence, and our discarnate past and future. Having come to know these entities in our prenatal history, we can now "recollect" precious fragments of that lost knowledge.

For the philosopher this "recollection" is a strenuously intellectual exercise. As I shall be explaining in chapter 4, its prerequisite is prolonged training in mathematics and dialectic. But it has also a different dimension which the great myth of the *Phaedrus* signals through poetic imagery. In "recollection" the philosopher grows the "wings" by which at death his soul will "ascend" to the "other" world:

T23 *Phdr.* 249C: "This is the reason why only the philosopher's intellect rightly grows wings: for to the best of his ability he is ever near in recollection to those things to which a god's nearness makes him divine."[154]

In popular belief the gods owe their privileged exemption from the fatality of death to their supernatural diet of nectar and ambrosia.[155] Plato in his myth upgrades, aetherealizes, those all-too-human gods of Homer. For feasting and carousing on Olympus his imagery substitutes processions of Form-contemplation (*Phdr.* 247Bff.) and he suggests that mind-contact with the Forms is precisely what makes his intellectualized divinities divine. His myth opens up the same privilege to men: we too have shared the nutriment of immortality in our prenatal state and now, in this mortal life, we may renew in recollection its immortalizing sustenance.[156] Creatures

---

152 "The region in which dwells the most blessed part of what exists" (τόπον... ἐν ᾧ ἐστι τὸ εὐδαιμονέστατον τοῦ ὄντος, *R.* 526E). "The noble and pure and invisible region, Hades" (τόπον... γενναῖον καὶ καθαρὸν καὶ ἀϊδῆ, εἰς Ἅιδου, *Phd.* 80D). "Hades," shorn of its harsh breathing, is derived by fanciful etymology from τὸ ἀϊδές, "the invisible"; a different, equally fanciful, derivation from πάντα τὰ καλὰ εἰδέναι at *Cra.* 404B.

153 "We should try to flee hence *thither* (ἐνθένδε ἐκεῖσε, *Tht.* 176A–B = "from this world to the other," Cornford, 1935])"; and cf. the description of the Forms as "the things *there* ([τὰ] ἐκεῖ) beheld by souls," *Phdr.* 250A.

154 πρὸς γὰρ ἐκείνοις ἀεί ἐστιν μνήμῃ κατὰ δύναμιν, πρὸς οἷσπερ θεὸς ὢν θεῖός ἐστιν: Burnet's text; I am following the translation in Hackforth, 1952. Same sense in Robin, 1950: "c'est à ces realités mêmes que ce qui est Dieu doit sa divinité."

155 Aristotle takes the belief seriously enough to argue against it: "How could they [the gods] be immortal, if they need food?" (*Metaph.* 1000a17).

156 The soul's "nutrition" through its contact with Form is highlighted in the description of its contemplation by the gods and by discarnate human souls (247D–E: "and contemplating truth she is nourished and prospers [θεωροῦσα τἀληθῆ τρέφεται καὶ εὐπαθεῖ]; "and when she has truly contemplated and feasted upon true being" [τὰ ὄντα

of time though we be, in contemplation of Form we may unite ourselves in knowledge and in love[157] with the eternal.

"Mysticism," according to the *O.E.D.*, is "the belief in the possibility of union with the Divine nature by means of ecstatic contemplation." As a definition this is much too narrow. For one thing, it overlooks non-theistic mysticism, as in Zen. For another, it ignores even theistic mystics who seek "union with the Divine nature" by means other than contemplation. But in its very narrowness it is a tribute to that aspect of Platonism which is genuinely mystical and has inspired mystical philosophies and theologies in the Western world.[158] "Ecstatic contemplation" fits perfectly the experience which Plato describes through verbs for seeing, viewing, gazing (ὁρᾶν, καθορᾶν, ἰδεῖν, κατιδεῖν, θεᾶν) and touching (ἅπτομαι, ἐφάπτομαι) for the terminal apprehension of Form. He thus alludes to the sort of intellectual experience in which prolonged exploration and searching, "suddenly"[159] culminates in insight that has the lucidity of vision and the immediacy of touch. Plato never says point-blank that in this experience "union with the Divine[160] nature" of Form is achieved. He rests content with imagery of union, both the nutritive one we have already seen and a parallel sexual one:

T24 *R.* 490A–B: "The true lover of knowledge, whose nature it is to strive towards reality, will not tarry among the objects of opinion which the many believe to be real, but press on with a love that will not faint or fail, until he has come in touch with the essential nature of each thing with that part of his soul which is fit to touch reality because of kinship with it; and having thus come close to true being and mixed with it,[161] he may give birth to intelligence and truth, may know and truly live and be nourished and thus find release from labour-pains – then, and not before."[162]

In the *Symposium* too (212A) the philosopher "gazing upon and

ὄντως θεασαμένη καὶ ἑστιαθεῖσα]), and is also prominent in the soul's contact with Form in the present life: τρέφοιτο at *R.* 490B (= T24 below); τρεφομένη at *Phd.* 84A (quoted in n.160 below).

157 Love is as salient a feature of the philosopher's relation to the Form as is knowledge: *R.* 490A–B (= T24) and 500C (the philosopher "lovingly associates," ὁμιλεῖ ἀγάμενος, with Form); *Smp.* 211D–212A (too long to quote).

158 Plotinus, the creator of the purest mystical philosophy of the Western world, is steeped in Plato; the label, "Neoplatonism," for the whole philosophical movement he spearheaded, is no misnomer.   159 *Smp.* 210E4–5, quoted in n. 129 above.

160 For the divinity of Form see e.g. *Smp.* 211E and *Phd.* 80B, 84A–B, and also *R.* 611E. And cf. the description of the "separate" Form in Xenocrates (fr. 30: cf. additional note 2.5, n. 95).

161 πλησιάσας καὶ μιγεὶς τῷ ὄντι ὄντως. For μείγνυμι as a common term for sexual intercourse see LSJ *s.v.* sense 4 (in the passive form: "in Homer and Hesiod most frequently of the sexes, *have intercourse with*").   162 The translation is modelled on Cornford's (1945).

consorting with" (θεωμένου καὶ συνόντος) the Form of beauty "will give birth (τεκόντι) to true virtue."

To evoke this experience Plato intimates that in vision of Form the philosopher achieves what the devotees of mystic cults seek to attain in their rites. At times he pictures it as a Dionysian mystery of divine possession – ἐνθουσιάζειν,[163] the state in which man becomes ἔνθεος ("god is in him").[164] Alternatively he depicts the prenatal contemplation of Form as though it were the celebration of an Eleusinian vision-mystery:

T25 *Phdr.* 250B–C: "Radiant beauty was there to see when with the happy choir we saw that blessed sight and vision and celebrated that rite which, with all due reverence, we may call the most blessed of all. Perfect were we the celebrants, untouched by any of those woes that befell us later. Perfect, simple, tremorless, blessed were those apparitions of the rite and celebration. In that pure light we too were pure, not yet entombed in this thing we now call 'body,' carrying it round, imprisoned in it as in an oyster-shell."[165]

As this quotation shows, Plato's Form-mysticism is profoundly other-worldly. The ontology of non-sensible, eternal, incorporeal, self-existent, contemplable Forms, and of their anthropological correlate, the invisible, immortal, incorporeal, transmigrating soul, has far-reaching implications for the mind and for the heart. In the heart it evokes the sense of alienation from "this" world where the body lives, a nostalgia for a lost paradise in that "other" world from which the soul has come and to which it longs to return. In the mind it arouses a hunger for the kind of knowledge which cannot be satisfied by investigating the physical world. All we can find here are images, copies, shadows of that real world which we shall fully know only when liberated from the "oyster-shell."[166]

One could hardly imagine a world-outlook more foreign to that of Socrates. He is unworldly: he cares little for money, reputation, security, life itself, in fact for anything except virtue and moral knowledge. But he is not otherworldly: the eternal world with which

---

163 *Phdr.* 241D2, E1; 253A.
164 Cf. Burkert, 1985: 109, explaining ἔνθεος as "within is a god": ch. 6, n. 55. And cf. *Phd.* 69D: "As those concerned with mystic rites tell us, 'Many are the wandbearers, few are the βάκχοι [those who have attained union with the god Bacchus].' Those βάκχοι in my opinion are none others than those who have philosophized rightly."
165 The oyster-shell image is a carry-over from the *Republic* (611D–612A): to see the soul as she really is we must "disencumber her of all that wild profusion of rock and shell (ὄστρεα), whose earthly substance has encrusted her" (translation after Cornford, 1945).
166 "It has been really shown us that if we are ever to achieve pure knowledge of anything we must get rid of the body... As the argument indicates, we shall have this after death, not while we live" (*Phd.* 66D).

Plato seeks mystical union is unknown to him. For Socrates reality –
real knowledge, real virtue, real happiness – is in the world in which
he lives. The hereafter is for him a bonus and anyhow only a matter
of faith and hope.[167] The passionate certainties of his life are in the
here and now.

167 As is made so clear in the closing paragraphs of the *Apology*. In the *Gorgias*, though the
eschatological myth is told to Callicles as a "true discourse" (523A), it is clearly bracketed
off from the foregoing elenctic discussion with him where truth was established by
rational argument.

3

THE EVIDENCE OF ARISTOTLE AND XENOPHON

At the start of the preceding chapter I staked out the claim that through a "Socrates" in Plato we can come to know the thought of the Socrates of history. By the end of the present chapter the reader should be in a fair position to judge if I am making that claim stick.

Let this much be agreed before I start: much as I need Plato's witness, I could not do the job if I had only his. The most we could learn from his writings is that in different periods of his life he puts into the mouth of Socrates philosophies which are not only different but, in important respects, antithetical. And that of itself would not give a particle of support to my claim. For there is no intrinsic reason why both of these philosophies, despite their polar differences, could not have been Plato's own original creations at different periods of his life. Within the present century we have seen a spectacular illustration of such a shift. In his *Tractatus* Wittgenstein produced a startlingly original philosophy and published it with the confidence that it would be his last word – indeed *the* last word – on the subject, announcing in the Preface: "The truth of the thoughts communicated in this work seems to me uncontestable and definitive. I am, therefore, of the opinion that the problems have in essentials been finally solved." But within less than ten years of the publication of that book we see him working anew on those same problems, moving now with a different method to reach results as opposed to those of the *Tractatus* as to the views of Russell or Moore or those of any other philosopher past or present. The same thing could have happened to Plato. If we are to believe otherwise it must be on the strength of evidence outside his own works. If we had no such evidence my claim would be hollow. But it so happens that we do. I shall set it forth in section II of the present chapter.

I   SOCRATES_E VS. SOCRATES_M: TWO MORE CONTRASTS

But first I must sharpen up further the difference between those two philosophies in Plato. Near the start of chapter 2 I listed Ten Theses outlining in laconic and dogmatic fashion ten contrasting traits in the two personae I have been calling "Socrates$_E$" and "Socrates$_M$." These are just the ten salient ones. If I had been trying for completeness I would have listed many more. Contenting myself with those ten, I passed quickly over Thesis I: this was meant to be programmatic, a highly general claim to be fleshed out as my argument proceeds. So I moved at once from Thesis I to Thesis II. This difference is so telling that a strong case for my main claim could have been made just from this even if it had stood alone: when we consult Aristotle's and Xenophon's testimony what we learn from it on just this Thesis would allow us to infer securely that the philosopher who believed in Socrates$_M$'s separable transmigrating soul and "separate" Forms could not have been S$_E$, the moral teacher in Xenophon's and Plato's Socratic writings who has no truck with metaphysical speculation. But if we are to bring those two witnesses into court let us give them more work to do. Let us confront them with two more of those Ten Theses: first, with Thesis IIIA, the disavowal of knowledge, characteristic of Socrates$_E$, foreign to Socrates$_M$, and then with Thesis IVB, the tripartite model of the psyche, prize achievement of Socrates$_M$, unknown to Socrates$_E$. So let me say a little about each of these two theses.

Thesis III: Socrates' un-Platonic disavowal of knowledge

Here is its clearest statement in Plato:

T1[1] *Ap.* 21B and D: "[a] For I am not aware of being wise in anything, great or small (οὔτε μέγα οὔτε σμικρὸν σύνοιδα ἐμαυτῷ σοφὸς εἶναι).[2] ... [b] It looks as though, while neither of us knows anything worthwhile,[3] he thinks he does; but as for me, while, as in point of fact, I have no knowledge, neither do I think I have any."[4]

---

1 Quoted as T1 in additional note 1.1 below.
2 As I point out below (additional note 1.1, n. 7), being σοφός in a given domain (or having σοφία in it), are used by Plato interchangeably with possessing the relevant ἐπιστήμη.
3 Literally, "beautiful and good" (καλὸν κἀγαθόν). I have followed above Grube's (1985) translation of the phrase.
4 Many readers (including myself [Vlastos, 1985: 29]) have misread this text, taking Socrates to be saying that he *knows he has no knowledge*. A closer reading will show that he says no such thing at either [a] or [b]: all he says at [a] is that he is not aware of having any knowledge, and at [b] that he has none. The difference is substantial: saying that one is not aware of having knowledge and that one, in fact, has none is not the same as (nor does it entail)

In Chapter 1 above and more fully in additional note 1.1, I have argued that this disavowal is a "complex irony" – a statement meant to be true in one sense, false in another. Here I may call attention to three closely related points.

The first is that Plato treats the disavowal as one of Socrates' most notorious traits, well known even to people who stand as far from the Socratic circle as does Thrasymachus. Plato represents the sophist as thinking of the disclaimer of knowledge as an egregious piece of sly hypocrisy which is Socrates' habitual, highly predictable, stance. This is how Thrasymachus responds to Socrates' mock-pathetic appeal for help in the search for the definition of "justice" which is eluding him and his friends

T2[5] *R.* 337A: "Heracles!" he said. "This is Socrates' habitual shamming. I had predicted to these people that you would refuse to answer and would sham[6] and would do anything but answer if the question were put to you."

Second: Plato never puts Socrates in the position of explaining what he means by that disavowal, which his friends simply ignore: hearing him say he has no knowledge to contribute to their inquiries, they continue to treat him as the wisest man they know,[7] never pressing him to say just what it is he claims to lack when he says he has no knowledge. This is what is to be expected if Thesis IA is true: Plato protects that earlier Socrates from having to address the question, "What is knowledge?" whose pursuit would have been diversionary from his all-engrossing eagerness for answers to moral questions, beginning with the most urgent one of all: How should we live?

knowing that one has no knowledge: only the latter threatens to embroil one in the logical paradox of the liar who says he is lying. (For a recent example of the latter reading see Kraut, 1984: 272, n. 44: "By putting his initial reaction to the oracle in the form of *a self-contradiction* [my emphasis] Socrates is telling his audience they should have realized from the start that he was wrong to disavow all claims to knowledge"; Kraut is evidently taking Socrates to be saying at [a] that he knows he has no knowledge, thereby incurring self-contradiction.) The misreading has ancient precedent. It is already in Cicero (*nihil se scire dicat nisi id ipsum*, *Acad.* 1.16) and doubtless goes much further back). But it is not in Aristotle: "he confessed (ὡμολόγει) that he had no knowledge" (*Soph. El.* 183b7, quoted in T13 below) does not go so far as saying that he knew he had no knowledge. (I am pleased to discover that my present reading of *Ap.* 21B has been reached independently by A. A. Long [1988: 158] and by Michael Stokes in his still unpublished paper, "Socratic Ignorance in Plato's *Apology.*"

5 Cited as T1 in chapter 1 above.

6 This translation of εἰρωνεία, εἰρωνεύσοιο was argued for in chapter 1 above, in comment on the same text, cited there as T1.

7 So e.g. in the *Laches*: everyone has heard Socrates say, "I have no knowledge concerning this matter" (186E) and so has Laches, who nonetheless declares, "To you I offer myself for you to teach and examine on whatever point you want" (189B, quoted in T9, in additional note 1.1); and at the conclusion Nicias too expresses unqualified confidence in Socrates as a teacher: he is the one to whom he would turn if he had sons in need of moral education (200C, quoted as T10 in the same additional note).

Third, and this is the most paradoxical aspect of the disavowal, its unique, absolutely unparalleled, feature: it may be voiced at the conclusion of an entirely successful elenctic argument in which Socrates has to all appearance, proved his thesis to the hilt.

T3 *G.* 508E–509A: "These things, having been shown in our earlier arguments to be as I state them, are clamped down and bound, if I may put it so bluntly, by arguments of adamant and iron, or so one would think... But as for me, my position is always the same (ἐπεὶ ἔμοιγε ὁ αὐτὸς λόγος[8] ἐστιν ἀεί): I do not know how these matters stand."[9]

Where, in all the annals of Western thought shall we find a philosopher saying in all seriousness that he has produced ultra-strong proof for his thesis – has tied it down by "arguments of adamant and iron" – *and* does not know if that thesis is true? Certainly not in any of Plato's dialogues after the *Meno*. In this respect Plato is like other philosophers, albeit less dogmatic than most, more acutely aware of vistas of undiscovered truth beyond any point to which his own inquiries have advanced. Thus at the conclusion of the long argument in the *Republic* (II–IV) which purports to have proved that justice is always the more advantageous of our options, Glaucon declares that now further inquiry has become ridiculous. Socrates agrees, though with a reservation:

T4 *R.* 445B: "Ridiculous indeed, I said. But having reached this point we must not weary of trying to see as clearly as possible that those things are so."

So the inquiry goes on and on for six more books. But to what purpose? Not to determine *if* "those things are so," but to see more clearly *that* they are.[10] But this prospect never prompts Socrates to say in this or any other work of Plato's middle period that he does not know at any given moment what he claims to have "proved" (*G.* 479E8) down to that moment.

8 λόγος here refers not to the theses he has defended against Callicles (to them he refers by ταῦτα at A5, as also previously at 508E6 and subsequently at 509B1) but to his disavowal of knowledge (cf. οὐδὲ εἰδὼς λέγω 506A3–4 with λόγος...ὅτι...οὐκ οἶδα at 509A4–5). Nor is λόγος being used to mean "argument" (so Irwin, 1979: *ad loc.*): Socrates disavows knowledge, as he did previously at 506A, but does not argue in justification of the disavowal in either passage. The sense is correctly rendered in Monique Canto (1987): "je dis et je redis toujours la même chose: que je ne sais pas."

9 ἐγὼ ταῦτα οὐκ οἶδα ὅπως ἔχει: he does not know whether or not his theses (whose truth he has established by "arguments of adamant and iron"!) are true.

10 Similarly at the conclusion of the arguments for immortality in the *Phaedo* (117B) Socrates encourages Cebes and Simmias to continue their inquiries, but with no indication that they are to do so for any other purpose than that of determining more clearly the grounds for that doctrine. In the *Republic* (611C) he declares: "That the soul is immortal is established beyond doubt [Cornford, 1945 for ἀναγκάσειεν ἄν] by the above argument and those others [presumably, the ones in the *Phaedo*, to which there is no direct reference in the *R.*]."

Nothing of that sort ever happens to Socrates$_M$ – not even in the *Theaetetus*, where Plato (for special reasons peculiar to this dialogue)[11] chooses a protagonist who professes at the dialogue's start to "make no assertions about anything because he has no wisdom" (150C).[12] This figure who has so much in common with Socrates$_E$[13] is nonetheless kept free of the crucial feature of the latter's disavowal of knowledge at T3 above, namely, reassertion of it *at the very moment at which he has produced evidence which appears to belie it*. Thus at 187A, where Socrates recognizes that appreciable progress has been made,[14] he does not *then* declare that he still does not know what, to all appearance, he has now come to know.[15]

At the conclusion of the whole dialogue he admits, indeed emphasizes, that he has not found the answer to the "What is the F?" question about knowledge. But in saying he does not know what knowledge is he is not reiterating the profession of ignorance in the global terms of its original assertion. What he says now is: "I have none of that knowledge possessed by all the great and wonderful men

11 Cf. Burnyeat, 1977.: 10–11: the midwife persona Plato creates for Socrates here is peculiarly useful for its creator in a dialogue which is "critical in intent and deliberately restrained in its positive commitments." This is how I understand the matter: in the *Parmenides* Socrates$_M$'s two-world metaphysical theory comes in for a furious battering (cf. additional note 2.5, n. 87) – old Parmenides hits it again and again with objections to which its young spokesman has not a word to say in reply (Socrates has been turned for the nonce into a juvenile inexperienced dialectician). Declining to meet head-on these formidable difficulties, Plato proceeds in the *Theaetetus* – which makes at 183E a pointed allusion to that (fictional) meeting between the aged Parmenides and the youthful Socrates – to assay a new beginning, starting with a clean slate.

12 οὐδὲν ἀποφαίνομαι περὶ οὐδενὸς διὰ τὸ μηδὲν ἔχειν σοφόν: for the sense of ἀποφαίνειν here, not "bring to light" as in Cornford 1935, but "make pronouncements" as in McDowell 1973, cf. χρὴ οὕτως ἀποφαινόμενον λέγειν, *Tht.* 151D.

13 Though unmistakably different from him in two ways: (1) the Socratic elenchus is no longer his method of philosophical investigation (see additional note 3.1 "Socratic elenchus in the *Theaetetus*?"); (2) he is now, heart and soul, what Socrates$_E$ had never been at all – an epistemologist, pursuing relentlessly the question "What is knowledge?" which Socrates$_E$ had never pursued, not even in the *Charmides* where it had been thrust upon him: cf. ch. 2, n. 12. For a parallel and no less fundamental difference of the Socrates of the *Tht.* from S_E see the antepenultimate paragraph of ch. 5, and n. 92.

14 "We have progressed so far" (τοσοῦτον γε προβεβήκαμεν); cf. also Socrates' remark to Theaetetus at 187B2: "see if you can get a better view now that you have progressed to this point (ἐπειδὴ ἐνταῦθα προελήλυθας)."

15 He has now reached the important insight that when we perceive the difference between two sounds we hear the sounds, but "two" and "difference" we do not hear or see or otherwise perceive through the senses. He takes this to entail that the "common" terms in perception are discerned not by the senses but by "the mind itself reaching out [to those terms] by itself" (186A). Comparing this with the doctrine of the *Phaedo* that the mind apprehends Forms "itself by itself" (65C7, 66A1–2, 67A1, 67C7, 83B1), by means of "pure" reasoning, uncontaminated by sensory content, "reaching out to reality, so far as possible without any contact with the body" (65C8–9), we can see that Plato has found in the *Tht.* a new route to some part of his previously held metaphysical doctrine – a route which proceeds *independently of that doctrine* by direct analysis of phenomenological data.

of the past" (210C). What he has come to know is minuscule by comparison with the spectacular attainments claimed by Heraclitus, Parmenides, and by Plato himself in preceding dialogues of his middle period. But it is more than he knew at the start of the inquiry and he says nothing here or hereafter which appears to cast doubt on what he has come to know in the course of it – nothing to assert, or imply, that he still does not know what he has learned in the course of the inquiry. The paradox in T3 is not reinstated. The difference between Socrates$_E$ and Socrates$_M$ remains intact.

Thesis IV: the unSocratic tripartite psyche in Plato

In Book IV of the *Republic*, at the height of his middle period, Plato projects a new analysis of the internal structure of the psyche which transforms his conception of the motivational dynamics of virtuous conduct and of the nature of virtue itself. Over against the rational part of the soul he sets two distinct non-rational components, as different from one another as from reason itself. One of them is passionate,[16] typically anger,[17] but also fear and no doubt other emotions as well.[18] The other is the "appetitive" (ἐπιθυμητικόν): hunger, thirst, sexual desire and other bodily cravings. The desire for the good remains what it had been for Socrates in the earlier dialogues: a powerful, ever-present drive,[19] associated with reason.[20] But whereas Socrates had thought reason all-powerful[21] this new tripartite model endows each of the three parts with independent dynamism: each is in principle autonomously motivating and may, therefore, successfully resist each of the other two. Thus each of the appetites is described as an urge for its own peculiar, highly determinate, objective:

T5 *R*. 437D–438A: "Now is thirst, so far as it is thirst, desire in the soul for anything other than simply drink?... We must be careful here lest we be caught off guard, disturbed by the objection that no one desires food, rather than good food, or drink, rather than good drink."[22]

---

16 Or "spirited" (as when we speak of "a spirited horse" or of "high spirits").
17 θυμός – hence θυμοειδές, Plato's term for this part of the soul.
18 Fear is added explicitly in the *Timaeus* (42A, 69D).
19 *R*. 505D–E: the good "is what every soul pursues and for its sake does everything it does."
20 τὸ λογιστικόν: the faculty which reasons out the implications of what we know or believe or wish to be the case.
21 *Pr*. 352C: "never overpowered by anything"; cf. the next note.
22 The point of saying that thirst *qua* thirst is desire for just drink, not for *good* drink, is understood and its contra-Socratic import is discerned (apparently for the first time in English-speaking scholarship) in Murphy, 1951: 28–9 (for the previous view see e.g. Adam, 1902, on 437E). And see now further Annas, 1981: 128–31.

To see what Plato is driving at let us remind ourselves that under extreme conditions thirst may be so intense as to make shambles of the constraints which our judgment habitually sets on acceptable drink, and we may then find ourselves impelled to drink anything at all that is drinkable rather than go without – mouthwash, aftershave lotion, even urine, as did the derelicts in the Arizona desert in the summer of 1978. Plato does not resort to such lurid examples. He is making a point he expects to carry conviction by itself once he has drawn attention to it. This is that thirst, like every other physical appetite, defines a generic object which in special circumstances may be desired with overpowering intensity in spite of flouting long-standing, rationally established, standards of desirability. Why should Plato insist on this so much? Because he wants to call attention to the fact that we may crave at times forms of gratification unacceptable to our reason.[23] He wants to say that this possibility cannot be excluded *a priori*, as it had been by Socrates, for whom desire for X had been necessarily desire for good X. On that psychological model we could desire a bad drink only if we failed to perceive that it is bad: discernment of its evil, Socrates$_E$ had thought, would free us[24] from the desire "to go" for it;[25] so if the desire retains its strength our rational judgment must be at fault.[26] In Plato's tripartite model there is no "must" about this: no inherent reason why desire cannot fixate on an object and keep clamoring for it in defiance of a judgmental veto.[27]

23 To his belief that the third part of the soul had autonomous motivational dynamism Plato was to give forceful expression many years later in his account of the physiology of sex: the male organ he describes as a "living creature" (ζῷον) in our body which is "heedless and self-willed (ἀπειθές τε καὶ αὐτοκρατές)," a creature that moves of its own accord, disobedient to reason, "bent on carrying all before it"; the female one is described in counterpart terms as having a life of its own, with a desire for intercourse which is entirely independent of reason (*Ti.* 91B4–D4).

24 Would "make inoperative the image" which holds us in thrall (ἄκυρον ἐποίησε τὸ φάντασμα, *Pr.* 356D) – would expose it as a misperception which loses its power to move us once we discern its delusiveness.

25 "It is not in human nature" to "want to go" (ἐθέλειν ἰέναι) for X instead of Y in circumstances in which we know that Y is our best option: *Pr.* 358C–D.

26 Socrates$_E$ knows well enough that at times a desire may flare up momentarily contrary to one's judgment of what is best: he would hardly be human if he did not. What he will not concede is that such a desire may *persist* in the face of reason's veto. Thus in the *Charmides*, catching a glimpse "of the inwards of the garment" of the seductively beautiful boy, Socrates is "inflamed and is beside himself," losing his customary self-possession, "barely able" to converse coherently with the boy (155D–E). But a moment later he has recovered his balance: no sign of the least abatement of Socrates' usual composure throughout the rest of the dialogue. They part with cool, ironically flirtatious, banter.

27 In the middle dialogues Plato recalls no less than three times (*Phd.* 94D–E; *R.* 390D, and 441B) that passage in the *Odyssey* (20.5ff.) depicting a desire whose indulgence is vetoed by reason but remains nonetheless disturbingly insistent (the impulse to dispatch on the spot

These contrary psychological assumptions dictate contrary strategies for the moral reformation of humanity. If Socrates' assumptions are correct, what is necessary *and sufficient* for moral reformation is intellectual enlightenment. The reformer's job is then to make us see that to indulge bad appetites or passion would be damaging to our own happiness. If he can bring us to understand our good we shall be bound to pursue it: our own desire for the good will drive us to it; incontinence (ἀκρασία) – doing the worse while knowing the better – will then be a psychic impossibility. Not so if the reformer were proceeding on Plato's tripartite analysis. Enlightened judgment would then be regarded as insufficient to produce right action unless the psyche has been brought into a condition in which judgment can have reliably practical efficacy. This condition Plato diagnoses as a harmonious integration of the psyche in which the passions play a critical role as reason's ally, giving its judgments the emotional backing required to control obstreperous appetite.

So Plato now puts high on his agenda a project which did not figure in Socrates' program at all: the hygienic conditioning of the passions. Since these are non-rational their moulding cannot be intellectual: argument cannot touch them. The only way to reach them is through the imagination. They are moved by images and can be shaped if exposed persistently to the right images in the right way at the right time – in our earliest years, when we are impervious to abstractions, while ultrasensitive to concrete, sensuously vivid stimuli. So Plato would coopt the image-makers: poets, story-tellers, songsters, and all other craftsmen who have power to put beauty into the man-made parts of our world. He wants them to play the major role in what he calls by synecdoche "musical" education, winning the hearts of children and adolescents through the power of fine art, saturating their environment with images in which virtue looks and feels enchantingly beautiful, vice repulsively ugly.[28]

Many things which are unclear or problematic about this process of "musical" education I leave aside. All that concerns me here is the overwhelming importance Plato attaches to it and his reason for doing so. When he discusses the courage of the military in his ideal state he observes that if they had missed that sort of education then, even if they had come by all the right beliefs, the result would not be true courage, but a cheap imitation of the real thing which should not even be called "courage":

the shameless wenches retains its force, keeping Odysseus awake, "tossing this way and that," long after he has realized that its immediate fulfillment would be unwise).

28 *R.* iii, especially at 401A–402A. Cf. Vlastos, 1981: 237–8.

т6 *R.* 430в6–9: "It is my opinion that correct belief about those very things [*sc.* about what is and is not truly fearful] induced without musical education would be brutish and slavish; you would not describe it as in accordance with our institutions[29] and would call it anything but 'courage.'"

In saying that this *ersatz* courage would be "brutish and slavish" he must mean that it would be activated by that purely external stick-and-carrot motivation through which we manipulate brutes and slaves and therefore cannot constitute genuine virtue, whose psychological controls must be internal. A truly brave man, Plato holds, will do the brave thing for its own sake – because he sees and feels that brave is beautiful and his perception of its beauty is what moves him to act bravely.[30] Hence if persons are to be genuinely brave they must be educated to resonate to the beauty of courage.[31] Such resonance, he believes, we must foster in our youth in their subteens and teens. If we miss that opportunity what we can do thereafter may be too little too late.

With this new[32] conception of moral education goes a new analysis of the concept of moral virtue. As an excellence of the tripartite soul courage turns out to be a different accomplishment from what it had been in Socrates' intellectualist psychology, where it had been defined as a kind of "wisdom":

т7 *Pr.* 360D: "Courage is wisdom concerning what is and is not fearful."

29 So Cornford, 1945 for οὔτε πάνυ νόμιμον ἡγεῖσθαι.
30 It is important to notice that when virtue is thus internally motivated it does not require *knowledge* of the good; true belief is sufficient if "musical" education has put on it the right emotional charge in one's formative years. Failure to grasp this fundamental point may produce the impression that in Plato's view genuine virtue is possible only for philosophers (so Cooper, 1977: 151ff. at 153, n. 7: Plato "very clearly requires wisdom and knowledge of anyone who is just"; and Cross and Woozley, 1964: 126: "true justice is the monopoly of philosophers" – so it would be, if only philosophers were capable of self-motivated virtue). And see the next two notes.
31 Cf. the gloss on т5 in Irwin, 1977a: 202: "A slavish man chooses virtue only because it produces the honours and pleasures he already seeks; but a musically educated man has learned to find virtue a source of pleasure and honour in itself; he enjoys and esteems virtuous action for itself... And Plato suggests that musical education produces the love of what is fair and admirable (*kalon*, 403c4–7) ... which would free [the musically educated non-philosopher] from slavish virtue." But then, curiously enough, Irwin proceeds (202–3) to contrast the "musically educated man" with the "virtuous man" on the ground that the former "does not choose virtue for its own sake, but only for its consequences" – a very odd thing to say in the face of his previous remark (quoted above) about the "musically educated man" that "he enjoys and esteems virtuous action *for itself*" (my emphasis).
32 New against not only the intellectualist view of moral conduct in the earlier dialogues but also against the imperfect understanding of the topic Plato had achieved at the beginning of his middle period. Cf. Vlastos, 1981: 137, n. 79, contrasting the restriction of genuine virtue to philosophers in the *Phaedo* (68c–69c).

If so, it is a cognitive achievement, an excellence of the intellectual soul. Compare Plato's definition:

т8 *R.* 442в–с: "And I believe we call a man 'brave' because of this [*sc.* the passionate] part of the soul, when it preserves through pains and pleasures the injunctions of reason concerning what is and is not fearful."

Here courage is an emotional achievement, an excellence of the passionate soul.[33] The contribution of the intellect – to provide "injunctions of reason concerning what is and is not fearful" – is, of course, essential.[34] But whether or not those injunctions of reason will have practical effect when we are put to the test is for Plato something for which only the spirited part of the soul can account. They will if, and only if, this part of our soul has power to hang on to those injunctions in moments of stress and keep them from scattering or blurring or, in Plato's own elaborate simile, from fading or washing out[35] when pain threatens or pleasure beckons at close range. And this, Plato thinks, will depend on whether or not the right "musical" education has given our rational judgments effective staying-power, fixed them in our soul by a kind of indelible chemistry, like colours made so fast in a cloth that they are proof against the harshest detergents.[36]

Here then, in what has now been added to what was presented in the preceding chapter, we have a fair (though still far from complete) view of far-reaching differences between the philosophy Plato puts into Socrates' mouth in the earlier dialogues and the one for which Socrates is made to speak in the middle ones. Armed just with these, we can now call first on Aristotle and then on Xenophon to learn from each what support if any, they would give to the claim

33 Note the clear implication of the quoted statement that the part of the soul to which we must look when determining if a man is brave is its passionate part (τὸ θυμοειδές). Our question has to be: Does *it* have "the power to preserve" under stress the correct judgments concerning what is and is not fearful? If so, the man is brave; if not, he is not.

34 Though not necessarily in the form of knowledge: cf. n. 30 above.

35 You know that those who want wool to take a purple dye, first choose wool which is naturally white, next treat it with great care to make it take the dye in its full brilliance, and only then dip it in the vat. Dyed in this way, wool gets a fast colour (δευσοποιὸν γίγνεται), which no amount of washing, with or without detergents, will rob of its brilliance" (429D–E; tr. mainly after Cornford, 1945). Plato pursues this simile for some 18 more lines to reinforce his point that "musical" education is what will make the right belief fast (δευσοποιός) in the soul of the soldiers so that it cannot be "washed out" by detergents as terrible as are "pleasure and pain, desire and fear" (430A–B).

36 Earlier he had used another, no less powerful, simile to get across the point which Socrates had completely neglected: that even with the finest rational beliefs about "what ought, and ought not, to be feared" one may still fail to carry out their prescriptions because one may lose those beliefs "by bewitchment [pleasure] or duresse [pain]" (413B–C). So something other than rational instruction is required to guard against these dread contingencies.

that the thought of the first of those two philosophies is true to that of the historical Socrates, while in the second Plato strikes out along new, unSocratic, lines of his own.

II ARISTOTLE'S TESTIMONY

T9 *Metaph.* 1078b9–17: [a] Now concerning the Ideas[37] (περὶ δὲ τῶν ἰδεῶν), we must first examine the theory of Ideas itself (τὴν κατὰ τὴν ἰδέαν δόξαν), taking it in the way in which it was originally conceived by those who were the first to assert the existence of Ideas (ὡς ὑπέλαβον ἐξ ἀρχῆς οἱ πρῶτοι τὰς ἰδέας φήσαντες εἶναι).[38]

[b] The theory concerning the Ideas (ἡ περὶ τῶν ἰδεῶν δόξα) occurred to those who asserted it because they became convinced of the truth of the Heraclitean doctrine that all sensible things are always in flux, so that if there is to be knowledge of anything, there must exist certain enduring natures beside the sensible ones, distinct from these; for of things in flux there can be no knowledge.

[c] Socrates, however,[39] was occupying himself with the moral virtues, having been the first to search for universal definitions of them ...

That Socrates has no part in the metaphysical theory of Ideas strikes Aristotle as so obvious that he feels no need to argue for it. He does not state it as a contestable thesis calling for defense. He is content to do no more than imply it at [c], where he comes to state what Socrates, in emphatic contradistinction from Plato, was searching for, namely definitions of the moral virtues – a far cry from Plato's central concern at [b] with the Heraclitean doctrine of the flux which led *him* to postulate Ideas. It was Plato, we are told at [b], who had made the inference from the perpetual flux of sensibles to the impossibility of knowledge concerning them, and had *therefore* postulated the existence of Ideas as invariant non-sensible entities to serve as the objects of knowledge.[40] That in this inference Socrates

37 Here and hereafter in this chapter I transliterate, instead of translating, ἰδέα, and I capitalize the English counterparts of ἰδέα, εἶδος in Aristotle's (interchangeable) use of these words as the key terms in his references to Plato's metaphysical "theory of Ideas."

38 Despite the generalizing plurals here and again in [b] and also in the quotations in n. 40 below, it is to Plato personally that Aristotle is ascribing the authorship of the theory of Ideas. This is completely clear in the doublet of T9 in the first book of the *Metaphysics* (987b29ff.) which begins: "After the aforesaid philosophies came *Plato's* investigation (μετὰ δὲ τὰς εἰρημένας φιλοσοφίας ἡ Πλάτωνος ἐπεγένετο πραγματεία)" and proceeds to expound the substance of this "investigation" in the same terms as in T9 above.

39 δέ, strongly adversative.

40 Though the Ideas have not yet been specified at [B] as "separate" entities (cf. Fine, 1984: 47ff.), they will be thus specified only a few lines later, fulsomely and reiteratively so, first at 1078b31 (quoted in T11), Socrates "did not regard the universals...as separate

had no hand Aristotle indicates by saying nothing about Socrates at [a] or [b], bringing him in only at [c] as the moralist, searching for definitions of moral attributes.

Additional testimony to Plato's exclusive authorship of the theory of Ideas comes in the phrases Aristotle uses in the *Nicomachean Ethics* to express his reluctance to voice criticism of the theory:

T 10 *Nic. Eth.* 1096a12–13:   This investigation [critique of Plato's theory of the Idea of the good] is painful because it was friends [of ours] who introduced the Forms (εἰσαγαγεῖν⁴¹ τὰ εἴδη).

Moreover a few lines after T9 in the *Met.* the difference between Plato and Aristotle on this point is singled out as the opposition in their respective conceptions of the universal, the latter being exactly what Aristotle thinks Plato's Forms should have been, and Socrates' forms in fact were:

T 11 *Metaph.* 1078b30–2:   But Socrates did not regard the universals or the [objects of] definitions as separate existents (οὐ χωριστὰ ἐποίει), while they [Plato] did separate them (οἱ δ' ἐχώρισαν), and this sort of entity they called 'Ideas.'"

Here we are told more specifically what it was about those non-sensible entities of Plato's which in Aristotle's view would have made those Ideas not only alien to Socrates' concerns, but flatly unacceptable to him: Plato made "separate existents" of the ethical universals⁴² Socrates had sought to define, which he did *not* regard as "separate existents."

Thus Aristotle offers no support to scholars who divide the theory of Forms in two, giving an earlier version of it to Socrates, a

---

existents" (οὐ χωριστὰ ἐποίει), but Plato did so (οἱ δ' ἐχώρισαν, 1079b36: χωρὶς εἶναι) and then again at 1079b36, where he makes his famous objections to the Platonic theory that "it makes the substance to exist separately (χωρὶς εἶναι) from that of which it is the substance."

41 Cf. the gloss on εἰσαγαγεῖν by Burnet, 1900 *ad loc.*: "the word is commonly used of introducing novelties, and suggests something arbitrary," as at *De Caelo* 271b11: "if one were to import minima (τοὐλάχιστον εἰσαγαγών) one would bring down the greatest truths of mathematics."

42 As I pointed out in my discussion of the categorial properties of the Platonic Form at chapter 2, section III, two of them (inaccessibility to the senses and exemption from flux), would have been perfectly acceptable to Socrates_E, but were answers to questions which Socrates_E, unconcerned with metaphysical issues, had never asked about the entities he sought to define. The third of those properties, their incorporeality, he might also have granted: there is no reason why he should have held (absurdly) that justice, beauty, etc. were physical objects. It is the fourth, their existing "separately" from the spatio-temporal world of our experience, which he could not have stomached: for Socrates justice, beauty, etc. exist *in* that world, and he never even hints that they exist "separately" in a world beyond it. At T11 Aristotle reveals his awareness that this is the crux of the difference between Socrates' and Plato's conception of the ἰδέα/εἶδος of their respective inquiries.

subsequent one to Plato.[43] As Aristotle understands the matter all of it is Plato's: Socrates has no part in it. So when Aristotle comes across statements in some of Plato's earlier dialogues which assert or imply the existence of things like justice, piety, beauty, and the rest,[44] he cannot be taking these to be Platonic Ideas or Forms, despite Plato's use of the terms εἶδος, ἰδέα as generic names for them in these and other[45] passages in some of his earlier dialogues.[46] Aristotle understands Socrates to be talking about what he (Aristotle) calls "universals" – as well he might since the Socratic εἶδος satisfies perfectly the definition he lays down for this term of art:[47]

T12 *Metaph.* 1038b11–12: For that is called "universal" whose nature it is to belong to a number of things (ὃ πλείοσιν ὑπάρχειν πέφυκεν).

How closely this formula fits the language. Socrates$_E$ uses to explain what *he* calls "form" can best be seen by noting that "F belongs to a" (τὸ Φ ὑπάρχει τῷ α) is ordinary Greek for asserting that *a has the property F*, which can also be expressed more simply by "*F is in a* " (τὸ Φ ἔνεστι τῷ α).[48] So when Socrates asks Euthyphro, "Is not the pious the same as itself *in every [pious] action*?"[49] he could have asked equivalently, "Is not the pious the same as itself *in all the actions to which it belongs*?" And what is "the same as itself" in all instances of the definiendum is, as we see in T12, precisely what Aristotle calls a "universal." Socrates$_E$'s question, "What is the εἶδος, piety?" Aristotle understands to mean exactly "What is the universal, piety?"

But Aristotle does not go so far as to say or imply that Socrates discovered *the concept* of the universal. Had he done so he would have made a metaphysician out of Socrates after all. And this he never does. He represents Socrates at [c] above as having been "the first to search for universal definitions *of the virtues*" – not as the first to search for the definition *of the universal* or to investigate *the nature of the universal*. When he praises Socrates for not having "separated" the

43 Allen, 1970 (cf, chapter 2, n. 46) puts this into the title of his book *Plato's "Euthyphro" and the Earlier Theory of Forms.* This view is by no means eccentric. It is widely shared.
44 T4 and T5 (*Euthyphro*); T7 (*Hippias Major*) in chapter 2 above; and *Meno* 72c7–8.
45 *HMa.* 289D, 298B; *Meno* 72D–E.
46 Though by no means all of them: the objects of Socrates$_E$'s definitional inquiries are never called εἴδη, ἰδέαι in the *Pr., Ch.* or *La.* This is a strong argument for assuming that all three of these dialogues are earlier than the *Eu.*, marking a stage in the development of Plato's understanding of Socratic philosophy at which he had not yet realized the peculiar fitness of those words to serve as generic names for the *F* of Socrates' "What is the *F*?" question.
47 The phrase τὸ καθόλου Aristotle had coined for this purpose he seems to have derived from an expression used by Socrates in the *Meno* (77A): "Keep your promise and try to say what virtue is as a whole (κατὰ ὅλου εἰπὼν περὶ ἀρετῆς ὅτι ἐστίν)."
48 Cf. chapter 2, nn. 131, 132.　　　　　49 T4 in chapter 2.

universals[50] he is not praising him for having formed the right theory about them, but for not having formed the wrong theory, because he had formed no theory about them at all, having had no occasion to do so since this sort of inquiry was not in his line. "Concerning himself with moral topics and not at all with the whole of nature,"[51] Socrates, in Aristotle's view of him, had never entered the metaphysical forest where Plato was to get lost. From the "embarrassments"[52] in Plato's metaphysical theory Socrates had been saved not by a superior theory but by theoretical innocence.

So my claim that the moral philosopher seeking definitions of moral terms in Plato's Elenctic and Transitional dialogues is Plato's recreation of Socrates, while the metaphysician inventing the theory of "separately existing" Forms is Plato, speaking only for himself, gets good confirmation from Aristotle. And so does my claim that Socrates$_E$'s profession of ignorance had been the stance of the historical figure:

T13 *Soph. El.* 183b7–8:   ...and this is why Socrates used to ask questions and give no replies: for he confessed that he had no knowledge (ὡμολόγει γὰρ οὐκ εἰδέναι).

In this closing chapter of the *Refutation of Sophistical Arguments* Aristotle pauses to look back to what he had said at the start of the treatise. There he had laid down the distinction between "dialectical" and "peirastic"[53] argument. In the former we refute our opponent's thesis by arguing from the reputable beliefs (τὰ ἔνδοξα) on that topic.[54] In the latter we refute him from his own beliefs:

T14 *Soph. El* 165b3–6:   Dialectical arguments are those which argue from what is reputably believed to the contradictory [of the refutand]. Peirastic are those which argue from the answerer's own beliefs.

T13, short as it is, gives us the precious information that in Aristotle's view Socrates declined to argue in both of these ways, and the reason

---

50 T11 above, where Aristotle goes on to say (1086b6–7): "separating them is the source of the embarrassing consequences of the Ideas (τὸ δὲ χωρίζειν αἴτιον τῶν δυσχερῶν συμβαινόντων περὶ τὰς ἰδέας ἐστίν)."

51 *Metaph.* 987b1–2 (the counterpart to [C] above in the doublet of T9 in Book I.

52 Cf. n. 50 above.

53 πειραστικός from πεῖραν λαμβάνειν, as in *Protagoras* 348A, ἐν τοῖς ἑαυτῶν λόγοις πεῖραν ἀλλήλων λαμβάνοντες καὶ διδόντες ("making *trial* of one another in the give-and-take of argument").

54 In Barnes, 1984 this rendering of ἔνδοξα supersedes "generally believed opinions" in the previous one, which I had followed uncritically in 1983a: n. 39 *et passim*. Burnyeat (1986) argues convincingly that the new rendering comes closer to capturing the intent of Aristotle's definition of ἔνδοξα ("what is believed by all or by most or by the wise and, of these, by all or by most or the most distinguished and most reputable (τοῖς μάλιστα γνωρίμοις καὶ ἐνδόξοις)," *Top.* 100a29–b23).

why he did decline: his disavowal of knowledge Aristotle understands to put out of bounds argument grounded on reputable belief; in telling his interlocutors that he had no knowledge, Socrates, in Aristotle's view, denied himself the use of reputable beliefs against them, for by his own admission he did not know if those reputable beliefs are true; so the only role Socrates could play in question-and-answer argument was peirastic,[55] i.e. to extract, by means of questions, admissions from his interlocutor which could serve as the premises from which Socrates would proceed, by syllogistic or epagogic argument,[56] to deduce the negation of the interlocutor's thesis. Thus on this count too my claim that in Socrates$_E$ Plato is recreating the historical Socrates is confirmed by Aristotle's testimony. Though Aristotle never refers elsewhere to that total disclaimer of knowledge which would have been as puzzling for him as it is for us,[57] he is nonetheless so confident that Socrates did make that disclaimer that he presents it as the very reason why Socrates confined himself to peirastic argument, impoverishing his argumentative arsenal in thus denying himself the resources of the form of reasoning Aristotle deploys so copiously in his own ethical treatises.

No less unequivocal is Aristotle's support for my claim that the tripartite division of the psyche, which enters Plato's corpus only in the course of his middle period, is foreign to the thought of the historical Socrates:

T15 Aristotle, *Magna Moralia*[58] 1182a15–26: Coming afterwards, Socrates spoke better and more fully [than did Pythagoras] about these matters [the moral virtues]. But neither did *he* speak correctly. For he made the virtues

---

55 In Vlastos, 1983a: 27ff., n. 39) I point out that, according to Aristotle, the accomplished dialectician will argue not only (a) *peirastically*, confining himself to the questioner's role, content to do no more than "exact an account" (λόγον λαμβάνειν) from his opponent, without expounding and defending alternative views of his own, but *also* (b), *dialectically*, assuming the answerer's role, "sustaining his thesis by rendering an account from the most reputable premises" (λόγον ὑπέχοντες φυλάξομεν τὴν θέσιν ὡς δι' ἐνδοξοτάτων). (b) describes what Aristotle does throughout his ethical treatises, where "demonstrative argument (ἀποδεικτικὸς συλλογισμός) from indubitably true premises (*Soph. El.* 100a27–b21) is unavailable; (a) is the way in which, he thinks, Socrates argues because he, unlike Aristotle, argues as one who professes to have no knowledge.

56 "For two are the things one would justly assign to Socrates: epagogic arguments (ἐπακτικοὺς λόγους: on these see additional note 3.2) and universal definitions" (*Met.* 1078a27–9).

57 Never in his surviving corpus does he venture to explain it or otherwise comment on it in any way.

58 Though probably not by Aristotle's own hand (but see Cooper, 1973: 327ff., for a cautious defense of its authenticity) there can be no reasonable doubt that this is an early peripatetic treatise and may be reasonably viewed as preserving faithfully Aristotle's understanding of the contrast between Socrates' and Plato's conceptions of the structure of the soul.

forms of knowledge (ἐπιστήμας ἐποίει), and this is impossible. For all forms of knowledge are activities of reason,[59] and reason arises in the intellectual part of the soul; so in his view all virtues arise in the reasoning part of the soul. In consequence, by making the virtues forms of knowledge, he does away[60] with the irrational part of the soul (ἀναιρεῖν τὸ ἄλογον μέρος τῆς ψυχῆς). And in doing this, he does away with both passion and moral character (ἀναιρεῖ καὶ πάθος καὶ ἦθος). This is why he does not treat the virtues correctly. But afterwards Plato divided the soul correctly into its rational and non-rational parts and assigned to each its appropriate virtues.[61]

Thus the Aristotelian view of Socrates unequivocally assigns to him, and to him in opposition to Plato, that intellectualist conception of motivation and of the nature of moral virtue which reduces courage and each of the other virtues to forms of knowledge, thereby ignoring the role of passion and moral character (πάθος καὶ ἦθος) in the determination of conduct. Aristotle[62] protests the identification of virtue with knowledge which, he feels, blinds Socrates to the difference between enhancing one's moral knowledge and improving one's moral character:

T16 *Eud. Eth.* 1216b2–9: Socrates the elder thought that the end is to know virtue, and he inquired what is justice and what is courage and what is each of virtue's parts. It is understandable that he should have done so. For he thought all the virtues were forms of knowledge, for [he thought that] when we have learned geometry and architecture[63] we are already geometricians and architects.[64]

Similarly the impossibility of incontinence, that most perplexing of the consequences of a reductively intellectualist psychology, Aristotle never attributes to Plato, but only to Socrates:

T17 *Nic. Eth.* 1145b23–7: For Socrates thought it would be strange[65] for knowledge to be in a man, but mastered by something else, and dragged

59 Literally, "with reason (μετὰ λόγου)."
60 I.e. ignores it, denies it due consideration.
61 I.e. intellectual virtue to the rational, moral virtue to the irrational part of the soul.
62 *Magna Moralia* 1183b8–18 (and cf. Irwin's trenchant paraphrase of Aristotle's criticism of the Socratic view: "he made the virtues pointless," 1977a: 198). Cf. also *Eudemian Ethics* 1216b2–25 from which I proceed to quote 16.
63 As some of his examples show (οἰκοδομία here, medicine in the *M.M.* passage), Aristotle's criticism is levelled directly at Socrates' argument against Gorgias at *G.* 460A–C.
64 Aristotle is putting his finger on the reason why that question, which in his own view (as also in that of Plato) is all-important, "how virtue is produced and by what means" (πῶς γίνεται καὶ ἐκ τίνων, 1216b10–11), should have gone by the board in Socrates' moral inquiries. He understands perfectly why Plato's concern with "musical" education is not matched in Socrates.
65 δεινόν, "terrible," "outrageous," which in this context must mean something like "incomprehensible."

around like a slave (περιέλκειν αὐτὴν ὥσπερ ἀνδράποδον).⁶⁶ Socrates rejected that view completely, holding that there is no such thing as incontinence (ὡς οὐκ οὔσης ἀκρασίας). For no one, he thought, supposes while he acts that what he does conflicts with what is best; [if one so acts, it is] because of ignorance.

Thus at each of those salient points marked off in the first four of the Ten Theses at which Socrates$_E$'s thought is antithetical to that of Socrates$_M$, Aristotle, when reading Plato's dialogues, unhesitatingly allocates to Socrates the views Plato puts into the mouth of Socrates$_E$, to Plato himself the views Plato puts into the mouth of Socrates$_M$.⁶⁷ What is so remarkable about this distributive allocation is that Aristotle should be making it without ever feeling called upon to argue in justification of it – so great is his confidence that his audience, taking this allocation for granted, does not expect him to provide any defense of it.⁶⁸ What could have given him this confidence? What else but the fact that the allocation was supported by all the information he had been getting from other sources – from that stream of Socratic dialogues by Aeschines, Antisthenes, Aristippus and the rest, and also orally from people Aristotle had met in Athens who had known Socrates in their twenties and thirties and were still around when Aristotle joined the Academy (367): Aristotle would have had ample opportunity to interrogate them.⁶⁹

66 As has often been noticed, here Aristotle is echoing Plato's simile, and even the wording, at *Pr.* 362C, περὶ τῆς ἐπιστήμης, ὥσπερ περὶ ἀνδραπόδου περιελκομένης.

67 In none of the passages from which I have drawn his references to Socrates (T9, T10, T12, T13, T15, T16, T17) does he use expressions which distance the referent of "Socrates" from the historical figure by indicating that the view in question is that of a character in a Platonic dialogue. Thus in T17, though echoing the very wording of the *Protagoras* (cf. the preceding note), Aristotle does not say ὁ ἐν Πρωταγόρᾳ Σωκράτης (like ὁ ἐν Φαίδωνι Σωκράτης, Σωκράτης ἐν τῷ ἐπιταφίῳ [the *Menexenus*], etc.), or even ὁ Σωκράτης (see Bonitz, 1870: 598A–B), but just Σωκράτης (on the difference and on the substantial, though not invariable, observance by Aristotle of the so-called "Fitzgerald's canon," Σωκράτης for the historical figure, ὁ Σωκράτης ["the Socrates"] for the Platonic figure, see Ross, 1924: xxxix–xli; and cf. the reference to the Aristophanes of Plato's *Smp.*: ἐν τοῖς ἐρωτικοῖς λόγοις λέγοντα τὸν Ἀριστοφάνην, *Pol.* 1262b11). Stenzel (1927: A.1, col. 882) also calls attention to the tense of the verbs in Aristotle's references: "he says," in referring to the Platonic figure of Socrates, "he *sought, thought, confessed*" etc. in referring to the historical Socrates. For a good example of the firmness of the differential allocation see Aristotle's criticism of Plato's utopia in the *Rep.* in *Politics* II, which starts off (1261a6), ὥσπερ ἐν τῇ Πολιτείᾳ τοῦ Πλάτωνος· ἐκεῖ γὰρ ὁ Σωκράτης φησί, and then proceeds to attribute consistently to ὁ Σωκράτης, without any further reference to Plato, the views Plato expounds in Books IV and V of the *Republic*.

68 The same distributive allocation is made by later authors who know Plato's dialogues at first hand, like Cicero: see n. 91 below.

69 From the fact that many of Aristotle's testimonia about Socrates seem derived directly from Plato's earlier dialogues (the dependence is very striking in the case of T17: cf. n. 67 above) it has often been inferred (most recently by Kahn, 1981: 305ff., n. 3) that Aristotle's testimony about Socrates is so largely derivative from Plato's as to have no independent

Suppose Wittgenstein had been, like Socrates, a purely oral philosopher and that an exceptionally gifted young student and friend of his, named "Paul" (alias Plato) publishes after his teacher's death a book in dialogue form entitled *Philosophy and Logic* whose protagonist is named "Wittgenstein" and has Wittgenstein's personal traits. And let us suppose, further, that a decade or so thereafter Paul published another book, *Philosophy and Language*. This too is in dialogue form and its protagonist is once again a figure named "Wittgenstein" with Wittgenstein's mannerisms. But this figure now expounds a philosophy which in method and content is at important points antithetical to the one put into his mouth in the earlier volume. And finally, to complete the parallel, let us imagine that after the publication of this second volume, a very bright eighteen-year old, named "Arnold" (alias Aristotle) comes to Cambridge to study with Paul and remains in Paul's circle for nearly twenty years. Arnold, knowing both of those books by Paul (knowing them so well that he can cite their very words by heart), treats their contents very differently: when he discusses *Philosophy and Logic* he speaks of its views as Wittgenstein's; when he talks about *Philosophy and Language* he takes its ideas to be exclusively Paul's *in opposition to Wittgenstein*. He does this without ever bothering to explain why he takes the same character in the two books to be "Wittgenstein" speaking for Wittgenstein in the first, "Wittgenstein" speaking for Paul in the second. If we were to see Arnold doing this, without ever feeling called upon to justify the practice, never expecting anyone to doubt that only the first "Wittgenstein" was Paul's teacher, while the second was a *nom de plume* for Paul himself, would there be any doubt in our mind that the reason for this behavior on Arnold's part is that everybody who is anybody in the philosophical world of Cambridge has been going for years and years on the same assumption, doing so because the older philosophers there, having themselves been Wittgenstein's familiars, were in a position to know that the views expounded in *Philosophy and Logic* were indeed Wittgenstein's, while everyone, young or old in Paul's circle, having first-hand knowledge of Paul's own views, would know without having to be told that the "Wittgenstein" of *Philosophy and Language* was only a mask for Paul?

value. But as Ross pointed out (1933, *ap*. Patzer, 1987: 225–39, at 234–5) there are items in Aristotle's testimony which could not have been fished out of Plato's text, for the information they convey is simply not there: thus Aristotle "could not have learned from [Plato's] dialogues that Cratylus was Socrates' first master in philosophy." In over a third of the 42 testimonia about Socrates included in Deman, 1942, there is no indication of a Platonic source.

III XENOPHON'S TESTIMONY

I shall not labour that fantasy by trying to make a place in it for Xenophon, if only because I would be hard put to it to find in Wittgenstein's entourage a plausible counterpart for that very proper Athenian. One could hardly imagine a man who in taste, temperament, and critical equipment (or lack of it) would differ as much as did Xenophon from leading members of the inner Socratic circle. The most important difference, of course, is that people like Plato, Aristippus, Antisthenes, Euclid, Phaedo were philosophers with aggressively original doctrines of their own, one of them a very great philosopher, while Xenophon, versatile and innovative litterateur, creator of whole new literary genres,[70] does not seem versed nearly as well as they in philosophy or as talented in this area.[71] This is the first thing we need to understand about him, if we are to use his witness about Socrates, as we must, for we cannot afford to neglect a single scrap of first-hand testimony, as Xenophon's no doubt is.[72]

For a start, consider two texts from the *Memorabilia*. First:

T18 Xen. *Mem.* 3.9.5: And he [Socrates] said that justice and every other virtue is wisdom. For just actions and all other virtuous actions are honorable and good; and those who know these things [i.e. the honorable and the good] would prefer nothing else to them, while those who do not know them are unable to practice them and will err if they try.

Since the preference Xenophon has in view here is practical – preference expressed in action – he is attributing to Socrates at this point the following thesis: when we are in the position of choosing

70 There is no known precedent in Greek prose for a pseudohistorical pedagogical romance, like the *Cyropaedia*, or for military memoirs, like the *Anabasis*. For Xenophon as "a pioneering experimenter" in these new forms of literature see Momigliano, 1971: 46ff.

71 For some of the shortcomings in Xenophon's perception of Socrates as a philosopher see Irwin's brilliant review of Leo Strauss, "Xenophon's Socrates" (1974: 490ff., at 411–12). For what can be said on Xenophon's behalf by a spirited, intelligently non-Straussian, defender, see Morrison, 1987: 9–22.

72 By his own testimony we know that he had no contact whatever with Socrates during the last two years or so of Socrates' life when Xenophon had left to join Cyrus' expedition in 401 (*Anabasis* 3.1.4). But he must have struck up some sort of personal acquaintance before that, else he could hardly have sought Socrates' advice when pondering the invitation to join Cyrus. But, since we do not have the slightest idea of the time at which the acquaintance had begun, nor of its intimacy, it does not lend the least credibility to his professions to have "heard" discourses he relates: from the internal evidence it is clear that such claims to ear-witness are bogus. See in chapter 2 (n. 14) above the reference to Robin, who presents a detailed refutation of the superficially plausible assumption (first voiced by Hegel, then adopted in all seriousness by the great Zeller and many lesser historiographers) that since Xenophon was a historian his accounts of Socrates have superior historical credibility and should therefore constitute the primary source for our knowledge of Socrates. Cf. also Momigliano, 1971: 54.

between exclusive and exhaustive alternatives one of which we know
to be honorable and good, the other dishonorable and bad,
"nothing" in the latter could make us prefer it to the former. It
should follow that when we are free to give effect to our preference,
we shall always choose what we know to be honorable and good,
regardless of countervailing attractions in any alternative option; so
we shall never act in conscious preference for the worse of the
alternatives open to us – i.e. never succumb to incontinence:
knowing the right thing to do will be a sufficient condition of doing
it. Isn't this the Socratic doctrine of the impossibility of incontinence?
It is a part of it, certainly; but by no means the whole of it. Nothing
has been said, or even hinted at, to explain why knowledge of the
good should have such a decisive effect on our desire for it. For
according to common belief, knowledge and practically effective
desire are two quite different things. "We know the good but do not
practice it (οὐκ ἐκπονοῦμεν)"[73] is asserted as a fact of common
experience in Euripides' *Hippolytus* (380–1) too well-known to call for
argumentative support.[74] Why should Socrates not only doubt but
categorically deny what everyone else takes to be the truth?
Aristotle's testimonia, brief as they are, address these questions.
Unlike Xenophon, he takes us under the surface of the Socratic
doctrine he reports, allowing us a glimpse of its foundation in a
conception of the structure of the psyche which was bound to lead an
intrepid thinker to flout common belief at this point.

In yet another way Xenophon's account of the Socratic doctrine
is defectively incomplete. Look at what is put into Socrates' mouth
in another passage of the *Memorabilia*:

T19 *Mem.* 4.5.6: "And don't you think that ἀκρασία, dragging men away
to pleasurable things, prevents them from attending to beneficial ones and
understanding them, and often so stuns men (ἐκπλήξασα) that, though
perceiving both the good and the bad, it makes them do the worse instead
of the better?"[75]

I have left ἀκρασία untranslated, for this is a translator's crux. If we
were to give it the same sense as it has in Aristotle's account of
Socratic doctrine,[76] rendering it "incontinence,"[77] we would have to

73 I can see no substantial difference in the import of the Greek phrase if, following Barrett,
    1964: 229, we translate it instead "do not bring it to completion (by means of πόνος)."
74 So too in Euripides' *Medea* (1078–80); cf. the comment on it in Vlastos, 1956: xliv.
75 Xenophon's Socrates here is made to teach *in propria persona* the popular view which Plato's
    Socrates rebuts at length (*Prt.* 355A–B *et passim*), that a man who knows the good may
    nonetheless act against it because he is "stunned" (ἐκπληττόμενος, 355B1) by pleasure.
76 T17 above.
77 As Marchant does in rendering T19 in his translation of the *Memorabilia* in the Loeb
    Classical Library.

charge Xenophon with something much worse than incomplete reporting: we would have to convict him of gross confusion in his comprehension of the doctrine he reports. For then the thing whose very existence Socrates is denying in T18 would be turning up in T19 alive and kicking, a real force that may "stun" us, making us do the very thing which we never do, according to T18, i.e. choose the worse alternative when this happens to be the more pleasant. But there is no need to read so complete a muddle into Xenophon's mind. To clear him of it we need only make the (perfectly reasonable) assumption that he is using the word ἀκρασία differently from Aristotle,[78] though by no means eccentrically – with perfect warrant from current usage[79] – as a synonym of ἀκράτεια, to mean not "incontinence" but "intemperance."[80] This would clear Xenophon of rank confusion, leaving us with a milder complaint: that nowhere in his elucidation of the Socratic view does he warn us, probably because he does not understand it himself, that the Socratic view denies the possibility of incontinence not only to the temperate but *to the intemperate as well*: the view allowed Socrates in 18, correctly understood, entails that neither are the unwise incontinent – intemperate, yes; incontinent, no. On that view no one is incontinent: the unwise and intemperate are no more incontinent than are the wise and temperate: the former too choose what they judge to be their best option; the trouble with them is not that their choice goes contrary to their judgment, but that their judgment is at fault.

This being the case, what should we do with Xenophon's testimony about Socrates' teaching? Bertrand Russell writes it all off with the remark that "a stupid man's report of what a clever man says is never accurate because he unconsciously translates what he hears into something he can understand."[81] But Xenophon is anything but a stupid man. His *Cyropaedia* is as intelligent a venture in belletrist didactic fiction as has come down to us from classical antiquity. Both in that work and copiously elsewhere Xenophon displays shrewd judgment of the world and of men. If I had been one of those ten thousand Greeks, left leaderless in the wilds of Anatolia, casting about for a commander we could trust to lead us

---

78 As also ἀκρατεῖς, twice at *Mem.* 3.9.4, correcting ἐγκρατεῖς of the codd., as a copyist's error for ἀκρατεῖς, agreeing with Marchant's translation, but not with his text (he retains the uncorrected text, but translates the corrected one).   79 See LSJ *s.v.* ἀκρασία.
80 Or "licentiousness," for which Aristotle uses ἀκολασία (*Nic. Eth.* 1107b6 *et passim*).
81 1945: 83. He has a better reason for cold-shouldering Xenophon's testimony about Socrates when he observes that he would rather have his personal philosophical views reported by a hostile philosopher than by a friend who has no understanding of philosophy.

safely back to civilization, I doubt if I could have hit on anyone better than Xenophon for the purpose; my vote would certainly have gone to him over Russell. If we cannot look to Xenophon for guidance through the treacherous subtleties of the Socratic doctrine of incontinence, there may still be many other things on which he might qualify as a highly instructive witness. Let us then pump him for information on those three pivotal Theses which are of special concern to us in this chapter: let us require him to speak directly to them, telling us whether or not at each of these three points the Socrates of his acquaintance is Socrates$_E$ or Socrates$_M$

One of our three questions has been put to him already: *Did Socrates rule out the possibility of incontinence?* To this, as we have seen, it is clear that his answer would be "Yes." That he does not give us all the elucidation we would have liked to get from him on this point, probably because his own understanding of it is imperfect, does not weaken the reliability of his assurance that Socrates did maintain the doctrine which, transposed in Aristotle's vocabulary would be the impossibility of ἀκρασία. And in the course of getting this assurance directly from him, we get indirectly an indication that he does not associate with Socrates in any way the tripartite psychology Plato expounds in book IV of the *Republic*;[82] for in that conception of the psyche incontinence would be all too possible.

Next, let us interrogate Xenophon on the first two of those Ten Theses in chapter 2. *Is his Socrates the daringly speculative thinker of Plato's middle dialogues? Or is he the metaphysically reticent moralist, of their predecessors, who resolutely restricts his inquiries to human concerns? And how does his Socrates stand on those highest flights of Plato's metaphysical theorizing, the separable, transmigrating, soul and the "separate", transcendent, Form?* Here Xenophon's testimony is firm and unambiguous. On Socrates' turning away from speculation on the nature of the whole universe. Xenophon is, if anything, even more explicit and emphatic than are Plato and Aristotle: in the *Memorabilia* Socrates does more than renounce that sort of inquiry; he denounces it as "folly."[83] The residual difference from Plato's testimony on this point is that in Xenophon Socratic piety is propped up by a teleological theodicy (*Mem.* 1.4 and 4.3) which it does not need and does not have in Plato's earlier dialogues. In chapter 6 I shall have something to say of Xenophon's ascription of this vein of speculative theologizing to Socrates. For the present suffice it to remark that to prove the existence of this providential deity

82 Of which there is, in any case, not the least sign in Xenophon's Socratic discourses.
83 τοὺς φροντίζοντας τὰ τοιαῦτα μωραίνοντας ἀπεδείκνυε, *Mem.* 1.1.11.

Xenophon's Socrates makes no appeal to the far-flung metaphysics of Plato's middle dialogues. So far from allowing Socrates a belief in the prenatal existence of the soul, Xenophon does not even credit him with the usual, old-fashioned, belief in the soul's survival in Hades.[84] Xenophon's Socrates is, if anything, even more earthbound than Socrates$_M$.[85] Nor does Xenophon ever assert, or even hint, that Socrates has a theory of non-sensible, eternally invariant, incorporeal, separately existing Forms.

So on each of those major points which would suffice all by themselves to make Socrates$_E$'s worldview antithetical to Socrates$_M$'s, Xenophon's testimony leaves no doubt that the Socrates of whom he speaks is as different from the Socrates of Plato's middle dialogues as is the Socrates of Aristotle and of Plato's earlier works. But when we come to the profession of ignorance there is a hitch. For, as I pointed out in chapter 1,[86] in Xenophon's Socratic writings that profession is never heard. Is this a minor point we can afford to overlook? By no means. If Socrates had disavowed knowledge as insistently and as frequently as he does in Plato's earlier dialogues, this would be too salient to have escaped Xenophon's notice. That he should never make Socrates allude to it has the force of implicit denial of what Plato, and Aristotle after him, take to be the fact. Whose testimony on this point shall we believe – Plato's and Aristotle's *or* Xenophon's?

Fortunately we have other witnesses. First, a fragment from a dialogue by Aeschines of Sphettus, who was for many years what Xenophon seems never to have been at all: a member of Socrates' inner circle:[87]

T20 Aeschines Socraticus, fr. 11C (Dittmar):[88] "...Though I had no knowledge through which I could benefit him by teaching it to him, nonetheless I thought that by associating with him I could make him better through my love.

---

84 The omission of any reference to Socrates' belief in the immortality of the soul has the effect of a denial. Belief in the possibility of survival after death Xenophon does ascribe to his other ideal figure, Cyrus (*Cyr.* 8.17–27), but to Socrates not even that.

85 The physico-theological baggage which Xenophon does allow his Socrates is of the same order: nothing could be more alien to Socrates$_M$'s gods communing with incorporeal forms in a supercelestial region than the anthropocentric deity of the *Memorabilia* whose whole *raison d'être* seems to be to care for man.   86 Pp. 31–2 above.

87 Plato, who never mentions Xenophon anywhere in his corpus, alludes to Aeschines' presence at Socrates' trial (*Ap.* 33E) and also at the death-scene (*Phd.* 59B). Aeschines' Socratic dialogues enjoyed high credibility in antiquity. Back-handed testimony to this comes from Menedemus' charge (late 4th to early 3rd century B.C.) that most of Aeschines' dialogues had been pirated from originals by Socrates' own hand left in the keeping of Xanthippe (D.L. 2.60; Athenaeus 611D). And see the other testimonia about Aeschines in Dittmar, 1912: 247ff. and 259ff.

88 Translated with comment in additional note 1.4.

This fragment is preserved in the seventeenth oration of Aelius
Aristides, a rhetorician of the second century A.D., well versed in the
Socratic literature of the fourth century B.C. In another of his
speeches he remarks:

T21 Aelius Aristides, *Or.* 45.2 (W. Dindorff II, p. 25): It is agreed that he
[Socrates] said that he knew nothing. This all who associated with him
declare.

Further evidence to the same effect comes from other sources
intermediate in time between Aeschines and Aristides. Here is
Cicero's, paraphrasing Antiochus of Ascalon, leading figure in
Plato's Academy at the time it turned away from the skepticism of
Arcesilaus and Carneades to return to its earlier tradition:[89]

T22 Cicero, *Acad.* 1.4.16: The method of discussion pursued by Socrates
in almost all the discourses so diversely and copiously recorded by those
who heard him is to refute others while affirming nothing himself, asserting
that he knew nothing except this very thing.[90]

Moreover we see that Cicero, following Antiochus, had made the
same discrimination in his reading of Plato's dialogues which we saw
Aristotle make earlier in the present chapter: when Cicero reads
dialogues of Plato's middle period he assigns its metaphysics – the
doctrine of the soul[91] and the theory of Ideas[92] – *only* to Plato, while
well aware of the totally different view of the soul's survival after
death, agnostic at worst, traditional at best, which Socrates voices in
the *Apology*: in his *Tusculan Dissertations* (1.97–9) Cicero quotes *in
extenso* Socrates' remarks at *Ap.* 40C–41C, never ascribing the theory
of the soul's pre-existence to him.

A parallel distinction between Socrates and Plato is made by
Colotes, the pupil of Epicurus. He too attributes only to Plato the

89 See Glucker, 1978: 16–17 *et passim.*
90 Cf. n. 4 above. Besides Plato's dialogues Cicero knows also (at least) dialogues by
Xenophon and Aeschines; he refers to dialogues by both of the latter (*De Oratore* 1.45).
Though he must be well aware of Xenophon's silence on this point, he treats it as of no
account.
91 In *Tusc.* 1.17 he speaks of the tradition that Plato "came to Italy to become acquainted
with Pythagoreans... and not merely agreed with Pythagoras about the eternity of souls
but gave reasoned proof for it as well"; at 1.22–3 he refers to "Plato's doctrine [of the
eternity of the soul] which is expounded by Socrates in the *Phaedrus.*" As for the theory of
recollection, he refers (1.57–8) to the exposition of it by "Socrates" in the *Meno*, but
ascribes the theory not to Socrates, but to Plato (as Aristotle had done before him: when
he read the *M.* he had referred the Socratic docrine at *M.* 73A–B that virtue is the same
in all human beings, regardless of sex or legal status, exclusively to Socrates [*Pol.* 1260a21];
but the Platonic doctrine of transmigration and recollection asserted so dramatically in the
same dialogue Aristotle never associates with Socrates in any way).
92 Plato holds "that nothing which arises and perishes *is*, but only that *is* which is always such
as it is: this he calls ἰδέα, while we call it *species,*" *Tusc.* 1.58.

theory of non-sensible, immutable forms,[93] while imputing to Socrates the profession of ignorance, albeit in a grotesquely simplistic form, which makes him an out-and-out skeptic:

T23 Plutarch, *adv. Colot.* 1117D: How could Socrates have been anything but a charlatan (ἀλαζών), when he said that he knew nothing, but was always seeking the truth?[94]

To this evidence we can add one more item – from a most surprising source:

T24 [= T7 in chapter 1]: Xen. *Mem.* 4.4.9: "By Zeus, you shall not hear it until you have stated what *you* think justice is. We've had enough of your ridiculing others, questioning and refuting everyone, while never willing to render an account yourself to anyone or state your own opinion about anything."

Only a Socrates who had habitually put to others questions to which, pleading ignorance, he would firmly decline to propose answers of his own could have elicited this reproach.[95] That Xenophon should have painted this into his portrait of Socrates in this single paragraph of the *Memorabilia* is his tribute – all the more impressive for having been doubtless inadvertent – to the truth suppressed throughout that work.

Thus if we submit to textual evidence the question, "Did Socrates make that profession of ignorance which Aristotle associates so closely with peirastic elenchus?" we get "No" if we consult Xenophon, only him, and not all of him; we get "Yes" if we consult Plato's earlier dialogues, Aristotle, Aeschines Socraticus, Aelius Aristides, Cicero, Colotes, and even Xenophon himself. Rarely in

93 "And Plato says that it is idle for us to regard horses as *being* horses and men as men," *ap.* Plutarch, Adv. Colot. 1115A (text as in Einarson & De Lacy, 1967). He is alluding to Plato's doctrine that only the Forms are fully real; from his examples, "men" and "horses," we may surmise with Einarson & De Lacy, 1967: 173, that he has *Phd.* 73E, 96D in mind.

94 Colotes is evidently under the misapprehension that Socrates impugned the evidence of the senses: he responds with a crude rebuttal ("we eat food, not grass," etc., *loc. cit.*) As I pointed out above (chapter 2, at the start of section II), the attack on the reliability of the senses as source of knowledge in the *Phaedo* is not anticipated by Socrates$_E$: there is absolutely nothing of the sort in Plato's earlier dialogues (nor in Xenophon). The realization of that difference was evidently beyond the powers of Colotes, and not only his: on this point the position of Socrates is conflated with that of Plato by Arcesilaus: Cicero, *De Oratore* 3.67: "Arcesilaus ... seized on the following in particular out of various writings of Plato and from the Socratic conversations: that nothing certain can be apprehended by *either the senses* or the mind."

95 Beckman (1979: 16) calls attention to the contradiction between Xenophon's representation of Socrates in T24 above as never stating his own opinion, but only asking questions, and Xenophon's usual depiction of Socrates throughout the *Mem.* as moral teacher and paradigm, whose avowed purpose is "to teach and recommend to others whatever good he knows ... teach[ing] to his friends all the good he can," *Mem.* 1.6.13–14.

the domain of philosophical historiography is it our good fortune to get evidence so decisive on a disputed issue of capital importance.

Let us take stock of the results. Asking our two main witnesses, Aristotle and Xenophon, to speak to the hypothesis that on four salient points (Theses I–IV) on which Socrates$_E$ differs from Socrates$_M$, the former speaks for Socrates in Plato, the latter only for Plato, we find Aristotle confirming the hypotheses on all four points, Xenophon confirming it on three out of four, disagreeing with Aristotle on only one out of the four, and on this disagreeing with himself. The hypothesis has been confirmed.

4

ELENCHUS AND MATHEMATICS[1]

At some time in the course of his life Plato acquired such thorough knowledge of mathematics that he was able to associate in the Academy on easy terms with the finest mathematicians of his time, sharing and abetting their enthusiasm for their work.[2] The *Academicorum Philosophorum Index Herculanensis* (ed. Mekkler, p. 17) goes so far as to picture Plato as "masterminding" (ἀρχιτεκτον-οῦντος) the researches of his mathematical colleagues. This we may discount as eulogistic blow-up. Not so its further statement that Plato "set problems" to the mathematicians. Elsewhere[3] I have argued for the credibility of the well-known report in Simplicius:[4]

T1 Simpl. *in De Caelo* 488.21–4: Plato had set this problem to those engaged in these studies: What uniform and ordered motions must be hypothesized to save the phenomenal motions of the wandering stars?

There is no good reason to doubt that Plato had been the first to project the idea that the apparently inconstant motions of the planets could be accounted for by compositions of invariantly

---

1 Material in this chapter was discussed in seminars at Berkeley (1984–7) and in a colloquium on Greek mathematics at King's College, Cambridge, where I presented a paper entitled "When did Plato become a mathematician?" The present text formed a Townsend Lecture at Cornell in 1986 and was published in *AJP* 109 (1988), 362ff. Its argument bears directly on the Fifth, Sixth and Tenth of the Ten Theses listed at the start of chapter 2 which stake out the salient differences between the Socrates of Plato's earlier dialogues and the synonymous figure that expounds Plato's original philosophy in the dialogues of his middle period. The present chapter undertakes to do for these three Theses what chapters 2 and 3 did for the Second, Third and Fourth, what chapter 1 did for the Eighth, and what chapter 6 will do for the Ninth. By the end of the book the First Thesis will also have been informally fleshed out.

2 His association with the leading mathematicians of the age and his zest for their science is amply attested in Eudemus, Γεωμετρικὴ Ἱστορία, fr. 133 (Wehrli), *ap.* Proclus, *Commentary on the First Book of Euclid's Elements* (Friedlein), 64ff, at 66.8–67.20. On Plato as a mathematician see in general van der Waerden, 1954: 138–42 *et passim*; Heath, 1921: vol. 1, chapter 9 on Plato. For detailed discussion of controversial points see especially Cherniss, 1951: 393ff.   3 Vlastos, 1975: 60 and 110–11.

4 I have argued (*loc. cit.*) that the report is made on the authority of Sosigenes, whose information arguably derives from Eudemus.

constant circular motions proceeding in different planes, directions, and angular velocities. If Plato could hit on this powerful and fertile notion which "under the name of the Platonic axiom was to dominate theoretical astronomy for twenty centuries"[5] and could propound it in a form which would strike Eudoxus and other practicing mathematical astronomers not as a pretty fancy but as a workable hypothesis, he must have been accepted by them as no dabbler in their business but as a student of their subject who understood it so well that his vision of progress in it might even be at certain points ahead of theirs.

But even if all those reports had perished, we would still be in a position to know that by the time Plato came to write the middle books of the *Republic* he had studied mathematics in depth. We could infer this directly from the place he gives it in the studies he prescribes for the rulers-to-be of his ideal polis. A whole decade of their higher education, from their twentieth to their thirtieth year, he reserves for the mathematical sciences of the day–number theory, geometry, celestial kinematics,[6] and theoretical harmonics – for just these subjects to the exclusion of every other, even philosophy.[7] From this prescription, coupled with Plato's stated rationale for it, we could infer two things:

(1) That by this time Plato's own mathematical studies had been sufficiently far-ranging and thorough to convince him that this was no subject for amateurs: if philosophers are to benefit from it, they must invest in it effort as intense and prolonged as that expected nowadays from those preparing for a vocation as research mathematicians.

(2) That it was in the course of pursuing such studies himself and to a great extent *because* of them that Plato had reached the metaphysical outlook that characterized his middle period.

The first inference is self-explanatory. The second I base on Plato's testimony to the power of mathematics to yield more than intellectual training – to induce a qualitative change in our perception of reality which may be likened to religious conversion:

T2 *R.* 521C1–523A: "Shall we next consider how men of this quality are to be produced and how they may be led upward to the light, as some are

5 Dijksterhuis, 1961: 15.
6 For Plato's conception of astronomy as celestial kinematics see especially Mourelatos, 1981: 1–32.
7 *R.* VII, 518B–531B; 537B–D. For brief comment see the explanatory remarks interspersed in Cornford's translation of the passage (1945); and Annas, 1981: 171–6.

fabled to have ascended from Hades to the gods?... This will be no matter of flipping over a shell, but the turning about (περιαγωγή) of the soul from a day that is as dark as night to the true day."

Immediately after saying this Plato proceeds to locate this turn-about of soul in the study of mathematics:

T3 *R.* 521c10-523a3: "Should we not ask which study has this power?... What is that study, Glaucon, that pulls the soul away from becoming to being (μάθημα ψυχῆς ὁλκὸν ἀπὸ τοῦ γιγνομένου ἐπὶ τὸ ὄν)?... It seems to belong to the study we are now investigating which naturally leads to insight, for in every way it draws us towards reality (ἑλκτικῷ ὄντι παντάπασιν πρὸς οὐσίαν), though no one uses it aright."

This passage comes immediately after the political corollary of the allegory of the Cave has been drawn, namely, that only those redeemed from the ontological bemusement which is the common lot of unregenerate humanity,[8] only those privileged few, may be trusted with the absolute power over their fellows to be enjoyed by Plato's philosopher kings. What the passage purports to disclose is how this soul-transforming change can come about – how creatures of time and sensuality may be liberated from the empire of the senses, translated into another form of life in which love for timeless truth will dwarf all other desires and ambitions. Improbable as such a mutation may seem, impossible as it would certainly be in Plato's view for the mass of mankind,[9] it can nonetheless be achieved, he believes, by those who study mathematics with the seriousness, the concentration, the prolonged application which is implied by that ten-year immersion in the science.

That only those twice-born souls would Plato credit with competence to make authoritative judgments on matters of right and wrong could be inferred from his conviction that in the moral domain, no less than others, *bona fide* knowledge requires ap-prehension of eternal forms.[10] But Plato does not leave this as a matter of inference. He insists that critical discussion of the basic concepts of morality is prohibitively risky for the populace at large, and not only for them – even for the philosophers-to-be prior to the completion of mathematical propaedeutics. Only after their decade of mathematical studies should they be permitted to enter discussion of right and wrong:

8 Cf. the text around T14 in chapter 2, and the next two paragraphs in section II of that chapter.
9 The ideal city will contain "many more" coppersmiths than "true" philosophers (*R.* 428D–E); "the multitude can never be philosophical" (*R.* 494A).
10 Cf. chapter 2, n. 90.

T4 *R.* 539A8–B2 : "If you don't want to be sorry for those thirty-year olds[11] of yours, you must be extremely careful how you introduce them into such discussions. One lasting precaution is not to let them have a taste of it while they are still young."

For if they come to it unprepared they would be sure to be corrupted. Premature exposure to such inquiry will undermine the beliefs about right and wrong inculcated in them from childhood and they will lose their moral bearings : they will be "filled with lawlessness" (538E4).[12]

Where in the annals of Western philosophy could we find a sharper antithesis to this restriction of ethical inquiry to a carefully selected, rigorously trained elite than in the Socrates of Plato's earlier dialogues? Not only does he allow question-breeding argument about good and evil to all and sundry, he positively thrusts it on them. He draws into his search for the right way to live the people he runs into on the street, in the market-place, in gymnasia, convinced that this outreach to them is his god-given mission :

T5 *Ap.* 28E : "The god has commanded me that I should live philosophizing, examining myself and others..."[13]

The central theme of this "philosophizing" is that for each and every one of us, citizen or alien,[14] man or woman,[15] the perfection of our own soul must take precedence over every other concern: money, power, prestige, and all other non-moral goods are trivial by comparison with the awful importance of reaching that knowledge of good and evil which is the condition of moral excellence and therewith the condition of happiness. Such knowledge one cannot expect to get from Socrates[16] or from anyone else, living or dead.

11 Who are now about to start the course in dialectics, the final lap of their higher education.
12 The importance of this passage for the contrast between the Socratic and the Platonic view of moral education, all too often missed by earlier commentators, is brilliantly highlighted in Nussbaum, 1980: 43ff.: "Plato charges his teacher (ironically, in his teacher's own *persona*) with contributing to moral decline by not restricting the questioning-process to a chosen, well-trained few...Plato, with Aristophanes, believes that for the ordinary man questioning [of moral values] is destructive without being therapeutic" (88).
13 His description of his daily activity in obedience to that command repeats the terminal clause of his self-description at 38A4–5: "daily discoùrsing about virtue and those other things you hear me discussing, examining myself and others."
14 "Anyone of you I happen to meet...everyone I meet, young and old, alien and citizen..." (*Ap.* 29D, 30A).
15 Women are not in the public places where Socrates could reach them. Not so in Hades, where those barriers are obliterated: "It would make me inconceivably happy to have discussion with the men *and women* there..." (*Ap.* 41C).
16 Socrates frequently implies as much, but never *says* so – not even to his intimate friends, as I tried to make clear in my discussion of his encounter with Alcibiades in chapter 1 above. That each of us must find out moral truth for ourselves is itself something which Socrates wants us to find out for ourselves. All he can do for us is to signal this by the complex irony in his disavowal of knowledge and of teaching: On these see additional note 1.1.

One must seek it for oneself by "examining" one's own moral beliefs and those of others:

т6 *Ap.* 38A: "The unexamined life is not worth living by man."

He invites everyone to join in this cooperative inquiry – most particularly the young,[17] from whom he gets a warm response.[18]

The method by which Socrates "examines himself and others," which I am calling "the elenchus" throughout this book,[19] involves the form of argument which Aristotle was to call "peirastic":[20] a thesis is refuted when, and only when, its negation is derived "from the answerer's own beliefs," *Soph. El.* 165b3–5). And the only constraint Socrates imposes on his respondents, apart from giving answers that are short and to the point, is that they should say only what they believe:

т7 *G.* 495A: "Callicles, you'll ruin our previous arguments and will no longer be examining the truth with me if you speak contrary to what you believe."[21]

As was pointed out in the preceding chapter, Aristotle contrasts the "peirastic" form of argument with another which he calls "dialectical," whose premises are "reputable opinions" (ἔνδοξα).[22] Peirastic argument could easily be mistaken for this alternative, since Socrates says nothing about the epistemic status of the premises from which he deduces the negation of the refutand:[23] so long as he is himself satisfied, for whatever reason, that those premises are true, he accepts the interlocutor's agreement to them without proceeding to

---

17 The elderly Lysimachus, casting about for advice on the education of his son, is told by Laches: "I am surprised you are turning to us for advice on the education of young men and not to Socrates... who is always spending his day in places where young men engage in any noble study or pursuit" (*La.* 180c).

18 Lysimachus tells the company: "When these boys are talking among themselves at home they often speak of Socrates, praising him warmly" (*La* 180E). Young Charmides tells Socrates: "There is much talk about you amongst us boys" (*Ch.* 156A).

19 Plato uses the same word in the *Republic* (534c) to refer to a very different method with which the *Socratic* elenchus should not be confused.   20 Cf. chapter 3 above т14.

21 "Say only what you believe" is a standing rule of elenctic debate, generally taken for granted, mentioned only when there is special need to bring it to the interlocutor's notice. Thus in the *Gorgias* there is no allusion to it in the whole of Socrates' argument with Gorgias and with Polus. In the *Pr.* nothing is said about it until the sophist reveals that he is unaware of the constraint (331c). In the *Cr.* Socrates brings it up (49c–D) only when it is critically important that Crito should realize the serious consequences of giving his agreement to the Socratic thesis: it is tantamount to taking his stand with Socrates *contra mundum.*   22 Cf. n. 55 in ch. 3 above.

23 Cf. the description of "standard elenchus" in Vlastos, 1983a: 38–9. I shall be making repeated references to this essay, which is foundational for my interpretation of Socrates, though in need of revision at some points; a corrected version of it will appear in the sequel to this book I announced in the Introduction.

ask or give any reasons for them in that argument.[24] *A fortiori* he does
not appeal to their being "reputable opinions," though this is in fact
what most of them are, and a superficial observer could easily get the
impression that he always argued from such premises. That
impression would be groundless. Socrates does not say or imply any
such thing. That multitudes, with "wise" men of high repute at their
head, subscribed to an opinion would leave Socrates cold. Opinions
matter for him only if they are the interlocutor's own:

T8 *G.* 427B–C: "If I cannot produce one man – yourself – to witness to
my assertion, I believe that I shall have accomplished nothing on the
matter we are debating. Neither will you, I believe, if you do not bring this
one man – myself – to witness for your assertions, letting all those others go.

The only other form of argument which Aristotle distinguishes
from the "peirastic" as firmly as from the "dialectical" is the one he
calls "demonstration" (ἀπόδειξις). This he defines as follows:

T9 Aristotle, *Topics* 100a27–b21: There is demonstration when the
premises are true and primary (ἐξ ἀληθῶν καὶ πρώτων). True and primary
are those which yield conviction not through some other thing but through
themselves (τὰ μὴ δι' ἑτέρων ἀλλὰ δι' αὐτῶν ἔχοντα τὴν πίστιν); for in
regard to the first principles of knowledge one should not proceed to ask the
reason why: each of the first principles should yield conviction just by itself
(αὐτὴν καθ' ἑαυτὴν εἶναι πιστήν).

What Aristotle is saying is best grasped with reference to the
axiomatized science geometry was coming to be by his time:[25] as
Greek mathematicians understood their science, the axioms[26]
constitute the reason which can be given for every proposition in it
while, short of an infinite regress, no further proposition could be
given in that science as the reason for any of them. For such
indubitably certain *termini* to inquiry there is no place at all in
Socratic elenchus. Here no opinion is ruled out for being out of line
with principles "known through themselves." Every thesis, no
matter how offbeat, is a fit subject for "examination" if put forward
seriously as the speaker's personal belief. What could be more
perversely eccentric than Thrasymachus' thesis that justice is the
interest of the stronger, or Callicles' view that to do injustice is more
honorable (κάλλιον) than to suffer it? But Socrates debates both
without the least reluctance – in fact, with enthusiasm: he is

24 Which is not to say that he has none, but that giving and defending them would be a topic
for *another* argument.   25 Cf. the quotations from Proclus in nn. 63 and 64 below.
26 I use "axioms" here and hereafter for the indemonstrables of a deductive system, be they
definitions, postulates, or "common notions" (as the last are called in Euclid; ἀξιώματα in
Aristotle).

overjoyed to have the chance to investigate propositions which he thinks many believe or half believe in their heart but lack the outspokenness[27] to own up to them in public.

From this description of the elenctic method as practice of peirastic argument four things follow.

1. In form the method is adversative. Declining at the start of an elenchus to give his own answer to the question under debate, Socrates' formal role in the debate is not to defend a thesis of his own but only to "examine" the interlocutor's.[28]

2. But since Socrates' real purpose is not merely to search out and destroy his interlocutors' conceit of knowledge but to advance the search for truth, if he is to find it by this method, while professing to know nothing, he must worm it out of *them*. He must derive it from true premises, accepted as such by his interlocutors. Hence the strategic import of the "say what you believe" rule. If his interlocutors were to decline compliance with this rule, Socrates would have no purchase on them; his argumentative procedure would be stymied.[29]

3. Since Socrates does expect to discover truth by this method, he must be making an exceedingly bold assumption which he never states[30] and, if he had stated it, would have been in no position to defend,[31] namely that side by side with all their false beliefs, his

27 παρρησία. Callicles is fulsomely praised for it, Polus reproached for lacking it (*G.* 487A3, B1, D5).
28 In the Elenctic Dialogues, when Plato wants to show Socrates attacking a Socratic thesis he hands that thesis over to an interlocutor, making him its proponent *pro tem*. So in the *Laches* 194Eff.) Nicias is made the spokesman for the definition of courage which we know to be Socratic (Socrates argues for it in the *Pr.* [360C–D] and uses it there with deadly effect against Protagoras). Alluding to its Socratic provenance (194D), Nicias is left holding the bag: he is made its sole supporter in this dialogue, required to defend it *against* Socrates. Though Socrates is intensely self-critical, confiding that he is always more eager to examine himself than others (*Ch.* 166C–D), the procedural form of elenctic argument prevents him from making any of his own doctrines the target of elenctic refutation by himself.
29 On two occasions Socrates tolerates a breach of the rule, though only as a *pis aller* (to circumvent the evasive tactics of an uncooperative interlocutor) and only *pro tem.*, as at *Pr.* 333Cff. (cited as T14 in Vlastos, 1983a: 37–8: see the comment on this text there), and again as *R.* I, 349Aff., resuming the application of the rule when it comes to the kill.
30 Though he may make statements which *imply* it: see the texts cited as T21, T22, T23, T24(b) in Vlastos, 1983a, and comment on those texts, 48–52.
31 He couldn't without turning epistemologist and metaphysician, ceasing to be the exclusively moral philosopher which he remains throughout Plato's earlier dialogues, where only moral truths are treated as elenctic theses (see the texts cited as T3, T4, T5, and comment on these texts, in Vlastos, 1983a). Exceptionally, Socrates debates an epistemological notion, as in the case of ἐπιστήμη ἐπιστήμης καὶ ἀνεπιστημοσύνης in the *Charmides* (167A–169B), on which see n. 12 in chapter 2).

interlocutors always carry truth somewhere or other in their belief system; hence if Socrates pokes around in their belief system he can expect to turn up *true beliefs entailing the negation of each of their false ones.*[32]

4. It follows, finally, that the elenchus is a *truth-seeking device which cannot yield certainty*, for it proceeds on an assumption – that everyone defending a false moral belief in elenctic argument can always be faulted for inconsistency – for which Socrates could only have offered, at best, inductive evidence, i.e. that it has proved true in his own experience: whenever he argued against interlocutors defending a thesis which he considered false, he had always succeeded in convicting them of holding beliefs, which he considers true, entailing the negation of that false thesis. And, of course, the fact that this has always proved true in the past offers absolutely no certainty that it always will in the future: it may have been vindicated in a thousand elenchi in the past and prove false in the very next one after that.

This shortfall in epistemic[33] certainty, inherent in the elenctic method, which only a self-deluded thinker could have failed to sense and only a dishonest one could have wished to conceal, is our best clue to what Socrates meant by declaring that he had no knowledge. As I have intimated in chapter 1,[34] the declaration is cast in the form of a "complex irony" – that peculiarly Socratic figure of speech in which the speaker both does and does not mean what he says. If certainty were the hallmark of knowledge (as it had been, still was, and would continue to be for centuries to come in the main line of Greco-Roman philosophy[35]), the Socrates of Plato's earlier dialogues[36] and of Aristotle's testimony[37] would wish to renounce moral knowledge absolutely, though only to reclaim it in another sense of the word, never invoked by any philosopher[38] before him, in which "knowledge" does not entail certainty, and may, therefore, be used to mean simply justifiable true belief – justifiable, in Socrates' view,

32 Proposition A (the "tremendous assumption") in section (3) in Vlastos, 1983a: 52.
33 See additional note 4.1 for the contrast between "epistemic" and "moral" certainty.
34 See especially additional note 1.1; cf. also Vlastos, 1985: 29–31.
35 Thus from *de omnibus quaeritur, nihil certi dicitur*, Cicero infers (*Acad.* 1.46) that Plato's position was skeptical – not materially different from that of the out-and-out skeptics of the New Academy, Arcesilaus and Carneades: Cicero is taking it for granted that if Plato renounces *certainty*, he is renouncing *knowledge*.   36 *Ap.* 21B–D *et passim*.
37 *Soph. El.* 183b8 (quoted as T13 in chapter 3 above).
38 I say "by any *philosopher*," not "by *anyone*"; non-philosophers (and even philosophers when off their high horse, speaking and thinking with the vulgar) would have had no hesitation in saying e.g. "I know my friend won't lie to me," while realizing perfectly well that in this case and in a million others like it epistemic certainty is unavailable: see additional notes 4.1 and 4.4.

by the highly fallible method of elenctic argument. In the *Gorgias* and the dialogues which precede it[39] the renunciation of certainty does not deter Socrates from using that method day in, day out, relying on it to vindicate the great theses on whose truth he stakes his life. The chanciness of his method does not cause the least wavering in his conviction that those theses are true. At the conclusion of his argument against Polus he declares:

T10 *G.* 475E: "So I spoke *the truth* when I said that neither I nor you nor any other man would rather do than suffer injustice."

About the parallel thesis that to do injustice is *ipso facto* to forfeit happiness, he tells Polus:

T11 *G.* 479E8: "Has it not been proved (ἀποδέδεικται) that what I said was *true*?"[40]

What then are we to make of the fact that this method, to which Socrates is committed down to and including the *Gorgias*, is dropped in the *Euthydemus*, the *Lysis*, and the *Hippias Major*?[41] This shedding of the elenchus Plato makes no effort to explain or justify. He does not even mention it. He indicates it by dramatic means, pairing Socrates with interlocutors who no longer give him any fight. In the *Lysis* they are teenagers, with no mind of their own on the theses he puts up to them[42] and, in any case, too well-bred and deferential to their older friend to cross anything he says. In the *Hippias Major* the

---

39 As I have previously noted (chapter 2, n. 3 above) commitment to the elenctic method as the final arbiter of truth in the moral domain (cf. n. 50 below) is common and peculiar to ten dialogues which, for miscellaneous reasons, have been often thought by a wide variety of scholars to constitute the earliest segment of the Platonic corpus which I have called Plato's "Elenctic Dialogues" in contradistinction to the "Transitional" ones, in which the elenctic method is discarded while consistency of moral doctrine with their predecessors is maintained. In the *Gorgias* I see a major chronological landmark, for I consider it the last of the Elenctic Dialogues, concurring with the widely held opinion that on good internal evidence it may be dated at, or close to, Plato's return from the first journey to Sicily: see e.g. Dodds, 1959: 19ff.; Irwin, 1979: 5–8.

40 Here Socrates is misspeaking himself: what he says, strictly read, suggests that a single elenchus could produce an elenctic refutation of a false thesis, which would be surely wrong; as I pointed out in Vlastos, 1983a: 49, all Socrates could claim to have proved in any given argument is that the thesis is inconsistent with the conjunction of the premises agreed upon in that argument. To make good the claim he is making in the quoted statement he would have to explain that if Polus were to escape the inconsistency by abandoning one of those premises Socrates would be in a position to find alternative premises in Polus' belief-system which would generate inconsistency within it so long as the false thesis was retained.

41 I so argue more fully in Vlastos, 1983a: 57–8, Appendix on "The Demise of the Elenchus in the *Eud.*, *Ly.* and *HMa.*"). Here I may note that the *Meno* is a special case, a hybrid, firmly elenctic down to 80E, firmly non-elenctic after that.

42 They follow sheeplike wherever he leads. When he takes a position they agree, when he objects to the position they agree with the objection.

interlocutor is mature enough, and more – a man of parts, *inter alia* accomplished mathematician and astronomer – but hopelessly inept in dialectical argument. His answers to the "What is the *F?*" question are so wild as to be wholly devoid of philosophical interest;[43] Socrates makes short shrift of them, invests little effort in their refutation. When interesting answers are introduced at long last, he gets them not from Hippias but from himself. Hippias welcomes each of them as they are put up, and is resentfully surprised when Socrates then turns against them. Here, as also in the *Lysis*, the promising theses are proposed by Socrates *and* refuted by him.

So in these dialogues Socrates is only half Socratic: the searcher remains, the elenctic critic has been cashiered. What we see of Socrates here is what Leavis tells us Wittgenstein's lecture audiences witnessed in Cambridge: "the sustained spontaneous effort of intellectual genius wrestling with its self-proposed problems."[44] This was all very well for Wittgenstein: but *he* had not said he had received a divine mandate "to live philosophizing, examining [himself] *and others*,"[45] declaring he would be faithful to that mandate, even at the cost of his life (*Ap.* 29C–30C). All through the Elenctic dialogues Socrates has done just that, examining himself *via* examining others, testing his own beliefs against the ones he refutes to vindicate his own. But now we see him dropping the two-in-one operation, turning his critical acumen only against his own proposals, examining only himself.

The change is no less marked in the *Euthydemus*. The visiting sophists are depicted as so outrageously and irresponsibly eristic that, try as he may, Socrates finds it impossible to lock horns with them in any kind of serious argument. So he gives up. In each of two long segments of the dialogue he turns his back on them, giving all his attention to Cleinias, a beautiful boy, who hangs on his lips. Here for the first time in Plato's corpus we see Socrates unloading his philosophizing on an interlocutor in the form of protreptic discourse[46] expounded in flagrantly non-elenctic fashion as a virtual

---

43 One could scarcely imagine less promising answers to the question "What is that by which *all* beautiful things are made beautiful?" (288A8–11 *et passim*) than "a beautiful girl" (287E), "gold" (289E), and the still more naively parochial one (too long to quote) at 291D–E.   44 Leavis, 1984: 63.

45 *Ap.* 28E (= T5 above) and 38A4–5 (quoted in n. 13 above).

46 Protreptic dialogue we get already in the interchange with young Hippocrates in the *Pr.* (310A–314B). There is no elenchus here – Hippocrates puts up no defense of the hare-brained premise with which he starts, that "Protagoras is the only one who is wise" (310D) – no adversative argument is needed to talk him out of it: a few pointed questions suffice to collapse it. So the episode is an edifying curtain-raiser to the elenctic drama it precedes.

monologue.[47] Socrates starts it off by laying down an indubitable truth, a proposition which, he says, it would be "ridiculous" (καταγέλαστον) and "senseless" (ἀνόητον) to question – strange departure from his practice in the elenctic Dialogues, where every thesis in moral philosophy is open to challenge. He proceeds to develop his thought entirely by himself, modifying it solely in response to caveats of his own. When the interlocutor is allowed at last an independent voice[48] it is only so he can interject something Socrates wants said but could not have put into his own discourse without digressing abruptly from its line of thought. So here, as in the *Lysis* and the *Hippias Major* the elenchus has been jettisoned. Moral doctrine of the highest import – the core of Socrates' moral philosophy[49] – is propounded in the *Lysis* and the *Euthydemus* unchallenged by an opponent.

I submit that to make sense of so drastic a departure from what Plato had put into his portrayals of Socrates from the *Apology* to the *Gorgias*, we must hypothesize a profound change in Plato himself. If we believe that in any given dialogue Plato allows the persona of Socrates only what he (Plato), at the time, considers true,[50] we must suppose that when that persona discards the elenchus as the right method to search for the truth this occurs because Plato himself has now lost faith in that method. This could have happened to him only after the *Gorgias*, where Socrates is still supremely confident that the elenchus is the final[51] arbiter of moral truth. Why then the

Protreptic speeches inside an elenctic dialogue we do get in the *Gorgias*, in great abundance (511C–513C; 517B–519D; 523A to the end), but there only after hard-won elenctic argument had established the great truths which the interlocutor is then exhorted to take to heart, while in the *Eud.* the exhortation displaces adversative argument.

47 So it remains during the whole of its first part (278E–280D) and at the start of the second (288D–290A). Here again, as in the *Lysis*, the interlocutor's attitude to Socrates is docility itself: the yes-man of the middle dialogues has made his entry into Plato's corpus.

48 At 290B–D: to be cited (in part) and discussed under T23 below.

49 In the *Ly.* Socrates lays out the doctrine of the πρῶτον φίλον: there is a supreme object of desire, such that all other things we may desire would be vain except in so far as that "first" object is reached (219B–220B). In the *Eud.* he teaches (1) that the only thing desired by all persons only for its own sake is happiness and (2) that for the attainment of happiness all goods *become evils* unless controlled by moral wisdom. One can hardly imagine stronger moral claims. In (2) the Socratic doctrine of the Sovereignty of Virtue (to be discussed in chapter 8) is pushed further in the words I have italicized than in any expression of that doctrine in Elenctic dialogues. But while heretofore Socratic doctrine had been maintained against opposition from a dissenting interlocutor, here it is unopposed.

50 This is the grand methodological hypothesis on which my whole interpretation of Socrates-in-Plato is predicated (I allude to one of its implications in n. 20 in chapter 2), with the qualification that in the *Symposium* and the *Parmenides* Plato creates new voices – Diotima in the former, Parmenides in the latter – to supersede that of Socrates *pro tem*.

51 It should go without saying that Socrates may have any number of reasons for believing that, say, to suffer injustice is always better than to do it. But when it comes to the crunch he never brings up any of these. When the issue is joined with those who think his claim

disenchantment with the elenchus at just this time in Plato's life? What could have happened in his intellectual development to account for this momentous change? Since Plato doesn't tell us, we have to guess, i.e. resort to a hypothesis. Mine is that now, in mid-career, Plato himself has taken that deep, long plunge into mathematical studies he will be requiring of all philosophers when he comes to write book VII of the *Republic* and that the effect is proving as transformative of his own outlook as he believed it would be of theirs. Direct evidence for his hypothesis we do not have. But of indirect evidence there is no lack. To find it in abundance we need only turn to the *Meno*, the first dialogue in which the impact of these new studies on the content and method of his philosophizing is allowed to surface freely. Here Plato's new enthusiasm bubbles out all over the text.

When Socrates announces[52] that all learning is "recollecting" and is asked if he has any way of exhibiting the truth of this startling proposition (82A5–6), he replies:

T12 *M.* 82A–B: "Call one of your attendants, any of them will do, that I may exhibit[53] this to you in his case."

What follows is the most sustained stretch of geometrical reasoning in the whole of Plato's corpus. Meno is to observe that the boy will "discover" (ἀνευρήσει)[54] the answer to a geometrical problem: find the side of a square which duplicates the area of a given square whose side is two feet long. The interrogation which follows has been

absurd and warn him that he is basing his life on a lie, he looks to the elenchus, and to nothing but that, to vindicate the truth of his position.

52 81A–C. The search for a definition, pursued in the familiar Socratic way (a replay of the elenchus to show it dead-ending), lands in impasse (80D–E: cf. n. 40 above). A radically new start is called for. Thereupon a *deus ex machina* is unveiled: the glorious doctrines of transmigration and its pendant, *anamnēsis* (T1, T2 in chapter 2), are revealed.

53 ἐπιδείξωμαι, not "prove" (ἀποδείξω); cf. T11 above.

54 A great point is made of this: "Watch whether you find me teaching and laying it out for him (διδάσκοντα καὶ διεξιόντα αὐτῷ) instead of querying his own opinions (τὰς τούτου δόξας ἀνερωτῶντα)" (84D). How so, when Socrates' questioning takes the boy *to* the solution step by step? I suggested a reply – too long to reproduce here in full – in Vlastos, 1965: 143ff. The boy, required to give *his own* opinion in answer to Socrates' questions, is in no position to base it on what he sees, or guesses, since Socrates thinks is the right answer. When he does try doing so he gets his fingers burned: both of his mistakes are due to his having placed unthinking trust in suggestions he reads into what Socrates has said (83B6–7; 83D3–5): the boy must say only what he judges to be true *for his own reasons*, prepared to defend it against Socrates. So when the interrogation reaches the point where Socrates fills out the diagram, giving a graphic presentation of the correct solution, the boy is in no position to say that this *is* the right answer unless he accepts it for reasons other than the suggestions made to him by Socrates both verbally and through the diagram: he must accept it only because *he has some understanding*, however rudimentary, *of the reasoning which warrants that conclusion*. (For fuller discussion see especially Nehamas, 1985: 1ff. at 24–30; Burnyeat, 1987: 1ff. at 8–24.)

thought a paradigm of Socratic elenchus.[55] Is it? Yes and no. Yes, where the boy's mistakes are being corrected. When he guesses that the side of the desired square is 4 feet long, or 3 feet long, he is shown that either of these answers must be wrong *because* each contradicts the boy's claim that the area in each case duplicates that of the given square with agreed-upon area of 4 square feet: the boy is brought to understand that if the side were 4 (or 3) feet long its area would be 16 (or 9) square feet, and 16 (or 9) is not twice 4. In correcting those two answers in just that way Socrates produces true-blue elenctic argument: false answer P is eliminated because P contradicts Q, and Q is what the answerer himself accepts as true. But how far does this take the boy? Only as far as convicting him of error. Elenchus is good for this, and only this. It does not begin to bring him to the truth he seeks. He could have gone on till doomsday trying out different integers or ratios of integers to be shown their falsehood by the same process, and none of this would have brought him an inch closer to the true answer. In Greek mathematics, which recognizes only integral numbers,[56] no integer or ratio of integers could yield the answer to Socrates' question. The problem admits of no arithmetical solution.[57] But it does admit of a geometrical one. This answer no elenctic badgering could have elicited from the boy.[58] To bring him to it Socrates *must shed the adversative role* to which persistence in elenctic argument would have kept him. Shed it he does. Extending the diagram, he plants into it the line that opens sesame, and *then* the boy "recollects" that the side of a square whose area is twice that of a given square is the diagonal of the given square.

What is so obviously new here is the resort to geometry. But let us note that this episode in the dialogue is not presented as deserting

55 Irwin, 1977a: 139: "the examination of the slave-boy is a scale-model of a Socratic *elenchos*." Same view in Nehamas, 1986: 16. It is expressed, or implied, in virtually all scholarly comment on the passage.

56 In Euclid "number" is *defined* as "a multitude composed of units" (τὸ ἐκ μονάδων συγκείμενον πλῆθος, *Elements* VII, Df. 2). A glance at the definitions cited *ad loc.* in Heath, 1926: II 280, will show that from the Pythagoreans in the fifth century B.C. to Theon of Smyrna in the second century A.D. this remains constant throughout their variations.

57 Nor does Socrates imply that it does. But the language he has to use in explaining the problem to the boy could hardly fail to suggest it to him. "Now if this side were 2 feet long and that side the same, how many [square] feet would the whole area be?" (82C). He continues using numbers when correcting the boy's mistakes. Only when he reaches the point at which the boy is put on the track of the right solution (84D) does he stop assigning numerical values to the sides of the proposed square to identify possible answers to the problem.

58 Only by imagining a preternaturally precocious slave-boy coming to the interrogation with the positive thesis that all magnitudes are commensurable (instead of the mere ignorance of the truth that they are not) could we set Socrates a task which he could solve by elenctic means, *sc.* helping the boy rediscover the proof of the irrationality of the square root of 2 in Euclid, *Elements* X, Appendix xxvii (Heiberg).

moral inquiry for mathematics. Its whole purpose is to illuminate the process by which according to this new, all-too-Platonic Socrates, *all* inquiry – and therefore all moral inquiry – must proceed:

T13 *M.* 81D: "For *all* inquiring and learning is recollecting."

As novel as is the theory of recollection itself and as significant an indication of the lines along which Plato's philosophical development is now moving is the fact that geometrical discovery is being taken as paradigmatic "recollection"[59] and therewith that knowledge of geometry is taken as the paradigm of all knowledge, including moral knowledge.

The same is true of a piece of geometry Plato had brought into the *Meno*, earlier on. To show by example how a "What is the *F*?" question should be answered Socrates had put up a geometrical paradigm. Picking "figure" as the definiendum, he proceeds:

T14 *M.* 76A4–7: "Is there something you would call a 'plane' (ἐπίπεδον), and something else which you would call a "solid' (στερεόν) as they do in geometry?... From this you can understand what I mean by 'figure' (σχῆμα). For of every figure I would say: that which is the limit of a solid (στερεοῦ πέρας), that is figure."

Contrast the line he had taken in the *Laches*, when giving the interlocutor a model to show him what sort of answer is required for a "What is the *F*?" question. The example he had used there is ταχυτής, "quickness" or "swiftness," a word in everyday speech, without scientific pretension;[60] and the model definition offered for it had been built up with bricks from the same kiln: the cases he wants it to cover are quick actions of "hands or legs or mouth or voice or thought." And the definiens he offers is a rough-and-ready, home-made job, owing nothing to scientific theorizing:

T15 *La* 192B: "The quality[61] of doing much in little time, both in speaking and in running and in all other things, is what I call 'quickness.'"

Not so in the *Meno*. The term to be defined here, σχῆμα, occurs both in common speech and in scientific discourse – one could use it to

---

59 When Plato's epistemology has matured, as it will by the time he comes to write the middle books of the *Republic*, he will be qualifying this first starry-eyed view of geometry, insisting that the axioms of geometry are not the first principles (ἀρχαί) which unphilosophical mathematicians take them to be: they should be regarded as "hypotheses" which are themselves in need of justification; mathematicians who treat them as final truths are only "dreaming about reality" (533B–C). In the *Meno* no such caveats are even hinted at.

60 In scientific discourse one would be more likely to speak of τάχος instead; thus Eudoxus' astronomical treatise was entitled περὶ ταχῶν (Simplicius, *in De Caelo* 492.31ff.). See Brandwood, 1976: *s.v.* τάχος for many examples in contexts of cosmological or astronomical or molecular theory in Plato; ταχυτής occurs only once in such contexts in Plato (*Pltc.* 284E5).　　　　61 For this rendering of δύναμις see Vlastos, 1981: 413.

refer to, say, the shape of a shield *or* to that of an intricate geometrical construction; Socrates cold-shoulders the former usage, ignores it completely, reminding his interlocutor that the critical words he will be using to produce the definition will be used as they are used in geometry: οἶον ταῦτα τὰ ἐν ταῖς γεωμετρίαις (76A2). That reference is not gratuitous. The vague way in which those words were used in common speech – ἐπίπεδον for flat, level ground, στερεόν for something firm, rigid, solid – would have disqualified them for the purposes of his definition. So he insists on that highly specialized use of those terms to denote abstract magnitudes, stripped of all physical properties except those implied by their extension in two or three dimensions – a sense which would never enter the heads of people using those words in everyday life.

And what is the provenance of the definition in T14? Almost certainly some contemporary geometrical axiom-set. From the scraps of the Eudemian history of geometry that survive in Proclus[62] we know that steps towards the axiomatization of geometry, first taken late in the fifth century by Hippocrates of Chios,[63] were continuing with growing success in the fourth.[64] By the end of the century they would reach that axiom-set, definitive for classical antiquity, which has survived in Euclid's *Elements*. Compare then what Euclid does by way of defining "figure." He takes it in two jumps, using "limit" (πέρας) to define "boundary" (ὅρος), and "boundary" to define "figure":

T16 Euclid, *Elements* I, Definition 13: Boundary is that which is the limit of something.

T17 *Ibid.*, Definition 14: Figure is that which is contained by a boundary or by boundaries.

62 Cf. n. 2 above (hereafter to be cited as "Proclus").
63 He "compiled elements (στοιχεῖα συνέγραψε) the first of those recorded to have done so," Proclus 66.1–8 – a pioneering venture of whose contents we know nothing beyond the fact that it identified geometrical "elements," i.e. propositions in geometrical argument, not derived from others, *from* which other propositions could be derived: cf. Proclus' definition of the term (72.3–6): "'Elements' are called those propositions which yield knowledge of all others and by which perplexities in these others are resolved."
64 Proclus 66.18–67.14: "At this time also lived Leodamas of Thasos [whose close association with Plato is reflected in the story that Plato taught him the method of analysis: Proclus 211.19–23], Archytas of Tarentum, and Theaetetus of Athens, by whom the theorems were increased and brought into a more scientific system. Younger than Leodamas were Neoclides and his pupil Leon, who added many discoveries to those of their predecessors, so that Leon was able to produce a system of the elements (τὰ στοιχεῖα συνθεῖναι) more adequate in respect of both their number and their utility for demonstrations...Amyclas of Heraclea, one of Plato's companions, Menaechmus, a pupil of Eudoxus, who also associated with Plato, and his brother Dinostratus, made the whole of geometry still more perfect...Theudius of Magnesia [member of the Academy]...produced an admirable system of the elements and made many partial theorems more general."

Why this more protracted procedure? It is dictated by the architectonics of Euclid's treatise, which defers solid geometry to its latest books. So it is understandable that Euclid should want to make no reference to "solid" until then: he will start off book XI by defining the term. But the source on which Plato is drawing when composing the *Meno* would be much earlier – two generations or more before Euclid, in the period when the axiomatization of geometry is making steady progress, but is still nowhere near the level reached in Euclid. At this earlier point in the development of geometrical axiomatics no need has been felt to avoid mention of the term "solid" from the very start. So we get the one in T14. above, more expeditious than Euclid's in T16 and T17. Its use by Plato shows that by the time he came to write the *Meno* he was so familiar with this branch of geometry that he found it natural to turn to it for a model of successful definition.

In the same context we get another novelty in Plato's writing: bringing in Empedocles' theory of effluences as the physical cause of sensation, he takes cognizance of physical speculation no less than of geometry. Socrates offers Meno a definition of "color" which incorporates the Empedoclean theory:[65]

T18 *M.* 76D: "color is an effluence from figures commensurate with vision and apprehensible to sense."

Expecting Meno to like this definition, Socrates teases him for fancying it – he calls it "theatrical" (τραγική), a sneer. With the geometrical definition in T14 he has no fault to find. The physical one in T18 he treats with condescension. Here again Plato is holding up geometry as paradigmatic science.

He does this on a grander scale in the part of the dialogue which follows the interrogation of the slave-boy. Reinstating the old Socratic question, "Can virtue be taught?" he announces that he is going to "investigate it from a hypothesis," identifying as follows the provenance of this phrase and explaining what he takes it to mean:

T19 *M.* 86E4–87B2: "By 'investigating from a hypothesis' (ἐξ ὑποθέσεως σκοπεῖσθαι) I refer to the way the geometricians frequently investigate. When they are asked, for example, as regards a given area, whether it is possible for this area to be inscribed in the form of a triangle in a given circle, they may reply: 'I don't yet know whether this area is such as can be so inscribed. But I think that a certain hypothesis would be helpful for that purpose. I mean the following. If the given area is such that when it has

---

65 Plato has no quarrel with it *qua* physical theory. He builds it into his own in the *Timaeus* (67C).

been applied [as a rectangle] to the given straight line in the circle, it is deficient by a figure similar to the one which is applied, then I think that one alternative results, while, on the other hand, another results if it is impossible for what I said to be done... So, setting up a hypothesis (ὑποθέμενος), I shall tell you what will follow from it for the inscription of the given area in the circle – whether or not the inscription is possible."[66]

An adequate commentary on this passage would require an essay longer than the present chapter all to itself. I restrict myself to the bare minimum of comment required for my argument.[67]

1. The geometrical example is ostentatiously technical. To understand its mathematics the reader would have needed considerable proficiency in a branch of Greek geometry, the "application of areas," to which modern histories of mathematics refer as "geometrical algebra."[68] Plato could certainly have chosen a simpler example. He is preening himself on his own expertise in geometry, warning his readers that if they have not already done a lot of work in that science they will have difficulty in following him, and this will be their loss, not his: to keep up with the best he has to offer they had best learn geometry. Though the detail of the mathematics is left obscure, the logical structure of the recommended method is entirely clear: when you are faced with a problematic proposition *p*, to "investigate it from a hypothesis," you hit on another proposition *h* (the "hypothesis"), such that *p* is true if and only if *h* is true, and then shift your search from *p* to *h*, and investigate the truth of *h*, undertaking to determine what would follow (quite apart from *p*) if *h* were true and, alternatively, if it were false. To adopt this procedure as a methodological model for research in moral philosophy is *to scuttle the elenchus*:[69] adherence to the model would entail systematic violation of the "say (i.e. assert) only what you believe" rule, which forbids debating an unasserted premise, while "investigating from a hypothesis" requires it. More generally: if one were to model method in moral philosophy on method in geometry

66 The translation, containing items whose meaning is controversial, follows in all essentials the one in Heath, 1921: 299.
67 For further comment see e.g. Heath, 1921: 298ff.; Karasmanis, 1987: 73ff.
68 See Proclus 420.23ff.; Heath, 1926: I 343–4; van der Waerden, 1954: 118ff.
69 To my knowledge, this claim has not been made in previous discussions of Plato's hypothetical method; it is implicitly contradicted in Cherniss, 1951: 419. It has not been realized that this method scraps the "say only what you believe" rule (cf. T7 above and n. 21) which *precludes argument from unasserted premises*, characteristic of both Zenonian and eristic practice (cf. Vlastos, 1983a: 27ff. at 28–9) and always normal in philosophical discussion, where the use of counterfactual premises is common and entirely unobjectionable.

one would be shifting definitively out of peirastic into demonstrative argument, and hence aiming to achieve in moral inquiry the certainty achievable in mathematical proof. For if you are practicing the geometrical method of "investigating from hypothesis" by tying the truth of p to that of h, you will be aiming to demonstrate that p is true (or false) because it is a necessary consequence of h which may be finally known to be true (or false) *because it (or its contradictory) is a necessary consequence of the axioms of the system.*[70]

2.   The use to which Plato's new Socrates wants to put this method is made clear at once. To continue the citation in T19:

T20 *M.* 87B2–4: "Just so, let us say about virtue: Since we know neither what it is (ὅτι ἐστίν) nor of what sort it is (ὁποῖον τι), let us investigate from a hypothesis (ὑποθέμενοι αὐτὸ σκοπῶμεν) whether or not it is teachable."

The problematic proposition is

p: Virtue is teachable.

The hypothesis to investigate p is

h: Virtue is knowledge.

And h we know to be a cardinal Socratic doctrine.[71] Here Socrates argues first for h (87D–89C), then[72] against it (96D–98C).[73] Neither

70 This point is not spelled out in the text, understandably so:.Plato is not undertaking a complete description of ἐξ ὑποθέσεως σκοπεῖσθαι. His mathematician readers would not need to be told that in their science when the logical convertibility of p with h had been established, the question of the truth of p would be left hanging in the air until it could be determined whether or not h is a "hypothesis worthy of acceptance" (ὑποθέσεως ἀξίας ἀποδέξασθαι, *Phd.* 92D), which could only be finally done by referring to the axioms.

71 *Pr.* 361B: Socrates holds that all the virtues are knowledge, "insisting" on it (or "urging it," ὡς σὺ σπεύδεις); and *La.* 194D: (Nicias speaking) "I have often heard you say that each of us is good in those things in which he is wise, bad in those in which he is ignorant." For Aristotle this is the crux of Socrates' moral psychology: Cf. T15, T16, and comment on these texts, in chapter 3.

72 There is no foundation for Robinson's view (1953: 116–17), followed by Karasmanis (1987: 85 and 99, n. 24), that the hypothetical procedure ends at 89C. The only reason given for this surprising claim is that "after 89 neither the word 'hypothesis' nor any methodological remark occurs in the dialogue" (Robinson, *loc. cit.*). This is true, but irrelevant. Plato is under no obligation to keep naming the method he is using or making methodological remarks about it.

73 It should be noticed that *only* this segment of the argument is directed against h: the long section, 89D–96C, argues not against h, but against p (its conclusion at 96D10, "Hence virtue is not teachable," is obviously the negation of p). So the inconclusiveness of the reasoning in 89D–96C (there are no teachers of virtue, *ergo* virtue is not teachable – lame argument, from *non esse* to *non posse*), does nothing to discredit h. The attack on h at 96D–98C is a perfectly solid argument, concluding that knowledge is not a necessary condition of right action (T21), from which it follows that knowledge is not necessary for virtue, as Socrates had thought (his theory makes no provision for controlled right action if the relevant knowledge is lacking).

argument is complete. In neither case is it pushed back to end-of-the-line ἀρχαί: Plato's epistemology is still in the making, still heavily programmatic; we can't expect too much all at once.[74] but what we do get in the text is quite enough to show that as between the two arguments, one for *h*, the Socratic doctrine, the other against it, the latter carries the day: Socrates satisfies himself that for governing action aright true belief is as good as knowledge:

T21 *M.* 98B–C: "And isn't this right too: when true opinion governs a course of action what it produces is in no way inferior to what is produced by knowledge? Hence in regard to action true belief is no worse or less beneficial than is knowledge."

When this conclusion is reached a whole row of Socratic dominos will have to fall,[75] including the fundamental conviction that

T6 (above): "The unexamined life is not worth living by man."[76]

For if true opinion without knowledge does suffice to guide action aright, then the great mass of men and women may be spared the pain and hazards of the "examined" life: they may be brought under the protective custody of a ruling elite who will feed them true beliefs to guide their conduct aright, without allowing them to inquire why those beliefs are true. Access to the critical examination of questions of good and evil, right and wrong, may then be reasonably withheld from all but the elite, and even from them until they have finished the mathematical studies which will prepare them for enlightenment (T4 above). So in the *Meno* we see Plato well started on a course that will take him to the other extreme from convictions he had shared with Socrates in the Elenctic Dialogues: the doctrine of the philosopher-king looms ahead.

But if Plato's mathematical studies are to be invoked to explain the fact that the elenctic method, so vibrantly alive in the *Gorgias* and

---

74 It would be reasonable to allow for substantial development between the *Meno* (where the new theory of Forms has not yet been formulated) and the *Phaedo* (where it is presented explicitly as the foundation of Plato's metaphysics: 65Dff., 100Bff.); so too *a fortiori* between the *Meno* and the middle books of the *Republic* (cf. n. 59 above).

75 The break-away from the earlier Socratic view is carried further in the immediate sequel (99B–100A): in the *Gorgias* Socrates had damned Athens' best leaders along with her worst (518C–519A: cf. Vlastos, 1983b: 495ff. at 501). Plato now recognizes Pericles as the "magnificently astute" (1983b: 495ff. 94B) statesman he surely was (Thuc. 2.60.5), allowing now for inspired statesmen (as Socrates had allowed for inspired poets: *Ap.* 22C, *Ion* 534B), who achieve much that is excellent (καλά) by divine dispensation (θείᾳ μοίρᾳ) without benefit of craft or science. (For a different reading of the passage, using vituperation in the *Gorgias* to undercut eulogy in the *Meno*, unwarrantably homogenizing their respective viewpoints, see Bluck, 1961: 368ff.; also Irwin, 1977a: 317, n. 22, rebutted by Kraut, 1984: 301–4.)

76 Cf. the antepenultimate paragraph of the Introduction above.

before it, goes dead in the *Lysis*, *Hippias Major*, and *Euthydemus*, would we not expect that some positive sign of this new preoccupation of Plato's will show up somehow or other *in* those three dialogues – not only after them, in the *Meno*? So we would, and in two of them the expectation is not disappointed.

A clear sign of what we are looking for occurs in the *Hippias Major*. It enters so inconspicuously that its import could easily pass unnoticed (as it in fact has in the scholarly literature).[77] It slips in as one of several examples of a point of logic. Socrates tries to get Hippias to see that there is a sort of attribute such that if each of two things has it in isolation from the other then each may, or may not, also have it when conjoined with the other; and, conversely, such that if things do have it in conjunction, each may or may not have it in disjunction:

T22 *HMa.* 303B–C: "[a] If I am strong and so are you, then both of us are strong. If I am just, and so are you, then both of us are just. And if both of us are just, then so is each of us. Is it similarly true that if I am beautiful and so are you, then both of us are beautiful; and if both of us are, then so is each? Or is it [b] like the case of even numbers: of two numbers which are even when taken together [i.e. when added] each could be an even number or again each could be odd; and again, as in the case of (magnitudes) which are severally irrational, but when taken together[78] may be either rational or irrational (καὶ αὖ ἀρρήτων ἑκατέρων ὄντων τάχα μὲν ῥητὰ τὰ συναμφότερα εἶναι, τάχα δ᾽ ἄρρητα)."

Still on the track of the "What is the *F*?" question for *F* = "beautiful," Socrates is undertaking to determine in which of two classes of attributes this particular *F* falls, identifying the two classes by example. Citing "strong" and "just" as examples of class [a], he proceeds to cast about for examples of class [b]. Whole numbers serve this purpose to perfection: thus from the fact that, $x + y = 10$,

---

77 I know of no previous notice of the fact (which I pointed out in 1985: 26, n. 65) that T22 is "the first clear indication in his corpus that Plato is now abreast of advanced mathematics."

78 I.e. added geometrically, since, as I explained above (n. 56), in Greek mathematics numbers are defined as discrete aggregates ("multitudes of units"), hence irrationals, not qualifying as numbers, are not susceptible of arithmetical addition. But they *are* susceptible of geometrical addition: thus two irrational line-segments may be joined to form a continuous one, segmented only by a dimensionless point. This has not been understood in the scholarly literature: Tarrant (1928: 83) remarks that "the use of the terms here is clearly inaccurate, for two ἄρρητα cannot become ῥητά by addition"; Woodruff (1982: 87) says that "Socrates may be enticing Hippias with a falsehood." (There is no textual foundation for the view [de Strycker, 1937: 317ff; 1941: 25ff.] that Plato is referring to the *product*, rather than the *sum*, of the two quantities: as Knorr [1975: 296, n. 77] points out, "the term συναμφότερος is regular for 'sum'", and ἀμφότερα had just been used in the parallel case of odd numbers having an even sum.)

which is an even number, we cannot tell whether or not x and y are even or odd: two even numbers would yield that sum, and so would a pair of odd ones. This example from elementary arithmetic, familiar even to youngsters, would have sufficed to make the point. Not satisfied with that, Socrates goes on to pick a second example. And where does he find it? In an area which at this time was at the frontier of mathematical research,[79] where only a mathematician, like Hippias, would have any idea of what the talk of "rational" and "irrational" magnitudes is all about. Plato writes with a lordly insouciance for the fact that those technical terms would mystify the layman, and does not deign to explain the theorem to which he is referring (simple enough for one who understands irrationals), namely, that suitably selected pair of irrational magnitudes (say, the segments of the "golden section," produced by cutting a line in "extreme and mean ratio")[80] would have a rational (geometric) sum, while a differently selected pair of irrationals (say, the square roots of 2 and of 3) would have an irrational one. Here again, as in the more complicated geometrical example in the *Meno* (T19 above), Plato gives clear evidence that his mathematical studies have taken him far from the interests and competences of his old teacher.

In the *Euthydemus* he does more of the same, though in a very different way, speaking through young Cleinias:[81]

T23 *Eud.* 290B–C: "No craft whose work is hunting goes further than pursuing and bagging its quarry. When [its] craftsmen have caught what they are after, they are not competent to use it themselves. And while hunters and anglers hand over their catch to cooks, geometricians and astronomers and masters of computation (λογιστικοί) – for they too are hunters: for they are not engaged in creating figures, but in discovering reality[82] – hand over their discoveries to the dialecticians, if they are not altogether stupid, since they themselves know only how to hunt, not how to use, them."

Here Plato names three of the four sciences which will constitute the curriculum of higher studies in book VII of the *Republic* and assures the people who are doing the work in each of them that while they do "discover reality," they are in no position to know what use is best made of their findings: this should be left to the διαλεκτικοί, the

---

79 Cf. additional note 4.2, n. 113.
80 As pointed out in Heath, 1921: 304, with references to Euclid, *Elements* II.11 and XIII.6 (cf. also Heath, 1926: I 137 and III 19). For an additional illustration of suitably selected irrationals having rational or irrational sums see Knorr, 1975: 276.
81 Cf. n. 83 below.
82 οὐ γὰρ ποιοῦσι τὰ διαγράμματα ἕκαστοι τούτων, ἀλλὰ τὰ ὄντα ἀνευρίσκουσιν. My translation is mainly after Cherniss, 1951: 422.

masters of philosophical argument.[83] If Plato is what we know him
to be – a sober, responsible thinker, not given to empty boasting –
he would not be making this extraordinary claim unless he already
felt when he wrote the *Euthydemus* that his own· understanding of
mathematical science had already advanced so far as to entitle him
to appraise the results reached by its experts and to rule on how they
should be used.

Thus in the *Hippias Major* and the *Euthydemus* there is solid, if
tantalizingly brief, evidence for the hypothesis that Plato was
already well advanced in mathematical studies by the time he came
to write those dialogues in which the elenchus goes dead. But in the
Lysis, where the elenchus is equally defunct, there is no allusion to
mathematics at all.[84] Does this present a difficulty for my hypothesis?
Not if we fix in the *Gorgias* as we should, the *terminus post quem* of this
new development in Plato's intellectual life.[85] This dialogue is the
natural turning-point. For while knowledge of advanced mathematics is displayed here no more than in any earlier work of
Plato's,[86] contact with geometry does show up,[87] well-motivated by
the fact that the *Gorgias* can be dated on good internal evidence[88]
soon after Plato's first journey to Syracuse.[89] There, Cicero tells us,

83 At this point Plato must have felt that to credit Socrates with such a task, so alien to the
    purely moral inquiries in which he had been wholly absorbed heretofore in Plato's
    portrayal of him, would place too heavy a strain on the dramatic consistency of the persona
    of the protagonist. So he presents the thought as an inspired fluke, a prompting from
    "higher powers" to a young innocent (291A).

84 Though there is to natural philosophy, paralleling the citation of Heraclitus (DK B82, B83)
    in the *HMa.* (289A–B): Socrates now finds wisdom in the writings of "those who discourse
    on nature and on the universe" *Ly.* 214B). Nothing of the kind happens in the Elenctic
    Dialogues. The nearest thing there to an allusion to natural philosophy is in saying he
    knows nothing "great or small" about such things when protesting the "nonsense" he is
    made to talk as a natural philosopher in the *Clouds* (*Ap.* 19C–D) and then, long after, in the
    last of the Eienctic Dialogues, the reference in the *Gorgias* (507E–508A) to the σοφοί
    (Pythagoreans? cf. Dodds *ad loc.*) who call the whole universe κόσμος because "it is held
    together by community and friendship and order (κοσμιότητα) and justice."

85 Cf. n. 39 above.

86 The description of computation as "investigating how numerous are the odd and the
    even both relative to themselves and relative to each other" (451C), regurgitating *verbatim*
    the one at *Ch.* 166A, does not presuppose advanced knowledge of mathematics: see
    additional note 4.2. Nor does the concurrent description of the subject-matter of astronomy
    as "the movements of the stars and the sun and the moon and of their relative speeds"
    presuppose more than a rudimentary understanding of what is going on in that science.

87 The continued proportion, "as cosmetics is to gymnastics, so is the sophistical to the
    legislative art, and as cookery to medicine, so is rhetoric to justice," is said to be *in the style
    of the geometricians* (εἰπεῖν ὥσπερ οἱ γεωμέτραι, 465C). This is the first time in the sequence
    of Platonic dialogues that Socrates says that he is speaking like the geometricians. The
    second is in the *M.* (T14 above) where he explains his reference to ἐπίπεδον, στερεόν as
    technical terms by saying that he is using the words οἷον ταῦτα τὰ ἐν ταῖς γεωμετρίαις.

88 See the references to Dodds and Irwin at the end of n. 39 above.

89 We have no reliable report of any earlier journey outside the Greek mainland: see
    additional note 4.2.

"he devoted himself to Pythagorean men and studies, spending much time with Archytas of Tarentum and Timaeus of Locri."[90] The latter is a shadowy figure;[91] not so the former. From first-hand evidence preserved in every history of Greek geometry[92] we know that Archytas was a perfectly brilliant mathematician. We know too that he was a leading statesman of his city, a democracy like Athens,[93] elected and re-elected "general" year after year.[94] Here is a new model philosopher for Plato, giving him everything he might have missed in his old one: Socrates had recoiled helplessly from Athenian politics, convinced it was irremediably corrupt. Archytas enters with stunning success the political fray in his own city. And Socrates had recoiled from metaphysics, while Archytas was a master metaphysician in the Pythagorean tradition.[95] Socrates, Xenophon assures us,[96] advised against the study of advanced mathematics, while Archytas was at the forefront of mathematical discovery.[97] If it was this personal association with Archytas that gave the impetus[98] to Plato's mathematical studies, we could hardly expect instant results. To his philosophers in their twenties Plato was

90 *Acad.* 1.10.16. The connection established with Archytas was to enable Plato to "bring about relations of friendship and hospitality" between Archytas and Dionysius II ([Plato], *Ep.* 7, 350A–B: this letter is a good source of information about the events it describes; if Timaeus of Tauromenium [*c.* 356–260 B.C.] "used it in the writing of his history" [Morrow, 1962: 37–9], it was read and thought trustworthy less than a century after Plato's death).

91 We have no information about him independent of Plato's description of the eponymous dialogue's protagonist: "second to none in wealth and birth, had held the highest and most reputable offices in his city and reached the peak of all philosophy" (*Ti.* 20A).

92 His solution of the problem of the duplication of the cube by an elegant construction in three dimensions, as described by Eudemus (DK A14: *ap.* Eutocius, preserved in Archimedes, vol. III.84 of his works [ed. by Heiberg]). For appreciative elucidation of its mathematics see e.g. van der Waerden, 1954: 150–1, writing about it with uninhibited enthusiasm ("Is this not admirable, Archytas must have had a truly divine inspiration when he found this construction").

93 Though a decidedly more conservative one: Aristotle, *Pol.* 1320b9–16.

94 "He held the office of general seven times, though no one else had held it in his city more than once, because the law forbade it" (D.L. 8.79). For his political views see DK 47 B3, comparing τὸ ἶσον ἕξειν here with ἡ ἰσότης ἡ γεωμετρική at *G.* 508A (quoted in part in n. 84 above).

95 Fragments 1, 2, 3 in DK. (For recent defense of the authenticity of fr. 1 see Bowen, 1982: 79ff.; Huffman, 1985: 344ff.)

96 *Mem.* 4.7.2–3: "In the case of geometry he said one should pursue it until one was competent to measure a parcel of land... He opposed carrying the study as far as the hard-to-understand proofs (μέχρι τῶν δυσσυνέτων διαγραμμάτων), though he was not himself unfamiliar with these." For comment see n. 6 in additional note 4.2.

97 He is named as the teacher of Eudoxus in Diogenes Laertius (8.86).

98 This, and exposure to Archytas' philosophical writings, is all we are in a position to assume on the basis of the available evidence. How much of Archytas' philosophical or mathematical thought Plato absorbed at this time we have no way of knowing: see n. 123 in additional n. 4.3, and cf. Knorr, 1975: 89.

to allow all of ten years to become accomplished mathematicians. If
Plato, himself, were coming to this science in his forties, he might
well be allowed an interval of more than that many months to go as
far. The natural place for the *Lysis* is early in that interval, when his
mathematical studies are advancing but have not yet reached so far
as to make him want to go public with this new accomplishment.
Give him another year or so and he will be giving signs of it in those
all-too-brief sallies in the *Hippias Major* and the *Euthydemus* and then
copiously and at deliberate length in the *Meno*.

That Plato's encounter with geometry was to prove no passing
infatuation, but a love-match, a life-long attachment as deep as it
was intense, is not hard to understand. We know how susceptible he
was to beauty. Is any product of the human imagination more
beautiful than are some of the proofs in Euclid? The elenchus is a
messy business by comparison. Still more appealing to him, if that
were possible, would be the epistemic achievement of Greek
geometry and number-theory. These disciplines, with their application to astronomy and harmonics, are the domain in which the
Greek aspiration to scientific knowledge had achieved its most
assured success. Whereas in other areas – natural philosophy,
medicine – there was no stable consensus, all was in controversy,[99]
with brilliant inventions galore, but nothing so settled that it could
not be unsettled by the next strong voice to come along, in
mathematics stable bases (the "elements" of the science) had been
ascertained from which ever new discoveries could be proved,
eliciting agreement among all qualified investigators to be in-
corporated in a common body of knowledge. Here Plato would see
inquirers within reach of a deductive system in which every
statement justifiable by rational argument is derivable from premises
which are "evident to all" (*R.* 510c)[100] – all except talented
cranks[101] – and confer similar indubitability on every conclusion

---

99 To Xenophon it seems a babble of doctrinaire in-fighting, speculative dogmas clashing in
    stark contradictions: "some hold that being is one, others that it is infinitely many; some
    that everything is in flux, others that nothing changes; some that all things are generated,
    others that nothing is generated and nothing perishes" (*Mem.* 1.1.14). Similar disgust with
    such contradictions among the natural philosophers in Isocrates (*Antidosis* 268–9).

100 "...assumptions, treated [by mathematicians] as the self-evident starting-points of
    mathematical deductions," Lloyd, 1979: 114. (I cannot follow the different interpretation
    of this text he adopts in 1983b: 12ff.)

101 Protagoras denying that the tangent meets the circle at (just) one point is not a
    mathematician opting for a finitist geometry, but a contrarian dogmatizing from the
    sidelines. Claims to have squared the circle come not from working geometricians
    (Hippocrates of Chios does not square the circle [cf. Lloyd, 1987a: 103ff.] but lunes
    inscribed in it [Simplicius, *in Phys.* 60.22ff.]), but from eristics or sophists: Bryson (Arist.
    Post. An. 75b40) and Antiphon (Arist. *Phys.* 185a14–17), provoking Aristotle's retort that

drawn therefrom by necessary inference, all of those results constituting necessary statements which, in Aristotle's phrase (*Post. An.* 71b15) "could not be otherwise."

Would it be any wonder if when the groundswell of this triumphant enterprise reached Plato it should sweep him away from his Socratic moorings and start him on the journey from the "Socrates" of the Elenctic Dialogues, in whom disciple and teacher had thought as one, to the "Socrates" of his middle period, pursuing unSocratic projects to antiSocratic conclusions, the great love of his youth still alive in his heart,[102] but his mind no longer in thrall?[103]

it is not the geometrician's business to rebut such claims, "for they are addressed to the many, who do not know what [proof] is, or is not, possible in a particular [subject]" (*Soph. El.* 172a5–7).

102 No dialogue composed before the *Phaedo* records greater depth and intensity of affection.

103 For comments which prompted revision of previous versions of this essay I owe thanks to exceedingly helpful criticisms from John Ackrill, Myles Burnyeat, G. E. R. Lloyd and the late Friedrich Solmsen. For other helpful comments I am indebted to Alexander Nehamas and Nicholas Smith. For residual errors I alone may be held responsible.

5

DOES SOCRATES CHEAT?[1]

That Socrates does not scruple to palm off on his interlocutors – for their own good, of course – premises he considers false or inferences he knows are crooked has been maintained repeatedly by scholars of high repute. E. R. Dodds:[2] "It looks rather as if Plato was content at this stage to let Socrates repay the Sophists in their own coin, as no doubt Socrates often did."[3] Paul Friedländer: Socrates believes that to educate deluded persons "he must resort to dialectical tricks";[4] and he "knows how to deceive better than all the sophists."[5] W. K. C. Guthrie: "Plato lets Socrates make a wickedly sophistical use of ambiguity when he likes."[6] Charles Kahn: Socrates uses "dialectical trickery"[7] to win his argument against Polus in *G.* 474c–475c.[7]

I am not suggesting that such views are now shared by a majority of Platonic scholars. My distinct impression is that quite the contrary is the case. Thus two of the best of recent philosophical commentaries on Socratic dialogues, C. C. W. Taylor's on the *Protagoras* (1976) and T. H. Irwin's on the *Gorgias* (1979),[8] give no quarter to the idea

---

1 In this essay I owe a special debt to Jonathan Barnes. He did me the kindness of reading an earlier draft and making me aware of a serious error in its reasoning which I have now pruned out. To what extent, if any, he agrees with the final product I do not know.

2 1959: 249. He is commenting on *G.* 474c.

3 Following Friedländer (1964: 254), he thinks that the fallacy in the Socratic argument at 474c–475c (to be discussed in section III below) is intentional.

4 1964: 181. He is echoing the view of Socrates whose most forceful formulation may be found in Kierkegaard: "one can deceive a person about the truth, and (remembering old Socrates) one can deceive a person into the truth. Indeed when a person is under an illusion, it is only by deceiving him that he can be brought into the truth" (quoted from Lowrie, 1938: 248, in Vlastos, 1985: n. 71). The same notion occurs, detached from reference to Kierkegaard, in Genet, "Il faut mentir pour être vrai" (quoted by Nigel Williams in *London Review of Books*, 18 May, 1989).

5 1964: 139.   6 1975: 246. Cf. also 143ff.

7 1983: 93. Cf. also the reference to similar views held by Michael O'Brien (1967) in chapter I above, n. 78.

8 Admittedly, in his previous book (1977a: 304–5) Irwin had tried to explain away Socrates' references to "parts of virtue" (*M.* 78D–79c) by maintaining that he "simply allows Meno this view [*sc.* that virtue has parts] to refute him" (in plainer English: pretends to believe

that Socrates resorts to sophistry when it suits his purpose.[9] Neither does the systematic examination – the most comprehensive on record – of the arguments in Plato's earlier dialogues in Gerasimos Santas' *Socrates* (1979). But the notion that Socrates is not above playing the sophist upon occasion dies hard. It keeps cropping up in the scholarly literature. One of the most impressively learned and strongly argued of recent papers, Kevin McTighe's,[10] maintains that Socrates "finds it more efficient to argue fallaciously ... than agree only to what he regards as true or strive for logical cogency."[11] In chapter 1 I made it clear that while I reject this point of view,[12] I do not propose to shrug it off. I started there my confrontation with it by exposing the misconception of Socratic irony which has often inspired it. I return to argue at greater length against it now.

I

The Socrates of my concern is, as before, and always, in this book, a Socrates in Plato[13] – *not* in Xenophon, for in the latter's case the question does not arise. The transparent guilelessness of this other figure, so wholesomely and artlessly straightforward in his philosophical talk, obliterates the problem. If our access to the historical figure had been only *via* Xenophon's hero, none of the scholars who have thought trickery Socrates' stock-in-trade would have believed they had a case. The present essay would have been pointless, for it would have had nothing to refute. What creates the problem is the Socrates of Plato's earlier dialogues – complicated, devious, cunning, and not averse to playing pranks on his interlocutors upon occasion.[14] Does *he* remain always free of resort to deceit? I want to argue that

it to facilitate the refutation). But this was only when he was hard pressed to uphold an untenable thesis despite the plainest evidence to the contrary in Plato's text (see Vlastos, 1981: 421–2; Ferejohn, 1984: 108–9) – a tactic Irwin has never repeated in later work, to my knowledge. See the next note.

9 In 1979 Irwin gives a sound diagnosis (1979: 127) of what causes the appearance of sophistry in a passage like *G.* 460A–C: the argument is "illegitimate" by reason of being "elliptical," not sophistic (there being no reason to believe that the tacit premises were suppressed with the intention of causing deceit.) Surely this is exactly right. For a sane stand on this issue, maintained consistently in his analysis of the Socratic arguments examined in his book, see Crombie, 1962: 26,   10 1984: 193–236.

11 1984: 226. The space accorded to this paper (more than twice the usual) in a journal of severe standards is *prima facie* evidence of its high claim to critical attention. The only published comment on it known to me so far, Roslyn Weiss, 1985: 314ff., refers to it as "a most valuable" article. So it is, in spite of the mistakes I shall be pointing out (nn. 74 and 84 below): it does more than anything published on its topic in the eighties to sharpen up the fundamental issues it pursues.

12 I had taken a strong stand against it already in 1981: see n. 17 below.

13 The "Socrates$_E$" of chapter 2.

14 The most elaborate of them, *Pr.* 339Aff., will be discussed directly in the text below.

he always does *when arguing seriously*: this is the all-important qualification. And we do have a way of telling when it applies. He tells us plainly when high seriousness may be expected from him no less than from his interlocutor:

T1 *G.* 500B–C: "By the god of friendship, Callicles, you mustn't think that you may play with me and say whatever comes into your head, contrary to your real opinion, nor, conversely, must you think of me as jesting. For you see what our discussions are all about – and is there anything about which a man of even small intelligence would be more serious than this: *what is the way we ought to live?*"

This is the touchstone of Socratic seriousness. When engaged in elenctic argument, searching for the right way to live, he is in dead earnest – as much so as anyone could be about anything at any time. In the *Apology* he represents the search as obedience to the command of god:

T2 *Ap.* 28E: "The god has ordered me, as I supposed and believed,[15] to live philosophizing, examining myself and others."[16]

He holds it up accordingly as the most sacred of all his obligations, overriding every other, even that of a loyal Athenian to obey the sovereign authority of his city's legal commands, giving fair notice that if the city were to order him to desist from his philosophizing he would disobey:

T3 *Ap.* 29D: "Athenians, I cherish and love you. But I shall obey the god rather than you."

So this is my claim: *when Socrates is searching for the right way to live, in circumstances in which it is reasonable for him to think of the search as obedience to divine command,*[17] his argument cannot involve wilful untruth. For elenctic argument is the very process on which he depends to test the truth of his own convictions about the right way to live, no less than those of his interlocutor:

T4 *Ch.* 166C–D: "How could you think that I would refute you for any reason other than the one for which I would search myself, fearing lest I

15 The import of this phrase will be pursued in chapter 6. It does not affect the present discussion.
16 The last clause is repeated at *Ap.* 38A, "discoursing daily on virtue and all those other things you hear me discuss, examining myself and others."
17 I am tying down a loose thread in an earlier essay (1981: 223, n. 5) where I denied "that Socrates would ever (knowingly, and in a serious vein) assert categorically a false premise or endorse a fallacious argument." What had been left unclear there is how we can tell whether or not Socrates *is* speaking "in a serious vein" in any given passage in Plato. The words I have italicized in the text above tell us how.

might inadvertently think I know something, when I don't know it? And this, I say, is what I am doing now: I examine the argument chiefly for my own sake, though no doubt also for the sake of my friends."[18]

To cheat his partners in this search would be to sabotage the process by which he hopes to discover moral truth himself; to cheat his interlocutors would be to cheat himself. I want to argue that such a thing could not happen within the limits of Plato's characterization of Socrates.[19] But first I want to turn the spotlight on what can and does happen at other times in an elenctic dialogue when Socrates is *not* "philosophizing, examining himself and others."

II

A longish section of the *Protagoras* – 338E–348A, nearly a seventh of the whole dialogue – portrays Socrates, engaging in a contest with the great sophist on the correct interpretation of a poem by Simonides. He treats the encounter as an out-and-out fight, a boxing match (T5 below). Maneuvered into it by Protagoras, he enters it reluctantly; but once in it he does everything he can to win. He plays the game in the spirit of that saying often quoted by semi-literates, a favorite of certain football coaches and of a late unlamented President of the U.S.: "Winning isn't everything; it is the only thing."[20] A smart opening move by Protagoras, greeted with loud applause from the bystanders, devastates our Socrates:

T5 *Pr.* 339E: "When he said this and the others cheered loudly, it felt like a body-blow from a fine boxer. I felt giddy and things got dark."

To recover from the set-back he tries a brazen maneuver and succeeds in pulling it off: he has the effrontery to claim[21] that when the poet says "it is hard to be good" he is using "hard" ($\chi\alpha\lambda\epsilon\pi\acute{o}\nu$) to mean "bad" – a willful travesty of the poet's meaning, for which he nonetheless manages to win support[22] by wheedling endorsement for it from a distinguished member of the company, Prodicus, master of the "correct use of words."[23]

18 It has been maintained that while Socrates thought his dialectic "the best method for educating others to think for themselves, he did not consider it a method of discovering truth for himself (Gulley, 1968: 67). How so if he pursues it "chiefly for his own sake"? Cf. also *G.* 453A1–4; 457E3–458B3; 505E–506C3.
19 A Kierkegaardian Socrates who outsophists the sophists (cf. nn. 3 and 4 above) is perfectly conceivable. But he would not be *Plato's* Socrates.
20 Those who quote it appear to be unaware of its logical import: its second clause belies its first; if winning "is the only thing" then it *is* "everything."
21 For the moment (341A–B). A few lines later (341D) he will be welshing on the claim, saying he made it only to test Protagoras.   22 341B–C.   23 ὀρθοέπεια. Cf. *Phdr.* 267C.

Socrates then goes off on a tongue-in-cheek digression (342A–343C). Its theme is that Sparta, whose culture everyone knows to be militarist to the bone, obsessively traditionalist, xenophobic, and anti-intellectual, was doing more than any other Greek state to foster philosophy.[24] Returning to his exegesis of the poem of Simonides after spinning out this pseudo-historical extravaganza, he resumes his manhandling of the text, torturing crypto-Socratic wisdom out of it, claiming, for instance, that in the following verses, "But all who do no baseness willingly / I praise and cherish," the punctuation should connect "willingly" with "I praise and cherish" instead of with "all who do no baseness"[25] because, forsooth, all wise men know the truth of the Socratic paradox that no one does wrong willingly,[26] hence the wise Simonides would have known that doing no baseness willingly is only to be expected from everyone, hence has no special claim to be "praised and cherished."

It can hardly be disputed that throughout this performance Socrates is pulling the wool over his hearers' eyes.[27] What is his game? Irony, certainly, but irony put to a very special use: mockery elaborately played out in sly concealment of its mocking intent. As I pointed out in chapter 1 above, irony is in its own nature innocent of deceit – so much so that it is *impossible* to use the ironical mode to deceive if the hearer is aware of its irony. But if we do want to use it to deceive we need only conceal the ironical intention. Is there any difficulty about that? Surely not. Other modalities of speech announce themselves. Thus English casts questions in a distinctive syntactical form. But even that is not foolproof. If we so choose, we can use interrogative grammar to indicative effect: we can say, "Did you, by any chance, make off with that book of mine?" to reproach someone for having done just that. In the case of irony grammar prescribes no special syntax. To give direct notice of it we must resort to extra-linguistic signalling like winking or making a face or shifting to another tone of voice. If we prefer to speak in deadpan the irony must be divined from the content of what is said or from its context. These are fragile matters, easily manipulated to contrive deceitful

24 It is sad to see the spoof mistaken for *confessio fidei* and cited as evidence of Socrates' laconism (Stone, 1988: 126ff.).

25 Cf. the comment in Adam & Adam, 1905: *ad loc.*, on this move: "it is only by the most perverse sophistry that Socrates reads [his own doctrine] into Simonides, ignoring entirely the words ἀνάγκη δ' οὐδὲ οἱ θεοὶ μάχονται."

26 No clearer, sharper, enunciation can be found in the Platonic corpus than the one Socrates smuggles into his mock-interpretation of Simonides' poem at *Pr.* 345D–E. For reassurance that this *is* what Socrates believes cf. *Ap.* 25E–26A and *G.* 509E5–7 (quoted as T19 below).

27 Particularly in the case of Hippias, not the least astute member of the group: Plato leaves us in no doubt that he is taken in (note especially what he is made to say at 347A6–7).

concealment. So they are by Socrates in this section of the *Protagoras* and at its end he lets us see that this was what he has been doing all along and why he chose to do it.

The debate on the poem had been wished on him by Protagoras, who had explained his rationale for it as follows:

T6 *Pr.* 348E: (Protagoras speaking) "In my view expertise in matters affecting poetry is the most important part of a man's culture. It consists in the ability to discern which poetic sayings are correct, which are not, and to tell them apart, giving reasons when asked."

People in that company who knew their Socrates, would feel him bridling at this pronunciamento, since to poetic exegesis Socrates gives bottom place, if even that, in moral culture – the only sort of culture that matters for him.[28] So when Alcibiades hears Socrates say poker-faced that it is bad to be good he knows that someone's leg is being pulled. But others in the company who are not in the know would be easily fooled. No signal of irony would come across to them from the wild constructions Socrates puts on Simonides' verse.[29] Nor would they have any sure way of knowing that the tall tale about the Spartans was a spoof. Only at the end of his long speech does Socrates give away the information from which his hearers, if they had the wit, could figure out that he had been putting on an act. For only then does he let on that he thinks the whole of the debate on what Simonides did, or didn't, mean had been an exercise in triviality, a complete waste of time, and a tasteless one – the sort of thing, he says, which only "dull and vulgar" people do at their drinking-parties: too uncultivated to entertain each other by intellectual talk, they hire educated whores to produce the entertainment:

T7 *Pr.* 347D: "But when the drinkers are *kaloi kagathoi* you'll find no hired females piping or dancing or chanting for them. They are quite capable of enjoying their own company without such stuff-and-nonsense, using their own voices in sober discussion, speaking and listening in turn."

He is protesting as a cop-out the shift out of question-and-answer

---

28 Cf. his use of παιδεία quasi-synonymously with δικαιοσύνη in *G.* 470E (discussed as T21 in chapter 8 below): Socrates would not call even the great king "happy" without knowing how he stands "in culture and justice." Note also the strongly moral connotations of παιδεία in the description of the wicked tyrant as ἄγριος καὶ ἀπαίδευτος at 510B.

29 As Friedländer (1964: 24–5) remarks, "the Socratic interpretation [of the poem] is as arbitrary as the sophistic and even surpasses it, in fact, in the consistency with which the speaker misinterprets the text." Hippias would not have commented so favorably on the interpretation (offering to match it in an epideictic speech of his own, 347A6–B2) if he had so much as suspected that the exegesis had been a spoof.

argument into poetic exegesis which Protagoras had instigated. He is allowing his hearers to infer that his part in it had been a labored joke. Trapped into it, he had played the fool to make fools of those who took it seriously.

Shorter extra-elenctic Socratic capers are scattered all through Plato's earlier dialogues in hyperbolic compliments to interlocutors and mock-anguished laments over his own ignorance and stupidity. He implores Euthyphro to take him on as a pupil (5A, 5C) so he may learn at last the nature of piety which had eluded him all his life. He bewails his fate when Euthyphro hurries off to another engagement:

T8 *Eu.* 15E: "Alas, my friend, will you leave me in despair? You have dashed my great hope of learning from you what is and isn't pious so that I may clear myself of Meletus' indictment..."

He pleads with Thrasymachus, "all a-tremor":

T9 *R.* 336E–337A: "Thrasymachus, don't be hard on us. Do realize that if we went astray in our discussion our mishap was involuntary... You must believe we are in earnest, my friend, but that the task is beyond our powers. It would be more seemly for you clever people to pity us than to be angry at us..."

He assures another sophist:

T10 *H. Mi.* 372A–B: "Hippias, you see I spoke the truth when I said[30] I was pertinacious in questioning wise men. And I think that this is my only good point, for I am full of defects and am always getting things wrong. My deficiency is proved to me by the fact that when I associate with one of you whose wisdom all Greece attests, it becomes evident that I know nothing."[31]

This is his characteristic irony[32] laid on thick. Is it meant to deceive his hearers? Adlai Stevenson used to say that flattery won't hurt you if you don't inhale it. He might have added that it won't deceive you either. If Hippias & Co. are so blind to the mockery in Socrates' praise, it is because they are already wallowing in self-deceit. If they did not think those compliments their just due, they would have had no trouble seeing through their hype. Socrates is not setting out to produce in them this deluded state of mind. Finding them deep in it

30 At 369D–E, where his self-deprecatory remarks had begun.
31 Translation adapted from Jowett's. For more on the *Hippias Minor* see additional note 5.1.
32 Which Thrasymachus misunderstands as "shamming" (cf. chapter 1, comment on the text cited there as T1), while Alcibiades refers to it, more discerningly, as "that extremely ironical way he always uses, very characteristic, his habitual manner (μάλα εἰρωνικῶς καὶ σφόδρα ἑαυτοῦ τε καὶ εἰωθότως)" (cf. the comment on the text cited as T9 in chapter 1 and the extended argument in that chapter for the claim that εἰρωνεία, εἰρωνικῶς must be read quite differently in the two texts).

already, he plays along, doling out to them extra-elenctic paregoric to induce them to submit to painful elenctic surgery.

III

Now let us get back on the main track where Socrates is not playing games, ironic or therapeutic, but engaged in the most serious business of his life, searching for the right way to live. I shall review two arguments he uses in that process.[33] Thought by several scholars to employ trickery,[34] the first has been much discussed in the recent literature. It has been investigated in detail no less than nine times within the last twenty-five years.[35] Though I have found many of these discussions helpful,[36] my greatest debt by far is to the ones by Irwin and by Santas. Each of them, without reference to work by the other,[37] puts his finger on the exact point at which Plato's argument goes fatally wrong, committing a fallacy which would have vitiated the whole argument even if everything else in it were flawless. This is no small achievement of the critical intelligence, considering that, to my knowledge, it is reached for the first time since the *Gorgias* was written, some 2,400 years ago.[38] Retaining as much of my previously published analysis of the argument as I still find sound, incorporating it into the one I offer here, I shall also use freely, without further acknowledgement, everything I have learned from subsequent comment on the passage in the scholarly literature.[39]

The thesis Socrates undertakes to prove to Polus in this section of the *Gorgias* (474B–475C) is at the heart of his vision of the good life. It is that he who commits injustice inflicts upon himself a greater injury than on the one he wrongs. Let us ponder this for a moment. Imagine someone living under a brutal dictatorship, accused of a

33 Exhaustive rebuttal of the view I am opposing would have required similar case-by-case analysis of a score or more of Socratic arguments – that is to say, a book all to itself. The best I can offer within the limits of the present book is a discussion of two major ones, either of which would otherwise constitute a crushing refutation of my thesis.

34 Cf. nn. 3 and 7 above.

35 By Friedländer, 1964: 256–7; Dodds, 1959: 249; Vlastos, 1967: 454–60; Santas, 1979: 233–46; MacKenzie, 1981: 179–81 and 241–4; Kahn, 1983: 84–97.

36 If I were more concerned with the minutiae of scholarship in this book, I would have found it mandatory to go through all of them, assessing in detail their respective merit. This would have required an essay no shorter than the whole of the present chapter. I leave the task to some graduate student aspiring to the Ph.D.

37 Irwin had no occasion for such reference: Santas had not yet discussed this particular argument in published work. Irwin's earlier discussion of the passage (1973, his Princeton dissertation) was known to Santas (it is listed in his bibliography); to what extent, if any, he may be indebted to it I cannot judge.   38 But see n. 57 below.

39 And I shall also use what I have learned in correspondence with Jonathan Barnes: cf. n. 1 above.

political crime, who saves himself by incriminating falsely a friend, whereupon the latter is apprehended and tortured, coming out of the ordeal a broken man to die soon after, while the accuser, well rewarded by the regime, lives on to a healthy and prosperous old age. Socrates is claiming that the perpetrator of this outrage has damaged his own happiness more than his victim's. Has any stronger claim been ever made by a moral philosopher? I know of none.

Here is the reasoning by which Socrates purports to prove[40] it to Polus, who admits (474c5–9) that doing injustice is "uglier" (αἴσχιον)[41] than suffering it, but finds the claim that it is "worse" (κάκιον) preposterous (473E). The reasoning falls into two parts. I start with a translation of part 1.[42]

TII G. 474D–475B: "In the case of all beautiful things (πάντα τὰ καλά), e.g. bodies, colors, figures, sounds, practices – don't you call them 'beautiful' with an eye to something?[43] Thus [a] in the case of beautiful bodies to begin with: don't you call them 'beautiful' either on account of their benefit for some purpose or because of a certain pleasure (κατὰ ἡδονήν τινα), if they delight their beholder in beholding them? In the case of the beauty of bodies can you mention anything further besides these two things?... [b] And thus also in the case of all the others?[44] Don't you call both figures and colors 'beautiful' because of some pleasure or some benefit or both?... [c] Doesn't this hold likewise (ὡσαύτως) for sounds and everything else pertaining to music?... [d] And surely also in regard to laws and practices: neither in their case does beauty fall beyond this, namely, benefit or pleasure?... [e] And doesn't the same hold for the beauty of fields of learning?... "

f(i)[45] "So when one of two beautiful things is the more beautiful, it must be so by surpassing in one or the other or both of these things: pleasure or benefit or both?... And [f(ii)] when one of two ugly things is the uglier, must it not be so by surpassing in pain or in evil?"

Let us examine this part of the argument from Polus' point of view. Premises [a], [b], [c] should cause him no trouble whatever, provided that a certain qualification, which Socrates makes expressly

40 Is this too strong for what he thinks he is doing? By no means. Looking back on the present argument he says to Polus: "Was it not proved (ἀποδέδεικται) that what I maintained is true?" (referring, in part, to his claim that "he who does wrong is always more miserable than he who is wronged").

41 Or "more shameful," "more disgraceful" (Woodhead, Irwin, Zeyl), "plus laid" (Robin), "plus vilain' (Canto).   42 Virtually the same as the one I used in 1967.

43 We should note at this point that the criterion "with an eye to which" we classify things as beautiful is meant to cover *all* five of the examples he proceeds to list, be they sensibly apprehensible, as in the case of the first three, or only intellectually discernible, as in the case of the fourth and fifth.

44 καὶ τἆλλα πάντα οὕτω, all of the examples he had mentioned: cf. the preceding note.

45 The conclusion (ἄρα) from premises [a], [b], [c], [d], [e].

in premise [a], is understood – as it should be from the wording in the text – to carry over into premises [b] and [c] as well. Bodies are said to be beautiful in premise [a] if (and only if) they are beneficial for their respective purpose or if they give *the viewer* "a certain pleasure" *in viewing them*. I italicize to indicate the qualification, which we know Socrates considers vital: in the *Hippias Major* (298D–299B) it is made completely clear that he does not consider the pleasurableness of an object of experience a sufficient condition of its beauty; to the suggestion that it might be, he presents what he considers a lethal counter-example: sexual gratification (τἀφροδ-ίσια), he observes, which everyone would count extremely pleasurable, is "ugliest to view (αἴσχιστον ὁρᾶσθαι)."

There can be no reasonable doubt that the same qualification is understood to apply to the pleasure we derive from beautiful figures and colors in premise [b] and then again *mutatis mutandis* pleasure from beautiful sounds and other elements of music as well in premise [c]. A close reading of the text should convince anyone that this is indeed what is meant. It is only for stylistic reasons that the phrase "because of a certain pleasure if they delight their beholder in beholding them" is not repeated in [b] or reproduced in a suitable variant in [c]: because the pace is quick and Socrates clips his sentences, reducing verbal baggage to the minimum. A second look at the text will show that when he says in premise [b] "and so too in the case of all the other things" he does expect the sense of the omitted phrase to be supplied from premise [a], thereby specifying as before the import of the qualifying pronoun in "because of a certain pleasure" (διὰ ἡδονήν τινα): that "certain" pleasure is evidently, once again, that which the viewer derives from viewing the object. The same thing, with a verb for hearing substituted for "viewing" must be meant to be understood in premise [c] to fill out the meaning of "likewise" (ὡσαύτως): the indicated parallelism would fail unless the pleasure to be had from beautiful sounds – melodies, rhythms, etc. – were derived just from hearing them, as distinct from some further use to which they might be put (giving consolation to mourners at a funeral, inducing erotic rapture, rousing the martial fervor of troops, or whatever).

Suppose now that, instead of going on to pile up more premises in the epagoge, Socrates were to draw its conclusion from [a], [b], [c]. To cover in the same way the beauty of "laws and practices" and of "fields of learning" along with the beauty of bodies, figures, colors, sounds, he would have needed in place of [f(i)] and [f(ii)] above some such formula as [f*(i)] When one of two beautiful things is the more beautiful must it not be so because it surpasses in pleasure or benefit or both *for one who contemplates it*? [f*(ii)] When one of two ugly things is the uglier must it not be so by surpassing in pain *for one who contemplates it*?[46]

Polus could have accepted this with perfect security: the admission would have been as harmless to his case as is that of the Socratic premises from which [f*(ii)] would be drawn. Nor could Socrates himself object to it, since it remains scrupulously faithful to his first three premises.[47] The difference from [b], and consequently also from [c], is nonetheless considerable: instead of pleasure/pain without qualification at [b] and [c], we have in [f*] pleasure/pain enjoyed by one who apprehends sensuously or views mentally an object or event.

This would make all the difference to the sequel in the elenchus, beginning with the first question Socrates springs on Polus in part 2 of the reasoning:

T12 *G.* 475C1-3: "First of all then let us consider if doing wrong is more painful than being wronged, and who are the ones who suffer the greater pain: those who do wrong or those who suffer it?"

When the question is put in this way – "Is wrongdoing more painful for the wrongdoer than for the wrongsufferer?" – it pretty well answers itself: if X wrongs Y with impunity,[48] Y will naturally suffer the greater pain. And if [f] (which puts no strings on who is to have the pleasure/benefit in the defining condition it lays down for the use of "beautiful" and who is to have the pain/evil in its defining condition for the use of "ugly") has been admitted as the agreed-upon understanding for the use of "beautiful" and "ugly," Polus would not be entitled to object to the cast of Socrates' question in T12. [f] would indeed empower one to settle which of two happenings is the uglier by inquiring which of the two causes greater pain without specifying *to whom*, thus making it entirely legitimate for Socrates to put the question as he does in T12, asking if doing wrong causes greater pain than being wronged *to those who do wrong or those who suffer it*. But if [f*] had been the agreed-upon understanding for the use of "beautiful" and "ugly," the question Socrates would have had to ask at T12 would be, "Which of the two causes the

---

46 Acceptable Greek for the italicized phrase would be: τοὺς ὁρῶντας ἢ ἀκούοντας ἢ θεωροῦντας.

47 As should be clear even from the suggested phrasing of [f*] in the preceding note: θεωρῶ, used in its primary sense of "seeing" in [a], can also carry (and often does, not only in Plato and Aristotle, but also in the orators and Epicurus: examples in LSJ, *s.v.*), the extended sense of "mental viewing," "contemplating," and I have put it to this use in the above formula for [f*].

48 That the wrongdoer has things his own way, escaping punishment or rebuff, is the presupposition of the whole discussion.

greater pain *to those who observe or contemplate* what happens to each of those concerned?" Would one who views the event in the example I used above be more pained at the thought of someone saving his skin by causing an innocent man's ruin than at that of his betrayed friend's catastrophic misfortune? And if *this* is to be the question, the answer to it is indeterminate.[49] Hence Socrates' argument would be stopped dead in its tracks at this point.

If, on the other hand, we were asking, as [f] would license Socrates to ask, "Which represents the greater pain to the directly affected person, the villain's success or the victim's disaster?" we would certainly be entitled to slant the question the way Socrates does, thereby assuring the answer he wants, "The latter, of course, would be more painful (to the victim) than would the former (to the villain, who could hardly be expected to suffer any pain at all)"; and Socrates' argument can then roll on as it does in the text. Let us follow its further course.

This is what it comes to, when excess verbiage is pruned out:

(1) Doing wrong is not more painful than suffering it (475C2–3: this is T13 above, its second question, rephrased affirmatively).[50]
(2) Doing wrong is either more painful or worse[51] than suffering it (475C4–5: this is [f] above, suitably rephrased). Ergo
(3) Doing wrong is worse than suffering it (475C8: follows directly from 2, given 1).

Here we have an impeccable inferential sequence. If Polus agrees to (1) and (2) he has no option but to grant (3). Has he then been refuted? Has it been "demonstrated"[52] to him that when one man wrongs another what he does is worse *for the wrongdoer* than it is *for his victim*? Anyone tempted to assent had best take another look at (2): we have seen the indeterminateness in "more painful," leaving us with the unanswered question, "More painful *for whom*?" Is the other disjunct, "more evil," any more determinate? Does (2) answer the question, "More evil *for whom*?"? Obviously not. By the same

---

49 Both are extremely painful to contemplate. Who is to say which is the more painful of the two? In my treatment of this point in 1967, I argued for a stronger answer to the question – *sc.* that the normal viewer is likely to find the wrongful benefit to the miscreant more disturbing than the undeserved damage to his victim. I now see that to press this answer against objectors (Guthrie, Santas, Kahn, Mackenzie) would be a waste of time since the weaker answer I adopt above is quite sufficient for the only thing that matters in this context – the correct analysis of the Socratic argument.

50 And stated in a disarmingly conservative way. On the premises Socrates could have said not just that successful wrongdoing is not more painful than suffering wrong but that it is distinctly less so: all too often not painful at all.

51 I avoid the translation of "more evil" for κακῷ ὑπερβάλλον since "evil" is more heavily freighted with moral connotations (unintended in this context) than is κακός "bad" in Greek.   52 *G.* 479E8.

token neither does (3) answer the question, "*for whom* is doing wrong worse than suffering it?" and so long as *that* question is still unanswered in the way it would have to be, to prove Socrates' great thesis, "worse *for the wrongdoer*," Socrates has not advanced an inch towards his objective. What he has to prove is that *the wrongdoer himself* – not somebody or other, the victim or the community at large – suffers more evil than does his victim, because of his wrongdoing. To warrant this conclusion, the premises in the sequence {1, 2, 3} would have had to read instead:

(1*)   Doing wrong is not more painful *for the wrongdoer* than is suffering wrong *for the victim*.
(2*)   Doing wrong is either more painful or worse *for the wrongdoer* than is suffering it *for the victim*. Ergo.
(3*)   Doing wrong is worse *for the wrongdoer* than is suffering it *for the victim*.

Look at the starred propositions, compare them with their unstarred counterparts, and ask yourself: Does what Socrates says in the text at T11 above warrant the substitution of {1*, 2*} for {1, 2}, and consequently that of (3*) for (3)? The substitution of (1*) for (1) is perfectly unproblematic since (1*) is innocuous: who would care to dispute it? But what about the next substitution? What has been offered in T11 to support the claim in (2*) that wrongdoing is more painful or worse *for the wrongdoer than for the wrong sufferer*? Nothing, once it is realized that [f], the conclusion in T11, was itself invalidly deduced from its own premises. If to remedy that error we had substituted [f*] for [f] it would be transparently clear that T11 thus amended could offer no support for (2*): its deduction from the amended premises would be a flagrant *non sequitur*.

Here then is a thoroughly unsound argument. How account for its presence in Plato's text? There are two possibilities. One is that he does not realize that the argument is faulty and puts it into Socrates' mouth believing that it is correct and sufficient to produce an elenctic refutation of Polus' thesis. The other is that, on the contrary, Plato understands that the argument is defective and represents Socrates as using it nonetheless because it is plausible enough to fool Polus and it will be good for Polus to believe that Socrates' thesis is true and soundly deduced from true premises. Consider both possibilities, inquiring which of the two offers the simplest explanation of the presence of the argument in Plato's text.

The first focuses on the fact that in this argument Socrates is represented as working with elliptical expressions for what he means, drawing inferences which are perfectly valid for what is *said* in this abbreviated form, though invalid for what is *meant*. If we were to take the argument as laid out in the text, T11, T12 above, and the inferential sequence {1, 2, 3} above, viewing the latter in abstraction from what the argument is meant to prove, treating its predicates as uninterpreted constants in a sentential calculus, we would get a logically tight deduction: the conclusion at (3) would follow impeccably from its premises, {1, 2}. The unsoundness of the argument shows up only when we substitute starred for unstarred sentences, the unstarred ones being clipped versions of the starred ones, the latter adding content which is not warranted by what is said in the text, and is critically essential to produce the conclusion which establishes Socrates' thesis. And the plausibility of the substitution of starred for unstarred counterparts is extreme, for the difference is one which Socrates would have had the strongest temptation to regard as only a stylistic matter, not affecting the substance of the thought.

I must emphasize this last point, for no attention has been paid to it in discussions of the argument in the literature. For Socrates to say (3) when (3*) is *exactly what he means* – using the former as though it were merely an abbreviated way of saying the latter[53] – is not exceptional. It is what he does throughout the whole of his argument with Polus.[54] Read through it and see if you can find even a single point at which Socrates spells out his great claim in the form of (3*). You will not.[55] It is always in the abbreviated form of (3), though there can be no reasonable doubt that (3*) is what he means: the context makes this unambiguously clear, as e.g. in the immediate follow-up to the argument:

53 Cf. the parallel use of abbreviations elsewhere in the *Gorgias*: ἃ δοκεῖ αὐτῷ ("what he thinks") at 467A–B and 468D as a contraction for ἃ δοκεῖ αὐτῷ βέλτιστα εἶναι ("what he thinks *best*") and οἰόμενοι βέλτιον εἶναι ("believing that it is better") at 468B as a contraction for οἰόμενοι ἄμεινον εἶναι ἡμῖν ("believing that it is better *for ourselves*"); cf. n. 71 below, and n. 14 in chap. 8.

54 He was doing it even before the argument started: already at 469B8–9 he is maintaining that "doing injustice is the greatest of evils," which entails that it is a greater evil than suffering it (and cf. the back-reference to this passage at 473A4–5: "in the foregoing I said that doing injustice is worse than suffering it"); and here the answer to the question "greatest of evils *for whom*?" is unambiguously clear: Socrates is announcing the paradoxical thesis that if he had to choose between doing injustice and suffering it himself he would prefer the latter (469C1–2), clearly implying that "doing injustice is the greatest of evils" is meant to be completed by "*for the one who does it*." So it is clear that when the phrase used at 473A4–5 is picked up again at 474B8 to serve as the refutand of our argument, "worse" here is meant as a contraction for "*worse for the one who does it than for the one who suffers it*."

55 Only later, when restating what he thinks had been established, does Socrates restate the conclusion in a way which makes it unambiguously clear that he takes [?*] to be the outcome: "that he who commits injustice is always more miserable than he who suffers it (ἀεὶ τὸν ἀδικοῦντα τοῦ ἀδικουμένου ἀθλιώτερον εἶναι)," i.e. that committing injustice is always worse *for the one who commits it* than is suffering it *for the one who suffers it* (479E).

T13 *G.* 475D4–E1: "Then would you choose *the worse* and the uglier in preference to what is less so?...Would any man?... So I spoke the truth when I said that neither I nor you nor any other man would rather do injustice than suffer it: for *it is worse.*"

He asks, "Would you choose the *worse*?" and concludes "for *it is worse*"; and here no one could doubt that what he means, duly spelled out, would be: "Would you choose what would be worse for you *if you were committing the injustice instead of suffering it*?"[56] Plato evidently feels that the shortened form of the question he puts into his text is so clear by itself that it would be superfluous to add all those extra words to make it clear. And since he is a master of prose style, who are we to tell him he is writing faulty Greek? If he wants to treat those extra words as pleonastic, he has a perfect right to do so. The omissions would be blameless if they did not trip up his reasoning in an unguarded moment, resulting in an error which is glaring once it has been pointed out, but so insidious that it went unnoticed for two and a half millennia, passing undetected until very recently through the hands of many generations of commentators,[57] including some who were particularly sensitive to matters of logic, as in the case of A. E. Taylor,[58] a learned Platonist who had been abreast of developments in modern logic bearing on the analysis of arguments in Plato's text;[59] his paraphrase of our argument in the *Gorgias* (pp. 113–14) betrays no suspicion that it falls short of cogency at any point. The same thing keeps happening half a century later: five years after the publication of Irwin's and Santas' discussions, R. E. Allen's account of the argument[60] regurgitates its fallacy in all innocence.

So this is one way to account for the presence of this rotten argument in the noble pages of the *Gorgias*: Plato's Socrates has made a slip. He is human, like the rest of us, and when he uses elliptical expressions as counters in a line of reasoning he may be led astray, slipping into inferential error. Now let us consider the

---

56 Parallel abbreviations are made with the like insouciance elsewhere in the *Gorgias*: cf. n. 52 above.

57 I know of only a single honorable exception – the one to which Irwin (1979: 158) calls attention *ad loc.*: George Grote (1865: II 107–10). He asks the right questions ("More beautiful to whom?" "Greater hurt to whom?") though he does not undertake the analysis that would be needed to show in detail how they affect the validity of the reasoning.

58 1937 (4th edition; first published in 1926, 3rd edition 1929).

59 In his "Parmenides, Zeno, and Socrates" (in *Philosophical Studies* [London, 1934], 28ff.). Taylor had transformed the diagnosis of Plato's Third Man Argument by spotting in it the use of "predicates predicable of themselves," which Russell had used in his analysis of logical paradoxes (Russell, 1933, at pp. 80 and 100ff., of the second edition).

60 1984: 204–5.

alternative hypothesis.[61] We are to suppose that Socrates is represented as well aware of the argument's invalidity, using the crooked reasoning nonetheless to fool Polus.[62] Charles Kahn argues for this thesis with incomparable skill. But he offers no help in understanding how such behavior would be consonant with Plato's conception of his master's character and activity as a philosopher.[63] For certainly Plato does not represent Socrates as playing games with Polus:

T14 *G*, 462C–D: "For the things we are disputing are hardly trivial but, as one might say, things which to know is noblest, not to know most base. For their sum and substance is just this: to know or not to know who is happy and who is not."

Polus has just been told[64] that when this most solemn of all themes is in dispute only one mode of refutation counts – the one that will "compel"[65] him to witness to the truth of the Socratic view which identifies the happy man with the virtuous one. Could Socrates be represented as saying this while intending to extract that "witness" from Polus by tricks? Could we be expected to think of Socrates as "examining" Polus (i.e. making Polus aware of contradictions in his beliefs) and "examining" himself thereby (i.e. allowing Polus the fullest opportunity to spot inconsistency in Socrates' own thinking which had escaped his notice heretofore) – getting results such as these by fooling his opponent? Resorting to deception in that procedure would be throwing dust in Polus' eyes, effectively ruining whatever hope Socrates might have had of giving to him or getting from him this kind of help.

To be sure Polus is represented as a dismal character, leeringly envious of the tyrant's high estate, undeterred by the foul crimes through which that success had been won. But would Socrates see in this a good reason for deceiving him? That *Polus* would not scruple to deceive Socrates goes without saying. But would Socrates? *He*

---

61 Its best defense in the scholarly literature is Charles Kahn's discussion of our passage (1983: 87–92).

62 I had faced that possibility in my earlier, less successful, examination of the argument (1967: 459), and answered it decisively in the negative. Referring to what Socrates says at 475E–476A, I had remarked: "It would have been a mockery of Socrates to put such words into his mouth if Plato had not thought them warranted by the facts. So Plato himself misjudged the facts which he depicted."

63 Kahn speaks of "the sense of awe before Socrates' personality" (1983: 116) Plato makes us feel. How so, if Socrates is portrayed as supporting his great thesis by fraudulent means?

64 472B–C. He will be assured of the same thing again at 473E–474B.

65 Cf. ἀναγκασθῆναι ὁμολογεῖν in the retrospective reference to the dialogue with Polus at 509D–E. Earlier on (472B) Socrates had taunted Polus for failing to "compel" him to "witness" to Polus' thesis.

does not believe in returning harm for harm[66] – and to deceive Polus in this argument would certainly be to harm him by aggravating his moral befuddlement, duping him into thinking those delusive inferences secure foundation for a tremendous moral truth. How could Plato have thought of Socrates as thus breaching his own precept and still remembered him, as he does in the closing words of the *Phaedo*, as "the wisest and *most just*" of all those he had ever come to know? If Plato had thought of Socrates as cheating Polus in this argument, he would have been faced with a crisis in his own characterization of his teacher.[67] Surely it is simpler to suppose that he is himself unaware of the fallacy.

IV

Now for another argument in which Socrates has been charged with deceit. It occurs in his earlier bout with Polus, which sprawls over more than two Stephanus pages of the *Gorgias*, 466B–468E5.[68] Evidently thinking that rough treatment is the right way to handle this impudent young upstart,[69] Socrates explodes a firecracker in his face. Conceding that (at the height of their influence) tyrants and orators (1) *can do as they please* in the cities where they hold sway – they can contrive, at pleasure, banishment, confiscation of property, even death for their enemies – Socrates nonetheless denies (2) that *they have great power*. Can Socrates honestly assert (1) while denying (2)? Can he believe that a man whose position in the power-structure enables him to do pretty much "as he pleases" (ἃ δοκεῖ αὐτῷ)[70] or "whatever seems best to him" (ὅτι ἂν αὐτῷ δόξῃ βέλτιστον εἶναι)[71] may nonetheless be virtually powerless? Or is this a trick to fool Polus?

First let us note that Socrates' denial of (2) is not meant to gainsay what both he and Polus take to be obvious, well-known, facts.[72] Had

---

66 *Cr.* 49C–D; *R.* 335A–E.   67 Cf. n. 17 above.

68 A rather messy layout (cf. Canto, 1987: 321, n. 34: "assez chaotique") in marked contrast to the neat and compact argument at 474C–475C which has just been discussed. Let us bear in mind that Plato is simulating a live conversation. When people are arguing on their feet not all of their arguments can be expected to come through in apple-pie order.

69 The difference between the respectful treatment Socrates accords Gorgias and the one he adopts when Polus butts in to take Gorgias' place at 461B2 has often been noticed: the charge that flattery is endemic in the craft of rhetoric, left implicit in Socrates' argument against Gorgias, becomes bluntly explicit when Polus takes over (463A8–B1). And cf. Dodds, 1959: 11 and 221, 249.   70 467A5 and B8.

71 466E1–2, 9–10; 467B3–4): the two expressions are used interchangeably; ἃ δοκεῖ τινι is treated simply as an abbreviation of ἃ δοκεῖ τινι βέλτιστον εἶναι (cf. n. 53 above).

72 Admittedly, they are subscribing to an absurdly exaggerated opinion of the power of orators in the democracies of their day (cf. Grote, 1865: II 145; Irwin, 1979: 138–9; Canto,

it been so meant, we would know that the reasoning which led to such a conclusion had gone off the rails somewhere or other along the line. But Socrates is saying nothing to contradict this supposed fact on which he and Polus are agreed. In full view of the enormous power which tyrants have to kill, exile, expropriate, and the like, Socrates denies that they have "great power."[73] Clearly then he is using "great" in a strongly evaluative sense, whose antonym would be not "small," "puny" but "mean," "contemptible." This use of "great" is made clear in the following exchange:

T15 *G.* 466E6–11: Socrates: "You said that having great power is good for him who has it." Polus: "I say so, indeed." Socrates: "Would you think it good if one mindlessly did whatever seemed best to one? Is this what you would call 'having great power'?" Polus: "I would not."

So "great power" is to be understood as power in the hands of a rational agent, acting rationally. On this too they are in agreement. So neither could this be a point at which Polus could be tricked.[74] Where then could trickery be supposed to occur?

The only plausible candidate for trickery in the course of the argument is the further claim Socrates proceeds to make shortly after the exchange in T15:

T16 *G.* 467B3–9: Socrates: "I maintain that they [tyrants and orators] do not do what they desire. Refute me!" Polus: "Did you not agree that they do what seems best to them?" Socrates: "I still do." Polus: "Are they not then doing what they desire (ἃ βούλονται)?" Socrates: "This I deny."

This is what evokes Polus' strongest protest (he explodes: "Socrates, what you say is shocking, monstrous"). It becomes the pivotal thesis

---

1987: 322, n. 43). But this is irrelevant to the analysis of the logical structure of the argument and to the estimate of its *bona fides*, where all that matters is that they agree on that premise and that the agreement is spontaneous: bringing that opinion to the discussion, Polus does not need to be argued into it. So *pace* McTighe, 1984: 218, the question of trickery on Socrates' part cannot arise at this point.

73 μέγα δύνασθαι, 466E3–4; 468E1–4.

74 Though it could and would if, as McTighe claims (1984: 220), Socrates' argument is predicated on the view that "power is *always* good [my emphasis]": if this claim were true it would suffice to impugn Socrates' *bona fides*, since we know that he believes the contrary (see e.g. *Eud.* 281D [to be discussed as T28 in chapter 8]: when the use of a non-moral good is not guided by moral wisdom, its possession is positively bad). But Socrates' argument does not need the premise McTighe allows him, and a look at the text will show that he does not use it: the "always" in McTighe's reconstruction of the Socratic argument is not warranted by what is said in the text at T15 above nor yet at 468E1–8. Socrates says nothing throughout our whole passage to misrepresent his true position, which is that, like all non-moral goods, power could be only conditionally good, hence not always good: if used under the wrong conditions it would be evil.

on which their disagreement turns. Socrates affirms and Polus denies
that

(3)   A man who is doing what seems best to him may not be doing
what he desires.[75]

To show Polus that (3) is entirely reasonable Socrates proceeds to
expound his fundamental doctrine that all our (voluntary) actions
are done for the sake of "some good" or "the good"[76] and that,
consequently, what we desire in each of them is not (just)[77] the
action itself, but the good for whose sake we desire to do it. From this
he concludes (3), i.e. that if x is bad[78] then while it may seem good
to us[79] (else we would not choose to do it), *we do not desire to do x.* Is
this a deliberate fallacy? Is it even a fallacy? Socrates' thought here
moves over terrain which is treacherous in the extreme. Even with
what we have learned about its semantic booby-traps from modern
analytical philosophy, it is hard to traverse it without misspeaking
ourselves. It would be a wonder if Socrates, without any such
equipment, were to manage a faultless performance.

The general sort of fallacy he might be suspected of palming off on
Polus has been identified by present-day philosophers under the
technical rubric "quantifying in psychological contexts." This
would be an example of that fallacy at its baldest:

He desires x; x happens to be y; ergo, he desires y.

Compare:

75 McTighe (1984: 194) paraphrases this proposition as "'doing what one desires' must be
    distinguished from 'doing what seems good to one'." He regards it as a deliberate
    misrepresentation of Socrates' considered view, injected into the argument to deceive
    Polus.
76 Cf. T17 and T18 below; also *Meno* 77E1–78B2. In all three passages "good" is to be
    understood, as usual in Plato, as "good *for us*," "good *for the agent*": cf. n. 53.
77 A vital qualification which Socrates does not state formally. But that he does intend it is
    clear at 468c: "So to slaughter someone or banish him or confiscate his property we do not
    desire *just like that.*" The italicized phrase is Irwin's apt rendering (following Dodds,
    1959: 239) of ἁπλῶς οὕτως (much the same in Robin, "comme cela tout simplement")
    – an offhand, imprecise, expression, which, however, is clear enough in context: to desire
    x "just like that" would be to desire it without reference to the good for whose sake x is
    in fact desired. It is unwarranted to report Socrates as holding that "we don't really want
    x if x is a means to some further end" (so Irwin, 1979: 141: see further on this additional
    note 8.4). Socrates explicitly affirms the contrary at 468c3–4: "but if these things [*sc.*
    things we want for the sake of something else] are advantageous, *we do desire them.*" Irwin
    takes due notice of this statement (1979: 145) and remarks that this is what Socrates *should*
    hold, but, surprisingly, does not recognize that this is what Socrates *does* hold.
78 As before "bad *for the agent.*"
79 And is thus, in Aristotle's terminology (*N.E.* 1113a16ff.), the "apparent" good, which in
    the case of misguided moral judgment is contrary to what is "truly good" (τὸ κατ'
    ἀλήθειαν ἀγαθόν, a25).

Oedipus desires to marry Iocasta; Iocasta happens to be his mother; ergo, he desires to marry his mother.[80]

But look again at the conclusion. On first hearing, that sentence sounds horrendously false. But if we keep thinking about it a sense comes into view in which the sentence would be plainly true for someone who has the information the gods had denied to Oedipus. Imagine two palace slaves, A and B, who know the secret of Oedipus' past. A says to B, "My god! Oedipus wants to marry his mother!"; if we understand him to mean that Oedipus wants to marry the woman who, unbeknown to him, *happens to be* his mother, we would see that what he says is perfectly true. And we can then imagine B retorting, "By Zeus, no! He does *not* want to marry his mother"; and this too we could take as clearly true if we understood it to mean, "He does not want to marry the woman *he believes to be* his mother." Is there some simple way of nailing down the feature of this situation which makes it perfectly intelligible that the identical sentence, "Oedipus wants to marry his mother," can be truly affirmed by A and as truly denied by B?

Let us coopt the powerful notion, brought into the philosophy of mind by Elizabeth Anscombe,[81] of "desiring under a description";[82] and let us also adopt the distinction between the "actual" and the "intended" object of desire employed by Santas in his illuminating discussion of the Socratic view.[83] In his example, we see a man who, we assume, is reaching for the salt-shaker across the table, getting hold of the pepper-mill instead. Did he get what he wanted? Clearly no, if he had wanted that object under the description "salt-shaker," for then what he got was not the "intended" object of his desire. As clearly yes, if, contrary to what we assume, he had wanted that same object under the description "pepper-mill," for then the "actual" object would be the "intended" one. In Oedipus' case his mother was indeed the "actual" object of his desire to marry Iocasta, but not its "intended" object: he did not desire to marry Iocasta under that description, but under some alternative one, like "that enchanting woman," "the adorable Queen who would make me so

---

80 I owe the example to McTighe, 1984: 205, who uses it to good effect for his own purposes.
81 1958: 65. I owe the reference to Santas. He used Anscombe's idea to attack successfully the Socratic paradoxes in the chapter on "The Socratic paradoxes" in his book (1979: 187 and 316), which reprints with revisions that ground-breaking paper (*Philos. Review*, 1964).
82 Irwin (1979: 145) makes an excellent application of the parallel notion of "considered under a description" in his discussion of our passage: "Socrates' question, 'Does *A* do what he wants?', is misleading, since he seems to suggest that it must have a yes-or-no answer, when in fact the answer may be yes when the action is considered under one description the agent believed true of it, and no when it is considered under another description."
83 1979: 186–9.

happy if she consents to be my wife," which does not include the phrase "my mother" or any intensionally equivalent one. Though A's statement seems the flat negation of B's, both can be true, because A's refers to the "actual," B's to the "intended" object of Oedipus' desire.

Applying this analysis to the Socratic sentence that struck Polus as so preposterous we may consider if the suspicion of trickery holds up: We know that Socrates takes the final object of human desire to be the good:

T17 *G.* 468B7–c6: "So it is for the sake of the good that all things are done by those who do them... For good things we desire, as you agree; things which are neither good nor bad, or things which are bad, we do not desire."

T18 *G.* 499E8–9: "The good is the final end (τέλος) of all actions and for its sake everything else should be done."

So it would be uncontroversial that what Socrates wants to say at (3) is that the "intended" object of our desire is always something good: whatever we may desire, we do so under the description "good." And in the not infrequent cases in which our action is bad he will want to say that while our "actual" object of what we desire in that action is indeed bad – best though it seemed to us at the time – the "intended" one is the good we pursued, however mistakenly, then, as always, in our actions.[84] Putting the new terminology to work let us, with its aid, produce an improved version of (3):

(3*) A man who is doing what seems best to him may not be pursuing the "intended" object of his desire.

This is surely what Socrates wants to say to Polus.[85] And if he had said it in some such terms as these, making it clear that this is what he meant, Polus would have found nothing "monstrous" about the thesis. For while he might have been sceptical about the Socratic

---

84 McTighe's interpretation of the Socratic doctrine is vitiated by his assumption that Socrates' claim that all men desire the good "means that they desire the apparent good" (1984: 206 *et passim*), which McTighe takes to be the "considered view" (216) which Plato expounds in every other relevant passage in the corpus. This assumption is false. The Socratic claim made in T17 and T18 is, on the contrary, that all men desire the "true" good even when it is tragically at variance with what "seems best" to them at the time, i.e. with "the apparent good." Though the discrepancy of what "seems good" to us with the ("true") good which we all desire is not expounded in any of the other passages to which McTighe refers (*Ly.* 216c–220b, *Eud.* 278e–282a; *Pr.* 258c–d) it is consistent with all of them. Thus at *Eud.* 281d, it would have been entirely in the spirit of the passage for Plato to have said, if this had been to his purpose there, that those non-moral goods which are in fact bad for us when our use of them is not guided by "wisdom" *seem* good to us when we so use them and are thus "apparent" goods, though contrary to our "true" good.

85 We might say that (3*) is the "intended" expression of Socrates' thought, while (3) is its "actual" one.

doctrine that we always desire the good, he would have seen that if he did grant it for the sake of argument, he would have no reason to be shocked by the inference that if people do bad things in the belief that those things are good, then they are not pursuing the intended object of their desire; hence Socrates would have had no reason to extract Polus' assent by sophistry. To rephrase (3) as (3*) – i.e. to make what Socrates means more perspicuous – is to disarm the suspicion of trickery.

But let us not make this the end of the matter. If Socrates is to be given the benefit of Santas' improved terminology why rest content with half-measures, which is all that has been achieved in (3*): what we have done there is apply the new terminology to the second clause of (3) – substituting "pursuing the 'intended' object of his desire" for "doing what he desires" – leaving the first clause, "doing what seems best to him," intact. Let us make a more thorough job of it. Since "what seems best" to him is the "actual" object, let us bring this into our improved version of (3), rewriting it accordingly as

(3**)   A man who is pursuing the "actual" object of his desire may not be pursuing its "intended" object.

The misguided agent is now represented as desiring not only the good which is the "intended" object of his desire but *also the evil which "seems best to him"* and is his desire's "actual" object. To put into this form what Socrates states in the form of (3) would have clarified his doctrine not only for Polus' benefit, but for his own as well, and the enhanced insight might well have led to a drastic revision in his expression of it. By rephrasing his claim in the form of (3**) instead of (3), he would have made it clear to others and to himself that *he has no reason to deny that those wicked tyrants and their ilk do desire* those horrible things – assassination, etc. – which "seem best" to them: under their misdescriptions of those actions as "good" they most certainly do desire them. Then Socrates would not have said, as he does say in retrospective reference to our passage, that he and Polus were "forced to agree" that

T19 *G.* 509E5–7: "... no one does injustice desiring it (μηδένα βουλόμενον ἀδικεῖν), but all who do injustice do it involuntarily (ἀλλ' ἄκοντας τοὺς ἀδικοῦντας πάντας ἀδικεῖν)."[86]

---

86 Cf. also *Meno* 77cff., a most instructive passage in which Socrates concludes that "no one desires evil things" (78A6). Santas' discussion of this passage (1979: 186–7) is excellent so far as it goes. But it fails to notice the trap in it: from the premise "everyone desires good things" Socrates is not entitled to infer "no one desires evil things." For once the premise,

Or, if he had said this, he would have added, "but to say this is not to deny that they do desire it, and do the injustice voluntarily." For as (3**) shows, Socrates has as good reason to say that unjust men do desire to do the evil that they do as that they do not desire it: just as those who know Oedipus' secret have as good reason to say that he does not desire to marry his mother, as that he does. If Socrates could have reformulated his (3) in some such form as (3**) he would have seen good reason to shed its most offensive feature, which is, surely, not that we do desire good things – there is no reason to object to that[87] – but that *we never desire the bad things* we do when we mistake bad for good.[88] His famous doctrine that all wrongdoing is involuntary[89] would dissolve.[90]

Thus the analysis which shows that Socrates has no reason to fool Polus also shows that Socrates has no reason to maintain the thing which Polus finds so outrageous, namely, that we do not desire the evil which "seems best" to us when evil is what we do. In clarifying his doctrine for Polus' benefit Socrates would have been himself the prime beneficiary of the clarification. It would have prompted him to disengage himself from the profoundly misleading dictum that all evil-doing is "involuntary," which if literally meant would wreck moral responsibility. (Properly understood the Socratic view leaves Medea fully responsible for the murders: they were the "actual", though not the "intended," object of her desire.) It is the sound perception that this dictum *is* so misleading and that Socrates would be better off without it which makes it so suspect to McTighe and motivates his ill-advised claim that Socrates only *pretends* to hold it so as to fool Polus.

properly disambiguated, following Santas' own directions, is understood to mean "good things are the "intended' objects of everyone's desire," it offers no ground for denying (or even for so much as failing to notice) that bad things are the "actual" objects of some people's desire.

87 As Santas (1979: 189) observes, this "seems to be one of the most common presuppositions made in accounting for human behavior, at any rate in situations of prudential choice." By concentrating on this part of the Socratic position Santas has no difficulty giving the whole of it a clean bill of health.

88 Anyone who doubts the ineptness of this doctrine if literally meant should consider how wildly unreasonable is the position into which Socrates would put himself if he were to deny that Cleon lusts for power, Medea thirsts for revenge. Saying that the terrible things those persons do are done "involuntarily" creates the impression that Socrates really does mean to deny they desire to do them – an impression which Santas does nothing to correct.

89 οὐδεὶς ἑκὼν ἁμαρτάνει (n. 26 above), which has so often been taken as one of Socrates' most fundamental doctrines.

90 That is to say, it would become clear that it is not meant to deny that persons may and do desire "actual" objects whose attainment would, unbeknown to them, defeat disastrously their desire for the good.

IN CONCLUSION

In my discussion of this and of the preceding argument in the *Gorgias* I have defended Socrates against the imputation of wilfully resorting to untruth in order to prevail against a disreputable opponent. To do so would have been to frustrate the effort to "search himself"[91] and his interlocutor by the elenctic method. None of the scholars who have seriously believed that Socrates employed insincere beliefs or consciously fallacious inferences in these and other arguments has ever tried to explain how such infidelity to the quest for truth could be reconciled with Plato's conception of Socratic philosophizing. To be sure, the portrayal of Socrates in the earlier dialogues does not represent him as the ideal philosopher pursuing truth in the ideal way in which Plato himself came to think, later in life, truth should be pursued. In the *Theaetetus* Plato gives us a glimpse of a different, much improved, Socrates, who has laid to rest the demon of contentiousness within him.[92] Instead of pouncing on his opponent's admissions to confound him, this nobler figure takes it upon himself to help his adversary correct and strengthen the position Socrates is challenged to refute, so that if the assault on it does succeed it will have achieved a demonstration of the intrinsic untenability of the targeted position, not of its current defender's failure to make the best case for it.

Not so here in the *Gorgias*. Throughout the dialogue and most particularly in his encounter with Polus the debater is more in evidence than the disinterested seeker after truth. Dealing with matters which cry aloud for clarification, he does nothing to clarify them for his opponent's benefit.[93] When that very surprising proposition, that tyrants and their ilk, doing what seems best to them, actually do what they do not wish, strikes Polus as a manifest absurdity, could not Socrates have done something there and then to explain that, startling though it may be on first hearing, that

---

91 *Ch.* 166c–d [= T4 above].

92 The reproach to Socrates is put into Protagoras' mouth: "It is most unreasonable that one who professes a concern for virtue should be constantly guilty of unfairness in argument [Cornford's apt rendering of ἀδικοῦντα ἐν τοῖς λόγοις διατελεῖν]. Unfairness here consists in failing to separate contention from discussion [χωρὶς μὲν ὡς ἀγωνιζόμενος τὰς διατριβὰς ποιῆται, χωρὶς δὲ ὡς διαλεγόμενος]. In contention one need not be serious and may trip up one's opponent as much as one can. In discussion one should be serious and help out one's interlocutor and point out to him slips and fallacies which are due to himself or to his earlier associations [and should be kept distinct from the substantive errors of the view he is defending]" (*Tht.* 167e–168a).

93 We may agree with Klosko (1983: 363–74) that from his interlocutor's point of view Socrates' arguments are "extremely poor," but not that "Socrates could not help but be aware of this" (373).

claim is really, when rightly understood, the plain truth in cases in which the agents are themselves deceived by what seems to them to be, but is not, their best option? Surely he could. But Socrates shows no interest in making any move in that direction. He flaunts his paradox in Polus' face, defying him to find anything wrong with it:

T20 *G.* 467B2: "I deny that they are doing what they wish. Refute me."

And when Polus sputters in baffled incomprehension, exclaiming that it is "shocking, monstrous," Socrates stonewalls him as before:

T21 467B11–C2: "Don't abuse me, peerless Polus... Do you want to question? Then show that what I say is false. If not, stand up to questioning."

With a true artist's reluctance to ingratiate his hero to us, Plato wants us to see Socrates as he is – as a man who has a one-track way to pursue truth, the method he practices with fierce devotion, without making any of those concessions to his opponent's weakness which magnanimity or compassion might dictate. If what we are looking for is generosity to a befuddled adversary, Plato makes sure that we shall be rebuffed. But as the foregoing interpretation may have suggested, Plato makes sure that we shall see Socrates giving Polus not less than he deserves. Enforcing on him to the letter the rules of dialectical disputation, Socrates leads him relentlessly to "bring witness against himself," without ever deliberately misleading him. If such a scheme as the one depicted in the *Gorgias* had flashed before Plato's eyes when he penned the closing words of the *Phaedo*, he would have seen no reason to qualify the tribute to Socrates as "the most just" of all the men he had ever come to know in his life.

6

SOCRATIC PIETY[1]

Socrates' commitment to reasoned argument as the final arbiter of claims to truth in the moral domain is evident throughout Plato's Socratic dialogues. He refers to it in the deliberation by which he justifies to Crito the decision to remain in prison and await execution:

T1 *Cr.* 45B: "Not now for the first time, but always, I am the sort of man who is persuaded by nothing in me except the proposition which appears to me to be the best *when I reason* (λογιζομένῳ) about it."

And yet he is also committed to obeying commands reaching him through supernatural channels. When explaining at his trial why the state's power of life and death over him could not scare him into abandoning the public practice of his philosophy, he declares:

T2 *Ap.* 33C: "To do this[2] has been commanded me, as I maintain, by the god through divinations and through dreams and every other means through which divine apportionment has ever commanded anyone to do anything."

Between these two commitments – on one hand, to follow argument wherever it may lead; on the other, to obey divine commands conveyed to him through supernatural channels – he sees no conflict. He assumes they are in perfect harmony.[3] Can sense be made of this? I want to argue that it can. This will be my first task in this chapter. But what concerns me even more is a larger objective: to understand Socrates' conception of religion. So before

---

1 This is a corrected and expanded version of a paper read to the B Club of the Classics Faculty in Cambridge in May 1988, published in the Proceedings of the Boston Area Colloquium (vol. v, 1989). Parts of it had been included in a Gifford lecture on "Socratic Piety" at St. Andrews (1981) and a Townsend Lecture at Cornell (1986).

2 I.e. to "live philosophizing, examining himself and others" (*Ap.* 28E, cited as T5 in chapter 4, and as T2 in chapter 5 above; cf. the comment on this text in those chapters.

3 As they must, since what is "commanded" him by the god in T2 is to engage in the activity which pursues the commitment to reason affirmed in T1.

closing I shall be returning to the point in the *Euthyphro* at which the search for the definition of piety is sidetracked in that dialogue.[4] I shall push that search a step further in the direction indicated there.

Let us begin by facing a fact about Socrates which has been so embarrassing to modern readers that a long line of Platonic scholarship has sought – in the most recent book-length study of the *Euthyphro*[5] is still seeking – to explain it away: Socrates' acceptance of the supernatural. I shall waste no time arguing against these scholars. The fact they are denying is so firmly attested in our principal sources – Plato's and Xenophon's Socratic writings – that to cut it out of them would be surgery which kills the patient. If we are to use Plato's and Xenophon's testimony about Socrates at all we must take it as a brute fact – as a premise fixed for us in history – that, far ahead of his time as Socrates is in so many ways, in this part of his thought he is a man of his time. He subscribes unquestioningly[6] to the age-old view that side by side with the physical world accessible to our senses, there exists another, populated by mysterious beings, personal like ourselves, but, unlike ourselves, having the power to invade at will the causal order to which our own actions are confined, effecting in it changes of incalculable extent[7] to cause us great benefit, or, were they to choose otherwise, total devastation and ruin. How they act upon us we cannot hope to understand. But the fact is that they do and their communications to us through dreams and oracles is one of the inscrutable ways in which they display their power over us. Born into this system of religious belief, Socrates, a deeply religious man, could not have shrugged it off.[8] And he could not have reasonably denied it without good reason: when a belief pervades the public consensus the burden of justifying dissent from it falls upon the dissident. And here his problem would be aggravated by the fact that the religious consensus has legal sanction. To flout it publicly is an offense against the state punishable by death.

4 At 14B–C Euthyphro is told that if he had answered the question he had been asked at 14A9–10, Socrates would have "learned piety [i.e. learned what piety is]": "you came right up to the point and turned aside." Cf. Brickhouse & Smith, 1983: 657–66, at 660.
5 By the late Laszlo Versenyi (1982). For effective critique see McPherran, 1985: 292–7.
6 In Plato's Socratic dialogue the gods' existence and power are never called in question – not even as an abstract possibility. In the *Memorabilia* the farthest anyone ever goes in that direction is to disbelieve in the power of the gods and their care for men (Aristodemus at 1.4, Euthydemus at 4.3). For Xenophon's and Plato's Socrates, as for the vast majority of Greeks, the gods' existence is almost as much of a "given" as is that of the physical world.
7 But by no means infinite extent. In striking contrast to the Hebraic and Christian deity of traditional theology, Greek gods are not omnipotent.
8 As did Thucydides, whose thoroughly secularized outlook makes it possible for him to ignore it, except as such beliefs afflict the subjects of his narrative.

A succession of brilliant thinkers, from Anaximander to Democritus, had solved this problem with the utmost discretion. From their new picture of the world they had expunged the supernatural quietly, without ever naming it in a critique: the Greek ancestor of our word for it was not in their vocabulary[9] and they did not need to invent it in order to obliterate its referent. They did the job in attending to their own business of *physiologia*, "science of nature," by so expanding the concept of nature as to make nature encompass all there is,[10] thereby creating a new conception of the universe as a cosmos, a realm of all-encompassing, "necessary"[11] order whose regularities cannot be breached by interventionist entities outside it because outside it there is nothing.[12] What room is there for god or gods in this new map of what there is? For supernatural gods there is none. For natural ones there is ample room – for gods existing not beyond nature, but in it. Not all of the *physiologoi* preserve deity under this name, for their world-picture is crafted to meet primarily scientific, not religious, needs; in principle they could complete it without any reference to god or gods. But they are not antireligious. Their temper is not that of the village atheist. When they postulate a cosmic intelligence to account for the intelligible order of their cosmos, most of them call it "god." So did Xenophanes, Heraclitus, and Diogenes of Apollonia, though not Anaxagoras:[13] in none of his fragments is the ordering mind which creates the world termed "god."

Thus in Ionian *physiologia* the existence of a being bearing that name becomes optional. What is mandatory is only that to have a place in the real world deity must be naturalized and thereby rationalized, associated with the orderliness of nature, not with breaches of its order, as it continued to be for the vast majority of Greeks. Even someone as enlightened as Herodotus was content to

9 ὑπερφυσικός is a late, Neoplatonic, concoction. As I have pointed out elsewhere (1975: 20) "the demolition of the supernatural is accomplished [in Ionian *physiologia*] without a single word about the victim."

10 This assumption is built into the very phrase by which they commonly designate their subject-matter: "the all" or "all things." Cf. the Word-Index in Diels–Kranz, 1952 (hereafter "DK"), *s.v.* τὸ πᾶν, τὰ πάντα, expanded into "the nature of all things" (ἡ τῶν πάντων φύσις), in Xenophon, *Mem.* 1.1.11 (quoted in part in T6 below) and 1.1.14.

11 Cf. the Word-Index in DK, *s.v.* ἀνάγκη: and cf. "necessary [causes]" in Xenophon's description of "what the experts call 'cosmos'" at T6 below.

12 For parallel accounts of the destructive impact of natural philosophy on the traditional religious world-view see "Die Wirkung der Naturphilosophie" in Gigon, 1959: 51–9; and "The displacements of mythology" in Lloyd, 1987b: 1–49.

13 Nor yet Anaximander, the true founder of Ionian *physiologia*, though this is controversial: cf. Vlastos, 1952: 97ff., at 113; *contra* Jaeger, 1947: 29ff. and 203ff.

minimize supernatural intervention in history without excluding it
in principle. When he tells the story of the prodigiously high tide that
overwhelmed the Persian army at Potidaea he endorses the local
belief that it was caused by Poseidon punishing the invaders for
desecrating his shrine.[14] Should we ever forget how tiny is the band
of intellectuals who accept *in toto* the point of view of the *physiologoi*,
we should recall what happened on the plain of Syracuse on August
27, 413 B.C. When immediate evacuation of the Athenian forces had
become imperative, and the departure had been decided by Nicias,
their commanding general, the full moon was eclipsed, whereupon,
writes Thucydides,

T3 Thuc. 7.50.4:   The mass of the Athenians was greatly moved and
called upon the generals to remain... And Nicias, who was rather too given
to divination and the like, refused to even discuss the question of the
departure until 27 days had passed, as the diviners prescribed.

Remain they did, with the result that Nicias' army was wiped out.
    From Plato's *Laches* we learn that Nicias knew Socrates well[15] and
had been influenced by his moral teaching: in that dialogue Nicias
is made the champion of the Socratic definition of courage. Nicias
could not have acted as he did at Syracuse if his teacher had been
Anaxagoras instead. That influence would have swept the super-
naturalist view of eclipses clean out of his mind.[16] His association
with Socrates had left it in place.[17] And we can see why. The way the
new "science of nature" had opened up out of that whole morass of
superstition Socrates could not have taught to his companions
because he had not found it himself.[18] From the investigations of the

14 8.129.3: "in my opinion at any rate, they [*sc.* the Potidaeans] speak well in saying that this
    was the cause." For other examples see Lloyd, 1979: 30, nn. 102–3.
15 Note especially *La.* 187D–188C: he had evidently known at close quarters the power of-
    Socrates' elenchus to "examine" the life, no less than the beliefs, of his interlocutors: cf.
    Vlastos, 1983a: 37. Cf. also *La.* 200C–D (cited as T11 in additional note 1.1).
16 As it did for Pericles: through his association with Anaxagoras, says Plutarch (*Life of
    Pericles* 6), he "was made superior to the fearful amazement which superstition produces
    on those who are ignorant of the causes of events in the upper regions."
17 Not that Socrates would have approved Nicias' decision to follow the advice of the diviners
    in defiance of military prudence. In the *Laches* (198E–199A) Socrates reminds his
    interlocutors that the law requires the diviner to obey the general, not the general the
    diviner. Thucydides (7.48.4: cf. Connor, 1984: 237) enables us to recognize the moral
    weakness which left Nicias vulnerable to the promptings of superstition at the fatal
    moment.
18 It is, therefore, a gross error to think of Socrates as a "typical representative of the Greek
    Enlightenment" (Joël, 1921: 759). As we know from the case of Pericles and Euripides, it
    is to natural philosophers, like Anaxagoras, that the partisans of the Enlightenment would
    look for leadership. Nor is it right to think of Socrates as "the intellectual leader of
    Athenian intellectuals" (Maier, 1913: 463). Certainly Plato does not so picture him: in his

physiologoi he had stood aloof.[19] Putting all his energies into ethical inquiry,[20] he took no more interest in natural philosophy than in metaphysics, epistemology, ontology, or any other branch of investigation that falls outside the domain of moral philosophy.

To be sure, it was bruited about that he pursued *physiologia* in private[21] and Aristophanes made immortal comedy of the canard. But our most reliable sources leave no doubt that the talk is groundless. Aristotle is so sure of this that he disposes of the matter in a parenthetic clause:

T4[22] Aristotle, *Metaph.* 987b1–2: But Socrates, occupying himself with ethical questions, *and not at all with nature as a whole* (τῆς ὅλης φύσεως) ...

In Plato's *Apology* Socrates repudiates as slander the Aristophanic caricature of the man in a basket up in the air scanning the skies.

T5 Plato, *Ap.* 19c: "Of such things I know nothing, great or small. Not that I would speak disparagingly of such science, if anyone really has it... But the fact is, O Athenians, that I have no share in it."

Xenophon, with his proneness to apologetic overkill[23] pulls out all the stops to clear Socrates of the suspicion of having been a crypto-*physiologos*, representing him as scornfully hostile towards natural inquiry:

T6 *Mem.* 1.1.11: Nor did he discourse, like most others, about the nature of the universe, investigating what the experts call "cosmos" and through what necessary causes each of the celestial occurrences are generated. *Those who did so he showed up as idiots.*[24]

Protagoras the great sophist compliments Socrates on his future promise, not on his present achievement: "I would not be surprised if you were to become highly distinguished for wisdom" (361E).

19 Which is not to say that he was scornful of it, as Xenophon would have us believe (T6 below). In Plato's *Apology* Socrates expressly repudiates that sentiment (T5 below). This is one of several cases (cf. de Strycker, 1950: 199ff. *passim*) in which, faced with a conflict between Xenophon's and Plato's testimony, we have good reason to prefer Plato's: he is less prone than Xenophon to tailor his representation of Socrates to apologetic ends (cf. n. 23 below).   20 Cf. Thesis IA in chapter 2.

21 In Aristophanes' comedy he teaches behind well-guarded gates. At his trial (*Ap.* 19B–D) Socrates appeals to members of the jury (which was bound to contain many men of his own age or even older) to speak up if any of them has ever heard him discuss such things, confident that no one has. Burnet (1914, in his note to 19D4) cites parallels from Andocides and Demosthenes which show that such an appeal would not be out of line with Athenian judicial procedure.   22 T9 in chapter 3.

23 For the strongly apologetic animus of the *Memorabilia*, which determines even the form of its construction, see Erbse, 1961: 17ff.

24 *Mem.* 1.1.1. In his account of Socrates' attitude to astronomy (*Mem.* 4.7.4–7) Xenophon makes Socrates side with the obscurantists, warning his associates that "he who ponders such things risks going mad like Anaxagoras."

Thus from Xenophon no less than Plàto and Aristotle, we get good
reason for withholding credence from the representation of Socrates
in the *Memorabilia*[25] as a dabbler in teleological cosmology in the
style of Diogenes of Apollonia, producing a physico-theological
argument for divine providence predicated on the man-serving
order of a variety of natural phenomena, from the structure of the
human organism to the solstitial motions of the sun.[26] Cosmological
argument for the existence of god is cosmologists' business. Why
should Socrates produce such argument when cosmology is none of
his?

To be sure, Socrates could hardly insulate his religious faith from
the formidable energies of his critical intellect. But to find scope for
these in his conception of the gods he would not need to desert moral
inquiry for physics and metaphysics. He could require his gods to
meet not metaphysical but ethical standards. The Ionians had
rationalized deity by making it natural. From within the super-
naturalist framework which they reject, Socrates makes a parallel
move: he rationalizes the gods by making them moral. *His gods can
be both supernatural and rational so long as they are rationally moral.* This,
I submit, is his program. Given his obsessive concentration on ethics,
a *natural theology* he could not have produced. But he could, and did,
produce a *moral theology*, investigating the concept of god no further
than is needed to bring it into line with his ethical views, deriving
from his new vision of human goodness norms binding on the gods
themselves.

Here is the first of the "outlines of theology," τύποι θεολογίας as
Plato calls them, in book II of the *Republic*:

T7 *R.* II, 379B: "Is not god truly good, and must he not be so
described?...

"And surely nothing good can be harmful?... And what is not harmful
does not harm?... And what does not harm does no evil?... And what does

25 1.4.1ff. (dialogue with Aristodemus); 4.3.3ff. (dialogue with Euthydemus).
26 As Jaeger (1947: 167 and notes) has pointed out, the arguments for the natural theology
which Xenophon here attributes to Socrates "are undoubtedly not Xenophon's own."
Following Theiler (1925: 18ff.), Jaeger suggests that the source is Diogenes of Apollonia.
In accepting the suggestion (*pace* Vlastos, 1952: n. 84) we should heed Theiler's caveat
(1925: 168) against reading into that source Xenophon's own naively anthropocentric
theodicy: there is no indication in Diogenes (DK B3) that the imposition of "measures"
on celestial motions was made for man's benefit. Xenophon, producing his natural
theodicy *ad hoc* in the interests of piety, is all too likely to have used borrowings from
Diogenes for edifying purposes of his own. The axiomatic faith of the cosmologists in the
unexceptionableness of the order of nature is alien to Xenophon's thought. He is as likely
to see evidences of the gods' care for men in providential breaches of the natural order as
in its maintenance for man's benefit: he believes (*Mem.* 1.4.15) that the gods send
"portents" (τέρατα) to enable men to foretell future events through the practice of
divination.

no evil could not be the cause of any evil?... And is not the good beneficent?... Hence the cause of well-being?...

"*So god cannot be the cause of all things, but only of good things; of evil things he is not the cause?*"[27] ...

I have italicized the final step in this sequence of inferences, the crucial one:[28] god cannot be the cause of everything in the life of men, but only of the good things in it. God's causation of those good things Socrates makes no effort to explain. Only the boldest of metaphysicians could have tried to excogitate how a supernatural being may produce any changes, good or bad, in the natural order. Socrates, no metaphysician, sticking to his own last, the moralist's, taking the fact of such causation for granted, is content to do no more than clamp on it moral constraints, reasoning that since god is good, he can only cause good, never evil.[29]

But why should god be credited with such unexceptionable beneficence? Is it because of the superlative wisdom which Socrates,[30] in common with traditional Greek sentiment,[31] ascribes to the gods? No, not just because of that. To allow one's gods

27 This comes from a passage in book II of the *Republic* where Plato lays down the first of the articles of theology to which all references to the gods by the poets should conform. What is presented here in a dialogue of Plato's middle period is pure Socratic heritage *employing no premises foreign to the thought of the earlier dialogues*. Only after this first τύπος θεολογίας has been staked out, does Plato make Socrates go beyond it (380Dff.), introducing the new, distinctively Platonic, metaphysical premise that gods cannot change, because this would involve "departure from their own form" (380D; cf. *Ti.* 50B; *Cra.* 439E), deriving from this the conclusion that gods cannot lie, since this would involve them in change.

28 Reiterated for emphasis at 379C2–7: "thus, since god is good, he is not the cause of all things that happen to human beings, *as the many say*, but of few of these: of many of them he is not the cause." I italicize the phrase in which Plato highlights the great novelty in Socratic theology by setting it off in defiant contrast to what is commonly believed, just as he highlights the great novelty in Socratic morality, the rejection of the *lex talionis*, by representing it as held in lonely opposition to the common view: it is not just to do evil to those who have done evil to us, "*as the many believe*" (*Cri.* 49D).

29 Of this cardinal feature of Socratic theology, which would obliterate the whole of the apotropaic aspect of Greek religion, there is not a word in Xenophon, understandably so, for there is no place for it in the conception of piety he ascribes to Socrates, which departs no further from vulgar notions than to teach that "modest sacrifices from persons of modest means are no less acceptable to the gods than frequent and lavish ones from those who have great possessions" and "the greater the piety of the giver the greater is god's pleasure in the gift" (*Mem.* 1.3.3), but still adheres to the *do ut des* rationale of sacrificing (cf. *Mem.* 4.3.17, quoted in additional note 6.3 below), as also to the conventional belief that the gods "have power to do *both good and evil*" (*Mem.* 1.4.16).

30 *Ap.* 23A–B. When Socrates discovers the true meaning of the oracle Chaerephon had received at Delphi he sees that compared with the divine wisdom man's "is worth little or nothing." In the *Hippias Major* (289B) Socrates endorses the saying of Heraclitus that "the wisest man is to god as an ape is to a man"; cf. Charles Kahn's gloss (1979: 183–5) on this fragment (no. 68 in his book).

31 Even subordinate divinities, like the Muses, are credited with cognitive powers vastly superior to the human (*Iliad* 2.485–6: "You are goddesses, you are present, you know everything," whereas what men know is only κλέος ('hearsay'); divine beings are privileged with that perfectly "clear" insight (σαφήνεια) which is denied to man (Alcmaeon, DK 24 B1).

infinitely potent intellect is not of itself to allow them flawlessly
moral will. It may only lead one to conclude, with Heraclitus, that
god transcends the difference between good and evil[32] and, with
Aristotle, that to ascribe moral attributes to god is to demean him.[33]
Why should Socrates reach the opposite conclusion? Because, I
suggest, for him the highest form of wisdom is not theoretical, but
practical.[34] And it is of the essence of his rationalist program in
theology to assume that the entailment of virtue by wisdom binds
gods no less than men.[35] He could not have tolerated a double-
standard morality,[36] one for men, another for the gods: this would
have perpetuated the old irrationalism. If Socrates is to rationalize
the moral universe as relentlessly as the Ionian *physiologoi* had
rationalized the physical universe when they made a cosmos out of
it, he would have to match in the moral domain their unstated
axiom that the regularities discernible in terrestrial events hold for
all events everywhere: if fire radiates heat and light in our fireplace,
it must do the same in the remotest star, and the bigger the fire, the
greater the heat and the brighter the light that it would have to
generate.

To be sure, Socrates never states the moral analogue of this axiom.
Do we know that he would stand by it? Would he want to say that
principles discoverable by elenctic argument on the streets of Athens
will be universally valid, holding for all moral agents, even if they are

32 DK 22 B102: "For god all things are beautiful and good and just, but men have thought
   some things unjust, others just." Of all the Presocratics it is Xenophanes who might be
   credited with "moralizing divinity" (cf. Vlastos, 1952: 97ff., at 116). Certainly none
   protested more strongly the *immorality* imputed to the gods in traditional belief (DK 21 B11
   and B12). But this is dictated by his protest against anthropomorphism (DK B23 and its
   immediate sequels in Clement, DK B14 and B15), *not* by the ascription of a specifically
   moral will to god as in Socrates' premise at T7 (ἀγαθὸς ὅ γε θεὸς τῷ ὄντι τε καὶ λεκτέον
   οὕτω, 379B1). I must, therefore, demur at the suggestion (Flashar, 1958: 109, n. 2) that
   the τύποι θεολογίας expounded in Rep. 379A–383C "have been taken over from
   Xenophanes." This first τύπος certainly has not, and whether even the second has is
   doubtful: there is appreciable difference between the denial of motion to god in
   Xenophanes (B 26) and the denial of "departing from his own form" (τῆς ἑαυτοῦ ἰδέας
   ἐκβαίνειν) in Plato: Xenophanes builds on a cosmological premise, Plato on a metaphysical
   one.
33 *Nic. Eth.* 1178b8: holding that "perfect happiness" (τελεία εὐδαιμονία), could only consist
   of purely theoretical activity, he infers that we would make the gods "ridiculous" if we
   imputed to them actions to which moral predicates apply.
34 *Moral* wisdom is clearly what he has in view in the doctrine that all the virtues "are"
   wisdom (*Pr.* 361B; cf. Aristotle, *Nic. Eth.* 1145b23, *Eud. Eth.* 1215b1; *Magna Mor.*
   1182b15). So if god's wisdom is perfect (n. 31 above) so must his virtue be.
35 This would follow from the unrestricted generality of the principle that "form is
   everywhere the same" (ταὐτὸ πανταχοῦ εἶδός ἐστιν, *Meno* 72D). And cf. the next note.
36 His search for definitions is predicated on the assumption that if any moral character *F* is
   correctly defined the definiens will apply to *every* action characterizable as *F* (cf. *Eu.* 5D: "Is
   not piety the same as itself *in every action*?").

gods? There is evidence in the *Euthyphro* that he would. He asks there:

T8 *Eu.* 10A: "Is piety loved by the gods because it is piety? Or is it piety because the gods love it?"

He is pressing Euthyphro to agree that the essence of piety – its rationally discoverable nature – has no dependence on the fact that the gods happen to love it.[37] So he is assuming that what piety *is* depends no more on what they, or anyone else, feel about it, than does the nature of fire depend on what anyone, god or man, happens to think that fire is. Piety, and by the same token, every other virtue, has an essence of its own which is as normative for the gods as it is for us: it determines what virtue is in their case as strictly as it does in ours. Thus Socrates would reason that if knowledge of good and evil entails moral goodness in a man it would entail the same in a god. And since the god's wisdom surpasses greatly that of the wisest man, god's goodness must surpass no less greatly that of the most virtuous man. And since he holds that goodness in a man can never cause evil to anyone,[38] he is bound to hold that *a fortiori* neither can goodness in a god: since god can only be good, never evil, god can only cause good, can never be the cause of evil to anyone, man or god.

To heirs of the Hebraic and Christian traditions this will hardly seem a bold conclusion. For those bred on Greek beliefs about the gods it would be shattering. It would obliterate that whole range of divine activity which torments and destroys the innocent no less than the guilty, as careless of the moral havoc it creates, as is, for instance, Hera in Greek traditional belief, who persecutes Heracles relentlessly throughout his life beginning with infancy, when she sends snakes to finish his life almost before it has started, and so on repeatedly thereafter until the day of his death, when she dispatches Lyssa, the divinity of madness, to unhinge his mind so that he murders his own wife and children in a fit of insanity – all this simply because Heracles had been the offspring of one of her consort's numerous infidelities: the calamities she contrives for Zeus's bastard is one of the ways in which she makes the son pay for his father's offenses to her.[39] It would be hard to find a human female acting more viciously

---

37 Cf. Crombie, 1962: 209–10; Taylor, 1929: 151–2; Cohen, 1971: 158–76.

38 *R.* 335*d*: "Is harming anyone, be he friend or not, the function (ἔργον) of the just man, or of his opposite, the unjust?" This is a crucial premise for his rejection of the *lex talionis* in the *Crito*: to return harm for harm is unjust, because "to harm a human being is no different from being unjust to him" (*Cr.* 49c).

39 I take the example from Lefkowitz, 1989a. She argues forcefully that such conduct by divine beings is portrayed in Euripides' plays not because the poet is "trying to get his

than this goddess does in the myths.[40] What would be left of her and of the other Olympians if they were required to observe the stringent norms of Socratic virtue which require every moral agent, human or divine, to act only to cause good to others, never evil, regardless of provocation? Required to meet these austere standards, the city's gods would have become unrecognizable. Their ethical transformation would be tantamount to the destruction of the old gods, the creation of new ones – which is precisely what Socrates takes to be the sum and substance of the accusation at his trial:

T9 *Eu.*   2B "They say I am a god-maker. For disbelieving in the old gods[41] and producing new ones Meletus has brought this indictment against me."[42]

Fully supernatural though they are, Socrates' gods could still strike his pious contemporaries as rationalist fabrications, *ersatz*-gods, as different from the ancient divinities of the cult as are the nature-gods worshipped in the godless Thinkery of the Aristophanic caricature.

Socrates could hardly have moved so far from the ancestral faith unless he had adhered uncompromisingly to the authority of reason, brooking no rival source of knowledge on any matter whatsoever,

audiences to question the gods' traditional nature, but because increased fears and resentments expressed by the characters are an aspect of Euripides' celebrated realism."

40 Another example from Euripides: because Hippolytus had provoked Aphrodite's enmity she destroys not only him but two third parties as well, Phaedra and Theseus, who had done no wrong whatever and had caused her no offense. In comments on my paper Professor Lefkowitz observed that in so acting the goddess "is playing by well-established rules" because "when there are many gods all should be honoured." But *this* rule is far too general. To fit the case the rule would have to be that a god or goddess offended by a mortal may destroy, along with him, innocent persons who had no hand in the offending action. Could there be a rule more obnoxious to the Greek, no less than our own, sense of decency?

41 I.e. the gods of the public cult ("the gods of the state") in whose existence he disbelieves according to the formal indictment (*Ap.* 24B; Xenophon, *Mem.* 1.1.1). Not once in Plato's *Apology* does Socrates plead innocent to this charge: that he believes in *gods* he makes clear enough; that he believes in the gods *of the state* he never says, as he does in Xenophon to rebut the charge (*Mem.* 1.1.2; *Ap.* 11 and 24). Here, as elsewhere (cf. n. 19 above), when Xenophon's testimony conflicts with Plato's we would be wise to believe Plato rather than Xenophon, whose Socrates, a model of conventional piety ("most conspicuous of men" in cult-service to the gods of the state, *Mem.* 1.2.64), would never have been prosecuted for impiety in the first place and, if he had been, would have had no trouble reassuring the jury (which was bound to be as heavily weighted on the traditionalist side as the mass of the army at Syracuse was weighted on the traditionalist view of eclipses: cf. T3 above) that in the abundance of his sacrifices the piety of his life compared favorably with theirs.

42 And cf. his subsequent remark (*Eu.* 6A), "Isn't this why I am being prosecuted – because when such things are said about the gods [tales of savage strife between them], I find them hard to stomach?" Socrates would know that he was not alone in objecting to such tales (Euripides, for example, puts the objection in the mouth of Heracles, Hera's victim (*Her. Fur.* 1340–6). What would be held against him, Socrates thinks, is that by pressing such objections in his *teaching* he undermines traditionalist faith ("the Athenians don't mind anyone they think clever, so long as he does not teach his wisdom; but if they think he makes others like himself, they get angry," *Eu.* 3C7–D1).

about the gods no less than about anything else. How could he have done so while believing, as we saw in T2 above, that communications from gods come regularly through extra-rational channels – reaching him, in particular, through dreams and through his personal "divine sign"?[43] Should this incline us to believe that Socrates is counting on two disparate avenues of knowledge about the gods, rational and extra-rational respectively, yielding two distinct systems of justified belief, one of them reached by elenctic argument, the other by divine revelation through oracles, prophetic dreams and the like?[44] If we did, then, since, as I remarked a moment ago, he shares the common Greek view that god's wisdom is vastly superior to man's,[45] we would have to conclude that he would look to the intimations of his *daimonion* as a source of moral knowledge apart from reason and superior to it, yielding the certainty which is conspicuously lacking in the findings of his elenctic searches.[46] I want to argue that, however plausible it may seem on first encounter, such a view is unsupportable by textual evidence and is in fact inconsistent with that evidence.

First let us look at the way Socrates views those dreams of his which he construes as divine monitions. Consider the one in the *Phaedo* (60E–61B):[47] He says that he had "often" had a dream "urging" and "commanding" him to "make music"[48] and that formerly he had *assumed* (ὑπέλαβον) that this meant he should be doing philosophy "since philosophy is the highest music" (61A), but that now in prison it has occurred to him that what the dream has been enjoining on him is "to make music in the popular sense of the word" (61A), i.e. to versify. So it has now "*seemed*" (ἔδοξε) to him

43 On Socrates' *daimonion* see additional note 6.1.
44 He does not specify the further means, to which he refers at T2 above by the phrase καὶ παντὶ τρόπῳ ᾧπέρ τίς ποτε καὶ ἄλλη θεῖα μοῖρα ἀνθρώπῳ καὶ ὁτιοῦν προσέταξε πράττειν. But we should note that he never attaches such significance to any of the extraordinary *physical* events which the Greeks consider "portents" (τέρατα: cf. Xenophon, *Mem.* 1.4.15, cited in n. 26 above) – unusual occurrences of lightning, thunder, earthquakes, floods, plagues, famine, eclipses, and the like – which figure so prominently as "signs" from the gods in the traditional religious view of the world (for examples see Vlastos, 1975: 11–13); as I remarked above, in Plato's earlier dialogues Socrates never alludes to anything of that sort as a divine "sign."   45 Cf. n. 30 above.
46 In chapter 4 (as also previously in 1985: 1ff., at 17–18 *et passim*) I stressed the shortfall in certainty in what Socrates expects to find through elenctic searching.
47 The passage is embedded in the piece of Socratic biography which introduces the philosophical argument of the dialogue: cf. ch. 1, n. 44.
48 The dream "urging" and "commanding" (61A2, τὸ ἐνύπνιον ἐπικελεύειν, 61A7, προστάτοι τὸ ἐνύπνιον) are, of course, contractions: it is the god that does the "urging" and "commanding" through the dream (cf. *Ap.* 33C5–6). Nonetheless it is significant that in Plato (less so in Xenophon) Socrates avoids as much as possible locutions which would suggest that god speaks to him, instead of merely giving him signs whose interpretation is left to him.

that "it would be safer not to depart [from life] before fulfilling a
sacred duty (πρὶν ἀφοσιώσασθαι) by composing verses in obedience
to the dream." The words he uses – "I assumed" in the first case, "it
has seemed to me" in the second – are not those he would have
chosen for knowledge-claims.[49] From what he relates and from the
language he uses in relating it we can infer that he thinks of the dream
as conveying to him a sign from the god susceptible of alternative
interpretations, the choice between them left entirely to his own
good sense.[50]

That he thinks of oracles too in the same way we can tell from his
conception of divination. Though he never expounds this directly,
we can reconstruct it from the theory of poetic inspiration which he
develops with great gusto in the *Ion*,[51] alluding to it also in the
Apology.[52] In the epic the poet had claimed confidently that he puts
into his verse knowledge imparted to him – "breathed into him"[53]
– by his divine mentor.[54] To this claim Socrates responds with a
characteristic ploy. His reply is, in effect: "Yes, what the inspired
poet puts into his poem is a wonderful, god-given thing; but *it isn't
knowledge* – it can't be knowledge for it is mindless." The poet's claim
to be the direct beneficiary of divine prompting, Socrates accepts; he
allows it at its strongest, conceding that at the moment of inspiration
the poet is ἔνθεος, "has god in him":[55] he is "god-possessed"
(κατεχόμενος).[56] But the very form in which Socrates allows inspired
poetry a superhuman source, debunks its claim to constitute
knowledge:[57]

49 Socrates uses similar language in relating an occurrence of his "divine sign" in *Phdr.*
   242B–C: "When I was about to cross the river...my customary divine sign came to
   me...and *I thought I heard* a voice (φωνὴν ἔδοξα ἀκοῦσαι), forbidding me to leave the spot
   until I had made atonement for some sin to god. Well, I am a seer (μάντις) – not a very
   good one but, like a poor reader, good enough for my own purposes."
50 The same is true in the case of the dream recounted more briefly in the *Crito*: it too, like
   the first dream in the *Phaedo*, employs allegory: in the verse of the *Iliad* (9.363) which
   foretells Achilles' death Socrates reads a prophecy of his own death; and here too he speaks
   only of "belief" or "seeming" (ἐδόκει, 44A10; ὥς γέ μοι δοκεῖ, 44B4).
51 See additional note 6.2 on the *Ion* below.   52 T10 below.   53 Hesiod, *Th.* 31ff.
54 For references see Dodds, 1951: 80–2 and notes.
55 The Greek word comes through the translations feebly as "inspired," losing its literal force
   (for which see e.g. Burkert, 1985: 109–11: he takes *entheos* to mean "within is a god"):
   Similarly weakened in translation is ἐνθουσιάζω, "to be inspired or possessed by a god, to
   be in ecstasy" (LSJ, *s.v.*); when ἐνθουσιασμός is anglicized as "enthusiasm" it becomes
   "ardent zeal" (*O.E.D.*); "frenzy" might come closer to its force.
56 The poets are described as "possessed by the god" (κατεχόμενοι: 533E7, 534A3–4 and E5),
   "possessed [by the god]" (κατεχόμενοι, 534A4 and 5); it is said that they βακχεύουσι
   ("speak or act like one frenzy-stricken," LSJ, *s.v.* βακχεύω).
57 And most particularly, the supposed knowledge which had made Homer "the educator of
   Hellas," widely thought to deserve "to be constantly studied as a guide by which to
   regulate our whole life" (*R.* 606E, Cornford's tr.; cf. Verdenius, 1943: 233ff. at 248).

T10 *Ap.* 22B–C: "I soon perceived that *it is not through knowledge* that poets produce their poems but through a sort of inborn gift[58] and in a state of inspiration,[59] like the diviners and soothsayers, who also speak many admirable things but *know nothing of the things about which they speak.*"[60]

In Socrates' view the effect of the god's entry into the poet is to drive out the poet's mind: when the god is in him the poet is "out of his mind," ἔκφρων,[61] or "intelligence is no longer present in him";[62] so he may find himself saying many things which are admirable (πολλὰ καὶ καλά)[63] and true[64] without knowing what he is saying. Thus to think of the poet as a recipient of divine *revelation*, i.e. as the beneficiary of "disclosure of *knowledge*"[65] to him by the god, would be to contradict Socrates' description of him as "speaking while *knowing nothing* of what he speaks": one who "has no knowledge of what one speaks" cannot have been been given knowledge.[66]

That this mediumistic theory of inspired poetry Socrates would apply also to divination follows directly from the fact that he regards divination as the theory's primary field of application: it is because he is *like* the diviner[67] that the inspired poet is "out of his mind" and

58 φύσει τινι, "by a kind of native disposition" (Allen), "some inborn talent" (Grube). Cf. Burnet, 1924: note on *Ap.* 22C1: "The word is used here in the sense in which it is opposed to habituation and instruction. It is the φυά which Pindar (*Ol.* 2.24) opposes to the ineffectual efforts of poets who have been taught, and is in fact 'genius' in the proper sense of the word." 59 ἐνθουσιάζοντες. Cf. additional note 6.1.

60 ἴσασιν δὲ οὐδὲν ὧν λέγουσι: "know nothing of the things they speak" (Allen); speak "without understanding of what they say" (Grube). The same phrase is applied to statesmen in the *Meno* (99c) when likened to the oraclegivers and seers who are bracketed with the poets in the *Apology*.

61 "Out of his mind, beside himself" (LSJ, *s.v.* ἔκφρων, principal use) – not ἄφρων, "silly," "stupid," as would have been the case if he had retained his own mind, albeit in an impaired condition.

62 ὁ νοῦς μηκέτι ἐν αὐτῷ ἐνῇ... οἷς νοῦς μὴ πάρεστιν (*Ion* 534C–D).

63 T10 above. So too in the *Ion*: in the state of divine possession "admirable" (καλά: 533E7, 534E4) sentences are uttered by poets – which is scarcely surprising since it is "god himself who speaks to us through them" (ὁ θεὸς αὐτός ἐστιν ὁ λέγων, διὰ τούτων δὲ φθέγγεται πρὸς ἡμᾶς, 534D3–4). It is reassuring to learn that Socrates did not consider inane or foolish the great poetry he hears on the stage or reads in Homer, whose words he has at his finger-tips and quotes freely (see the numerous listings *s.v.* Ὅμηρος and its inflections in Brandwood, 1976). His stubborn resistance to the popular Greek view that one may learn how to live by reading, hearing, and memorizing the poets (cf. n. 57 above), instead of searching critically for the truth, does not keep him from admitting that there is much wisdom *in* poets who speak "by divine grace" (θείᾳ δυνάμει, 534C, and are used by god as his mouthpiece (534D3–4). 64 *Ion* 534B: καὶ ἀληθῆ λέγουσι.

65 *O.E.D., s.v.* "revelation." On this see further additional note 6.1 on the *daimonion*.

66 He might have true beliefs, yet lack that understanding which would enable him to see why they are true and draw the right inferences from them. The knowledge denied to the poets is reserved to the god who speaks through them or in them: *Ion* 534D: "it is not they [the inspired poets] who utter those priceless words while bereft of understanding (οἷς νοῦς μὴ ἐνῇ), but that the god himself is the speaker (ὁ θεὸς αὐτός ἐστιν ὁ λέγων)."

67 *Ap.* 22B–C: "they compose their verses not by skill but by a sort of natural endowment and divine inspiration, *like the diviners and oracle-givers*" (ὥσπερ οἱ θεομάντεις καὶ οἱ χρησμῳδοί).

"knows nothing of the things of which he speaks." So neither could Socrates think of the diviner as receiving knowledge in his mantic states: how could a mental state in which there is no νοῦς, no understanding, in which a person "knows nothing of what he speaks," constitute *knowledge*? For Socrates diviners, seers, oracle-givers, poets are all in the same boat. All of them in his view are know-nothings, or rather, worse: unaware of their sorry epistemic state, they set themselves up as repositories of wisdom emanating from a divine, all-wise source. What they say may be true; but even when it is true, they are in no position to discern what there is in it that is true. If their hearer were in a position to discern this, then *he* would have the knowledge denied to them; the knowledge would come from the application of *his reason* to what these people say without reason.

Though Socrates does not apply this theory explicitly to prophetic dreams or to his own "divine sign" the connection with the latter is unavoidable, since he refers to the functioning of his *daimonion* as his "customary divination" and to himself as a "seer,"[68] without ever denying, directly or by implication, that what is true of divination generally would also apply to that homespun variety of it with which "divine dispensation" has favored him. So all he could claim to be getting from the *daimonion* at any given time is precisely what he calls the *daimonion* itself – a "divine sign,"[69] which allows, indeed requires, *unlimited scope for the deployment of his critical reason* to extract whatever truth it can from those monitions.[70] Thus without any recourse to Ionian *physiologia*,[71] Socrates has disarmed the irrationalist potential

In the *Ion* (534C) god uses poets *and* oracle-givers and "those of the diviners who are divine" as his servants by "taking away their understanding from them" (ἐξαιρούμενος τούτων τὸν νοῦν). We should note that both passages speak of "oracle-givers," *not* of the "oraclemongers" (χρησμολόγοι), who are treated with such scorn by Aristophanes and whom Socrates ignores as unworthy of any notice at all.

68 *Ap.* 40A; *Phdr.* 242C (cf. n. 49 above).   69 Cf. additional note 6.1.

70 It is in this direction that Plato develops his own theory of divination in *Ti.* 71E: a god-given sop to human weakness (ἀφροσύνῃ θεὸς ἀνθρωπίνῃ δέδωκεν), enabling us to enjoy divinatory powers in certain abnormal states (dreams, or illness, or enthusiasm) whose import we may try to understand when we revert to a normal condition: "it is for the rational nature (τῆς ἔμφρονος φύσεως) to comprehend (συννοῆσαι) the utterances, in dream or waking life, of divination and possession."

71 As does Democritus, producing a naturalistic theory of divination (DK 68A136-8), the complement of his naturalistic theory of poetic inspiration that fine poetry is produced by its creators "with enthusiasm and a holy spirit" (DK 63B18; cf. B21). The divine influx into the poet's mind is explained, like everything else in Democritus' natural philosophy, in corpuscularist terms (Plutarch, *Moralia* 734F-735C: cited as Democritus' fragment A77 in DK, with which A79 and B166 in DK should be compared). For a detailed exposition of the Democritean theory see Delatte (1934: 28ff.) who, however, assumes (56ff.) that the theory of inspiration in the *Ion* was derived from Democritus – a groundless guess, which would have had considerable plausibility *if* we knew that Socrates had been receptive to

of the belief in supernatural gods communicating with human beings by supernatural signs. His theory both preserves the venerable view that mantic experience is divinely caused *and* nullifies that view's threat to the exclusive authority of reason to determine questions of truth or falsehood.[72]

Thus the paradox I confronted at the start of this paper dissolves: there can be no conflict between Socrates' unconditional readiness to follow critical reason wherever it may lead and his equally unconditional commitment to obey commands issued to him by his supernatural god through supernatural signs. *These two commitments cannot conflict because only by the use of his own critical reason can Socrates determine the true meaning of any of these signs.* Let me apply this result to the signs from the god on which Socrates predicates his philosophic mission in the *Apology*.[73]

Some scholars have expressed bafflement, or worse, incredulity, that from the Pythia's "No" to the question "Is there anyone wiser than Socrates?" he should have derived the command to philosophize on the streets of Athens.[74] Wouldn't that be pulling a rabbit out of a hat? Quite so. And is there any difficulty about that, if you are licensed to put the rabbit into the hat yourself in the first place? Socrates makes no secret of how subjective had been the process by which the god's command[75] had reached him:

the speculations of the *physiologoi*, while, as we know, he insisted that he had no truck with them (*Ap.* 19C).

72 It is hard to find a clear recognition of this in any account of Socrates' view of divination in the scholarly literature. Beckman's (1979: 84–5) comes closest to doing so, for he rightly credits Socrates with "a strict refusal to grant the status of knowledge to any such 'revelations.'" But he stops short of allowing Socrates a clean break with the traditional view, remarking that nonetheless Socrates retains "an orthodox view of divine inspiration" (*loc. cit.*). How so, when the assumption that divine inspiration yields *knowledge* was of the essence of the orthodox view?

73 I shall be following exclusively Plato's version of the oracle story. In Xenophon's *Memorabilia* there is no reference at all to the oracle Chaerephon brought back from Delphi (a curious discrepancy with the Xenophontic *Apology*, where the oracle story forms the centerpiece of Socrates' defense), and the whole motif of a command from God is suppressed – understandably so, given the apologetic animus of the former work: for that purpose the claim to have received a divine commission would be counter-productive – it would be seen as self-serving megalomania, which is indeed how Socrates fears it is being viewed by many of his judges in the Platonic *Apology*: "if I were to say that this [abandoning his mission to obtain acquittal] would be to disobey the god and this is the reason why I could not keep silent, you would not believe me, thinking that I was shamming" (37E). (Further comment on the difference between Plato's and Xenophon's versions of the oracle story in additional note 6.3.)

74 Hackforth (1933: 88ff.) is greatly exercised over this, as are the other commentators to whom he refers. He claims that to make sense of the narrative in Plato's text "we must deduct from that story the element of the imperative in the oracle" (93). The claim is refuted convincingly by Brickhouse & Smith, 1983: 657ff. (cf. n. 4 above).

75 The wording in T11 (τοῦ θεοῦ τάττοντος) and the analogy with the orders on which a soldier is assigned to his "post" (*loc. cit.*), as well as the reiteration of the idea in T2 above

T11 *Ap.* 28E: "The god commanded me, *as I supposed and assumed*, to live philosophizing, examining myself and others."

Here again the same language as in recounting the dream in the *Phaedo* where he had "assumed" (*Phd.* 60E) that "make music" meant "do philosophy." So even if that oracle from Delphi had been the only sign Socrates had received from the god, he could still have pried out of the Pythia's "No" the command to engage all and sundry in philosophic discourse: he could do so by "supposing and assuming" that this had been the hidden meaning in the riddling declaration[76] that no one alive was wiser than himself, though he was painfully "aware of being wise in nothing, great or small" (21B). But in point of fact that oracle was by no means the only sign Socrates had received. It was only the first of many. Let me cite T2 once again:

T2 "To do this has been commanded me... *through divinations and through dreams and every other means through which divine apportionment has ever commanded anyone to do anything.*"

So there had been more divinations (some of them no doubt from his own *daimonion*) and more than one prophetic dream. Suppose that one of these had spelled out fully what the god wanted him to do, ordering him to do it in the very words in which he describes his own activity:

T12 *Ap.* 30A–B: "I do nothing but go about persuading you, young and old, to have your first and greatest concern not for your body or for your money but for your soul, that it should be as excellent as possible."

Suppose the dream had ordered him to do just that. Would this have given him the certainty that the command comes from god? How would he know that this is not one of those lying dreams which the gods have been traditionally thought to send to men when they want to deceive them?[77] And how could he tell that it does not come from his own fancy instead? There is only one way he could have proceeded to still that doubt. He would have had to ask himself: Do I have *reason* to believe that this is work the god wants done by me? Is he that sort of god? What is his character?

Fully explicit in the text is one item in the character Socrates

---

(προστέτακται) leave no doubt on this point. I cannot understand why Brickhouse & Smith (*loc. cit.*) follow Guthrie in claiming that "Socrates sees the oracle as a 'message' and not as a 'command'" (1983: 663, n. 14).

76 Which he had found so baffling on first hearing (21B): "I kept thinking: What does the god mean? What is he hinting at?... For a long time I was baffled..." (Cf. Burnet's note on 21B3.)   77 As e.g. in *Iliad* 2.6ff.

imputes to the god upon first hearing the report Chaerephon brought back from Delphi:

T13 *Ap.* 21B: "Surely he is not lying. That would not be right (θέμις) for him."

Why so? The gods in whom the city believes have no such scruples. They have been lying since Homer.[78] Why should Socrates think his god would be so different? Because, as we saw earlier, unlike their gods, Socrates' god is invariantly good, incapable of causing any evil to anyone in any way at any time. Since to deceive a man is to do evil to him, Socrates' god cannot be lying. And since his goodness is entailed by his own wisdom,[79] which is boundless, his goodness must be boundless too. And since his good will is directed to Socrates' fellow-townsmen in Athens, no less than to Socrates himself,[80] he must wish that they should put the perfection of their soul above all of their other concerns.

How could the god implement this wish for them? How could he bring everyone in Athens to see that "they should have their first and greatest concern for their soul that it should be as excellent as possible?" He could send them signs to that effect, dreams and oracles galore. But *unless they brought the right beliefs to the interpretation of those signs, they would not be able to read them correctly.* And they could not have come by those right beliefs unless they had already engaged in the quest for moral truth.[81] So the god is stuck. Vastly powerful in innumerable ways though he is, in this matter he is powerless to give effect to his will by his own unaided means.[82] He must, therefore, depend on someone who does have the right beliefs and can read signs correctly to assist the god by doing on his behalf for the people of Athens what the god in his boundless good will for them would be doing himself in person, if he only could. This being the

78 See e.g. Deichgräber, 1952. That the traditional gods think nothing of deceiving each other is one of the first criticisms the Ionian rationalists directed against the deities of popular belief (Xenophanes B11). Would such gods scruple to deceive men? "Athena has deceived me," Hector reflects (*Il.* 22.299) in that duel with Achilles which is to be his last.

79 Cf. p. 164 above.

80 Socrates assumes that he had been commissioned to be Athens' gadfly because of the god's care for the Athenians (30E–31A).

81 As Socrates already had, else *he* could not have read correctly the signs the god sent him. Scholars who think that Socrates' moral inquiries begin with his receipt of the Delphic oracle (Ross, 1933, in Patzer, 1987: 227; Ferguson, 1964: 70–3) seem unaware of this fundamental point.

82 A parallel (and entirely independent) use of this idea is made by C. C. W. Taylor, 1982: 109ff., at 113: "But there is one good product which [the gods] can't produce without human assistance, namely good human souls." That Socrates "sees the pious man as a kind of craftsman" who aims at the production of an "all-glorious" *ergon* in service to the god is rightly stressed by Brickhouse & Smith (1983: 665; cf. n. 4 above).

case, is it not understandable that Socrates should have seen his street-philosophizing as work done on the god's behalf and should, therefore, have a rational ground for "believing and supposing" that this is what the god is commanding him to do, declaring that no man is wiser than Socrates, not to give Socrates cause to preen himself on that account,[83] but to make it possible for him to guess that a unique responsibility was laid on him to use in the god's service what little[84] wisdom he has?

We can now move to that point in the *Euthyphro* to which I said at the start of this chapter I would return near its close. In the search for the answer to "What is piety?" Euthyphro had got as far as saying that piety is "service" to the gods.[85] But when pressed to say what sort of service this would be, he could only regurgitate the traditional answer:

T14 *Eu.* 14B: "Speaking and doing what is pleasing to the gods by praying and sacrificing – this is piety."[86]

Sniffing out here the age-old *do ut des* conception of worship – swapping gifts of sacrifice for prayed-for benefits – Socrates rebuffs it brutally. He says that, if so, piety would be "an art of commercial exchanges between gods and men" (ἐμπορική τις τέχνη, 14E6), exchanges which would make no sense since they would be so one-sided: the gods stand in no need of gifts from us, while we are totally dependent on their gifts to us – "there is no good in our life which does not come from them" (15A) – so we would be the exclusively advantaged party; if piety is holy barter it is a bargain for us, a swindle for the gods. So the definition in T14 is decidedly on the wrong tack. To forestall that wrongheaded, diversionary move Socrates had asked:

T15 *Eu.* 13E10–11: "In the performance of what work (ἔργον) does our service to the gods assist them?... In Zeus's name, tell me, what is that glorious[87] work the gods perform by using us as their servants?"

That is the critical point in the search. Socrates remarks a moment later that if that question had been answered correctly, the goal of

---

83 As he does in the Xenophontic *Apology of Socrates* (15–17) where mention of the oracle (blown up to declare that "no one is more liberal, more just, or wiser" than Socrates), triggers a lengthy outburst of self-congratulation.

84 "Human wisdom," he calls it, admitting that this much he *can* claim (20D–E) in the very context in which he declares that he "is not aware of being wise in anything, great or small" (21B: cf. additional note I.I).   85 13D: ὑπηρετική τις...θεοῖς (13D7).

86 This is virtually the same as the definition of "piety" Xenophon puts into Socrates' mouth in the *Memorabilia*: "The pious man is rightly defined as 'he who knows the νόμιμα concerning the gods'" (4.6.14); these νόμιμα are the lawfully prescribed sacrifices (1.3.1).

87 πάγκαλον, "all-beautiful," "marvellously fine."

the search would have been reached: Socrates would have learned what piety is.[88] That is a very broad hint. But how could Euthyphro have taken advantage of it? The clue he is offered is lost to him because the notion that the gods have work to do,[89] work in which human beings could assist them, is foreign to Greek religion.[90]

But just suppose that Euthyphro had been allowed a preview of the speech Socrates was to give at his trial – that part of it which recounts the oracle story and Socrates' response to it. Would it be too much to hope that even Euthyphro's sluggish mind would have picked up the needed clue? For then he would have realized that Socrates saw his own work in summoning all and sundry to perfect their soul as work he did at the god's command, as his own service (λατρεία, ὑπηρεσία) to the god.[91] And that Socrates did consider this a "glorious work" could hardly have escaped Euthyphro if he had heard Socrates assuring the judges

T16 *Ap.* 30A: "I believe that no greater good has ever come to you in the city than this service of mine to the god."

With these pieces of the puzzle before him Euthyphro should have been able to see what piety means in Socrates' own life: doing on the god's behalf, in assistance to him, work the god wants done and would be doing himself if he only could.[92] To derive from this a definition of piety Euthyphro would then have had to generalize, contriving a formula that would apply not only in Socrates' case but in every possible case of pious conduct. This is a tall order and it is by no means clear that Socrates himself would have been able to fill it. But this technical failure would not shake – would scarcely touch – the central insight into the nature of piety with which, I submit, we can credit Socrates on the strength of what Plato puts into his mouth

88 Cf. n. 4 above.

89 The imputation of an *ergon* to the gods has been thought a conclusive objection to taking the question in T15 as a true lead to the discovery of what piety is: Burnet, Allen, Versenyi have claimed that Socrates could not have predicated his search on a notion which is so patently foreign to the common Greek conceptions of the gods: for refutation of this claim see Brickhouse & Smith, 1983: 660–2 (cf. n. 4 above) and McPherran, 1985: 292–4 (cf. n. 5 above).

90 The nearest thing to it in Greek mythology is the "labors" of Heracles. Socrates, clutching at a straw, alludes to them at one point in his defense: he speaks of the hardships of his mission (22A) "as if they were labors I had undertaken to perform" (ὥσπερ πόνους τινὰς πονοῦντος), choosing to ignore the fact that Heracles' labours had been a torment inflicted on him by the ill-will of Hera, while Socrates' labors had been the source of the greatest possible happiness in his life (38A). (Professor Lefkowitz in her comment reminds us of Ion's "labor" (πόνον, Eur. *Ion* 128) for Apollo; but this case is not illuminating: Ion is a religious professional, a temple-servant.)

91 23B–C (in T16), τὴν τοῦ θεοῦ λατρείαν, and 30A6–7: τὴν ἐμὴν τῷ θεῷ ὑπηρεσίαν. The former had especially strong religious evocations; cf. *Phdr.* 244E, "prayer and service to the gods" (θεῶν εὐχάς τε καὶ λατρείας) for "religious activity." 92 Cf. n. 82 above.

in the *Apology* and the *Euthyphro*. *Piety is doing god's work to benefit human beings* – work such as Socrates' kind of god would wish done on his behalf, in service to him. Whether or not a formula could be devised to encapsulate this insight in an elenctically foolproof definition, this much should be already clear: Socrates has hit on a new conception of piety, as revolutionary in the religious domain, as is his non-retaliatory conception of justice in the moral one.

How radical, how subversive of traditional Greek belief and practice this conception of piety would be, we can see if we reflect that what had passed for religion to-date had been thick with magic. By "magic," I understand[93] the belief, and all of the practices predicated on it, that *by means of ritualistic acts man can induce supernatural powers to give effect to his own wishes*. In black magic one exorcises supernaturals to do evil to one's enemy. In white magic one seeks to prevail on them through prayer and sacrifice to do good to oneself and to those for whom one cares – one's family, friends, nation, and the like: good which, but for those ritualistic performances, the gods would have withheld. As practiced all around Socrates, religion was saturated with just that sort of magic.[94] From religion as Socrates understands it magic is purged – all of it, both white and black. In the practice of Socratic piety man would not pray to god, "My will be done by thee," but "Thy will be done by me." In this new form of piety man is not a self-seeking beggar beseeching self-centered, honor-hungry gods, cajoling them by gifts of sacrifice to do good which without that gift their own will for good would not have prompted them to do. Man addresses gods who are of their very nature relentlessly beneficent: they want for men nothing but what men would want for themselves if their will were undividedly will for good.

If some such thing as this is what Socrates' conception of piety would do for Greek religion, we may still ask what it would do for Socrates himself. What is it that doing god's work on god's behalf to benefit his fellow-townsmen brings to Socrates' own life and character that would not otherwise be assured for it? Here is my

---

93 The primary sense of "magic" according to the *O.E.D.* is "the pretended art of influencing course of events by occult control of nature or of spirits"; among the senses for "occult" that dictionary lists "mysterious, beyond the range of ordinary knowledge, involving the supernatural." Taking "occult" in this sense of the word, petitionary prayer whose efficacy is predicated on the incinerating of a sacrificial offering on an altar in accordance with the established ritual, could very well be reckoned magic (white if benign, advancing the welfare of the petitioner or his friends, black if malevolent, causing harm to his enemies).

94 Most petitionary prayer accompanying sacrifice, as conceived by the Greeks, would have to count as white magic: the sacrificial gift to the gods is designed to elicit a reciprocal favor to the worshipper. See additional note 6.4.

answer in nutshell form: it brings a release from that form of egocentricity which is endemic in Socratic eudaemonism, as in all eudaemonism. In that theory the good for each of us is unambiguously our own personal good: the happiness which is the final reason for each of our intentional actions is our own personal happiness.[95] To what extent we should care for the good of others will then depend on those contingencies of blood or fortune which so bind their good to ours that we can perceive their good as our good, their happiness as a component of ours. In Socratic piety that link between our good and that of others is made non-contingent through devotion to a disinterestedly benevolent god who, being already perfect, does not require from us any contribution to his own well-being but only asks each of us to do for other persons what he would be doing for them himself if he were to change places with us. To the spiritual toxins in eudaemonist motivation high religion here provides an antidote. Were it not for that divine command that first reached Socrates through the report Chaerephon brought back from Delphi there is no reason to believe that he would have ever become a street-philosopher. If what Socrates wants is partners in elenctic argument, why should he not keep to those in whose company he had sought and found his eudaemonist theory – congenial and accomplished fellow-seekers after moral truth? Why should be take to the streets, forcing himself on people who have neither taste nor talent for philosophy, trying to talk them into submitting to a therapy they do not think they need? The physician who seeks out people who fancy themselves in the best of health, taking it on himself to persuade them that they are mortally sick, is undertaking a thankless task. Would Socrates have given his life to this task if his piety had not driven him to it?

In closing let me offer a passage which is a far cry from Socrates' own world and shows what his piety would be like if transposed into the language of an altogether different religious creed and practice:

T17 *The Book of the Perfect Life*:[96] When men are enlightened by the true light they renounce all desire and choice and commit and commend themselves to the Eternal Goodness, so that every enlightened man would say: "I fain would be to the Eternal Goodness what his own hand is to a man."

95 As I point out in chapter 8, n. 14, this assumption is so deeply embedded in Socratic eudaemonism that no need is felt to make it explicit, but its presence is easily detectable when the text is closely read. Thus in explaining the general principle that in all our actions we pursue the good, Socrates moves from "because we think it better" (*G.* 468B, οἰόμενοι βέλτιον εἶναι) to "because we think it better *for us*" (οἰόμενοι βέλτιον εἶναι ἡμῖν) without any apparent awareness that what is expressed in the second phrase is substantially different from what is expressed in the first.

96 By an unknown German mystic of the fourteenth century.

The language is that of mystical religion, and Socrates is no mystic. And "renunciation of all desire and choice" would be decidedly out of the question for him as a declared eudaemonist. But this much he would have in common with that medieval mystic. He too would fain be to an infinitely wise and belevolent being what his own hand is to a man or, better still, what a man's argumentative voice is to a man.[97]

97 In revising this essay for publication I have benefited from Professor Lefkowitz's comments on it (1989b) and have made some revisions in my text in the light of remarks of hers which I consider just. But I am puzzled why she should think the gods she has in view here (and in her paper [1989a] to which I refer in n. 39 above) worthy of *reverence* (σέβας: piety *is* εὐσέβεια). Think of Hippolytus. Eccentric in his straitlaced abstention from "the works of the night" over which Aphrodite presides (fornication and adultery these would be in his case, since he is unwed), he commits no moral wrong: chastity is no crime, even when it is overdone. Can he *revere* the deity who destroys him – "powerful, proud, intolerant, and quite without scruple or pity" (Barrett, 1964: 155)? Fear of her power would have given him reason enough to refrain from provoking her fury. But could such concessions to power devoid of moral quality be reckoned εὐσέβεια, and the sentiment which animates it σέβας?

7

SOCRATES' REJECTION OF RETALIATION[1]

If therefore the light that is in thee be darkness, how great is that darkness.   (Matt. 6:23)

In the last and most famous of his *Theses on Feuerbach* Marx observes: "The philosophers have done no more than interpret the world. The point, however, is to change it." Substitute "morality" for "world" and the observation would be true of almost all the leading philosophers of the West. Moralists as powerfully innovative as are Aristotle, Hume, and Kant take the morality into which they are born for granted. The task they set themselves is only to excogitate its rationale. It does not occur to them to subject its content to critical scrutiny, prepared to question norms ensconced in it which do not measure up to their rational standards. But there have been exceptions, unnoticed by Marx, and of these Socrates is the greatest. Proceeding entirely from within the morality of his own time and place, he nevertheless finds reason to stigmatize as unjust one of its most venerable, best established, rules of justice.

By the morality of a society I understand those norms of right and wrong, rules of conduct or excellences of character, publicly acknowledged within it, whose function it is to foster human well-being. The sense of justice centers in the concern that those norms be applied impartially. So if in a given society we were to find them habitually observed in a discriminatory way – applied strictly for the benefit of some and loosely, if at all, for that of others – we would know that to this extent the morality of the society is defective. When we scrutinize the morality of ancient Greece with this in mind two large areas of such deficiency come into view. (1) The application of its moral norms is grossly discriminatory in conduct towards personal enemies. (2) It is no less so, though for different reasons and in different ways, in the conduct of citizens towards their social inferiors – women, aliens, slaves. Coming to Socrates' practical

---

1 An ancestor of this essay formed the first of my Gifford Lectures at St. Andrews in 1981, and was published in *Archaiognosia* (1 [1980]: 301–24). Drastically revised in response to criticism, it was presented as a Townsend Lecture at Cornell in 1986.

moral teaching with this in mind we can see in good perspective the most strikingly new thing about it: its root- and-branch rejection of that first form of discrimination. And we can also see the limits of its innovative thrust: it has nothing to say against the second. Revolutionary on the first, it is conformist on the second.

To assess justly Socrates' contribution to the Greek sense of justice we must treat *it* impartially, recognizing its achievement without disguising its failure. Accordingly, though in this book I speak only of the former, I shall not lend it a false grandeur by concealing the latter. There is no evidence that Socrates' moral vision was exempt from that blindspot in the Athenian civic conscience which made it possible for Demosthenes, addressing a lot-selected court, to put compassion at the forefront of his city's ethos,[2] yet no less possible for his contemporary, Lycurgus, addressing a similar court, to declare that it is "most just and democratic (δικαιότατον καὶ δημοτι-κώτατον)" to make it mandatory that court evidence by slaves should be given under torture.[3] To subject citizens to such treatment would be unthinkable in the Athenian judicial system.[4] Nowhere in our sources is there the slightest indication that this and other forms of grossly discriminatory conduct towards slaves, sanctioned by the prevailing moral code, drew any protest from Socrates. His critique of the code leaves institutional morality untouched. It is directed solely to that area of conduct which falls entirely within the limits of the habitual expectations sustained by the institutional framework.

I

Harming one's enemy to the full extent permitted by public law is not only tolerated, but glorified, in Greek moralizing. The sentiment is ubiquitous.[5] Solon (fr. 1 Diehl), aspiring to "good repute among all men," prays that that he may be "sweet to friends, bitter to enemies." Medea, scorning the role of feminine weakling, determined to be as strong as any male, vows that she will be "harsh to foes, gracious to friends, for such are they whose life is most glorious."[6] In Plato's *Meno* Socrates' interlocutor builds it into the formula meant to capture the essence of manly excellence:

2 *Against Timocrates*, 170.
3 *Against Leocrates*, 29. Some scholars have claimed that this was rarely applied. Their claim is more of a wishful projection of humanitarian sentiment than a sober conclusion from evidence: see Marie-Paule Carrière-Hergavault, 1973: 45–79; also MacDowell, 1978: 245–7.
4 It was forbidden by law: MacDowell, 1978: 247 and n. 563.
5 For a rich documentation of this pervasive feature of Greek morality and for extensive references to comment on it in the scholarly literature, see especially Blundell, 1989: ch. 2.
6 Euripides, *Med.* 807–10: "Let no one think me a low and feeble thing, / A quiet one, but of that other sort, / Harsh to foes, gracious to friends, / For such are they whose life is most glorious."

T1 Plato, *M.* 71E: "Socrates, if you want to know what manly virtue is, it is this: to be able to conduct the city's affairs doing good to friends and evil to enemies, while taking care not to be harmed oneself."

Isocrates, mouthing traditional commonplaces, counsels Demonicus:

T2 Isocrates, *To Dem.* 26: Consider it as disgraceful to be outdone by enemies in inflicting harm, as by friends in conferring benefits.

If one is nurtured in this norm, what constraints on harming a foe would one accept? The authorities which recommend it lay down none. Consider Pindar, golden voice of conventional wisdom:

T3 Pindar, *2 Pyth.* 83–5: Let me love him who loves me, / But on a foe as foe I will descend, wolf-like, / In ever varying ways by crooked paths.[7]

The image – wolflike, stealthy, crooked attack – conveys the thought that underhanded malice, normally contemptible, would be in order here. If you were to deceive your enemy, corrupt his slave, seduce his wife, ruin his reputation by slander, you would not be ashamed of it, you could be proud of it. Are there then no limits to be observed in deviating from decent conduct at your foe's expense? So long as you keep the public law, traditional morality lays down none,[8] except those set by the *lex talionis*, the ancient doctrine of retaliation.

The metaphor through which this notion grips the moral imagination of the Greeks is the repayment of a debt: verbs for "paying" (τίνειν, ἀποτίνειν, ἀνατίνειν) and "paying back" (ἀντι-τίνειν) are the ones regularly used to express it. The idea is that if you do someone a wrong or a harm, you have thereby incurred a debt and must discharge it by suffering the same sort of evil yourself – a wrong or harm "such as" (*tale*, hence *talio*[9]) to repay what you did to him. At first blush this extension of the money-debt resists generalization. If you had stolen one of your neighbor's sheep, and he were then to steal it back, his action could be plausibly pictured as making you repay a surreptitious loan you had previously extracted from him. But what if you had killed one of his sheep, and he were now to retaliate by spitefully killing one of yours?. What semblance of reason would there be in thinking that he thereby secures *repayment*? Does he get back his sheep by killing one of yours,

---

7 I was reminded by the late Friedrich Solmsen that Schadewaldt (diss. Halle, 1928: 326, n. 1) had objected that Pindar could not have associated his own person with "crooked" action, and had amended the text accordingly (πατέων to πατέοντ') to make "crooked" refer to the adversary. But the received text is palaeographically impeccable, and no reason has been offered for assuming that Pindar would balk at "crooked paths" *against an enemy*.

8 In Euripides' *Ion* (1046–7) the elderly slave remarks as he goes forth to carry out Creusa's errand (to poison the youth), "When one wants to do evil to enemies, no rule (νόμος) bars the way." Here νόμος does not refer to statute law (else the sentiment would make no sense), but to the moral code.

9 Blundell (cf. n. 5 above) notices that this is the Latin legal term for "repayment in kind."

leaving its carcass on the hillside to be picked off by jackals? But this is not to say that he gets nothing from the retaliatory act: he may get something he prizes much more than a sheep.[10] The passionate desire for revenge – i.e. to harm another person for no reason other than that he or she harmed one in the first place – is as blind to calculations of utility as to every other rational consideration. One may get all the greater satisfaction from an act of pure revenge, freed completely from concern for restitution. And this, precisely, is the *raison d'être* of the *lex talionis*. it aims to put a lid on the extravagance of passion by stipulating that for any given harm no greater may be inflicted in return.

T4 Exodus 21 : 24–5: ...eye for eye, tooth for tooth, hand for hand, foot for foot, burning for burning, wound for wound, stripe for stripe.

If someone has knocked out one of your eyes you might well feel like knocking out both of his – or more, if he had more.[11] The rule says: Only one.

This constraint on revenge by a limit of equivalences so commends the *talio* to the moral sense of the Greeks that when their first philosophers come to think of the natural universe as an ordered world, a cosmos,[12] they project on it their idea of justice by picturing the grand periodicities of nature as enacting cycles of retaliatory retribution. In Anaximander's famous fragment (T5), the hot and the dry, encroaching upon the cold and wet in the summer, must "pay" for their "injustice" by suffering in return the like fate in the winter, when the cold and wet make converse aggression upon the erstwhile aggressors, completing one retaliatory cycle, to start another in endless succession:

T5 Anaximander, fr. 1 (Diels–Kranz): For they render justice and repayment (δίκην καὶ τίσιν) to one another in accordance with the ordering of time.

So too the first recorded definition of "justice" identifies it with τὸ ἀντιπεπονθός, whose literal force, "to suffer in return," is lost in the unavoidably lame translation, "reciprocity":

T6 Aristotle, *Nic. Eth.* 1132b21–7: Some believe that reciprocity (τὸ ἀντιπεπονθός) simply *is* justice. So the Pythagoreans thought. For they defined "justice" as "reciprocity."

10 At this point I am indebted to Terry Irwin for criticism of an earlier version of this paper.
11 Blundell cites (1989: 30) Hesiod, *Op.* 709–11 ("If he starts it, saying or doing some unpleasant thing, be sure to pay him back twice as much") among other expressions of the sentiment. As she notes, though Hesiod favors "twice as much," he does not say this would be just: cf. T7 below.
12 Cf. Vlastos, 1975: chapter 1 ("The Greeks discover the cosmos").

Ascribing this archaic formula to Pythagorean philosophers, Aristotle does not accept it as an adequate definition of "justice." But he concurs with its sentiment,[13] citing Hesiod in its support:

T7 Hesiod, fr. 174 Rzach: For if one suffered what one did, straight justice would be done (εἴ κε πάθοι τά τ' ἔρεξε, δίκη κ' ἰθεῖα γένοιτο).

From the many testimonies to the currency of this notion I pick one from the *Oresteia*:

T8 Aeschylus, *Choephoroi* 309–14: "'For hostile word let hostile word / Be fulfilled (τελείσθω),' Justice cries aloud / As she collects the debt (τοὐφειλόμενον πράσσουσα). / 'Let homicidal blow the homicidal / Blow repay (τινέτω). Let him who did suffer in return (δράσαντι παθεῖν),' / The thrice-venerable tale declares."

Aeschylus reaffirms the hallowed tradition of his people that to satisfy justice the wrongdoer must be made to suffer in return the evil he or she has done another. But as the action moves on, it becomes apparent that the maxim leaves the poet gravely troubled. As Orestes drags his mother offstage to kill her the poet makes him say:

T9 Aeschylus, *Choephoroi* 930: "Since you killed whom you ought not, now suffer what you ought not (κανοῦσ' ὃν οὐ χρῆν καὶ τὸ μὴ χρεὼν πάθε)."[14]

Why so? If the *talio* is quintessentially just, why should not Orestes be saying instead, "Since you killed whom you ought not, now suffer what *you ought*?" Orestes is in a bind. Instructed by Apollo that Clytemnestra should be made to pay with her own blood for the family blood she had spilled, he is still unable to shake off the horror of matricide.

In the *Electra* of Euripides we see him in the same bind. He remonstrates with Electra: "How shall I kill her who bore me and brought me up?" When she retorts, "Just as she killed your father and mine," he goes along but without conviction, railing against the "folly" (ἀμαθία) of Apollo, "who prophesied that I should kill a mother, whom I ought not to kill."[15]

For further evidence that the rule of just repayment elicits less than full conviction from the conscience of those who invoke it, consider Euripides' *Medea*. Though her object is to extract from

13 More to the same effect from Aristotle below: T13, T14.
14 Translated by G. Thomson (1938) as "Wrong shall be done to you for the wrong you did."
15 Euripides, *Electra* 969–73: Orestes: "How shall I kill her who bore me and brought me up?" Electra: "Just as she killed your father and mine." Orestes: "O Phoebus, you prophesied a great folly." Electra: "Where Apollo errs, who could be wise?" Orestes: "He prophesied that I should kill a mother whom I ought not to kill."

Jason "just repayment with God's help,"[16] she nonetheless reflects that "she has dared a most impious deed."[17] The modern reader cannot but wonder how she could have brought herself to believe that the grisly crimes by which she retaliates against Jason are "just repayment"[18] for his infidelity. By what stretch of the imagination could the murder of their two children along with that of his new bride qualify as wrongs "such as" his wrong to her? Yet neither the Chorus nor any of the principals – Medea herself, or Jason, or Creon – take the least notice of the grotesque disproportion of what she does to what she suffered. To anyone who protested the mismatch she would doubtless say that the pain Jason had caused her was as great as the one she is bent on causing him. Euripides makes us see that when revenge is accepted as just in principle the limit of just equivalences turns out in practice to be an all-too-flexible fiction.

We see more of the same when we turn from myth in the tragedians to tragic history in Thucydides. The people who filled the theatre to see the *Medea* in 431 B.C. reassemble on the Pnyx four years later to debate a more infamous proposal than any ever previously moved in the Athenian Assembly:[19] that rebellious Mytilene, now subdued, should be exterminated, all its adult males executed without trial, and all its women and children sold into slavery. In the speech for the proposal Cleon invokes justice on its behalf[20] and, as we might expect, it is the justice of the *talio*:

T10 Thucydides 3.40.7: "Coming as close as possible[21] in thought to what you felt when they made you suffer, when you would have given anything to crush them, now pay them back (ἀνταπόδοτε)."[22]

16 803: ὃς ἡμῖν σὺν θεῷ τίσει δίκην.   17 796: τλᾶσ' ἔργον ἀνοσιώτατον.
18 261: δίκην τῶνδ' ἀντιτίσασθαι κακῶν.
19 The obliteration of Histiaea in 447/446 (Thuc. 1.14.3) had also been brutal in the extreme and would even be bracketed with that of Melos, Scione, and Torone in retrospect (Xen. *Hell.* 2.2.3). But so far as we know the action was not taken after formal debate in the Assembly but through summary decision in the field by military command; and the city was wiped out by expulsion of its people and parceling out of their land among Athenian cleruchs rather than by wholesale executions and enslavement.
20 Emphasis on the violation of justice by the Mytileneans (3.38.1; 3.39.1 and 6) comes early on in his speech, and it culminates in the appeal that both justice and interest require the proposed action (3.40.4–7).
21 He had argued earlier (3.38.1) that retaliatory action should be as prompt as possible because "the response upon the heels of what one suffered exacts a vengeance that most nearly matches the offense."
22 Throughout the ages retaliation has been the standard justification for genocidal acts and policies. Pogroms in medieval Europe and then in Poland and the Ukraine in modern times were ostensibly carried out in retaliation against "Christ-killers." Massacres of Armenians in Anatolia were perpetrated in retaliation for an incendiary assault against the Bank of Turkey in Istanbul by Armenian terrorists. The Nuremberg outrages against the Jews which paved the way for the Holocaust gained a measure of mass support from the belief that Jewish bankers had conspired to "bring Germany to her knees."

To justice so debased Diodotus, the spokesman for decency, makes no appeal. He lets Cleon have it all to himself, turning to cool expediency instead. Conceding that the Athenians have been wronged, Diodotus wastes no words haggling over what would or would not be an equivalent return.[23] He asks them to reflect instead that they have more to lose than gain by an action which would bear down as harshly on the Mytilenean *dēmos* as on its oligarchic masters, prime movers of the revolt. He argues that such indiscriminate terror will lose Athens her best asset in the war – the sympathy of the democrats in each of her subject cities. He does come around to justice near the end of his address, warning the Athenians that if they were to destroy the *dēmos* who had forced the city's surrender when arms were put into its hands, "they would wrong their benefactors" (3.47.3). *But this is not the justice of the talio.* As to that, he implies, the Athenians would be better off as its victims than as its executors:

T11 Thucydides 3.47.5: "I think it more conducive to the maintenance of our empire to allow ourselves to suffer wrong (ἀδικηθῆναι) rather than destroy, however justly (δικαίως), those whom we ought not to destroy."[24]

The flaw in the justice of the *talio* shows up with startling clarity in the lightning flash of a crisis in which sane moral counsel is most desperately needed. The sense of justice – which should have been the best resource of decent Athenians in their resistance to the promptings of blind, unreasoning, hatred – here strengthens the very force they seek to contain. Instead of giving Diodotus the backing he needs, the justice of the *talio* is a bludgeon in Cleon's hand.[25]

23 "If we are sensible we shall not make the issue turn on their injustice (οὐ γὰρ περὶ τῆς ἐκείνων ἀδικίας ἡμῖν ὁ ἀγών), but on what is the wise course for us to follow (περὶ τῆς ἡμετέρας εὐβουλίας) ... We are not involved in a lawsuit with them, so as to be concerned about the justice of their case; we are deliberating about them to determine how our treatment of them may best serve our interest" (3.44.2–4).
24 Failure to notice that at 3.47.3 Diodotus has momentarily shifted to a different conception of justice, not tied to the *talio*, to which he returns at 3.47.4–5, may result in a misunderstanding of the position allowed him by Thucydides: it may lead one either to ignore the previous remark, thereby making Diodotus rest his whole case on imperial expediency (so Andrews takes him to "present his own case entirely in terms of expediency" [1962: 72]) or else to dismiss as "hollow" the remark in T11 that the Athenians should let themselves "suffer wrong" (so Macleod, 1978: 77, who doesn't see that by the justice of the *talio* they *would be* letting themselves be wronged if, in pursuit of self-interest, they were to forgo retaliation).
25 In her essay on the Melian Dialogue, Jacqueline de Romilly (1963: part III, ch. 2) connects that Athenian atrocity (identical with the one they were to inflict, later in the war, on Scione and Torone) with Thrasymachean immoralism (*R.* 1, 338cff.) and Calliclean antimoralism (*G.* 483Aff.). She might have reflected that the Athenians would not need to go so far as that to justify genocide against a powerless enemy: wherever they could see

How was it then that the *talio* had won and kept so long its commanding place in the moral code? Because it had been confused with one or more of three closely related, though entirely distinct, concepts: restitution, self-defense, punishment. The most widespread and, superficially, the most plausible of the three confusions is the one with restitution. If retaliation *were* restitution in principle, it *would* be paradigmatically just: what could be more just than the repayment of a debt? As for self-defense, at first blush it looks like a far cry from retaliation, but it will not if we notice that ἀμύνειν, ἀνταμύνειν, "to ward off from oneself," "to defend oneself" were *also* used to *mean* "to retaliate,"[26] and reflect that when retaliation is the expected response to unjust aggression, failure to retaliate will be construed as weakness, inviting further assaults. By easy extension the preemptive strike becomes acceptable as righteous self-defense: those who see themselves as likely objects of attack feel justified in cracking down before the anticipated aggression has occurred.

In the case of punishment the linguistic bond is still more potent. It is positively tyrannical throughout the archaic period. Down to the last third of the fifth century, τιμωρία, whose original and always primary sense is "vengeance," is *the* word for "punishment." The specialized word for the latter, κολάζειν ("chastening," "disciplining" – with no collateral use for "taking vengeance"), does not acquire currency until we reach the prose of Thucydides and Antiphon. Earlier, as for example in Herodotus,[27] language traps one into using "vengeance" (τιμωρία), even when "punishment" is exactly what one means.[28] What is the difference? Rightly understood punishment is the application of a penalty (ποινή), that is to say, of a norm-mandated sanction of norms. As such, it differs from revenge in three closely connected ways.[29]

themselves as returning wrong for wrong (as at Mytilene, Scione, and Torone): the ultra-respectable *talio* could supply the hard-liners with a righteous fig-leaf.

26 Thus the Athenians, executing the Spartan ambassadors in retaliation for what the Spartans had done to them, are said to have acted δικαιοῦντες τοῖς αὐτοῖς ἀμύνεσθαι (Thuc. 2.67.4; and cf. τ17). Creon uses the verb (Soph. *Ant.* 643) to say that a man hopes for sons who will retaliate on his behalf by doing evil to his enemies (τὸν ἐχθρὸν ἀνταμύνωνται κακοῖς). Socrates uses the term himself in expressing his own rejection of returning harm for harm: οὔτε κακῶς πάσχοντα ἀμύνεσθαι ἀντιδρῶντα κακῶς (*Cr.* 49D8–9).

27 In his prose νουθετεῖν, which may also be used for "punishing" in the classical period, is never used for this purpose, but only in its literal sense of "admonishing."

28 Even Socrates, who rejects revenge, is allowed by Plato occasional use of τιμωρεῖν when "punishing" is what he means (so e.g. at *G.* 472D–E, 525B–E), though κολάζειν, νουθετεῖν are his preferred expressions for it.

29 For a more complete analysis of the differences between revenge and deserved punishment ("retribution") see especially Nozick, 1981: 366–8. He clears up well what remains most unclear in the common use of "revenge": cf. the definition of the word in the *O.E.D.* to which I refer in the text below.

1.   While inflicting a harm on the wrongdoer is common to punishment and revenge, doing him a wrong is not: to punish a wrongdoer is not to wrong him. To the return of wrong for wrong, which is normal in revenge, punishment gives absolutely no quarter: those who apply the penalty are not licensed wrongdoers, but instruments of norm-enforcement, agents of justice.

2.   To give relief to the resentful feelings of victims is not, as in revenge, the dominant motivation of punishment, whose principal aim is not to do evil to the evildoer but to implement the community's concern that its norms should be observed and hence that norm-violators should be called to account by being made to suffer the lawful penalty.

3.   Hatred for the wrongdoer, the core-sentiment in revenge, need not be present in punishment; those who apply the penalty to him should be impelled not by malice, but by a sense of duty in loyalty to the norms which he has breached and by fellow-feeling for the victims of wrongful harm. This motivation is entirely consistent with fellow-feeling for the wrongdoer himself: since he has alienated himself from his fellows by violating the common norms, it is for his own good, no less than that of others, that he be reunited with the community by submitting to the pain the community mandates for norm-violators.

The distinction of punishment from revenge must be regarded as one of the most momentous of the conceptual discoveries ever made by humanity in the course of its slow, tortuous, precarious, emergence from barbaric tribalism. With characteristic impartiality Plato assigns the discovery not to his personal hero, but to Protagoras, Socrates' arch-rival. We see it in the Great Speech Plato gives the sophist in the debate with Socrates in the *Protagoras*.[30] In support of his thesis that virtue is teachable, Protagoras in that speech propounds a comprehensive theory of the origins of culture which views all cultural institutions, including morality, as inventions through which men win the struggle for existence against wild beasts. He constructs a consequentialist argument for the universal

---

30 Were it not for its occurrence in this text we would not have known that Protagoras was the discoverer: there is no record of it in any of our other, all-too-meager, sources for his thought. So powerful an innovation could only have come from a daring and original thinker. When Plato (who has no motive for favoritism to the sophist) assigns it to him we have good reason to accept the assignment, as is done by the majority of scholars (for some references see Guthrie, 1969: 64, n.1).

distribution of the "political art": all men must have been endowed with sensitiveness to moral norms ("share in shame and justice")[31] else humanity would have lost that struggle: it would not have survived. Viewing punishment in this light, he explains it as a device designed to promote deterrence from wrongdoing:

T12 Plato, *Pr.* 324A–B: "No one punishes (κολάζει)[32] wrongdoers putting his mind on what they did and for the sake of this – that they did wrong – not unless he is taking mindless vengeance (τιμωρεῖται), like a savage brute. One who undertakes to punish rationally[33] does not do so for the sake of the wrongdoing, which is now in the past – for what has been done cannot be undone – but for the sake of the future, that the wrongdoing shall not be repeated, either by him or by the others who see him punished (κολασθέντα)... One punishes (κολάζει) for the sake of deterrence (ἀποτροπῆς ἕνεκα)."

Assuming[34] that this is a fair, if harshly abbreviated, statement of the Protagorean view, we must admit that the theory on which it predicates its analysis of the rationale of punishment is indefensibly lopsided. It invokes only deterrence to justify the practice. And this is clearly wrong. For while the reference of a penalty is indeed strongly prospective – to discourage recurrence of the offense – it must be also no less strongly retrospective, if it is to be just: it must apply to the offender the harm which he deserves to suffer under the norms because of *what he did*. We punish a man justly for a given breach of the rules only if we have reason to believe that *he* is guilty of it – that it is he, and no one else, who did commit just that offense. To visit that punishment on a surrogate who could serve as well its exemplary purpose would be the height of injustice, though the deterrent effect could be as great if the false accusation were well concealed. So *pace* Protagoras we do, and should, punish a wrongdoer "for the sake of what he did": our theory must recognize the retributive nature of the practice which we accept for the sake of its deterrent effect. Hence Protagoras' theory of the social function of punishment is unacceptable. It cites, correctly enough, deterrence as the *raison d'être* of the institution, but fails to see that the institution itself is unavoidably retributive.

But even so, though working with a defective theory, Protagoras succeeds brilliantly in sorting out punishment from revenge – he distinguishes perfectly the rational application of a penalty, designed to reinforce compliance with norms aiming at the common benefit,

---

31 *Pr.* 322D: αἰδοῦς καὶ δίκης μετέχειν.
32 Plato makes Protagoras use this word for "punishment" throughout the passage in clear distinction from vengeance, reserving τιμωρεῖν for the latter.
33 ὁ μετὰ λόγου ἐπιχειρῶν κολάζειν.
34 We have no positive reason for thinking otherwise.

from the indulgence of anarchic vengeful passion. He disentangles what had been hopelessly jumbled for millennia in the past and was to remain entangled in popular thought for millennia to come. A leading Victorian jurist, James FitzJames Stephen, was still declaring, in 1883, that criminal justice is legally sanctioned revenge: "the criminal law," he claimed, "stands to the passion of revenge in much the same relation as marriage to the sexual instinct."[35] This articulates what many people believed at the time, and still believe today. That punishment is institutionalized revenge is still a popular view, voiced even by some philosophers,[36] and not without support from the dictionary: for "revenge" the *O.E.D.* gives "inflict punishment or exact retribution."

But after giving Protagoras full credit for having been two and a half millennia ahead of his time, we must still observe that neither does he undertake to give revenge its long overdue come-uppance. It is one thing to distinguish it clearly from punishment, quite another to discern that when thus distinguished revenge is morally repugnant. The first step by no means assures the second, as we can see in Aristotle. He draws the distinction in a way which leaves the moral acceptability of revenge untouched.[37] He still puts harming enemies morally on a par with helping friends:

T13 Arist. *Top.* 113a2–3: Doing good to friends and evil to enemies are not contraries: for both are choiceworthy and belong to the same disposition (αἱρετὰ καὶ τοῦ αὐτοῦ ἤθους).

He still exalts retaliation as "just and noble":

T14 Arist. *Rhet.* 1367a19–20: It is noble (καλόν) to avenge oneself on one's enemies and not to come to terms with them: for retaliation (τὸ ἀνταποδιδόναι) is just (δίκαιον), and the just is noble, and not to put up with defeat is courage.

---

35 The quotation (which I owe to Allen, 1980a: 137) is from Stephen's *History of the Criminal Law* (1883: 83) where he argues that "it is highly desirable that criminals should be hated, that the punishment should be so contrived as to give expression to that hatred..., gratifying an healthy natural sentiment." It did not occur to Stephens that, while punishment does indeed have an "expressive" function (see Feinberg, 1970: 95ff.), the sentiment it should express in a humane society is concern for the enforcement of justice and for the welfare of the community, which criminal legislation is designed to protect in solicitude for *all* members of the community (the law-breaker himself not excepted; see Vlastos, 1962: 55: "The pain inflicted on him for his offence against the moral law has not put him outside the law...does not close out the reserve of goodwill on the part of others which is his birthright as a human being").

36 See e.g. Oldenquist (1985: 464–79), who calls penal justice "sanitized revenge." By the same token marriage would be sanitized fornication.

37 Arist. *Rhet.* 1369b12–14: Revenge and punishment (τιμωρία καὶ κόλασις) differ: for punishment is for the sake of the person punished, revenge for that of the one who does the punishing, to satisfy [his feelings] (ἵνα ἀποπληρωθῇ)." (At this point I am indebted to oral and written comments from John Procopé.)

Worse yet, Aristotle takes the desire for revenge to be a constant in human nature, as deep-seated and ineradicable in the psyche as is the emotion of anger. Defining "anger" as "desire to inflict retaliatory pain,"[38] he identifies the emotion of anger with vengeful impulse, strangely overlooking the absurd consequences of the supposed identity: what sense would it make to hold that when one is angry at oneself (a common enough occurrence) one desires to be revenged on oneself and that when one is angry at one's child (also common) one desires to be revenged on it?

Admittedly т13 and т14 do not come from Aristotle's ethical writings and do not express original moral insights of his own. But they do show that his creative moral thought does not transcend the traditional sentiment in which the justice of the *talio* is enshrined. Great moralist though he is, Aristotle has not yet got it through his head that *if someone has done a nasty thing to me this does not give me the slightest moral justification for doing the same nasty thing, or any nasty thing, to him.* So far as we know, the first Greek to grasp in full generality this simple and absolutely fundamental moral truth is Socrates.

II

Innovations in history don't come out of the blue. Somewhere or other in earlier or contemporary Greek literature we might expect anticipations of Socrates' rejection of the *talio* or at least approximations to it. Let me put before you some of the best approximations I could find and you can judge for yourself if Socrates' originality suffers by comparison.

In the *Oresteia* Aeschylus confronts the futility and horror of the intrafamilial blood-feud and makes the trilogy culminate in a celebration of the supersession of private vengeance by the majesty of civic law. But he never recants on the principle that "each must suffer the thing he did" enunciated by the chorus as "ordained" (θέσμιον) in the *Agamemnon* (1564) and as the "thrice-venerable tale" in the *Choephoroi* (т8 above). In *Seven Against Thebes* Antigone invokes it (1049–50) to justify her brother's retaliatory assault against Thebes and does not question the validity of the principle: she only rebuts its application in the present case.

Nor does Herodotus succeed where Aeschylus falters. His

---

38 *De Anima* 403a29ff.: explaining the difference between the natural and the dialectical understanding of a psychological phenomenon, he says that in the case of anger (ὀργή) "the διαλεκτικός would say that it is desire to cause retaliatory pain (ὄρεξις ἀντιλυπήσεως) or something of the kind, the φυσικός would say that it is boiling of the blood and the hot element about the heart." In the *Rhetoric* (1378a31ff.) he gives a fuller definition of anger, whose core is "pained desire for conspicuous revenge" (ὄρεξις μετὰ λύπης τιμωρίας φαινομένης).

Pausanias (9.78–9) rejects indignantly the proposal that he avenge Leonidas by doing to Mardonius' corpse what he and Xerxes had done to that of the Spartan hero. But what are his reasons for rejecting the proposal? (a) That to desecrate the dead "befits barbarians rather than Greeks," and (b) Leonidas has been already avenged in the huge casualties suffered by the Persians. The propriety of revenge is not denied in (a), and is assumed in (b). Herodotus' Xerxes (7.136), declining to retaliate against Sperthias and Bulis for what Sparta had done to his ambassadors, explains that "what he had blamed in the Spartans he would not do himself." This remarkable statement[39] *could* be used to derive Socrates' Principles II and IV below. But it is not. There is no hint of the insight that since one may not do oneself what one condemns in another, *therefore* one should not return wrong for wrong or harm for harm.

A third candidate comes from Thucydides in the speech of the Spartan envoys at Athens in 425 B.C. Their force at Sphacteria, now cut off, is in desperate straits. A truce has been patched up. Negotiations are afoot. The spokesmen for Sparta plead:

T15 Thuc. 4.19.2–3: "We believe that great enmities are not best brought to secure resolution when the party that got the best of the war, bent on retaliation (ἀνταμυνόμενος),[40] forces on the other a settlement on unequal terms, but rather when, though the victor has the chance to do just that, yet, aiming at decency (πρὸς τὸ ἐπιεικές), he rises higher in virtue (ἀρετῇ αὐτὸν νικήσας) to offer unexpectedly moderate terms. For if what the other now owes is not retaliation for what was forced on him (ἀνταμύνασθαι ὡς βιασθείς), but a return of virtue (ἀνταποδοῦναι ἀρετήν), a sense of shame will make him readier to stand by the agreement."

The Spartans plead: Don't go by the *talio* this time or, better still, work it in reverse: leave us generosity, not injury, to repay. Defeat on these terms we could live with. Your moderation would evoke our best, not our worst, and you would have that further surety that the peace will endure.

Clear in this passage is the perception of a better way to settle a long-standing dispute. Morally better, certainly – perhaps even prudentially, since the victor might have more to gain from

---

39 The principle that it would be unseemly for you to do *x* if you are indignant when *x* is done by someone else (a special form of the "Universalization Principle" in ethics) is not without acknowledgement in Greek moral reflection. It is anticipated in the *Iliad* (6.329–30 and 23.492–4) and the *Odyssey* 6.285–6).

40 Good example here and in the next occurrence of the word in this text of the traditional conflation of the concepts of retaliation with self-defense which made ἀνταμύνομαι a common expression for "to retaliate" (cf. n. 26 above). In both occurrences it is clear that only retaliation is meant: the victor is no longer in the position of having to defend himself against his defeated enemy; the only question is whether he should retaliate for the real or fancied wrong he has suffered.

enhanced security that the agreement will be kept than from any immediate advantage he could extort. But is there so much as even a hint that the Spartans, and Thucydides himself who credits their spokesmen with this fine sentiment in this passage, perceive that the *talio* itself is unjust? None that I can see. To say that, if you did not drive the hardest bargain your present advantage puts within your grasp, your restraint will be admirable and will also pay off, is not to say that if you did prefer the other course you would be acting unjustly.[41]

My last candidate is the character of Odysseus in Sophocles' *Ajax*. The mad protagonist of this tragedy, imbued with mortal hatred for Odysseus, had planned to put him to a slow, tortured, death. He had announced the plan to Athena in Odysseus' hearing and reaffirmed the determination to carry it out despite her plea that he refrain. Knowing this, Odysseus takes no joy in the calamities which now afflict his enemy. When burial is denied to Ajax, Odysseus pleads with Agamemnon to rescind the edict.

T16 Sophocles, *Ajax* 1332ff.: "Listen, For the gods' sake, do not dare / So callously to leave this man without a grave. / Do not let violence get the better of you / So as to hate this man so much that you trample justice. / To me too he was bitterest enemy... / But nonetheless, though he was all of that, / I would not so dishonour him in return (οὐκ ἀντατιμήσαιμ' ἄν) as to deny / He was the best of us who went to Troy, / Save for Achilles... / It is not just to injure a good man / After his death, even if you hate him.

From the standpoint of our own Christianized morality Odysseus' reaction to his enemy's downfall, however admirable, is not extraordinary. In his own time and place it is so far above anything that could be expected of a decent man that it takes Athena by surprise. She had offered Odysseus to parade before him Ajax in his disordered state, thinking it would please her favorite to see his rival, once so mighty, now laid low. She asks Odysseus,

T16 *Ibid.* 79: "When is laughter sweeter than when we laugh at our foes?"[42]

When he declines the offer we are moved to agree with Albin Lesky that here "the man is greater than the goddess."[43]

Can we then say that what we see here is a man who has come to

---

41 As MacDowell (1963: 127ff.) observes, the virtue the Spartan envoys are recommending to Athens is not justice ("there are no laws or rules that a foreign state defeated in war must be treated mercifully") but generosity ("giving one's opponent more than he could reasonably expect").

42 Cf. Stanford (*loc. cit.*): "Athena here expresses... the normal heroic attitude, that nothing is more pleasant than to be able to exult and gloat over the misfortunes of one's enemies."

43 1967: 100.

understand that retaliation itself is unjust? We cannot. What we see is a man of exceptional moral stature realizing that this particular application of the principle – in denial of burial (contrary to divine law) to this man (next to Achilles the best of the Achaeans) – would be unjust.[44] What we do not see is a man who would scruple to apply it in any circumstances against any man. Elsewhere in the play his Odysseus accepts the justice of retaliation as a moral commonplace. He remarks in another connection,

T18 *Ibid.* 1322–3: "If he gave insult for insult I pardon him."

Odysseus has not come to see that the *talio* as such is wrong, a precept not of justice but of injustice. Neither has the poet for whom he speaks.

If we go back to to an earlier scene, near the start of the play, when Agamemnon's decree had not yet fouled the waters, and ask ourselves how Sophocles accounts for the pure nobility of Odysseus' rancorless response to his stricken enemy's state, we can tell, I believe, that the poet wants us to see it rooted in the sense not of justice but of compassion. He evokes what we all may feel for a fellow-creature when touched by the sense of our common frailty, our common defencelessness against implacable fate:

T19 *Ibid.* 119–26: Athena: "Here was a man supreme in judgment, unsurpassed in action, matched to the hour. Did you ever see a better?"[45] Odysseus: Not one. And that is why, foe though he is, I pity his wretchedness,[46] now yoked to a terrible fate. I have in view no more his plight than mine, I see the true condition of us all. We live, yet are no more than phantoms, weightless shades."

This is the mood of the eighth *Pythian*:

T20 Pindar, *Pyth.* 8.1–2:   Day-creatures. What is it to be or not to be? Man is a shadow in a dream.

It is the mood of Herodotus' Solon when he remarks, "Man is all accident."[47] It is as old as the *Odyssey*. We hear it in book 18 in Odysseus' sombre musings (vv. 130–7) on the theme "Earth breeds

---

44 The grounds on which Odysseus protests Agamemnon's decree show very clearly that his objection has nothing to do with the moral impropriety of revenge. To leave the corpse of Ajax unburied would "trample justice" (a) because it would violate the divine interdict on denying burial to anyone at all in any circumstances whatsoever and would breach "the divine laws", 1343, to which Sophocles refers as "the unwritten unshakeable laws of the gods (*Antigone* 454–5) which constrain Antigone's obedience at frightful cost to herself, and also (b) because the high and well deserved esteem in which Ajax had been held entitles him to posthumous respect (1340–1; 1345).

45 My translation here follows E. F. Watling's rendering of these lines in *Sophocles, Electra and Other Plays* (Baltimore, 1953).

46 ἐποικτίρω... δύστηνον ἔμπας. Later in the play he reproaches Agamemnon for his lack of compassion; cf. ἀναλγήτως βαλεῖν, 1333, σκληρὰν... ψυχήν, 1361.

47 πᾶν ἐστι ἄνθρωπος συμφορή (1.32.4).

no creature feebler than man." The moral import of the sentiment we see after the massacre of the suitors in book 22. When Eurycleia lets out a whoop of vengeful joy at the sight of the gore spattered about the banquet hall, Odysseus rebukes her sternly,

T21 *Od.* 22.411–12: "Keep your gloating to yourself, old woman. Shut up. Don't yell. It isn't pious to exult over corpses."[48]

More successfully than Pindar or Homer Sophocles distills moral therapy from the sense of man's brittleness. He reveals how it can purge the heart from the toxins of spite and hatred. But when he has done this, we still want to know: Has he seen that the *talio* is a fraud, its justice a delusion? To this we must reply that he has not even faced the question. So we return to Socrates, who did, and reasoned out an answer.

III

The reasoning which leads him to it is laid out in that short section of the *Crito* (48B–C)[49] which starts the deliberation by which Socrates justifies the decision to remain in jail and await execution. He calls this the ἀρχή of the deliberation, its "starting-point" or, as we would say, reading the metaphor differently, its foundation. This comprises five principles laid out in rapid-fire succession:

T22 *Cr.* 48B4–C9:

I. "We should never do injustice (οὐδαμῶς δεῖ ἀδικεῖν)."
II. "Therefore, we should never return an injustice (οὐδαμῶς δεῖ ἀνταδικεῖν)."
III. "We should never do evil (κακουργεῖν) [to anyone]."[50]
IV. "Therefore, we should never return evil for evil [to anyone]" (ἀντικακουργεῖν)."
V. "To do evil to a human being is no different from acting unjustly to him (τὸ γὰρ κακῶς ποιεῖν τοὺς ἀνθρώπους τοῦ ἀδικεῖν οὐδὲν διαφέρει)."

Of these five principles the one that would hit Plato's readers hardest are II and IV. Here Greeks would see a fellow-Greek cutting out of their morality part of its living tissue. Socrates is well aware of this. For after laying out all five principles he proceeds to zero in on just these two:

T23 *Cr.* 49C10–D5:[51] "Therefore, we should never return a wrong [Principle II] or do evil to a single human being (οὐδένα ἀνθρώπων) no matter what we may have suffered at his hands [Principle IV]. And watch

---

48 Stanford (1963:67) remarks that Odysseus is the first character in Greek literature to proclaim that it is impious to exult over a fallen foe.
49 A fuller encounter with this crucial text must await chapter 8, section III *sub fin.* Here I take a first look at its language and reasoning.
50 For the justification of the expansion I have added in square brackets here and again in IV note how Socrates himself rephrases IV when he refers to it in T23.
51 Will be quoted again in chapter 8 (there as T13).

out, Crito, lest in agreeing with this you do so contrary to your real opinion (παρὰ δόξαν). For few are those who believe or will believe this. And between those who do and those who don't there can be no common counsel (οὐκ ἔστι κοινὴ βουλή). Of necessity they must feel contempt for one another when viewing each other's deliberations."[52]

What Socrates says here he never asserts about any other view he ever voices in Plato: with people who do not agree with him on these two principles which enunciate the interdict on retaliation he would be unable to take "common counsel" about anything. Is he saying that this disagreement would cause a total breakdown of communication? No. Socrates is not saying that he cannot *argue* with anyone who rejects Principles II and IV. Obviously he can: he does so, copiously, with Polus, Callicles, Thrasymachus, and who knows how many others. But what he *is* saying is serious enough: if agreement cannot be reached on these two principles there can be no common *deliberation*: the gulf created by this disagreement will be unbridgeable when it comes to deciding what is to be done. The political consequences of his remark I shall be unable to pursue in this book.[53] Here I must concentrate on Principles II and IV as norms of personal action within the limits fixed for the individual by public law.[54]

While they mark Socrates' break with the established morality they do not account for the break by themselves. Each is derived from one or more other principles in the set. Principle II is derived directly and exclusively from Principle I.

I. We should never do injustice. *Ergo*:
II. We should never do injustice in return for an injustice.

From the proposition that we should refrain from doing injustice in any circumstances whatever ("never" do it), Socrates infers by simple deduction that we should refrain from doing it in the special circumstances in which *we* have been victims of injustice ourselves. To derive IV he uses I again, this time in conjunction with V:

---

52 So far from allowing Socrates the same position on this fundamental point, Xenophon gives him its opposite, making him endorse repeatedly the traditional help-friends-hurt-enemies ethos: the good man "toils to win good friends and to worst his enemies" (*Mem.* 2.1.19); "it is thought worthy of the highest praise to anticipate enemies in causing them evil and friends in causing them good" (*ibid.* 2.3.14); "you have come to know that a man's virtue consists in outdoing friends in conferring benefits and enemies in inflicting harm" (*Mem.* 2.6.35; cf. T1 above). On why Plato's testimony should be preferred to Xenophon's on this point see additional note 7.1.

53 If Socrates cannot join in a common deliberation with people who disagree with him on Principles II and IV he excludes himself from the decision-making processes of Athens' participatory democracy: the "multitude" that staffs those processes would indeed disagree with him on his rejection of the *talio*, as he himself emphasizes in T23.

54 Cf. what was said in the third paragraph of this chapter above.

v.   Doing any evil to a human being is the same as doing injustice to that person.

And since

i.   We should never do injustice,

it follows from this in conjunction with Principle v, that

iii.   We should never do any evil to a human being. *Ergo*
iv.   We should never return evil for evil.

From the proposition that we should refrain from doing evil to anyone in any circumstances whatever ("never" do it), he infers as before that we should not do it when evil has been done to us.

The commanding importance of Principle i in this reasoning should be evident: it is the sole premise for the derivation of Principle ii, and it is used again for the derivation of Principle iv in conjunction with the further premise, Principle v. How would Socrates justify the latter? What reason would he give us to agree that to do any evil[55] to anyone is no different from doing that person an injustice? There is no fully satisfactory answer to this question anywhere in Plato's Socratic dialogues. The nearest Socrates comes to confronting the question is in that passage of *Republic* i where he refutes the conventional notion that justice consists of doing good to friends *and* evil to enemies (335A8–10). To rebut the second term in that conjunction Socrates picks what he believes to be the worst evil that could be done to a human being – to impair that person's justice – and argues that this would be *impossible*: justice in one person could not produce injustice in another – no more than heat in one thing could produce cold in another or drought in one thing produce moisture in another (335B–D). The force of these analogies is problematic.[56] And even if the validity of the reasoning were granted in this case, where the retaliatory evil would impair the enemy's justice, how it would be extended beyond it is not made clear: if the just man cannot impair another man's justice, how would it follow that neither could he harm another in any of innumerable ways in which one could do evil to an enemy *without* impairing the enemy's justice? The one thing that is made clear in this passage – and this is what we must settle for – is Socrates' intuition that true moral

55 I.e. any *morally avoidable* evil – any evil which is not purely incidental to the execution of a non-malicious intent, as in the case of self-defense (where harm is inflicted on an aggressor solely to prevent him from causing wrongful harm) or that of punishment (where infliction of the evil of the penalty Socrates takes to be moral therapy for the wrongdoer [*G*. 480A–D, 525B] and/or retribution and deterrence [*G*. 525A–527A]).
56 Cf. the discussion of this argument in Annas, 1981: 31–4.

goodness is incapable of doing intentional injury to others, for it is inherently beneficent, radiant in its operation, spontaneously communicating goodness to those who come in contact with it, always producing benefit instead of injury, so that the idea of a just man injuring anyone, friend or foe, is unthinkable. This version of undeviatingly beneficent goodness guides Socrates' thought at so deep a level that he applies it even to the deity; it leads him to project a new concept of god as a being that can cause only good, never evil.[57] Let us then accept it as such, as a powerful intuition whose argumentative backing remains unclear in Plato's presentation of Socrates' thought.[58]

So the full weight of the justification of Socrates' rejection of retaliation must fall on Principle i. From this alone, without appeal to any further consideration whatsoever, Socrates derives the interdiction of returning wrong for wrong in Principle ii and therewith the surgical excision of that malignancy in the traditional morality which surfaces in actions like the genocide Athens had all but inflicted on Mytilene and then, as the war dragged on, did inflict on Scione, Torone, and Melos.[59] Plato's awareness of the importance of Principle i shows up in the way he leads up to it in the text of the *Crito* which immediately precedes T22 above.[60] He takes the whole of that paragraph to introduce it, stating and restating it no less than three times,[61] reminding Crito that they had often agreed to it in the past and that he cannot go back on it now just because to stick to it would be to die.

How then should we read the modal language Socrates uses in the first two of those three statements of Principle i in that paragraph?

57 Cf. chapter 6 (discussion of the text quoted there as T7).

58 Plato's recreation of Socratic thought may limp at this point, possibly because he had not been fully in sympathy with this particular aspect of Socrates' teaching. The ethic expounded in the middle books of the *Republic* lacks the unqualified universalism of Principle iii, "We should never do evil *to any human being*." In *R.* v, 470A Socrates does not demur when Glaucon declares that the atrocities Greeks now commit against one another when fighting fellow-Greeks (devastation of the land, desecration of corpses, enslavement of prisoners) should be forbidden to "our citizens" when they are fighting fellow-Greeks, but "towards barbarians they should behave as Greeks now behave to one another."

59 An apologist for Athens, like Isocrates, belittles the enormity of such actions, explaining them away as "severe discipline" of states which had made war on Athens, and alleges that the Spartans had done much worse (*Paneg.* 100, defending the Athenian action against Melos and Scione; and *Panath.* 70, excusing what Athens had done to unnamed "islets"). His apologia would have been hollow if it had not presupposed the justice of the *lex talionis* to which, as we heard from Cleon in the debate on Mytilene (T10 above), advocates of such actions would have appealed.

60 *Cr.* 49A4–B6. I shall be returning to the discussion of this passage in chapter 8. Now I am rounding out my discussion of the passage which starts with the text quoted as T15 in chapter 8 and culminates in the text quoted as T13 in that chapter.

61 A4–5; A5–7; 49B4–7.

T24 *Cr.* 49A4–B6: "Do we say that in no way *should we* intentionally do a wrong (ἑκόντας ἀδικητέον)? Or that *we may* do wrong in some ways but not in others (τινὶ μὲν ἀδικητέον τρόπῳ τινὶ δ' οὔ)? Or that to do a wrong is never good or noble (οὔτε ἀγαθὸν οὔτε καλόν), as has been often agreed between us in the past?"

In the preamble to a moral deliberation it would be natural to read the modal operators as signifying the "should" or "ought" of moral obligation, the "may" of moral acceptability. We must resist that reading: it would be too narrow: it would give us only part of what Socrates means. For he is not saying that if an action does a wrong then it is morally forbidden no matter what might be the circumstances. That would itself be a strong thing to say. But Socrates must mean much more than that. For he proceeds to ask, rephrasing the question with which he began, "Or that to do a wrong is never either *good* or noble – οὔτε ἀγαθὸν οὔτε καλόν?"[62] Of these two adjectives, ἀγαθόν, καλόν, the latter is the one normally used to express what is morally right as such. The use of the former is much broader – fully as broad as that of "good" in English, ranging over the whole spectrum of values: not only moral ones, but also hedonic, economic, political, psychological, physiological, or whatever.

Now it is all too obvious that there are circumstances in which by doing a wrong to someone we may reap a rich harvest of non-moral goods: win a huge sum of money, realize a long-cherished dream, gratify the dearest wishes of a much-loved friend; in the present case it would make the difference between life and death.[63] In saying that it is never *good* to do a wrong, and making this the foundational reason for breaking with the accepted morality, Socrates must be using the word in its most inclusive sense. He must be saying: "If an act of yours will wrong another, then it is bad for you, the agent, so bad that no other good it offers could compensate you for its evil for you. If everything else you value – pleasure, comfort, security, the good opinion of your fellows, the affection of those for whom you care, your own self-preservation – required you to do an unjust action, the mere fact that it is wrong would give you a final,

---

62 He had already implied as much in the preceding remark (48B4–9), where, as I shall be pointing out in chapter 8, the juxtaposition of εὖ ζῆν with καλῶς καὶ δικαίως ζῆν anticipates that of ἀγαθόν with καλόν in T23).

63 Socrates is satisfied that if he were to save his skin by availing himself of the opportunity to escape, his action would be destructive of his city's laws, which command that one should submit to the authority of the verdicts of the courts (even if they are wrong in one's own opinion) (*Cr.* 50B8), and would thus flout the interdict on returning evil for evil (*Cr.* 54C2–4).

insuperable, reason to refrain. Were there a world to win by wronging other persons, you must refrain. Life itself would not be good if you could keep it only by wronging someone else."

Compare Thoreau: "If I have wrested a plank from a drowning man, I must restore it to him though I drown myself." Here too the force of the modality must be the same. Were we to take Thoreau's "must restore" to mean no more than "I am morally required to restore" we would flatten out his dictum, we would squash it into a platitude. For then the consequent would follow with dreary obviousness from the antecedent. Who would gainsay that I am morally obligated to undo an immoral act which is about to cost another man his life? But Thoreau is not asking us to endorse a moral commonplace. He wants us to declare for the most difficult choice anyone could ever be asked to make. Socrates is asking us to do the same – to acknowledge not only the validity of the claim of Principle I on us, but its sovereignty over all other claims. How Thoreau would justify that hard "must" in his dictum is not our affair: his transcendentalism would be a far cry from Socrates' eudaemonism, which is all that matters for us here; Principle I is an immediate consequence of Socrates' commitment to the Sovereignty of Virtue and therewith of his construction of eudaemonism. This takes us to the deepest stratum of his ethical theory. To understand it we must explore his conception of the relation of virtue to happiness – the theme of chapter 8.

8

HAPPINESS AND VIRTUE IN SOCRATES' MORAL THEORY[1]

I ARETĒ, EUDAIMONIA: THEIR TRANSLATION

The key terms in the title pose problems of translation. On "virtue" for aretē I need not linger at all, for whatever may be the general usage of this word, Socrates' own use of it to designate precisely what we understand by moral virtue must have been apparent throughout this book. Any lingering doubt on this point in my readers' mind may be resolved by referring them to the fact that whenever he brings the general concept under scrutiny – as when he debates the teachability of aretē in the Protagoras and the Meno[2] – he assumes without argument that its sole[3] constituents or "parts" (μόρια,[4] μέρη[5]) are five qualities which are, incontestably, the Greek terms of moral commendation par excellence: andreia ("manliness," "courage"), sōphrosynē ("temperance," "moderation"), dikaiosynē ("justice," "righteousness"), hosiotēs ("piety," "holiness"), sophia ("wisdom").[6]

---

1 Originally presented to the Cambridge Philological Society, and printed in its Proceedings (210 [N.S. 30], 1984), 181–213; reprinted in Topoi 4 (1985), 3–22. Now substantially revised.
2 Pr. 319Aff.; M. 70Aff., 79Cff.
3 That he takes his list to be complete is a reasonable inference from the fact that whenever he enumerates the "parts" of virtue (cf. nn. 4 and 5 below) or spells out what it takes to be a "perfectly good man" (ἀγαθὸν ἄνδρα εἶναι τελέως, G. 507C), none but these are mentioned. When non-moral or dubiously moral qualities come into view (as at M. 88A–B; καὶ εὐμαθίαν καὶ μεγαλοπρέπειαν καὶ πάντα τὰ τοιαῦτα) they are not called ἀρεταί, but placed, along with the moral virtues, under the more general heading of τὰ τῆς ψυχῆς ἐπιχειρήματα καὶ καρτερήματα, loc. cit.
4 Pr. 329Cff., 349Cff., 359Aff.; La. 199E; M. 79A–D.
5 La. 190C; M. 89A. On this Socratic doctrine, sadly misunderstood by some recent writers on that topic, see "Socrates on the Parts of Virtue" in Vlastos, 1981: 418–23.
6 This narrowly moral construction of ἀρετή is characteristically Socratic. Aristotle's usage, which allows qualities like "magnificence" and "greatness of soul" (μεγαλοπρέπεια and μεγαλοψυχία) to count as ἠθικαὶ ἀρεταί, would be closer to popular usage, which is still more relaxed and would count, e.g., δεινότης ("cleverness") as ἀρετή (so undoubtedly in Thucydides' [8.68.1] praise of Antiphon as "inferior to none in ἀρετή"), while for Aristotle δεινότης is a conspicuously non-moral quality (E.N. 1144b1–4). However, Socrates' use of

"Happiness" for *eudaimonia* is a more contentious matter. Leading Aristotelians, Ross[7] and Ackrill,[8] have claimed that "well-being" would be a better translation. But in their own translations of the *Nicomachean Ethics* (hereafter abbreviated to "*E.N.*") both[9] stick to "happiness" all the same. It is not hard to see why they would and should. "Well-being" has no adjectival or adverbial forms. This may seem a small matter to armchair translators, philosophers dogmatizing on how others should do the job. Not so if one is struggling with its nitty-gritty, trying for clause-by-clause English counterparts that might be faithful to the sentence-structure, no less than the sense, of the Greek original. And "well-being" suffers from a further liability: it is a stiff, bookish phrase, bereft of the ease and grace with which the living words of a natural language perform in a wide diversity of contexts. *Eudaimonia* fits perfectly street-Greek and Aristophanic slapstick, yet also, no less perfectly, the most exalted passages of tragedy. Even ecstasy is not beyond its reach, as in the cult-hymn in the *Bacchae*,

T1 Euripides, *Ba.* 72–3: O blessed (*makar*) he who, happy (*eudaimōn*) in knowing the rites of the gods, lives in holiness...

and the epiphany in the *Phaedrus*,

T2 Plato, *Phdr.* 250B–C: "Radiant beauty was there to see, when with the happy (*eudaimoni*) choir we saw the blessed (*makarian*) sight and vision and celebrated that rite which, with all due reverence, we may call most blessed (*makariotatēn*) of all."[10]

Eudaimōn reaches easily the highest registers of intensity, keeping pace with *makar*, *makarios*, matching their tonality and resonance, evoking so marvellous a felicity that the gods themselves could ask for nothing better for themselves[11] and we in turn could ask no greater gift from them:

ἀρετή, though innovative (as it would have to be to implement his profoundly new conception of moral excellence), is not eccentric. It retains good contact with popular usage, whose vagaries even allow upon occasion startling anticipations of Socrates, as in Theognis 147, "in righteousness all ἀρετή is comprehended" (on which, however, see Dover, 1983: 35–48 at 48) and, in any case, frequent use of ἀρετή *more Socratico* in stark contrast to conduct dominated by considerations of pleasure or profit, as in the description of Spartan conduct by Athenians in Thucydides (5.105.4): at home "they stick to ἀρετή for the most part," abroad "they identify what is pleasant with what is honourable and expediency with justice."

7 Ross, 1923: 190. So too, earlier, Sidgwick, 1907: 92.   8 Ackrill, 1980: 14.
9 Ross in Ross & Smith, 1910–52; Ackrill, 1973 – his version of the one by Ross.
10 The ineptness of "well-being" for εὐδαιμονία in contexts of this sort speaks for itself. So should that of "human flourishing" (defended by Cooper, 1975: 89, n. 1; rejected by Kraut, 1979: 167–70). For a vigorous defense of the traditional translation see also Dybikowski, 1981: 185–200.   11 *E.N.* 1178b9–10 and 20–3.

T3 Arist. *E.N.* 1097b11–13:   If there is any gift from gods to men, it is reasonable that *eudaimonia* should be god-given. Of all things human this is most fit to be god-given, for it is the best.

What then, really, is the objection to "happiness" for *eudaimonia*? What is there about the meaning of the English word which is supposed to make it a mismatch for the Greek one? Consider what our dictionaries make of "happiness":

T4 *O.E.D.* (second of three entries, the only relevant one):   the state of pleasurable content of mind which results from success or the attainment of what is considered good.
   Webster's: a state of well-being and pleasurable satisfaction.

Two features of the concept are recognized in both: a subjective (pleasurable contentment or satisfaction) and an objective one (attainment of good, well-being). But whereas in the *O.E.D.* happiness is identified with the first, only causally connected with the second (it *is* the pleasurable mental state, it *results from* attainment of what is considered good), in *Webster's* the two factors are conjunctive, on a par. Now consider the standard objection to "happiness" for *eudaimonia*: "Whereas 'happiness' means a state of feeling, differing from 'pleasure' only by its suggestion of permanence, depth, and serenity, Aristotle insists that *eudaimonia* is a kind of activity."[12] True, but what does it show? That *eudaimonia* may be used to refer to the activities in which persons find happiness, not that it must be so used. That it need not should be clear from the fact that the Greek hedonists have no difficulty in calling what they consider the good for man *eudaimonia*:

T5 Epicurus, *ap.* Diogenes Laertius 10.122:   We must study the things which produce *eudaimonia*, for when it is present we have everything; when it is absent we do everything to obtain it.

But while for Aristotle this end is an activity, for Epicurus it is pleasure and the absence of pain. Thus if hedonism is a mistake, having *eudaimonia* as your word for "happiness" won't save you from it; if your theory requires it, you can use εὐδαιμονία to mean pretty much what the *O.E.D.* takes "happiness" to mean. If Aristotle's interpretation of *eudaimonia* is closer to normal Greek usage than is that of Epicurus, as it doubtless is,[13] the difference in meaning between *eudaimonia* and "happiness" in their normal use would still

12 Ross, 1923: 190.
13 As is clear enough from the common use of εὐδαιμονία for "prosperity."

be no greater than that between alternative definitions of "happiness" in major English dictionaries. This is ample reason for sticking to the traditional translation, provided only we bear in mind that in its pre-theoretical uses *eudaimonia* puts a heavier loading on the objective factor in "happiness" than does the English word.

II THE THREE POSITIONS IN EUDAEMONISM

I may now introduce the principle I shall call "the Eudaemonist Axiom," which, once staked out by Socrates, becomes foundational for virtually all subsequent moralists of classical antiquity. This is that happiness is desired by all human beings as the ultimate end (*telos*) of all their rational acts.[14] The best clue to what this means is in a remark in Plato which every Greek moralist would applaud:

T6 Plato, *Smp.* 205A2–3: "Of one who wants to be happy there is no longer any point in asking, 'For what reason (ἵνα τί) does he want to be happy?' This answer is already final (ἀλλὰ τέλος δοκεῖ ἔχειν ἡ ἀπόκρισις)."

In the imaginary dialogue A asks B, "What is your reason for doing *x*?" and if B replies, "Because it will get me *y*," A persists until the point is reached where B replies, "Because it will make me happy," and then the question stops: to renew it after that would be pointless. Thus to say that happiness is "the τέλος of all our actions[15] is not to say that this is what we are always, or often, thinking of when choosing what to do in our daily life, but only that this is the last of the reasons we could give if pressed to give our reason for choosing to do anything at all – the only one which, if given, would make it senseless to be asked for any further reason.[16]

This being the case, the question, "Why should I be moral?" which some modern moralists would find tendentious – perversely

---

14 Here desire for happiness is strictly self-referential: it is the agent's desire for his own happiness and that of no one else. This is so deep-seated an assumption that it is simply taken for granted: no argument is ever given for it in the Platonic corpus. (For this assumption in the context of T6 cf. the gloss on *Smp.* 206A and 207A in Vlastos, 1981: 20, n. 56 *sub fin.*). For the same assumption in Socratic dialogues see e.g. how Socrates shifts *without argument* from βέλτιον εἶναι ("to be better") at *G.* 468B2 to ἄμεινον εἶναι ἡμῖν ("to be better *for us*), at 468B (cf. n. 53 in ch. 5), and how his use of the phrase "injustice is the greatest of evils" (μέγιστον τῶν κακῶν... τὸ ἀδικεῖν) at 469B8–9 just takes it for granted that ["to the unjust man himself"] will be understood after "evils" (nn. 52, 53 in ch. 5).
15 Cf. T24 below.
16 Hume's explanation of the notion of "ultimate ends" of conduct is the same (though the plural, to which I would call attention, "ends" vs. τέλος, constitutes a fundamental residual difference): *Enquiry concerning the Principles of Morals*, Appendix I, section v ("It is impossible there can be a progress *in infinitum*; and that one thing can always be a reason why another is desired. Something must be desired on its own account...').

predicated on the reduction of morality to interest[17] – is for all Greek moralists a perfectly proper and unavoidable one, the most urgent of all the questions they must confront. It is on this issue that they divide. They agree that the right reply is "Because moral conduct offers me the best prospects for happiness." They disagree on the reason why this is so: they differ radically among themselves on the relation of virtue to happiness:

(1)   For some the relation is purely instrumental; they hold that virtue is desirable only as an instrumental means[18] to happiness, not at all for its own sake.

(2)   For others the relation is constitutive, but only partly so; they hold that virtue is a principal, but not the only, thing desirable for its own sake.

(3)   For still others, who go further in the same direction, the relation is constitutive *in toto*: for them virtue *is* happiness – the only thing that makes life good and satisfying.

Position (1) is held by one of Socrates' own intimate companions, Aristippus,[19] and, after him, by Epicurus and his many followers. Identifying happiness with pleasure and the absence of pain, they hold that virtue should be preferred to vice because, and only because, it is the more likely of the two to yield hedonic benefit. This identification of happiness (or "the good")[20] with pleasure Socrates attacks in the strongest terms in the *Gorgias*. He argues that it could[21]

17 So H. A. Prichard argued in his famous essay, "Does Moral Philosophy Rest on a Mistake?" (first published in 1912; reprinted in Prichard, 1949).
18 Cf. the reference above (Introduction, n. 30) to Irwin's definition of the term (1977a: 300, n. 53).
19 *Pace* Xenophon's hostile portrayal of him (*Memorabilia* 2.1 and 3.8), this "sophist" (Aristotle, *Metaph.* 996a32) was undoubtedly a member of Socrates' inner circle, one of Socrates' closest, most devoted friends, mentioned as present at the death-scene by Plato (*Phaedo* 59c2–3); cf. also Aristotle, *Rhet.* 1398b28–31 (Aristippus responding to a peremptory remark by Plato by saying "our comrade (ἑταῖρος), Socrates, would not have spoken thus") with comment by Maier, 1913: 81, n. 1, who reckons it a "personal reminiscence" (I would suggest that it is most likely to be one of those anecdotes that went the rounds in Athens, when Aristotle was there, among Socratics resentful of Plato.)
20 Neither Socrates nor Plato feels called upon to *argue* that happiness is man's good: they use the terms interchangeably. For Socrates' usage see e.g. how freely he interchanges the terms in his statement of the Calliclean thesis at *G.* 494E–495B: "those who have pleasure, pleasure of whatever sort, are *happy*," or again, without any intervening explanation, "this is the *good* – to have pleasure of whatever sort."
21 Not that it must: nothing is said in the *G.* to commit the hedonist to a Calliclean strategy of pleasure-maximization (whose imprudence is clearly indicated [488D–489B]). Had Socrates thought that hedonism entails antimoralism, his association with Aristippus would be unintelligible.

sanction a life of obscene self-indulgence – the life of a catamite (494E). Since the moral theory I shall be exploring in this chapter is precisely the one Socrates holds in the *Gorgias*[22] (consistently with what he says in every Socratic dialogue)[23] in opposition to the identification of the good with pleasure,[24] we must conclude that whatever else Socrates may or may not have been, he certainly was no hedonist.[25]

Position (2) is Aristotle's and Plato's. It has taken philosophical scholarship some time to catch up with this fact. Earlier in the present century leading lights in Oxford were strongly inclined to believe, and some of them did believe, that if Plato and Aristotle were eudaemonists they would have had to be utilitarians: H. A. Prichard, a stubborn Kantian, so argued with conviction.[26] What he and others had failed to understand is how it was possible for Plato and Aristotle to hold that everything is chosen for the sake of happiness *and* that some things are chosen for their own sake, which is, of course, what Aristotle says in so many words:

T7 *E.N.* 1097B1–5: [Happiness] we choose always for itself, never for the sake of anything else. But honour, pleasure, intelligence, and every virtue we choose indeed for themselves – for if nothing resulted from them, we would still choose each of them – but we choose them also for the sake of happiness.

Can Aristotle hold without inconsistency that something can be desired for its own sake and also for the sake of something else? He certainly can, and if so fine an Aristotelian as Ross had failed to see

---

22 More than a third of the texts on which I base my account of the Socratic view below are from the *G.*, and these are so informative that at a pinch the whole account could have been worked up just from them: all four categories in the Socratic scheme of value in which I sum up my findings at the end of section v could be documented from the *G.* alone.

23 Including the *Pr.*: see additional note 8.1 below. (The interpretation of *Pr.* 351B–358D is a highly controversial matter. (Strong defenses of the contrary in Irwin, 1977a: ch. 4, and Gosling & Taylor, 1982: chs. 2 and 3.)

24 The nature of this antithesis is misunderstood when it is argued (so Gosling & Taylor, 1982: 62–4) that the sentiment voiced by Socrates in the *Ap.* and the *Cr.*, that dying should be preferred to living unjustly, is not inconsistent with hedonism, since Socrates could have maintained (however implausibly) that the preference is justifiable on hedonistic grounds. This misses the point that for Socrates justifying the preference for a just to an unjust alternative by their respective yield in hedonic value is excluded *ab initio*, for no value accruing to the unjust option should be considered at all (cf. T10, T11, T12, to be discussed below), and that moreover pleasure enjoyed in an unjust course of conduct is evil rather than good (T28, to be discussed below).

25 Which is not to say that he would have put hedonism on the same level with immoralism, antimoralism, or mindless moral opportunism. See additional note 8.1.

26 In the essay cited in n. 17 above and in several other essays in the same volume, also in his Inaugural Lecture, *Duty and Interest* (1928).

this,[27] it was only because, bullied by prevailing philosophical dogmas, he had not paid due attention to the fact that for Aristotle happiness *consists* of goods like those named in T7 – in fact *is* nothing but such goods:

T8 *Magna Moralia* 1184A26–9: For happiness is composed of certain goods. For it is not something other than these, distinct from them: it *is* these[28]

Scruples over the authenticity of the *Magna Moralia* could, conceivably, have kept Ross[29] from taking this text seriously. However, he could have got the same message from a passage in the *E.N.* which, long before, had been understood and glossed correctly:

T9 *E.N.* 1144A1–6: [About σοφία and φρόνησις] let us first say that they are choiceworthy for their own sake – as they would have to be... even if neither of them produce anything, for they are virtues. But then [let us observe] that they do produce something, though not in the way in which medicine produces health: σοφία produces happiness in the way health does.[30] For being a part (μέρος) of complete virtue it makes one happy by being possessed and exercised.[31]

As Stewart[32] and Greenwood[33] saw, here we are told how certain things can be desirable both for their own sake and for the sake of happiness: because they are "component parts" (Greenwood), "constituent elements" (Stewart) of the happiness they are said to "produce."

Is there any difficulty in understanding such a relation? Suppose I am very fond of the Andante of a Beethoven symphony. If this had been the only part of it that had survived, I would play it "for its own sake." But luckily enough I do have the whole symphony and

---

27 He wrote "morality for [Aristotle] consists in doing certain actions not because we see them to be right in themselves but because we see them to be such as will bring us nearer to the 'good for man'" (1923: 188). To get truth instead of falsehood from this statement delete "not" and substitute "and" for "but."

28 ἡ γὰρ εὐδαιμονία ἐστὶν ἐκ τινων ἀγαθῶν συγκειμένη... οὐ γάρ ἐστιν ἄλλο τι χωρὶς τούτων, ἀλλὰ ταῦτα. I am indebted to Mr. J. O. Urmson for bringing this extremely important passage to my attention.

29 1923: 15. For a reasonable defense of the "substantial authenticity of the *Magna Moralia* and its importance for the study of Aristotle's moral philosophy" see Cooper, 1973: 327–49.

30 Understanding [εὐδαιμονίαν ποιεῖ] after ὡς ἡ ὑγιεία contrary to Ross in his translation of the *E.N.*, who understands [ὑγιείαν ποιεῖ], in the same place, thereby missing the point that, in any case, the terminal clause of T9 gives a perfect example of a state choiceworthy both for its own sake *and* for the sake of happiness.

31 I have followed I. Bywater's text of the *E.N.* (1894).

32 Stewart, 1892: II 48.

33 Greenwood, 1909: 295.

I treasure all of it. So when I listen to the Andante I do so both for its own sake and for the sake of the whole ordered sequence of movements to which it belongs. This is how Aristotle thinks of the relation of virtue to happiness,[34] except that the relation he has in view is multidimensional and synchronic, as well as diachronic, and virtue is only one of the "parts" of happiness, each of which may be desired both for its own sake and for the sake of the whole. Thus consider the case of temperance. If we follow Aristotle we should choose to be temperate both for its own sake (temperance is καλόν) *and* for the sake of pleasure (in exercising that virtue we get a special pleasure which we could get in no other way) *and* for the sake of health (temperate indulgence in food and drink is essential for health) *and* for the sake of honor (if we live among morally sensitive people we win their esteem by our temperance) *and* for the sake of happiness which consists of all these "parts" of it and of many more besides.[35]

Plato's view of happiness in *Republic* II–x and in the *Philebus* is not expounded as fully or explicitly as in the works of Aristotle. Unlike the latter, Plato never uses the "parts/whole" terminology for the relation of intrinsically valuable goods to happiness. Nor does he speak of them as being desired both for their own sake and for the sake of happiness. But what he does say can be put together in a pattern substantially like the one in Aristotle. What is essential for my purpose is sufficiently indicated in the trichotomy of goods with which Glaucon begins his speech in *R.* II (357B–358A):

(a) Goods desirable only for their own sake. Example: harmless pleasure.

(b) Goods desirable both for their own sake *and* for their consequences. Examples: thinking, seeing, health; justice (and, by implication, all the virtues).

(c) Goods desirable only for their consequences. Examples: physical training, medical treatment, money-making.

The goods in class (c) are desirable only for the sake of those in classes (a) and (b). Since the trichotomy is exhaustive, it follows that all those whose possession will make us happy must fall into those two classes. So each of the goods in (a) and (b) must be components

---

34 For this ("inclusive") conception of happiness in Aristotle see especially Ackrill, 1974: 339–60.

35 See the long list of "parts" of happiness in the *Rhetoric* (1360b19ff.). That several of these items may be desired for the sake of other things is no objection to reckoning them "parts" of happiness when desired for their own sake.

of happiness, for this is the only way in which they could be desired both for their own sake (as they are said to be) and for the sake of happiness (as they must be, for as we saw in T6 above, happiness is "the question-stopper" – the final reason why anything is desired, hence, why pleasure, health, thinking, virtue or anything else is desired).

Position (3), the view that virtue is the only constituent of happiness – that virtue *is* happiness, the whole of it – is held by that strange man, Antisthenes, the progenitor of Cynicism, who was one of Socrates' closest friends and associates,[36] and was later held not only by the Cynics – the philosophical hippies of classical antiquity – but also by that incomparably more numerous and influential, ultra-respectable, philosophical sect, the Stoics.[37] Of the content of Antisthenes' doctrine we know all too little. But its general tenor is indicated by the saying attributed to him by Diogenes Laertius (6.3): "I would rather go mad than experience pleasure" (ἔλεγέ τε συνεχές "μανείην μᾶλλον ἢ ἡσθείην").[38] From the identity of virtue and happiness a eudaemonist would unavoidably infer, as did the Stoics, that all non-moral goods are matters of indifference. Could this be Socrates' view of the relation of virtue to happiness?

I believe that the best attack on this question can be made from a central principle of Socrates' practical moral teaching which I shall call, for reasons to be explained directly, the "Sovereignty of Virtue." Though this makes no reference to happiness as such, it nonetheless gives the best insight into the problem. Here we can best see how Socrates, in his total innocence of the *problematik* not only of modern moral theory but even of Hellenistic and Greco-Roman philosophical ethics, approaches the matter. For this purpose I shall begin with three thoroughly familiar, yet sadly neglected[39] passages,

36 Plato, *Phaedo* 59B8; Xenophon, *Mem.* 3.17 ("Apollodorus and Antisthenes never leave me," says Socrates to Theodote) and *Smp. passim.*

37 It was the view of the founders, Zeno and Chrysippus, and of leading Stoics thereafter that "virtue is self-sufficient for happiness" (Diogenes Laertius 7.127), ensuring all by itself happiness at the maximum, "admitting of neither diminution nor enhancement of intensity (μητ' ἄνεσιν μήτ' ἐπίτασιν ἐπιδέχεσθαι)" (*ibid.* 101). Everything else ("life, health, pleasure, beauty, strength, wealth, good repute, high birth" and the like) they considered not goods (i.e. constituents of happiness), but indifferents (ἀδιάφορα) (*ibid.* 102).

38 Sextus Empiricus quotes the saying twice (*P. Hyp.* 3.181; *Adv. Math.* 11.73) without naming its source. For other quotations of the saying see Giannantoni, 1983: II 365.

39 No notice of them is taken in either of the great landmarks of ninteenth-century Socratic scholarship: Eduard Zeller, *Philosophie der Griechen*, George Grote, *Plato and the Other Companions of Socrates*. They continue to be generally ignored in the present century; they do not figure in the *index locorum* of the two book-length accounts of Socrates in the sixties: Gulley, 1968 and Guthrie, 1969. But see Maier, 1913: 305ff., for a notable exception: he quotes (at 308, n. 1) *Ap.* 28B (= T10 below) and also (at 309, n. 2) *Cr.* 48B (= T15 below),

two of them in the *Apology*,[40] the third in the *Crito*, where Socrates declares the Sovereignty of Virtue his supreme principle of practical choice. The third passage[41] is particularly illuminating, for it reveals the structural design of the fundamentals of Socrates' moral theory: the passage shows how he gets to that principle and what he gets from it.

III SOCRATES' PRINCIPLE OF THE SOVEREIGNTY OF VIRTUE

He states it twice over in the *Apology*, invoking it to explain why he had followed for so many years that singular course of conduct which has now put him in peril of his life. If someone were to reproach him for that, he says, this would be his reply:

т10 *Ap.* 28в5–9:[42] "Man, you don't speak well, if you believe that a man worth anything at all would give countervailing weight (ὑπολογίζεσθαι) to danger of life or death, or give consideration to anything but this when he acts: whether his action is just or unjust, the action of a good or of an evil man."

He reiterates the principle a few lines later, using again the verb I am translating "give countervailing weight"; for, as Riddell points out,[43] what is conveyed by ὑπο- in ὑπολογίζεσθαι is not subtraction but rather, as he puts it, "meeting from an opposite direction" – as in ὑπαντᾶν, ὑπωμοσία ("affidavit to stop proceedings"), ὑπο-τιμᾶσθαι (equivalent to ἀντιτιμᾶσθαι):

т11 *Ap.* 28d6–10: "This is the truth of the matter, men of Athens: Wherever a man posts himself on his own conviction that this is best or on orders from his commander, there, I do believe, he should remain, giving no countervailing weight to death or anything else when the alternative is to act basely."[44]

along with passages from the *Gorgias*, to document his lucidly anti-instrumentalist interpretation of the Socratic ethic ("die Tügend an sich selbst schon nicht Glück bringt, sondern – Glück ist," 319) to which I had referred in my review of Irwin, 1977a (cf. the *Introduction* above, pp. 6–10). (I am correcting my faulty reference to Maier in Vlastos, 1984b: n. 51.)

40 The advantage of starting with the *Apology* is that here we find the most explicitly personal, least theory-laden, account of Socrates' conception of the good life. Any construction of Socratic theory which does not do justice to this primary base would be suspect.

41 *Crito* 48в4–49е3. I quote pieces of it (т12, т13, т14, т15) in chopped-up fashion, disregarding their order in the text. This should not keep the reader from viewing the passage as a continuous exposition of Socratic doctrine.

42 Quoted in the Introduction, p. 8 above.   43 Riddell, 1867: 66 and 167.

44 μηδὲν ὑπολογιζόμενον πρὸ τοῦ αἰσχροῦ. For the recognition of т10 and т11 as enunciating a "principle of choice [A1], or at any rate, a principle that tells us what sorts of things to consider in making a choice," and of т11 as doing the same [A2], thereby explaining

In the *Crito* we meet the principle for a third time. Plato's fastidious prose, shunning regurgitation, allows itself repetition of just the one word, ὑπολογίζεσθαι, to tie this further statement of the principle to that in each of the preceding texts:

T12 *Cr.* 48c6–D5: "But for us, since the argument thus compels us (οὕτω...αἱρεῖ) the only thing we should consider is...whether we would be acting justly...or, in truth, unjustly...And if it should become evident that this action is unjust, then the fact that by staying here I would die or suffer anything else whatever should be given no countervailing weight when the alternative is to act unjustly."

In each of these three texts Socrates is confronting that fatality of our lives which forces us to choose between competing values or, in the more down-to-earth language he uses himself, between competing "goods" (ἀγαθά). He would recognize (cf. e.g. *Eud.* 279A–B) a wide variety of such goods – physical, to begin with: bodily health and strength, good looks; life itself as a biological fact – living, as distinct from living well. Next on his list would come those social and intellectual goods which Socrates takes to be morally neutral, seeing no moral merit in their possession or stigma in their dispossession. Such he thinks wealth, social connections, good reputation and prestige, success in politics or war. Such too he thinks that cleverness or quickness of mind which the wickedly cunning may have on a par with the wisely good.[45] Over against all these he sets the moral goods, his five canonical virtues, all of which, given his well-known doctrine of the unity of the virtues, stand or fall together as "parts" of virtue:[46] whatever stake any of them has in a given choice, each of the other four has the same. So the principle announced in the above three texts comes to this: Whenever we must choose between exclusive and exhaustive alternatives which we have come to perceive as, respectively, just and unjust or, more generally, as virtuous and vicious, this very perception of them should decide our choice. Further deliberation would be useless, for none of the non-moral goods we might hope to gain, taken singly or in combination,

---

momentous personal decisions made by Socrates throughout his life, see Santas, 1979: 32–3. In the present paper I show how A1 and A2 in Santas are variant expressions of a general principle of practical choice, reiterated in the *Cr.* (48c6–D5 = T12), where it is derived from a thesis concerning the relation of virtue to the good (T15 below) which entails, either directly or through that principle, the absolute interdicts on ἀδικεῖν, ἀνταδικεῖν, ἀντικακουργεῖν.

45 δεινότης at n. 6 above.

46 They are interentailing: "if one has any of them one will necessarily have all of them," *Pr.* 369E4.

could compensate us for the loss of a moral good. Virtue being the sovereign good in our domain of value, its claim upon us is always final.

To take the measure of this commitment we should compare it not with Thrasymachean immoralism or Calliclean antimoralism, nor yet with the skin-deep morality of the *homme moyen sensuel*, but with that deep regard for virtue we could expect only in the finest characters of the time. Consider Neoptolemus in the *Philoctetes*.[47] When first propositioned by Odysseus he recoils with disgust: just to listen to that dishonest proposal, he says, causes him pain, and he "abhors" the thought of carrying it out (*Philoct.* 87).[48] This is his first reaction and, as the drama shows, it will be also his last: he returns the bow, well aware of the sorry consequences for himself. And when Odysseus berates the recklessness of that choice, he retorts (1246): "If it is just, it is better than prudent."[49] This is his true character. The bow is in his hands, he need only keep it to be the glorious captor of Troy, and who would know, or care, that he had got it by cheating an embittered, paranoid cripple? Giving it back of his own accord, he proves that he means what he had said at the start: "I would rather fail acting nobly, than win by acting basely" (94–5).[50] That sentiment has a Socratic ring. It is what Socrates tells the court after the sentence had been passed: "I would much rather die, having defended myself as I did, than do as you would have had me do and live" (*Ap.* 38E). At that point the graph of Socratic morality intersects that of other admirable people in his own world who, like him, vindicate in a crisis the genuineness of their concern for justice by living up to its demands at painful cost to their worldly fortunes. Sophocles was counting on the presence of such people in his audience in those last dismal years of the Peloponnesian War. And so was Isocrates half a century later when he wrote in his *Panathenaicus*: "Victories won in violation of justice are more despicable than are morally clean defeats" (185).[51]

47 For my understanding of the moral import of this play I am indebted to Nussbaum, 1976–7: 25–53 and, even more, to Blundell, 1989: ch. 6.
48 πράσσειν στυγῶ.
49 ἀλλ' εἰ δίκαια, τῶν σοφῶν κρείσσω τάδε. The best commentary on the sense of σοφῶν here is the dialogue at 100–20, where the course of action which is plainly dishonest and is recognized as αἰσχρόν (108), is justified by its "prudence" (σοφός τ' ἂν αὐτὸς κἀγαθὸς κεκλῇ' ἅμα, 119).
50 βούλομαι δ', ἄναξ, καλῶς | δρῶν ἐξαμαρτεῖν μᾶλλον ἢ νικᾶν κακῶς. This is his retort to Odysseus' admission that the trickery is ἀναιδές (83) and, by implication, unjust and impious, but must nonetheless be dared as the means to victory (81–2).
51 I am not suggesting that Isocrates adhered consistently to this noble sentiment. I see no defense against the blistering critique in the essay on Isocrates by Norman H. Baynes in his *Byzantine Studies and Other Essays* (1955).

But think how much further the people who would share those fine sentiments would have to go before they could embrace Socrates' principle of the Sovereignty of Virtue. Had Neoptolemus got that far, Sophocles would have lost his play: the stichomythia which starts with Neoptolemus voicing loathing for deceit (100) and ends twenty verses later in abject capitulation (" I'll do it – I'll dismiss the shame") could not have occurred: Odysseus would never have had his chance to dangle the prize before the young man's nose. As for Isocrates, it is one thing to hold up to the admiration of his public a rare deed of high resolve, a glittering moral exploit, like the self-immolation of Leonidas and his band, quite another to make the total subordination of comfort, safety, life itself, to virtue the inflexible rule of everyday conduct. The difference becomes palpable in the *Gorgias* when Socrates argues that to suffer wrong oneself is always better than to wrong another. We know what Isocrates would say to that: "Forced to choose between two options, neither of them ideal, [our fathers] thought it a better choice to do evil to others than to suffer it themselves" (*Panath.* 117). This, he adds, is what every sensible man would prefer – in fact everybody, except some few "who pretend to be wise" – as pointed an allusion to Socratic doctrine as can be found in the Isocratean corpus.

In chapter 7[52] I argued for the ground-breaking originality of Socrates' interdict on retaliation. Here I must refer again to his own awareness of the unbridgeable gulf this interdict creates between his morality and that of all the adherents of the traditional code:

T13 *Cr.* 49C10–D5:[53] "Therefore, we should not return wrong for wrong (ἀνταδικεῖν) nor do evil to a single man, no matter what he may have done to us. And watch out, Crito, lest in agreeing with this you go against your own belief. For I know that few believe or will believe this. And between those who do believe and those who don't there can be no common counsel: of necessity they must despise each other when they view each other's deliberations."

In section III of chapter 7 we saw how Socrates reaches this position in the *Crito*. That we should never return injustice is

---

52 Which supersedes my first shot at the Socratic doctrine (Vlastos, 1980: 301–24, especially at 318–23), which I have since revised with help from colleagues at St. Andrews, where the substance of that paper had formed the first of my Gifford Lectures (1981), and also from Irwin, who had pointed out to me that the mathematical model I had used in that paper is strictly inconsistent with the Identity Thesis (to be defined in section IV below) I had endorsed there: if virtue were the only component of happiness, then the analogy of infinite to finite quantities to elucidate the relation of moral to non-moral goods would be inapplicable, since on the Identity Thesis the value of any or all of the latter would be zero.
53 Quoted as T22 in chapter 7.

presented as an immediate consequence of the premise that we should never commit injustice: from "we should never commit injustice" (οὐδαμῶς ἀδικεῖν) he derives directly "we should never return injustice" (οὐδαμῶς ἀνταδικεῖν). The matching interdict, on returning harm for harm (ἀντικακουργεῖν), he derives from that same premise taken in conjunction with the further premise that to do evil to a person is to do injustice to that person. And if we were then to ask, "Why should we grant that first principle, which is used for the derivation of that twofold renunciation of the *lex talionis*?" it is from the principle of the Sovereignty of Virtue that we would get our answer – all the answer we need at this point. If, when we see that an option is unjust, we should reject it instantly without giving any consideration at all to countervailing benefits, then, naturally, we should never commit injustice.[54] And then the question becomes: how does he derive the principle of the Sovereignty of Virtue?

The *Apology* does not disclose the answer; but the *Crito* does. What is laid down as an unargued principle in the *Apology* (T10) and T11) is presented in the *Crito* as the conclusion of a line of reasoning. Recall how T12 begins: "But for us, since the argument thus compels us" ("thus catches us," if we give with Burnet[55] its literal force to the verb in ἐπειδὴ οὕτω ὁ λόγος αἱρεῖ). The same explicit indication of an inferential link to what precedes had been given earlier in the same paragraph, as its start:

T14 *Cr.* 48B11–C2: "From what has been agreed let us consider this: would it be just or unjust to leave this place without the consent of the Athenians? If it is just, we shall. If it is not, we shan't."

Here we see a proleptic application of the principle of the Sovereignty of Virtue: the decision between those life-or-death alternatives – to break jail or to stay put to drink hemlock – is to be made solely on the justice or injustice of the matter, shutting out every other consideration. Why so? Because of "what has been agreed." And what is that? It is spelled out in the immediately preceding lines:

54 The way οὐδαμῶς ἀδικεῖν ("we should *never* commit injustice") is in fact derived in the text (49A5–7) exhibits it as an entailment of the previous "agreements" (ὡς πολλάκις ἡμῖν καὶ ἐν τῷ ἔμπροσθεν χρόνῳ ὡμολογήθη) that ἀδικεῖν (committing injustice) is never good (49A6) for the agent (49B). These "agreements" would *also* entail the principle of the Sovereignty of Virtue (and could have been used to derive the latter had they preceded it in the text); and they are themselves interentailing with the statement (48B8–9 = T15) from which the Sovereignty of Virtue is derived in the text (as I proceed to explain in the text above).

55 Burnet, 1924. See his gloss on ὁ λόγος αἱρεῖ, supported by references to Herodotus, the orators, *et al.* (196–7).

T15 *Cr.* 48B4–10: "Do we still hold, or do we not, that we should attach highest value not to living, but to living well?" – "We do." – "And that to live well is the same as to live honorably and justly: do we hold that too, or not?" – "We do."

IV   THE IDENTITY AND SUFFICIENCY THESES

What should we make of T15?[56] Many scholars[57] have passed it over as a truism.[58] If we take a closer look at it we will see that it is anything but that.[59] For since "well" is the adverbial form of "good" and since for Socrates, as for all Greek moralists, the good for man is happiness,[60] the *prima-facie* meaning of his statement is that the happy and virtuous forms of living are identical, that is to say, that the form of life we call "happiness" when viewing it under desirability criteria (as the most deeply and durably satisfying kind of life) is *the same form of life* we call "virtue" when viewing it as meeting moral criteria (as the just, brave, temperate, pious, wise way to live). Could any proposition in moral philosophy be less of a commonplace than this? For if this is what Socrates holds, it commits him unavoidably[61] to the third of the positions laid out above: he is holding that virtue *is* happiness – virtue its sole component, the only thing that makes life good and satisfying. This is the *prima-facie* import of T15. I shall call it "the Identity Thesis of the relation of virtue to happiness" or "the Identity Thesis" for short. But why should I keep saying that this is "the prima-facie" import of the text? Why that qualification? Could there be any doubt on this score? There could indeed. Let me explain.

What we are offered in this text is meant to state the rationale of

56 The only reference to it in Gosling & Taylor, 1982, is at 45, where it is not connected with T12 and is explained away as "vacillation." On the interpretation I am presenting here there is no need so to regard it: T15 fits into a stably coherent moral theory.

57 Cf. n. 39 above.

58 Presumably for this reason: I can think of no other to explain why so many scholars who were thoroughly familiar with this text should have made nothing of it.

59 One's whole interpretation of Socrates' moral theory could be altered by taking notice of the true import of this crucial text. Thus Guthrie, who does not cite T15 (or T10, T11, T12), would not have written, "The utilitarian conception of good is certainly Socratic" (1969: 463); Frankena, 1963: 3–5 and 16, who ignores T15 in his extended account of *Cr.* 47C–51C as a paradigm of moral reasoning, would not have thought the interdicts on returning injustice for injustice and evil for evil teleologically ungrounded and so would not have bracketed Socrates with Kant as a "rule-deontologist." Both of these diametrically opposite misinterpretations of Socratic ethics could have been blocked if the role of T15 in its passage had been properly understood.

60 See additional note 8.2.

61 See additional note 8.3.

the principle of the Sovereignty of Virtue in T12: the phrases "from what has been agreed" in T14 and "since the argument thus compels us" in T12 make this doubly clear. And, of course, the Identity Thesis would warrant the implication if we share Socrates' eudaemonist axiom, which makes the attainment of happiness the final reason for every rational choice.[62] Given this further premise – the tacit premise of the argument – then, certainly, once we are satisfied that of two possible courses of action the one is just, the other unjust, the identity of virtue and happiness would immediately decide the choice: the unjust course would not deserve even a second look if it is known to be the unhappy one. So for a eudaemonist the Identity Thesis would indeed meet the requirement of compelling acceptance of the principle of the Sovereignty of Virtue. But *it over-satisfies that requirement.* The principle does not require so strong a premise: the Identity Thesis "catches" the principle, but the principle does not "catch" the Identity Thesis. The principle only tells us how we should choose when the alternatives are virtuous and vicious respectively. It does not tell us how we should choose when the alternatives are not of that sort at all – when both options are acceptable from a moral point of view. Yet choices of this latter sort may make an appreciable difference to our happiness, while on the Identity Thesis they should make none: if virtue is identical with happiness, then options equally consistent with our virtue should be equally consistent with our happiness. But in point of fact they are not.

To illustrate: imagine that in a strange house where I must spend the night I have the choice of two beds. One is freshly made and the sheets are clean. The other was slept in the night before by someone in a drunken stupor who vomited on the bed: the sheets are still soggy from the remains. Since my virtue would be unimpaired if, clenching my teeth and holding my nose, I were to crawl in between those filthy sheets for a bad night's sleep, why should not my happiness be similarly unimpaired? I trust the grossness of the example will not offend: misplaced delicacy is an impediment to clear thinking on moral topics, as Socrates would be the first to observe. I trust also that the example will not be brushed aside on the ground that it concerns the happiness of a few hours, while the happiness Socrates is talking about is a long-run, ideally, a life-long business: I could easily concoct examples to fit that bill: say, life in a concentration camp. If happiness were identical with virtue, an

---

62 Cf. the comment on T6 above, and T24 below.

inmate of Gulag should be as happy as an equally virtuous inmate of a Cambridge college. Or, to use a Biblical fable, if happiness were identical with virtue, Job should be as happy after Satan's work has been done as he was before – the loss of his seven thousand sheep and five thousand camels and of all his kin, the running sores that cover him from head to foot, should not result in the slightest diminution of his happiness.

Is there then no alternative to the Identity Thesis which would provide a ground for rational preference between courses of action indistinguishable in respect of virtue but differing materially in other ways? There surely is. Let me sketch a possible model of it. Keeping virtue in its place as the sovereign good, both necessary and sufficient for happiness, let us allow happiness a multitude of lesser constituents in addition to virtue. Everything on Socrates' list of non-moral goods (cf. *Eud.* 279A–B) would come in under this head. *In disjunction from virtue each would be worthless.*[63] But when conjoined with virtue (i.e. when used virtuously) they would enhance happiness in some small degree.[64] Variations in happiness which, on the Identity Thesis, would be a function of a single variable, on this alternative model would be a function of many variables: all of those non-moral mini-components of happiness would be incremental in some small way if conjoined with virtue; each would make a mini-difference, greater in the case of some than of others (thus the enhancement of Job's happiness would be greater if he regained his health than if he got back his camels).

63 This feature of the model (entailing that the value of all non-moral goods would be conditioned on their conjunction with virtue) suffices to distinguish it from the doctrine of Antiochus of Ascalon (*ap.* Cicero, *De Fin.* 5.78ff., *Tusc.* 5.22–3), which matches the model in allowing that virtue suffices for a "happy" life, though not for the "happiest" (*beatam...neque tamen beatissimam, Tusc.* 5.22), maintaining (against the Stoics: cf. n. 3 above) that happiness admits of degrees (*De Fin.* 5.84), allowing that non-moral evils are decremental (though the decrements are very small: *exigua et paene minima, De Fin.* 5.78); but there is no indication that Antiochus makes non-moral goods decremental only when disjoined from virtue and incremental only when conjoined with virtue, stipulating that virtue is a necessary condition of non-moral goods having any value whatsoever for their possessor, as does the model above.

64 A virtuous person would be *happy*, regardless of possession of non-moral goods, but happi*er* with than without one or more of them (at a level higher than the minimal needed for the exercise of knowledge, below which virtue itself would be impossible and life would not be worth living: cf. n. 69 below). We know that Socrates believes that a man who is *unhappy* (because he acts unjustly) will be unhappi*er* if his injustice goes unpunished (the former state is δεύτερον τῶν κακῶν μεγέθει, the latter is μέγιστον καὶ πρῶτον κακῶν, *G.* 479D); and that of two foolish persons the less enterprising would err less and would therefore be "less unhappy" (ἄθλιος ἧττον, *Eud.* 281C2). It is reasonable to infer that his conception of happiness will similarly admit of degrees: good and evil, straightforward contraries, could hardly fail to be symmetrical in this important respect.

Here we see the possibility of two alternative theories of the relation of virtue to happiness, predicated on different conceptions of happiness. A unicomponent model of happiness would yield the Identity Thesis. The multicomponent model I have just sketched would yield, alternatively, what I shall call the Sufficiency Thesis,[65] since on this model virtue, remaining the invariant and sovereign good, would of itself assure a sufficiency of happiness – enough of it to yield deep and durable contentment – but would still allow for small, but not negligible, enhancements of happiness as a result of the virtuous possession and use of non-moral goods. I want to argue that, appearances to the contrary notwithstanding, the Sufficiency, not the Identity, Thesis gives the right insight into the Socratic view. Let me probe those appearances. What do the texts really say?

Doesn't T15 *say* that the happy and the virtuous life are identical? It says that they are ταὐτόν. Isn't that as good? It would be, if it were certain that ταὐτόν is being used here to express identity. Could there be any question as to that? There could indeed. Aristotle, the first Greek thinker to investigate that innocent-looking term,[66] concludes that when two general terms, A and B, are said to be ταὐτόν, any one of three different things could be meant. These are his first two:[67]

(1)   that A and B are synonyms or that they "are the same in definition";

(2)   that B is, in technical Aristotelian terminology, a "proprium" (ἴδιον) of A, i.e. that while B is not the "essence" of A, the two are nonetheless necessarily interentailing.[68]

The first, which Aristotle takes to be the "primary and principal" use of the term, will not fit our text at all: "happiness" and "virtue" are certainly not meant to be synonyms, nor are they supposed to have the same definition. What about the second? It clearly fits on the

---

65 That should not be confused with the standard Stoic doctrine that "virtue is self-sufficient for happiness," by which they understand precisely what I am calling the "Identity Thesis," that virtue is the only component of happiness, the only good (cf. n. 37 above). Still less should it be confused with what Irwin calls "the sufficiency of virtue" (1977a: 100–1), which stands at the other extreme from the Stoic view and also from what the Socratic view would be on either the Identity or the Sufficiency Theses, since Irwin takes the relation of virtue to happiness to be purely instrumental, while I take it to be strictly constitutive on the Socratic view as also, of course, on the Stoic.

66 *Topics* 103a23–31, b10–12.

67 His third, "accidental sameness," is irrelevant to the analysis of T15.

68 ἀντικατηγορεῖται, i.e., that for all x, x has A if, and only if, x has B.

Identity Thesis, where "happiness" and "virtue" are the same form of living differently described. But it also fits on the Sufficiency Thesis: when *A* and *B* are necessarily interentailing, then, necessarily, *x* has attribute *A* if, and only if, *x* has attribute *B*, and then *x* may (but need not) have certain additional attributes, say, *C* and *D*, necessarily interentailing with attributes *E* and *F*, respectively, On the Sufficiency Thesis *A* would stand for virtue, *B* for the happiness which is found necessarily and exclusively in virtue; *C* and *D* might stand for, say, virtuous health and virtuous wealth,[69] and *E* and *F* for the increments of happiness associated with health and wealth, respectively, when these are virtuously used. On these terms "happy" and "virtuous" would be interentailing and would, therefore, qualify for being "the same" in sense (2), though the degrees of happiness experienced by virtuous persons differently circumstanced with respect to non-moral goods would differ.[70] Thus the Sufficiency Thesis would fit T15 no less than would the Identity Thesis.[71]

We may now investigate three texts which, like T15, appear to give the very strongest possible support to the Identity Thesis but, as I shall argue, turn out on closer scrutiny to be equally consistent with its rival. I start with the one which I take to give the clue to the right reading of all three of these texts:

T16 *Ap.* 30C5–D5: [a] "You should know well that if you kill the sort of man I say I am you will harm yourselves more than me. Me neither

---

69 That is to say, at a level higher than that strictly necessary to sustain virtue: If health fell below a certain minimal level, *x*'s mental processes would fail – he or she would be incapacitated for the exercise of knowledge and therewith for that of virtue, since Socrates holds that virtue "is" knowledge. (We may surmise that some such sub-minimal physical state is what Socrates has in view at *Cr.* 47D–E and *G.* 512A: a body so ravaged by disease that life is no longer preferable to death.) *Mutatis mutandis* the same would be true of "wealth," i.e. of the means of subsistence.

70 I am not crediting Socrates with anticipating the Aristotelian analysis of the various senses of "the same" – far from it: had he done so he would have saved himself a pack of trouble (cf. Vlastos, 1981: 431–3 and 444–5). I invoke the Aristotelian analysis to show that a student of multivocity (which, alas, Socrates was not) attests a use of "the same" which is the only one that fits T15 (since neither homonymy, nor definitional identity, nor accidental identity will). In T21[b] and then again, more elaborately, in T22 below we shall see Socrates use interentailment to express the relation of virtue to happiness, doing so without resort to any word suggestive of identity in that context, while continuing to maintain that καλόν and ἀγαθόν are ταὐτόν in adjacent contexts: at *G.* 474C9–D2 he takes his dispute with Polus to pivot on the latter's denial of this proposition.

71 And note that the Identity Thesis is not suggested at all in the statements in the *Crito* at 49A5–6 and 49B4–6 which (as I remarked above: n. 54) "*also* entail the principle of the Sovereignty of Virtue (and could have been used to derive the latter)": no more than interentailment of ἀγαθόν and δίκαιον (or καλόν) is asserted (49A5–6 states that ἀδικεῖν is never ἀγαθόν, 49B4–6 that ἀδικεῖν is always κακόν). The identity of ἀγαθόν to καλόν and of κακόν to αἰσχρόν is not even suggested in these statements.

Meletus nor Anytus could harm;[72] they could not, for it is not permitted that a better man be harmed by someone worse than himself.

[b] "He could kill me, perhaps, drive me into exile, deprive me of civic rights. He and others might think that these are great evils. But I don't. Much greater is the evil he is attempting now – to send a man unjustly to death."

Does Socrates really mean that Meletus and Anytus could not harm him, knowing well that they could bring about his death, exile, *atimia*? If he did, he would be asserting that these – and, by the same token, any other – non-moral evils would make zero difference to his happiness. But look at what he goes on to say in part [b] of our text: not that they can do him *no* evil, but that they can do him no *great* evil. Is he dithering, thinking those calamities non-evils at [a], mini-evils at [b]? There is no need to suppose that there is any vacillation at all; he can be reasonably understood to be making the same point in both parts of the text. To see this we must take account of that special use of negation, available in all natural languages, Greek no less than English, whose purpose is not to deny the applicability of the predicate, but to de-intensify its application. You ask, "Might I trouble you to post this letter for me?" and I reply, "It would be no trouble – none at all," though I know and you know that the errand would take me several blocks out of my way. You understand me to say "no trouble" and mean "a mini-trouble – too trivial to be worth mentioning." If we were entitled to read in that way the negation in T16[a], what is said there would fit the Sufficiency Thesis fully as well as does what is said in T16[b].

Are we then entitled to read T16[a] in this way? There is reason to think so. Consider what Socrates had been saying a few lines earlier in the *Apology*:

T17 *Ap.* 30A8–B4: [a] "[I ask you] to make your first and strongest concern not wealth but the soul – that it should be as virtuous as possible."

[b] "For virtue does not come from wealth, but through virtue, wealth and everything else, private and public, become good for men (ἀλλ' ἐξ ἀρετῆς χρήματα καὶ τὰ ἄλλα ἀγαθὰ [γίγνεται] τοῖς ἀνθρώποις ἅπαντα καὶ ἰδίᾳ καὶ δημοσίᾳ)."[73]

---

72 This is Epictetus' favourite Socratic text. He cites it repeatedly (always in the same pungent paraphrase: "Anytus and Meletus can kill me but cannot harm me"): *Diss.* 1.29.17; 2.2.15; 2.23.21.

73 I am adopting Burnet's construction of the terminal clause ("ἀγαθὰ is predicate," *ad loc.*) which has been ignored in every subsequent translation known to me except Robin's (1956) in the *Pléiade* Plato, I, where the same construction ("mais c'est le vrai mérite qui

In [a] he is reiterating the sentiment he had voiced just before:

T18 *Ap.* 29E5–30A2: "…if he appears to me not to have the virtue he says he has, I shall reproach him for setting least value on the things of the greatest value and setting the greater on inferior (φαυλότερα) things."

What Socrates is saying here fits perfectly the framework of the Sufficiency Thesis. He is not saying that the non-moral goods he has been talking about (money, reputation, prestige) have no value at all, but that their value is vastly inferior to that of the most precious thing in life, perfection of soul. In T17[b] he explains why the latter should hold so preeminent a place in our scheme of value: this is what makes all other things good;[74] without this nothing else would be good. Since there is no reason to think that his perspective on non-moral goods has altered, less than a page later, in T16, we are justified in reading the message in T16[a] in the same way, hence as the same message as in T16[b].

Should there still be hesitation on this point, here is a further consideration to allay the doubt: In that special use of "no trouble" in my example, negation functions as an implicit comparative: the phrase is, in effect, a contraction for "no trouble by comparison with the vastly greater trouble I would gladly take to give you pleasure."[75] Apply this to the remark in T16[a] that Meletus and Anytus "could not harm him": what he is trying to get across in both parts of T16 is the triviality of the harm his prosecutors could do to him by comparison with the enormity of the harm they are doing themselves. In [b] this thought is fully explicit ("much greater is the evil he is attempting now"); it follows the denial that what Meletus could do to Socrates would be "the great evils" that they are commonly thought to be and explains how that denial should be understood. In [a] the same comparison ("you will harm yourselves more than

fait bonne la fortune," etc.) is being followed (without argument, without reference to Burnet and without appeal to his suggested syntax). For a rejection of the traditional translation (even without opting for Burnet's syntax) and an alternative suggestion for avoiding its perverse reading of the text (which would make Socrates recommend virtue as a money-maker) see Myles Burnyeat, "Virtues in Action," in Vlastos, 1971: 209–34 at 210.

74 Cf. *Ch.* 156E6–9 ("all good and all evil, whether in the body or in the whole man, come from [the condition of] the soul"); *Pr.* 313A7–8 ("the soul, on whose deterioration or improvement your whole welfare depends"); *Eud.* 291D–E: things which would be good if wisely (hence virtuously) used would otherwise be evil. (John Ackrill has pointed out to me that Aristotle has a similar doctrine: "those goods with which prosperity and adversity have to do, *simpliciter* are always good, but for a particular person are not always good," *E.N.* 1129B2–4: they would not be good for a bad man. He compares also *E.N.* 5.1.9; *E.E.* 8.3 (esp. 5) and *Pol.* 1332a19–27.)

75 Or, perhaps, "by comparison with the value I attach to our friendship."

me") introduces the denial that Meletus or Anytus could harm him and similarly shows how it is to be understood. The point of saying in [a] that he could not be harmed is the same as that of saying in [b] that he could not be *greatly* harmed: both are instruments of the same comparison,[76] alternative ways of expressing the same thought.

We may now look at two more texts which, if taken at face-value, would be conclusive evidence for the Identity Thesis:

T19 *Ap.* 41c8–d2: "But you too, my judges, must be of good hope towards death and bear this truth in mind: no evil can happen to a good man either in life or in death."

T20 *R.* 1 335c1–7: "And shall we say the same about men, that when they are harmed they are made worse in respect of human excellence?" – "Certainly." – And is not justice human excellence?" – "Absolutely." – Hence, necessarily, when men are harmed they are made more unjust."

In T19 he says "no evil" can happen to him. In T20 the conclusion – that when men are harmed they are necessarily made more unjust, entails, by modus tollens, that when they are not made more unjust they are not harmed. Can Socrates say this, knowing quite well that men may be robbed, imprisoned, tortured, blinded, without being made more unjust? He obviously can on the Identity Thesis. But so too on the Sufficiency Thesis if we carry forward into our reading of each of these new texts what we learned in T16[a] via T17 and T18 and the de-intensifying use of predicate negation. If in T16[a] Socrates could use "no evil" as a simple variant for "no great evil" in T16[b], then what he says in T19 and T20, each of them to all appearance hard evidence for the Identity Thesis, can be similarly read as consistent with its rival.

There is still another text where, as in T16 above, the initial impression of unambiguous support for the Identity Thesis dissipates when the text is read as a whole:

T21 *G.* 470e4–11: "Obviously, then, you'd say you don't know even if the Great King is happy." – "And that would be the truth, for I don't know how he stands in culture and justice." – "What? Does all of

---

76 Cf. the use of negation at *Ap.* 23a, where Socrates takes the god to be declaring that human wisdom is "worth little or nothing." That here "nothing" is a disguised comparative becomes clear in the sequel (b2–4): the god is to be understood as telling men that the wisest of them is he who "has come to realize that, in truth, he is worthless πρὸς σοφίαν" – worthless not absolutely but by comparison with the god's own superlative wisdom.

happiness depend on that?[77] – [a] "Yes, Polus, I would say so, indeed. [b] For I say that the honorable and good man and woman is happy, the unjust and wicked is miserable.

If what Socrates says in [a] were literally meant – that all of happiness depends on "culture and justice" – he would be ruling out the eudaemonic value of everything but virtue; he would be saying that virtue is the only good.[78] The foregoing argument for deflating the quantifier in т16[a] – for taking "no harm" to mean "no great harm" – prompts the question whether the same semantic operation might not be also in order here.[79] The question admits of a firm "Yes" once we note two things about the follow-up to [a] in [b]: first that [b] purports to give the reason (γάρ) for what is asserted in [a], thereby implicitly explaining what is meant at [a]; secondly, that the relation of virtue to happiness which is expressed in [b] is, unmistakably, interentailment, not identity: Socrates does not say that happiness is that very thing which (τοῦτο ὅπερ) virtue is[80] but that one will have happiness if, and only if, one has virtue. And if we want reassurance that precisely this constitutes his mature, fully considered view, it is supplied us in full measure later on in the dialogue, when Socrates sums up as follows the upshot of his long argument against Callicles:

т22 *G.* 507в8–c7: "So there is every necessity, Callicles, (i) that the temperate man who, as we have seen, will be just and brave and pious, will be a perfectly good man, and the good man will act well and nobly in whatever he does, and he who acts well will be blessed and happy; and (ii) that he who is wicked and acts badly will be miserable..."

---

77 The alternative translation "Does all of happiness consist in that?" is possible (so Robin in his translation of the *Apology* [1956] and Santas, 1979: 266), but improbable in view of the plethora of passages which attest the wide use of the phrase to mean "depends on" or "rests in": Soph. *O.T.* 314, *O.C.* 248; Eur. *Alc.* 278; Thuc. 1.74.1 and 3.13.54; Plato, *Pr.* 354E7; Dem. 18.193 (I am indebted to Irwin for the first three references, to Ian Kidd for the rest). To opt for the latter translation is not to give hostages to the instrumentalist interpretation of the Socratic theory: the dependence could be constitutive (i.e. entailment, not causal consequence); the issue remains open, to be decided on other grounds.

78 This is how the Stoics read т21. Cicero's (*Tusc.* 5.35) gloss on Polus' last question is, *Videtur omnem hic beatam vitam in una virtute ponere?*

79 And similarly in *G.* 507D6–E1: "This, I do believe, is the mark (σκοπός) to which one should look throughout one's life, that *everything* in one and in one's city should tend to the presence of justice and temperance in one who is to be blessed," where "everything" raises the same question as does "all" in т21 above: does Socrates mean that virtue is our *only* good, or rather, the all-important one which should have absolute priority over all of our other goods, since it is the condition of the goodness of anything else?

80 Or that "happiness is nothing but virtue" or, as in Cicero's gloss (n. 78), "[Socrates] makes happiness repose solely in virtue."

Simplifying this more elaborate statement, trimming it down to just those assertions which are essential for my present argument, what is said here comes to this:

(1)   if one were perfectly virtuous then, necessarily, one would be happy, i.e. that virtue necessarily entails happiness,

and moreover

(ii)   if one were wicked then, necessarily, one would be miserable, i.e., that wickedness necessarily entails unhappiness and thus (by modus tollens) that happiness necessarily entails virtue.

Putting (i) and (ii) together, we get

(iii)   virtue and happiness are necessarily interentailing.

This is what Socrates feels he has established in the *pièce de résistance* of the whole dialogue. Thus interentailment is indubitably the relation of virtue to happiness in T21[b] and T22, therefore also in T21[a], confirming the previous argument that just this was the relation expressed *via* ταὐτόν in T15. So the relation of virtue to happiness asserted in all three of these texts is equally consistent with the Identity and with the Sufficiency Theses.

What should we conclude from this review? Suppose we could have put our question to him: "Tell us, Socrates, which of those two theses we blocked out for you represents your view. What does your picture of happiness look like? Is it a monochrome, all of the space for happiness filled by a solid color, say, blue, standing for virtue? Or is the picture a polychrome, most of it painted blue, but flecked out with a multitude of other colors, each of those specks making some tiny but appreciable contribution to the design?" We scan several dicta of his, trying to read from them his answer, and we are disappointed by their failure to speak out loud and clear. Several of them – T15, T16[a], T19, T20, T21[a] – at first look like flat endorsements of the Identity Thesis.[81] But when scrutinized more closely all of them are seen to be consistent with the Sufficiency Thesis too, as is the case from the start in T16[b], T21[b], T22, while

81 Any of these texts, read without the correction for which I have argued above, would amply suffice to make the Stoics believe that their view of the "all-sufficiency of virtue"(cf. nn. 37 and 78 above) was pukka Socratic.

two of them, T17 and T18, are more than just consistent with the Sufficiency Thesis: they speak from its own point of view, that of the incomparably higher value of virtue, not of its exclusive value. So the evidence so far considered, taken as a whole, cannot be said to favor the Identity Thesis to the exclusion of the Sufficiency Thesis. But I do not wish to stop with that. I want to argue that Socrates has a compelling reason to opt for the Sufficiency Thesis, and shall produce textual evidence that he is in fact committed to it.

V   FOR THE SUFFICIENCY THESIS

I may put that reason bluntly: if Socrates had opted for the Identity Thesis he would have made a perfectly senseless decision. I do not mean to echo Aristotle's sally against those thinkers who, he thought, were crediting the virtuous man's happiness with impossible invulnerability to misfortune:[82]

T23 Arist. *E.N.* 1153B19–21: Those who say that a man who is being tortured and has suffered terrible calamities is happy if he is a good man are willy-nilly talking nonsense.

Why nonsense? If Aristotle were charging conceptual error – which I do not think he is – I would disagree. If Socrates believes that human beings could remain happy in the most extreme suffering, I would marvel at his faith in the sublime capacities of human nature, but I would see no contradiction in it, no logical reason why it could not be true. It is not for this that I would fault the Identity Thesis. After all, on this point it is no different from its rival: in either case Socrates would be making heroic demands on human nature. But the Identity Thesis does something more. It requires that all those values which are strictly non-moral on his reckoning should make zero difference to happiness.

Consider the consequence, given his view that

T24 *G.* 499E7–8: "The good [= happiness][83] is the final end (τέλος) of all our actions; everything must be done for its sake."

i.e. that happiness is the final reason which can be given for any purposeful action, hence for any rational choice between alternative

---

82 The target could be Antisthenes (D.L. 6.11, "he held virtue to be sufficient for happiness without need of anything further except Socratic strength"). If Aristotle's reference is to Socrates we could not infer that the Identity Thesis is being imputed to him: the Sufficiency Thesis could have provoked the same objection.

83 Cf. n. 20 above.

courses of action. It follows that if Identity were the true relation of virtue to happiness, *we would have no rational ground for preference between alternatives which are equally consistent with virtue* – hence no rational ground for preference between states of affairs differentiated only by their non-moral values. And if this were true, it would knock out the bottom from eudaemonism as a theory of rational choice. For many of the choices we have to make in our day-to-day life have to be made between just such states of affairs, where moral considerations are not in the picture at all. Shall I walk to my destination or ride the bus? Shall I have my hair cut today or next week? Shall I have Burgundy or Rosé for dinner, or no wine at all? We do make such choices all the time, and we want to make them: we would resent it fiercely if they were taken out of our hands. And the grounds on which we have to make them are clearly non-moral: hedonic, economic, hygienic, aesthetic, sentimental, or whatever. This being the case, if the Identity Thesis were true it would bankrupt the power of eudaemonism to give a rational explanation of all our deliberate actions by citing happiness as our final reason for them. On that theory, if happiness were identical with virtue, our final reason for choosing anything at all would have to be only concern for our virtue; so the multitude of choices that have nothing to do with that concern would be left unexplained.[84] To avoid this consequence all Socrates would have had to do is opt for the Sufficiency Thesis, whose mini-goods fill exactly the gap in the explanatory scope of the eudaemonist theory if the Identity Thesis were true. Were Socrates to deny himself this option he would be making an utterly gratuitous choice, since the Sufficiency Thesis would serve as well the moral purpose of his theory of the relation of virtue to happiness.[85]

Can we say more – not only that this would have been the right decision for Socrates to make, but that he gives positive evidence of being committed to it? We can.

84 Would this objection tell also against the Stoic view (cf. n. 37 above)? This had a doctrine of natural elective affinity (οἰκείωσις) for life, health, etc., which makes such things naturally "akin" (οἰκεῖα) to us and, therefore, "preferred" (προηγμένα) to their contraries, though "indifferent" (ἀδιάφορα) nonetheless, since they are not goods. But does it really make sense to say of life, health, etc. that they are "preferred" *and* "indifferent"? Unable to pursue this question within the limits of the present book, I still venture to suggest that the multicomponent model of happiness I am sketching for Socrates in the present chapter would have served the Stoics better than their strange doctrine of "preferred indifferents" or any other on their market, including the doctrine of Antiochus (cf. n. 63 above): it would have enabled them to hold that their προηγμένα *are* goods without jeopardizing their concern that virtue be both necessary and sufficient for happiness.

85 I argue above (second paragraph of section III) for this function of T15. For that purpose the Identity Thesis is postulational overkill.

T25 G. 467E1–468B4: "Now is there anything in existence that isn't either good or bad or intermediate between the two: neither good nor bad?... And you call 'goods'[86] wisdom and health and wealth and other things of that sort?... and by 'neither good nor evil' don't you mean things of this sort: which partake now of the one now of the other and at times of neither – for example, sitting and walking and running and sailing; and again stones and sticks and other things of that sort?... And when people do those intermediate actions, do they do them for the sake of the good things, or the good things for the sake of the intermediates?... So it is in pursuit of the good that we walk when we walk, thinking this would be better, and when, on the contrary, we stand, this too we do for the sake of the good? Is it not so?"

Here "everything in existence" is trichotomized into things (objects or actions) which are either (a) good or (b) evil or (c) neither good nor evil ("intermediate between good and evil," hence "intermediate" for short). Into box (c) he puts everything which can have only instrumental value – physical objects, like sticks and stones, and physical actions, like sitting or standing, which, it is assumed, we would never perform for their own sake, but only for the sake of some end external to themselves.[87] Into box (a) he puts all "goods" – all those things for whose sake we may want any "intermediate" whatever. As examples he gives a moral good, wisdom, and two non-moral goods, health and wealth. This would be unintelligible if he were accepting the Identity Thesis, which identifies the good with virtue and assigns purely instrumental status to non-moral goods: if Socrates were tacitly opting for the Identity Thesis he obviously would not have put health and wealth into box (a), which is exactly where they do belong on the Sufficiency Thesis, which assigns intrinsic value to non-moral goods, accepting them as components of the good,[88] without thereby elevating them to preference-parity with the moral goods – nothing of this sort is suggested in T25 nor anywhere else in the *Gorgias*; the absolute subordination of all other goods to virtue is maintained as strongly in this dialogue as anywhere in the Platonic corpus.[89]

Further evidence for the Sufficiency Thesis is available in the *Gorgias*:

---

86 I.e. constituents of the good, as is shown by the interchangeability of "goods" with "good" throughout the passage: Socrates uses the plural to refer disjunctively to the same things to which he refers conjunctively by the singular (τὸ ἀγαθόν) which is *identical* with happiness.

87 Cf. additional note 8.4.   88 Cf. n. 86 above.

89 The great argument against Polus and Callicles that to suffer wrong is always better than to commit it turns on that principle. It is implied in 507D6–E1 (cited in n. 79 above).

T26 *G.* 469B12–C2: Polus: "Would you then wish to suffer injustice rather than do it? Socrates: "For my part I would wish neither. But if I were forced to choose between suffering injustice and doing it, I would choose to suffer it."

Confronting two states differentiated only by their non-moral value – in one he suffers injustice, in the other he doesn't – Socrates says flatly that he would not wish the former. Why so, when, as he believes, suffering injustice would not impair his virtue? If his sentiments were in conformity with the Identity Thesis, he would be saying that neither would it affect his happiness – so why should he care whether or not he suffers injustice? Since he does care – he is not a masochist, he objects to being victimized by predators – he cannot be accepting the Identity Thesis: only its rival would justify a preference for courses of action which are morally on a par over alternatives to which they are superior only on non-moral grounds – because they would spare him the loss of property or reputation or health or any of those other non-moral goods which would be filched from him if he suffered injustice.

We get more to the same effect in the discussion of pleasure in the *Gorgias*:

T27 *G.* 499C6–500A3: "Some pleasures are good and some bad. Is it not so?... And the good ones are the beneficial, the bad ones the harmful?... Now is this what you mean: of the bodily pleasures – of eating and drinking, for instance – are not the good ones those that produce bodily health or strength or some other bodily excellence, the bad ones those which do the opposite?... Then pleasant actions, as well as [all] others, should be done for the sake of the good, not the good for the sake of pleasure?"

As between two courses of action, both pleasant, both acceptably moral,[90] but differing in their effect on health, Socrates finds this a sufficient basis for deciding which of the two pleasures is the better. So here again, as previously in T25, he is counting non-moral values as bona fide constituents of happiness – mini-constituents, to be sure, not worth a second look if they would tempt us away from the path of virtue but, even so, once the demands of virtue have been satisfied, sound guides to right choice between alternatives.

This position is maintained in the protreptic discourse in the *Euthydemus* (278E–282D) and in its miniaturized doublet in the *Meno* (87E–88E) where the Socratic thesis that virtue "is" knowledge is

90 For if they were not, moral criteria would decide that one of the two should be preferred.

defended.[91] I quote the lines in which the discourse in the *Euthydemus* comes to a head:

T28 *Eud.* 281D2–E1: [a] "In sum, I said, it would appear, Cleinias, that in the case of all those things which we first said were good,[92] our view is that it is not their nature to be good just by themselves.[93] But this is the truth of the matter, it seems: if ignorance controls them they are greater evils than their contraries to the extent of their greater power to serve their evil leader; while if they are controlled by sound judgment and wisdom they are greater goods, though both are worthless just by themselves. [b] What follows from what has been said? Is it anything but this: *that none of those other things is either good or evil* [just by itself], while there are two things of which one – wisdom – is good [just by itself], the other – ignorance – is evil [just by itself]?

That non-moral goods of whatever description are good only in conjunction with virtue ("wisdom") is the position we have seen Socrates hold all along: explicitly in the *Apology* (T17[b]: "virtue is what makes wealth and all other things good for men "),[94] implicitly in the *Gorgias* (T21[b], T22: virtue is a necessary condition of happiness, hence of the eudaemonic value of everything else). In T28[a] this thought is pushed one step further: wealth, health, etc, good though they are when used virtuously, would be positively bad, "greater evils than their contraries," if they were viciously used.

So far things are plain enough. But in part [b] of our text there is trouble – or, rather, there would be, if we were to take at face value the phrase I have italicized in the citation. For if we did, we would

91 Before being attacked (89Dff.) and finally rejected (96D–98C) in favour of the unSocratic thesis that for the right guidance of action true belief is as good as knowledge. (Cf. chapter 4, n. 73.) I take it that the initial defense of the Socratic thesis represents the point of view maintained throughout the Socratic dialogues, while the subsequent attack on it presents the new position which Plato will be putting into Socrates' mouth throughout the middle dialogues.

92 The reference is to the non-moral goods which head the list of goods at 279A–B and return in great style at 281C3–D1 to illustrate the point which is being made here that when goods are misused they turn into evils instead. It might appear that the indictment of non-moral goods on this score would also extend to moral ones (courage and temperance appear as examples at 281C6 sandwiched in between two sets of non-moral goods). But a moment's reflection will show that the control by "*ignorance*" of attributes whose very essence is wisdom is a counterfactual: if (*per impossible*) courage and temperance *could* be controlled by ignorance (as all of those non-moral qualities in the list uncontroversially can be), *then* they too would be a blot on our happiness. In the doublet of this passage in the *M.* (88A6–D3) the counterfactual use of ἀνδρεία is fully explicit (88B3–5: εἰ μή ἐστι φρόνησις ἡ ἀνδρεία ἀλλ' οἷον θάρρος τι), indicating that σωφροσύνη too (B6) should be understood in the same way. Cf. Irwin, 1977a: 52 and 295–6, n. 16.   93 See additional note 8.5.

94 It is also the position expounded in the *Charmides* (173A–174E), well summarized by Ferejohn (1984: 105–22 at 114): "the beneficial powers of all other 'goods' are entirely nil in the absence of wisdom. " (But I see no justification for putting: "goods" in quotes: there is no indication of anything suspect about the goodness of the products of the crafts under discussion, headed by health, if they are wisely used.)

have to understand Socrates to be saying that health, wealth, etc. are neither good nor evil which, it will be recalled, was the description in T25 above of division (c) of the trichotomy he had laid out there: things which are (a) good, (b) evil, (c) neither good nor evil. This scheme has established the categorial difference between constituents of the good in (a), which included both moral and non-moral goods (both "wisdom" and "health and wealth" are cited as examples of "goods" in (a)), and the things in (c) which have no intrinsic value, are never desirable for their own sake, but only for the sake of some good. Socrates had kept faith with this categorial scheme throughout the *Gorgias*: his adherence to it shows up later in the dialogue, in T27. In dialogues which follow the *Gorgias* the non-moral goods continue to be placed in division (a): in the *Lysias* (218E) Socrates asks about health, "Is it good or evil or neither?" (the same trichotomy as in T25) and answers firmly, as before, "It is good"; in the *Meno* (78c), he asks, "And by 'good' don't you mean such things as health and wealth?", leaving no doubt as to the answer.[95] The same thing happens in the *Euthydemus* prior to T28 and independently of it: health and wealth appear again as straightforward examples of "goods" (279A–B) no less than are the moral goods (279B–C). Thus if Socrates were to assert in T28[b] that health, wealth, etc. are neither good nor evil, thereby transferring them from (a) to (c) in the trichotomy,[96] he would be deserting a categorial scheme he had maintained in all the dialogues which speak to the issue from the *Gorgias* to the *Meno*, including the *Euthydemus* prior to T28. The inconsistency would be palpable. Is there no way of reading that italicized phrase in T28[b] which would preserve consistency?

There surely is, and the best clue to it is in the very words with which T28[b] leads off: "What follows from what has been said?" Well, what does follow from the truth expounded in T28[a], namely that the possession of non-moral goods will enhance our happiness if, and only if, we possess the wisdom to guide our use of them aright? What does follow, surely, is precisely what I have indicated in my citation of the text by the interpolated expansions: namely, that no non-moral good is good just by itself (αὐτὸ καθ' αὑτό), but only in

95 Same thing in the doublet of this passage, *M.* 87E–88A.
96 And the Socratic view would then collapse into the Stoic: "…they say that what may be used both well and ill is not good: wealth and health can be used well and ill; hence wealth and health are not good" (D. L. 7.103; cf. Sextus, *Adv. Math.* 11.61). Thus without the suggested expansion at T28[b] Socrates would be saying with the Stoics that health *is not good* (hence "indifferent"). Commentators who represent him as teaching in T28 that everything except wisdom and ignorance is neither good nor evil seem unaware of the far-reaching consequences for his whole conception of the relation of virtue to happiness if he were to assert in good earnest, like the Stoics, that health, wealth, etc. are not good.

conjunction with wisdom and, by the same token, no non-moral evil is evil just by itself, but only in conjunction with ignorance (since conjunction with wisdom or with ignorance is what will decide if either non-moral goods or non-moral evils will enhance or impair their possessor's happiness) while the moral good, wisdom, is good just by itself and, by the same token, the moral evil, ignorance, is evil just by itself (since in their case the enhancement of their possessor's happiness or unhappiness does not depend on anything but themselves). Thus if we read the expression "either good or evil" as a contraction for "either good [just by itself] or evil [just by itself]" perfect sense will result, its entailment by what was said in T28[a] will be assured,[97] and no violence to the categorial scheme established in the *Gorgias* will be done: health, wealth, etc. will hold their place in division (a) of the trichotomy at T25 as constituents of happiness, but their hold on it will be conditional or contingent:[98] each will be a constituent of their possessor's happiness if, and only if, he or she has wisdom.[99]

Collecting the results obtained in the present section and splicing into them what may be learned from another major passage, which (in the interests of economy) I have not utilized in the above analysis, the account of the *prōton philon* in the *Lysis* (219B–220B), we get the following scheme of value.

   1.   The final unconditional good is happiness. It is the only good we "pursue" or desire only for its own sake and thus the "end" (τέλος) of all our actions (T24).[100] It is the *prōton philon* for whose sake

---

97 We should note the logical invalidity of the inference "*x* is *F* only in conjunction with *W*, *ergo x* is not *F*." The valid inference from that premise would be "*ergo x* is not *F* in disjunction from *W*."

98 I must emphasize that there is nothing the least suspect in the notion of conditional constituents of happiness, i.e. of things which are indeed desirable for their own sake but only under certain conditions.

99 This reading of the italicized phrase in T28[b] will dictate the same reading of two further occurrences of the phrase later on (292B–D): the remark about non-moral civic goods at 292B6–7 must be read, "all those things [prosperity, freedom, civic harmony] have been seen (ἐφάνη) to be neither good nor evil [*themselves by themselves*]"; the back-reference to T28 – where such non-moral goods were seen to be neither good nor evil just by themselves, good only when conjoined with wisdom – is an essential guide to the meaning of what is said here: in Socrates' view even such conspicuous civic goods as prosperity, freedom, and social harmony, depend for their goodness on their wise and virtuous use. The reference to "neither evil nor good" which follows at 292D2–3 must be understood in the same way. For confirmation we may note that in the doublet of T28 in the *Meno* (88C–D) the observation that non-moral goods are beneficial only when rightly used leads to the conclusion that "they are neither beneficial nor detrimental *themselves by themselves*" but do become beneficial or detrimental when they occur "in conjunction with wisdom or ignorance."

100 The terms "benefit," "beneficial" (unless otherwise qualified by context) Socrates reserves for whatever gives direct, unconditional, support or enhancement to our happiness. Thus at *Ch.* 174D–E the science of good and evil is the only one which is

all other dear things are dear, "while it is not itself dear for the sake of any other dear thing" (*Ly.* 330B1–5), since the sequence "*x* is desired for the sake of *y*, *y* for the sake of *z*, etc." cannot be unending.[101]

2.　The supreme non-final unconditional good, both necessary and sufficient for our happiness, hence the sovereign constituent of our good is virtue (wisdom and, by *synecdoche*, each of its associated moral virtues too). The achievement of this good should be the aim (σκοπός) by which all our actions are guided (*G.* 507D6–E1), for regardless of what other goods we may gain or forfeit, if we achieve this constituent of the good we shall possess the final good: we shall be happy (T21, T22).

3.　The subordinate, non-final and conditional goods: health, wealth, etc.[102] The difference to our happiness these can make is minuscule. But goods they are (T25, T27, *Ly.* 218E, *Eud.* 279A–B, *M.* 78C and 87E); we shall be happier with than without them, but only if we use them aright, for they are not "good just by themselves": if separated from wisdom they will go sour on us and we shall be worse off with them than we would have been without them (T28, *M.* 87E–88D).

4.　The "intermediates" (T25), which are reckoned "neither good nor evil" because they are not constituents of the good: their value is purely instrumental; they are never desired for their own sake, but only for the sake of goods.

CONCLUSION

In section IV above we start with texts whose *prima-facie* import speaks so strongly for the Identity Thesis that any interpretation which stops short of it looks like a shabby, timorous, thesis-saving move. What else could Socrates mean when he declares that "no evil" can come to a good man (T19), that his prosecutors "could not harm" him (T16[a]), that if a man has not been made more unjust he has not been harmed (T20), that "all of happiness is in culture and justice," that living well is "the same" as living justly (T15)? But then doubts begin to creep in. Recalling that inflation of the

---

"beneficial" (ὠφέλιμος, ὠφελοῖ ἡμᾶς). In the *Eud.* (289A–B) we would be no better off (ὄφελος οὐδέν) with immortality, than we are now without it, if we did not know how to make the right use of it. In the *M.* (87E–88E) it is the presence of wisdom that makes any good ὠφέλιμον, its absence βλαβερόν.

101　Same reasoning as in Plato (T6 above) and Aristotle (*E.N.* 1093a20–1).

102　In the arguments for the *prōton philon* at *Lysis* 219C–D they are represented by health at 219C and in the immediate sequel (219D–220A) by the wealth the father is ready to spend to save the boy's life.

quantifier is normal and innocuous in common speech ("that job means everything to him, he'll do anything to get it, will stick at nothing") we ask if there is really no chance at all that "no evil" in T19, "not harmed" in T20 might be meant in the same way? The shift from "no harm" at T16[a] to "no great harm" at T16[b], once noticed, strengthens the doubt. It gets further impetus in T21[b] when to explain how "all of happiness depends on culture and justice" he depicts a relation (recurring more elaborately in T22) which, though still enormously strong, is not nearly as strong as would be required by identity. The doubt seeps into T15 when we note that current usage did allow just that relation as a respectable use of "the same."

At that point we begin to wonder if resort to the Identity Thesis might not be just a first approximation to a subtler, more finely nuanced, doctrine which would give Socrates as sound a foundation for what we know he wants to maintain at all costs – the Sovereignty of Virtue – without obliterating the eudaemonic value of everything else in his world. We cast about for a credible model of such a relation of virtue to happiness and hit on that multicomponent pattern sketched on pp. 215–16 above. We ascertain that this will afford a comprehensively coherent eudaemonist theory of rational action, while its rival would not, and will fit perfectly a flock of texts in section v which the latter will not fit at all. Are we not entitled to conclude that this is our best guide to the true relation of virtue to happiness in Socrates' thought – the one for which he would have declared if he had formulated explicitly those two alternatives Theses and made a reasoned choice between them?[103]

103 An alternative analysis of the Socratic scheme of value which has much in common with the one I have presented here has been recently offered by Brickhouse & Smith, 1987: 1–27. Unhappily its major novelty is textually groundless, for it is built on a supposed "Socratic distinction between [a] virtue considered as a condition of the soul, and [b] (virtue considered as) virtuous activity" (2 *et passim*), which has no foundation in our Socratic texts: such a distinction is never mentioned in any of Plato's earlier dialogues nor could it be expressed in their vocabulary, as its proponents would have realized if they had asked themselves how the quoted statement could be translated into Greek without resort to Aristotelian idiolect, ἕξις for [a], ἐνέργεια for [b]. To give Socrates' moral theory the benefit of one of Aristotle's salient innovations would be plainly anachronistic.

EPILOGUE: FELIX SOCRATES

To single out one of the many values in our life, elevating it so far above all the rest that we would choose it at any cost, is one of the many things that have been called "romanticism" in the modern era. Its typical expression there is sexual love. To the hero of a romance winning a particular woman's love may be worth more than are all the other things he covets put together. He may gamble all else for it. But it has other expressions too, not always tagged "romanticism." What else but this is "Give me liberty or give me death"? In the great religions of the world the same attitude may be found, though it has never been so described:

T1 Matthew 13:44–6: Again, the kingdom of heaven is like unto treasure hid in a field, the which when a man hath found, he hideth, and for joy thereof goeth and selleth all that he hath and buyeth that field. Again, the kingdom of heaven is like unto a merchant man, seeking goodly pearls, who, when he had found one pearl of great price, went and sold all that he had, and bought it.

What answers to romanticism in Greek antiquity is the heroic code. Socrates appeals directly to it in self-justification. Confronting an imaginary detractor who reviles him for having lived in a way which now puts him in danger of being executed as a criminal, he replies:

T2 *Ap.* 28B–D:[1] "Man, you don't speak well if you believe that someone worth anything at all would give countervailing weight to danger of life or death or give consideration to anything but this when he acts: whether his action is just or unjust, the action of a good or of an evil man. Mean, on your view, would be those demigods who died in Troy, the rest of them and the son of Thetis... Do you think *he* gave any thought to life or death?"

The comparison is breathtaking in its boldness. Socrates is a plebeian, Achilles noblest of the heroes, darling of the aristocracy.

1 Quoted in part already in the Introduction, p. 8 above, and then again as T10 in ch. 8.

233

Socrates is the voice of reason, Achilles a man of passion rampant over reason. Socrates abjures retaliation, while Achilles, glutting his anger on Hector's corpse, gives the most terrible example of vengeance in the *Iliad*. What can Socrates and this savagely violent young nobleman have in common? Only this: absolute subordination of everything each values to one superlatively precious thing: honour for Achilles, virtue for Socrates.

To keep faith with that subordination Achilles gambles happiness for honor, prepared to lose. And lose he does. He dies grief-stricken. Anticipating his own death in that last scene with Priam, he is as anguished as is the father of the man whose corpse he had dragged in the dust:

T3 *Iliad* 24.522–6: "Sit here and let our pain / Lie still in our heart, despite our anguish, / For cold lament gets nowhere. / Such is the lot the gods have spun for mortals, / To live in grief, while they are sorrow-free."

So too other heroic figures in the tragic imagination of the Greeks die overwhelmed by grief. Antigone goes to her death in unrelieved gloom,[2] fearing that even the gods have forsaken her.[3] Alcestis is so devastated, she thinks of herself as having already "become nothing" before her death.[4] But not Socrates.

In the whole of the Platonic corpus, nay, in the whole of our corpus of Greek prose or verse, no happier life than his may be found. He tells the court how happy he has been plying daily his thankless elenctic task, expecting them to think what he tells them too good to be believed:

T4 *Ap.* 38A: "And if I were to tell you that there can be no greater good for a man than to discourse daily about virtue and about those other things you hear me discuss, examining myself and others – for the unexamined life is not worth living by man – you will believe me even less."[5]

If we are to "count no man happy before the end," we have Plato's assurance that his hero's happiness would meet that test:

T5 *Phd.* 117B–C: "He took the cup most cheerfully,[6] O Echecrates, without any change of color or expression on his face[7]... He drained it very easily, in good humor."[8]

---

2 She goes to Hades "more miserably by far" (κάκιστα δὴ μακρῷ) than any of the members of her ill-fated family (Sophocles, *Ant.* 895).

3 "Why, hapless one, should I look to the gods any more? What ally should I invoke?" (922–3, Jebb's tr.).

4 ὡς οὐκετ᾽ οὖσαν οὐδὲν ἂν λέγοις ἐμέ (Euripides, *Alc.* 387), οὐδὲν εἰμ᾽ ἔτι (390).

5 To go on doing the same in Hades, he confides (41C), "would be inconceivable happiness" (ἀμήχανον ἂν εἴη εὐδαιμονίας).   6 μάλα ἵλεως.

7 οὐδὲν τρείσας οὐδὲ διαφθείρας οὔτε τοῦ χρώματος οὔτε τοῦ προσώπου.

8 μάλα εὐχερῶς καὶ εὐκόλως. Xenophon uses a variant of the phrase to describe the whole of Socrates' foregoing life ("most admired of men for living cheerfully and in good humour"

Is this surprising? If you say that virtue matters more for your own happiness than does everything else put together, if this is what you say and what you mean – it is for real, not just talk – what is there to be wondered at if the loss of everything else for virtue's sake leaves you light-hearted, cheerful? If you believe what Socrates does, you hold the secret of your happiness in your own hands. Nothing the world can do to you can make you unhappy.

In the quest for happiness the noblest spirits in the Greek imagination are losers: Achilles, Hector, Alcestis, Antigone. Socrates is a winner. He has to be. Desiring the kind of happiness he does, he can't lose.

(ἐπὶ τῷ εὐθύμως τε καὶ εὐκόλως ζῆν, *Mem.* 4.8.2), maintained to the end: he departs from the trial "blithe (φαιδρός) in glance, in mien, in gait" (*Ap. of Socrates* 27; Marchant's translation); death he "anticipates and meets cheerfully" (ἱλαρῶς, *ibid.* 33).

ADDITIONAL NOTES

0.1 "CHARITY" AS A PRINCIPLE OF INTERPRETATION[1]

When controlling alternative interpretations of a text in search of *truth* – concerned only to know which is the more likely to be the one that captures the writer's intended meaning – why should "the principle of charity" ever decide the issue? The principle has the look of legitimizing an appeal to sentiment to decide a question of truth. Not so. It has a sound basis in the fact that *belief is dispositional*: to claim that someone believes *p* is to claim much more than that he asserts it at just this moment; it is to claim that this is what he *would continue to assert* unless something happens to change his mind. So if we have reason to think that a person would not wish to hold both *p* and *q*, and would not do so if he realized that they are inconsistent, then we have that much reason for doubting the claim that he does believe both and would assert each as his personal opinion; in the absence of direct evidence for the claim that he does believe both of them, we have that much reason to reject the claim that he does, and opt for an alternative interpretation of his words which preserves consistency. This is the principle on which we decline to take persons to mean statements in which they recognizably misspeak themselves: we feel justified in imputing to them the corrected statement they did not actually make, substituting it for the erroneous one they had inadvertently made.

1.1 SOCRATES' COMPLEX PHILOSOPHICAL IRONIES[2]

In chapter 1 above, to simplify the exposition, I laid out only two of them for a start. But a third is closely connected with the second and

---

1 Cf. n. 36 in the Introduction.   2 Cf. ch. 1, pp. 31–2.

therewith also with the first.[3] All three are best understood when viewed as a group:[4]

(1)   Socrates disavows, yet avows, knowledge.[5]
(2)   He disavows, yet avows, the art of teaching virtue.
(3)   He disavows, yet avows, doing politics (πράττειν τὰ πολιτικά).[6]

The disavowals are explicit. Here are examples of each:

(1)   Disavowal of moral knowledge:

T1 *Ap.* 21B4–5; D5–6: "I am aware of being wise[7] in nothing, great or small (οὔτε μέγα οὔτε σμικρὸν σύνοιδα ἐμαυτῷ σοφὸς ὤν);...as in fact I have no knowledge, neither do I think I have any (ὥσπερ οὖν οὐκ οἶδα, οὐδὲ οἴομαι εἰδέναι)."[8]

(2)   Disavowal of the art of teaching virtue:

T2 *La.* 186D–E: "Socrates says he has no knowledge of the thing [the art of teaching virtue] and is unable to tell which of you is speaking truly [about it]."

(3)   Disavowal of doing politics:

T3 *Ap.* 31D–E: "You know well, O Athenians, that if I had undertaken to do politics long ago I would have perished long ago and done no good either to you or to myself."

---

3 And there is also a fourth, discussed at some length in ch. 1: Socrates' eroticism. This I now put aside to concentrate on the three I mention above.

4 And also in the light of Socrates' use of complex irony evidenced in non-philosophical contexts, as in Xenophon (T6 in chapter 1, and associated texts) and at *Ap.* 20B–C.

5 Here, as *always* in such contexts, we should understand "moral" before "knowledge." Knowledge in the moral domain is the sole object of Socrates' epistemic concern: as Maier (1913: 303–5) has stressed, Socrates was the evangelist of a "purely moral salvation," though it is incorrect to infer, as Maier does (103), that Socrates "was no philosopher" ("gar kein 'Philosoph' war"): the correct conclusion is that he was an exclusively *moral* philosopher. Cf. Thesis IA and n. 12 in ch. 2. Cf. also Vlastos, 1983a: 27ff. at 32–3.

6 As this was understood in Athens it meant active participation in the procedures through which public policy was determined in this highly participatory democracy (cf. *Ap.* 31C–32A, cited in n. 19 below). Many actions which would be counted nowadays as political *par excellence* would not be regarded in Athens as "doing politics" at all. Thus Socrates' vigorous objection in the Assembly to the illegal motion to try the generals *en masse* and his refusal to obey the order of the Thirty to help arrest Leo the Salaminian (*Ap.* 32A–D) would *not* have counted as "doing politics" at the time. This is clear e.g. in the context of T3: Socrates brings up his honorable record in these two cases after explaining why he had *not* "done politics" (32E, where πράττειν τὰ δημόσια = πράττειν τὰ πολιτικά at 31D–E).

7 "Wisdom" (σοφία) and "knowledge" (ἐπιστήμη) are being used interchangeably: see e.g. *Ap.* 19C6, where Socrates shifts in the same breath from having "knowledge" in a given domain to "being wise" in that domain. And cf. *Tht.* 145e: "so knowledge and wisdom are the same thing."   8 Cf. n. 8 in ch. 3.

If these disavowals had been simple ironies the avowal in each case would be left entirely tacit, communicated solely by counting on his hearers to understand from the context that in each of them he wants to convey something contrary to what he says. But there are occasions on which Plato makes him step out of this simple ironical mode. I shall try to show this for all three, beginning with the first.

In an earlier discussion, I had listed no less than nine texts in which Socrates states, or unambiguously implies, that he *does have* knowledge.[9] Those texts cannot be disarmed by maintaining that the knowledge he avows in these texts concerns knowledge of different truths from the knowledge he disavows elsewhere.[10] They cannot, for the simple reason that the knowledge Socrates disavows so explicitly in T1 is global, sweeping enough to be flatly incompatible with knowledge of *anything* "great or small." Nor can the difficulty be dissolved by taking the knowledge which Socrates disclaims to be restricted to "expert knowledge," leaving himself free to claim non-expert or "common" knowledge.[11] For if Socrates did claim the latter sort of knowledge he would be claiming to have a great deal of knowledge – all he needs to guide his actions aright from day to day – which would be excluded by the sweeping generality of what he says at T1. Is there no other way of defusing the blatant contradiction of disclaiming, and yet claiming, moral knowledge? There is.[12]

He gives a clear indication of it in the *Apology*, where he has special reason to take the members of the court into his confidence, doing his best to help them judge him fairly by understanding him correctly; he promises to tell them "the whole truth,"[13] reiterating his assurance he had given them at the start of his address: "from me you will hear the whole truth" (17B8).[14] Responding to what he considers to be the oldest, most widespread and most threatening of

---

9 1985: 1ff. at 7–10, texts T9, T10, T11, T12, T13, T14, T15, T16, T17.
10 So Lesher, 1987: 275–88 at 282: "Socrates' denials of moral knowledge are denials of knowledge concerning the truth of certain basic theses about virtue, the good, and the noble, and are therefore compatible with claims to knowledge about the moral character of specific actions."   11 So Woodruff, 1987: 79–114 at 92–9 *et passim*.
12 My earlier discussion of this crucial feature of my position (1985: 26–9), emphasizing the avowal of what he calls "human" wisdom at *Ap.* 20D–E (= T4) which precedes and implicitly qualifies the disavowal of wisdom in the oracle story at 21B–D, has been inexplicably overlooked by critics. Neither Lesher nor Woodruff (1987) takes account of it. A third critic (Morrison, 1987: 8ff. at 11–13) also ignores it completely, though it is an essential feature of the interpretation he rejects: he makes no reference to what I say at pp. 26–9 of the paper which is the butt of his critique.   13 πᾶσαν τὴν ἀλήθειαν, 20B.
14 The same words he would use again at 20B. So careful a stylist would not repeat himself carelessly; this is one of the rare passages in which he does, and we can be confident that he does so for the purpose of emphasis.

all the public misconceptions of him fostered by the Aristophanic caricature of him as a natural philosopher, theorizing about "things in the heavens and under the earth" and as a sophist "making the weaker argument the stronger" (19B), he explains:

T4 *Ap.* 20D–E: "I came by this reputation, O Athenians, only by a sort of wisdom. What sort? Exactly that which is, no doubt, human wisdom. It looks as though in this I really am wise. But those of whom I spoke just now would be wise in a wisdom that is more than human[15] – I don't know how else to speak of it."

The members of his audience would have been singularly obtuse if, after hearing him say this, they had failed to catch the irony in the total disavowal of knowledge he would proceed to make just a few lines later (T1 above). A man who says, "I have *no* wisdom" cannot expect to be understood to mean simply what he says if a moment before saying it he has admitted that he does have "a certain sort of wisdom" – the kind he calls "human wisdom." Only the most sluggish intellect could have failed to draw the obvious inference: Socrates *is* avowing that "*human* wisdom," which, he believes, may be claimed by a man determined to stay inside the limits of the "mortal thoughts" (θνητὰ φρονεῖν) which befit the human condition;[16] therefore, when, so soon after saying this, he turns around and says that he has "*no* wisdom, great or small," he can only be referring to that "more than human" wisdom he has disavowed as god's exclusive prerogative.[17] Thus in the case of the first of those three paradoxes Socrates gives ample warning that he is using "wisdom" in two sharply contrasting senses, avowing it in one of the two, when it refers to "human" wisdom, while disavowing it when it refers to a kind of wisdom he deems above man's reach.[18]

15 μείζω τινὰ ἢ κατ' ἄνθρωπον σοφίαν σοφοὶ εἶεν. For the force of the underlined phrase cf. its use in the warning given Ajax by the seer in Sophocles (*Ajax* 760–1) that terrible calamities are in store for one who "though born with human nature does not think human thoughts" (μὴ κατ' ἄνθρωπον φρονῇ). Stanford (1963: 159) remarks that these two verses "contain the moral of what is almost a miniature sermon by Calchas here (and is also the main lesson of the whole play, as of many other Greek tragedies), that if a man wishes to avoid disaster he should recognize the limitations of human nature and not try to exceed them."

16 Cf. the preceding note, and the verses of Euripides (*Ba.* 395–7) and Sophocles (*Trach.* 473), cited in my earlier discussion of the paradox (1985: 28–9), where I had alluded to Socrates' difference on this fundamental point from Plato (who believes that man should "so far as possible liken himself to god (ὁμοιοῦσθαι τῷ θεῷ)," *R.* 613B, *Tht.* 176B1) and also from Aristotle, who explicitly *rejects* the traditional precept that "one who is human should think human thoughts (ἀνθρώπινα φρονεῖν ἄνθρωπον ὄντα)," *E.N.* 1177b31–3.

17 The only true wisdom, by comparison with which man's is "worth little or nothing" (*Ap.* 23A).

18 Why then doesn't he *say* so? First, because he feels under no obligation to turn didactic, "distinguish the two senses of ['knowledge'] and state his position clearly in terms of

The other case where the avowal is as explicit as the disavowal involves the third paradox as it appears in the *Gorgias*. Socrates' disavowal of "doing politics" is as conspicuous in this dialogue as it is in the *Apology* at T3 above. In his argument with Polus he freely admits to being a stranger to political affairs:

T5 *G.* 473E: "Polus, I am not a political man (οὐκ εἰμὶ τῶν πολιτικῶν)."

And when Callicles berates him for spending his life "sunk in a corner, whispering with three or four juveniles," not man enough to show his face in "the forums and markets of the city where, as the poet says, 'men prove their mettle'" (485D),[19] Socrates does not demur: he concedes that the life he has chosen for himself had no place for "doing politics."[20] Nevertheless, without retreating an inch from this position, he declares:

T6 *G.* 521D: "I believe that I am one of few Athenians, not to say the only one, to engage in the true political art (ἐπιχειρεῖν[21] τῇ ὡς ἀληθῶς πολιτικῇ τέχνῃ) and of the men of today I am the only one who does politics."[22]

Thus after telling Polus in T5 in Callicles' hearing that he does not engage in politics, Socrates assures Callicles in T6 that he does, and what he means in giving him that assurance should be perfectly understandable in the light of what Socrates had said to him a little earlier:

T7 *G.* 515A: "And now, most excellent man, that you are beginning to engage in the city's affairs (ἄρτι ἄρχῃ πράττειν τὰ τῆς πόλεως πράγματα)

each," as Morrison (1987: 12) says he should, reproaching him for defaulting on a philosopher's obligation to his public. But this is not *Socrates'* way of doing philosophy; he wants his hearers to find their way through the paradox for themselves (just as he wants Alcibiades to find out for himself the meaning of Socrates' love for him). Secondly, because (as I explained in 1985, in comment on *Ap.* 23A–B) he could not have done so without turning epistemologist, shifting out of the role of pure moralist to which he sticks with single-minded fidelity in Plato's representation of him.

19 On Callicles' reference to Euripides' *Antiope* to rub in this charge see Carter, 1986: 173–5.
20 In the *Apology* (31C–32A) he explains why he has been following this policy throughout his life: "it may seem queer to you that while I go round and play the busybody (πολυπραγμονῶ, cf. Burnet's note *ad loc.*, and Carter, 1986: 185), I don't dare to mount the rostrum and offer advice to the Assembly."
21 ἐπιχειρεῖν here should not be weakened to "attempted" (as in Helmbold, 1952, and in Irwin in his Commentary *ad loc.* [1979: 240]): ἐπιχειρεῖν *can* mean "performing," not just "attempting to perform" (LSJ *s.v.*, duly listing the former sense, cites Hippocr. *Ep.* 5.20: ἐπεχειρήθη, "the operation was performed"); and that this is what it does mean here is clear from the immediate sequel: the doctor to whom Socrates compares himself at 521E–522A is not represented as *attempting* to practice those harsh, though salutary, medical procedures, but as practicing them (ταῦτα πάντα ἐποίουν, ὦ παῖδες, ὑγιεινῶς).
22 καὶ πράττειν τὰ πολιτικὰ μόνος τῶν νῦν.

and you invite me to do the same, reproaching me for not doing so, shall we not examine[23] each other and ask: 'Come, has Callicles made any of the citizens a better man? Is there anyone – alien or citizen, slave or freeman – who, previously a bad man, unjust, intemperate, foolish – has become a good and honorable man (καλός τε κἀγαθός) because of Callicles?'"

No one who heard Socrates say this could be left in doubt that by "the true political art" at T6 Socrates could only mean the art whose exercise improves the moral character of one's fellow-townsmen (whoever they may be, even slaves!). So Callicles would know that when Socrates has the effrontery to say that he, who has made staying away from politics the rule in his life,[24] is nonetheless the only man in Athens who "does politics," he is using this phrase *ad hoc* in a wilfully idiosyncratic sense:[25] he is saying that, while he does *not* do politics in the accepted sense of the word, nevertheless he most certainly does in that other sense in which to do "the city's business" would be to improve the moral character of the people who live in it.

Once the first and the third of our three paradoxes have been certified as complex ironies by Socrates himself, it could hardly be doubted that the second too must be a statement of the same kind. Anyone tempted to take at face value Socrates' disavowal of the art of teaching virtue in the *Laches* (T2 above) should notice how he uses the disclaimer to point up the contrast with the sophists' fraudulent claim to possess this art. Consider the form in which he gives the court his assurance that he is no teacher of virtue:

T8 *Ap.* 20B: "I counted Evenus fortunate indeed if he really does possess that art and teaches for such a modest fee.[26] For my own part, at any rate, I would be puffed up with vanity and pride if I had such knowledge. But, fellow Athenians, I just don't have it."

---

23 ἐπισκεψόμεθα, whose sense becomes clearer when he shifts to ἐξετάζῃ at 515B1.
24 Cf. T3 above.
25 As he does also with πολυπραγμονεῖν (n. 20 above). Cf. Carter, 1986: 185: "Socrates is in fact both *apragmōn* and not."
26 οὕτω ἐμμελῶς διδάσκει. The complex irony in ἐμμελῶς should not be missed. The stated fee, 500 drachmae, a whole year's earnings for the poorer members of the jury, would still be cheap enough, the bargain of the century, if Evenus could really deliver what he promises. But since the promise is a fraud his product is outrageously expensive at any price. Contrast Xenophon's handling of the matter. He does no more than report: "He never promised (ὑπέσχετο) to be a teacher of such a thing [sc. virtue]... he never promised (ἐπηγγείλατο) this [sc. to be a teacher of virtue] to anyone" (*Mem.* 1.2.3 and 8). Nehamas, 1986: 276, construes this as evidence that Socrates not only did not *promise* to teach virtue, but *did not teach it*, and did not even *try* to teach it, which Xenophon does not say and certainly does not mean; cf. *Mem.* 4.7.1: "whatever he knew himself it behooves a good and honorable man to know he *taught* to his associates more eagerly than did anyone else (πάντων προθυμότατα ἐδίδασκεν)."

So the ability to make his hearers good citizens and good men (of which Evenus is so confident that he offers to do the job for anyone who will meet his stated fee) Socrates vehemently disclaims: he says that he would have to be afflicted with megalomania, "puffed up with vanity and pride," to make such a claim. But he has no qualms about making this very claim at T6, when he declares himself to be "one of the few Athenians if not the only one" who practices the "true political art" whose hallmark is (T7) making better men of his fellow-townsmen – improving the moral character of the people on whose behalf he practices that art.

I have made the argument turn narrowly on T6 because the avowal there is so fully explicit. But, of course, there is plenty of evidence elsewhere in Plato's earlier dialogues that the disavowal at T8 is ironic. Given Socrates' known criteria for "good," would he have said that "no greater good had yet come to you in this city than this service of mine to the god" (*Ap.* 30A), unless he were convinced that in those elenctic ministrations to his fellow-townsmen which were his "service to the god" he *was* practising the art of teaching virtue? Though he does not himself so describe it – he does not call it "teaching" – his elenctic arguments are most certainly so understood and so described both by his enemies[27] and also, what is more to the point, by those who know him and are eager to be themselves the beneficiaries of his teaching:

T9 *La.* 189B (Laches speaking): "To you, O Socrates, I offer myself for you to *teach* (διδάσκειν; cf. διδάσκεσθαι, διδασκόμενον just before) and refute (ἐλέγχειν) in any way you will."

T10 *La.* 200C (Laches again): "I advise Lysimachus and Melesias here to let go of you [Nicias] and me as educators of these youngsters and not to let go of Socrates, as I was saying earlier on. That is what I would do myself if I had sons of that age."

And Nicias chimes in, endorsing with enthusiasm the same tribute to Socrates as a moral teacher. He assures Lysimachus and Melesias:

T11 *La.* 200C–D: "If Socrates were willing to take charge of the boys, one shouldn't look for anyone else. If he were willing I would entrust Niceratus [his own son] to him with the greatest of pleasure."

27 In the *Apology* (29C) Socrates refers to the prosecutors' warning to the court that if he were acquitted "your sons, practicing what *Socrates teaches* will all be wholly corrupted." In the *Euthyphro* (3B–C) Socrates remarks to his interlocutor that the Athenians "don't worry much if someone is that sort of person [who 'innovates in religious matters,' 3B], but does not teach his own wisdom; but if they think of him as [so doing] and turning others too into that sort of person, they become angry."

1.2 DELPHIC PRECEDENTS

In a favorite mode of the oracular responses which figure so prominently in the folk-history of the Greeks we find statements which are meant to be true in one of their possible readings, false in another. Here are some examples. "Upon crossing the Halys a great power will Croesus destroy" (Hdt. 1.53.3; Arist. *Rhet.* 1407a38): true if understood only in the sense missed by Croesus in his folly – that the power he would then destroy would be his own. So too when the Phocaeans found a city on Corsica ("Cyrnus") at what they take to be the direction of the oracle and then, twenty years later, "learn from a man of Posidonia that the Phythia had prophesied that they should establish worship to Cyrnus the hero, not set up a city in the island Cyrnus" (Hdt. 1.165.1).[28] Here again, correctly interpreted, the Delphic sentence is perfectly true, false only if understood as it originally had been by the Phocaeans. In a third example[29] "the prophesied moment of Heracles' release from toils (μόχθοι) turns out to be the moment of agonized death (Soph. *Trach.* 1164–74) and, in a double twist, of his apotheosis." If he had grasped the meaning of the prophecy, he would have known the truth, that the end of his toils would be *also* the end of his life and *also* his divinization.

But Heracles is not meant to see this. He is given a response whose true meaning he could not have been expected to recognize unless he already possessed the gods' knowledge of the future which they deny to men. So too in Croesus' case: he is virtually certain to miss the ominous truth. Nor were the Phocaeans at all likely to understand the meaning of the oracle and get the right directions from it. In all three cases the god is making fools of those who earnestly seek his help. He allows his mouthpiece to utter sentences which are meant to be true only in a sense their hearers are virtually sure to miss.

Not so in Socrates' complex ironies. Here everything is open; there is no sly concealment. In Xenophon's *Symposium* Socrates' hearers are not left in the least doubt as to the special sense in which "procurer" and "beautiful" are meant to be true of him though sadly false in their ordinary sense. So too in the case of the philosophical ironies put into his mouth in Plato. Here Socrates does not address hearers whom he expects to miss their intended sense for lack of information which would enable them to catch the sense in which both their affirmation and their denial are meant to be true.

28 I owe this example and much else – the stimulus for this whole section of the note – to a perceptive comment (by letter) from Helen Bacon, a fellow-participant in a symposium on Socrates at Santa Cruz, where I had presented the essay on "Socratic Irony."
29 Also given me by Helen Bacon: the quotation is from her letter.

If he has reason to believe that they do not already have the requisite information, Socrates supplies it *ad hoc*. In the *Apology* he tells his fellow-citizens that he is "aware of being wise in nothing great or small" (T1) only after having admitted that what he lacks is "wisdom that is more than human," while "human wisdom" he does have (T4). In the *Gorgias* Callicles is told Socrates does possess the "true political art" (T6), but only after the critical test for the possession of this art had been explained to him (T7). In the *Laches* the dark saying that Socrates knows nothing about the art of teaching virtue is not made immediately clear; but Nicias, who knows Socrates well, does not need to be told that Socrates is indeed a master of the art of teaching virtue; and the others too would find out soon enough if they stayed close to Socrates.

The oracles of the gods are notoriously inscrutable.[30] Apollo's suppliants are left unsure whether the surface meaning of his response is its true meaning. Socrates' interlocutors are not left in the like uncertainty. Given moderate intelligence and good will,[31] no one who hears Socrates say that he has no knowledge, that he cannot teach, and that he "does politics," would have reason to think that what he means in each case is simply the literal sense of what he says.

It is at just this point that Socratic irony has been subtly misunderstood in the account of "Socratic irony" in Fowler's *Modern English Usage*,[32] where it is taken as the archetypal instance of "a form of utterance that postulates a double audience, consisting of one party that hearing shall hear and not understand, and another party that, when more is meant than meets the ear, is aware both of that more and of the outsiders' incomprehension." As should be already clear from what I have said in this note and in chapter 1 above, the italicized part of Fowler's statement is simply false as a description of the mode in which Socrates addresses his own interlocutors in Plato. So too in Xenophon: Theodote is obviously meant to understand that those "girlfriends" are no *girl* friends (Socrates makes sure by giving her their names). His fellow-guests at the banquet are no less obviously meant to see the double sense of "procurer" and "beautiful" as applied to Socrates: none of them is

---

30 δυσμαθῆ (Aeschlyus, *Ag.* 1255). The oracles do not hide the truth (cf. Heraclitus B93: "The lord whose oracle is in Delphi neither states the truth nor conceals it, but gives a sign"); but neither do they supply the clues by which their riddling message can be correctly deciphered.

31 That the latter, no less than the former, is a necessary condition is clear from Thrasymachus' reaction to Socrates' profession of ignorance. If one comes to Socrates to pick a fight one would be strongly predisposed to construe his ambiguous self-referential statements as dishonestly evasive ploys.   32 *S.v.* "irony," 305ff. (2nd edn.).

in the least danger of "hearing and not understanding" when Socrates says he is a procurer and has an enchanting nose.

But we can still get something illuminatingly true from Fowler's definition of irony as "the use of words intended to convey one meaning to the uninitiated part of the audience and another to the initiated, the delight of it lying in the secret intimacy set up between the latter and the speaker." This is indeed acceptable as a description of *Platonic*, rather than Socratic, irony, holding up even in the case of dialogues like the *Euthyphro*, *Ion*, and *Hippias Major*, where there can be no question of a double audience inside the setting of the dialogue (in all three cases there are no bystanders: Socrates is alone with the interlocutor), if we count as the "initiated" part of the audience the one which Plato addresses in those dialogues, i.e. his readers. The ironies with which Socrates plies his interlocutor in each of those dialogues, lost on his interlocutor, are certainly not meant by Plato to be lost on the readers: they are the "initiated" who are meant to grasp the meaning that eludes the interlocutor's comprehension. And when we turn to other dialogues, like the *Protagoras* or the *Gorgias* we can easily find there within the dialogue persons we may include among the "initiated," for they are represented as being privy to Socrates' little ways and would be in a position to enjoy that "intimacy" with the speaker that Fowler has in view: Alcibiades in the *Protagoras*, Chaerephon in the *Gorgias*. So too a sense of belonging to the "initiated" section of the double audience would be no small part of the amusement Socrates' youthful claque derived from watching him stick pins into prestigious Athenian windbags, the spectacle inspiring them to try their hand at the game themselves (*Ap.* 23c).

1.3   ἔρως καλός: ITS HAZARDS FOR THE BOY[33]

Third parties close to him who are concerned for his own good – parents and friends within his peer group – feel he would be well out of such affairs:[34]

Smp. 183c5–d2: "Fathers put tutors in charge of the boy and won't let him talk with lovers: the tutors are ordered to forbid it. And friends of his own age revile him (ὀνειδίζειν)[35] if they see him going in for anything of this sort, and their reviling isn't vetoed by their elders – they don't say the abuse is undeserved."

---

33 Cf. n. 64 in ch. 1.   34 Cf. Dover, 1978: 81–91.   35 And cf. ὄνειδος, *Phdr.* 231e3–4.

Phdr. 255A4–6: "If formerly, bad-mouthed by his friends, who had been saying that dallying with a lover is a disgrace (αἰσχρόν), he had repelled the lover..."

However glamorized in the fashionable νόμος, the boy's role remains *risqué*; he is placed in an ambiguous and vulnerable position. Still in his teens, emotionally immature, his character barely formed, without seasoned judgment of men and the world, suddenly, if he happens to be καλός, he finds himself in possession of an asset in short supply and high demand,[36] for access to which an older man will grovel[37] at his feet, prepared to offer great prizes in return for "favors." Would he not be under the strongest of temptations to barter his new-found treasure in ways which would corrupt him?

Suppose he does form an honorable liaison within which his lover gets all he wants. Will the boy escape the stigma which in Greek sentiment taints the sexual pathic?[38] Dover thinks he will, because he holds (103 *et passim*), within the νόμος orgasmic contact remains solely intercrural. Deeply conscious of my debt to him for what little understanding I have of this difficult matter,[39] I remain strongly sceptical of this particular thesis of his. The vase paintings supply his sole evidential ground for it. But can we exclude the possibility that prevailing convention screened out the depiction of what was in fact the normal mode of gratification? That this is no idle conjecture we know from the literary evidence. As Dover recogizes, his thesis gets no support from this quarter: "In Greek comedy [anal copulation] is assumed (save in *Birds* 706),[40] to be the only mode of [homosexual

---

36 The demographic facts should not be overlooked: bloomers are to potential bloom-chasers as are the καλοί within a five-year age-group to most of the adult males. Of the scarcity of the καλοί within their age group we get some sense in the opening scene of Plato's *Charmides*: droves of youngsters in the palaestra and one καλός, all eyes on him, "gazing on him as on a statue" (154C).

37 "Praying, entreating, supplicating, vowing upon oath, sleeping at the door, willingly enduring slavery worse than any slave's" (*Smp.* 183A).

38 Dover, 1978: 103–4: "By assimilating himself to a woman in the sexual act the submissive male rejects his role as a male citizen" and chooses "to be the victim of what would be, if the victim were unwilling, hubris." For a plethora of references to the dishonor the passive partner in a homosexual relation is supposed to suffer in Athenian opinion see especially Cohen, 1987: 5–15.

39 Cf. my tribute to him in my earlier discussion of Platonic ἔρως (1981: 40).

40 I do not concede that this verse of Aristophanes is an exception. There is no textual evidence for Dover's supposition (1978: 98) that the word used here, διαμηρίζειν, was "almost certainly" the original term for intercrural copulation or that it ever meant anything but the usual type of full sexual intercourse, vaginal with a female, anal with a male, as it uncontroversially does in Zeno Stoicus (H. von Arnim, *SVF* 250 and 251, *ap.* Sextus Empiricus, *P. Hyp.* 3.245, *Adv. Math.* 11.190). The three earliest occurrences of the word are all in the *Birds*. In 1024 it refers unambiguously to vaginal copulation, as Dover recognizes. I submit that it must refer likewise to the usual type in its two other occurrences

consummation]; and when Hellenistic poetry makes a sufficently unambiguous reference to what actually happens on the bodily plane, we encounter only anal, never intercrural, copulation" (1978: 99). But even if the thesis were conceded *in toto*, it would still not obliterate the shadow on the boy's good name. If submitting to anal copulation carries a stigma, the boy would always be under suspicion of it. Who is to say what goes on between him and his lover in the privacy of their *amours*?[41]

1.4 AESCHINES SOCRATICUS, FR. 11[42]

Here is the fragment in translation:

[*a*] (Socrates speaking) "If I thought I could benefit him through some art, I would stand convicted of great folly. But in fact I thought that in the case of Alcibiades this [*sc.* to benefit him] was given me by divine dispensation (θείᾳ μοίρᾳ), which is nothing to be wondered at."

[*b*] "For of those who are sick many are made whole by human art, but others through divine dispensation. Those cured by human art are healed by doctors, while in the case of those cured by divine dispensation it is desire that drives them to improve: they desire to vomit when this would be good for them, and they desire to go hunting when strenuous exercise would be good for them."

[*c*] "As for me, because of the love I had for Alcibiades, my experience was no different than that of the bacchantes. For the bacchantes, when they are god-possessed, draw milk and honey from wells where others cannot even draw water. And so I too, though I had no knowledge through which I could benefit him by teaching it to him, nonetheless I thought that by associating with him I could make him better through my love."

It is hard to resist reading into part [*c*] of this fragment what we know of the "mad lover" of the *Phaedrus* and assuming that what we are being told is that Socrates' love for Alcibiades is a state of ἐνθουσιασμός like that of the bacchantes. Yielding freely to the

in this play: Euripides, declaring, διαμηρίζοιμ' ἂν αὐτὴν ἡδέως (699), could hardly be lusting after ersatz gratification. And if it were agreed that the word is used to signify phallic penetration in 699 and then again in 1024, as also by Zeno in the Stoic fragments cited above, we would have no textually grounded evidence for supposing that in 706 Aristophanes has shifted to a different sense which is never unambiguously attested in a single surviving Greek text and is not required by the immediate context: no reason is discernible in the text why the birds' vaunted power to fulfill men's longings should accord to their favorites something less than the usual thing.

41 As David Cohen points out (1987: 19), "a boy who was seen at the home of a man or seen alone with a man in a deserted place (particularly after dark) was compromised and might become the object of blackmail": see his references in n. 69 on p. 19.

42 Cf. n. 71 in ch. 1.

impulse A. E. Taylor (1924: 15) takes its teaching to be that Socrates' love for the youth is a "fine frenzy," like the state of the bacchantes when they are god-possessed. Barbara Ehlers (1966: 22), realizing how poorly this will fit a Socratic depiction of the master, but still clinging to the notion that Socrates is being credited with ἐνθουσιασμός, invents a special form of this experience, more appropriate for Socrates (of which there is not the least sign in the text): "because of his love for Alcibiades Socrates' elenctic powers rise to highest, most compelling, clarity."[43] I submit that both Taylor and Ehlers are indulging liberally in *hineinlesen*. If we read the text more strictly, this is all we can get from it: At [a] it is said that the longed-for result (moral improvement of Alcibiades) will *not* be achieved by means of art but "by divine dispensation" (the stress falling on the negation: it would be "great folly" to think otherwise); at [b], that in the treatment of the sick a wonderful result (the patient gets well) may be reached *not* by art but "by divine dispensation" – just by letting the patient do pretty much what he feels like doing; at [c] that Socrates will bring about for Alcibiades the longed-for result *not* through art, but through love, as in the case of the bacchantes who, when possessed, get *their* wonderful result without art. There is nothing in [c] to support Taylor or Ehlers in taking the point of the comparison with the bacchantes to be that in his love for Alcibiades he too is, like them, god-possessed.

2.1   THE COMPOSITION OF *REPUBLIC* I

By the criteria specified in the Ten Theses near the start of chapter 2 ("The Ten Theses"), the first book of the *Republic* clearly belongs to Group I, while books II–X as clearly belong to Group II.

Thesis I. In book I Socrates investigates only propositions in the moral domain, announcing at 344E that his goal is "to determine the conduct of our life – how each of us should conduct himself to live the most advantageous life" and then again, at 352D, that what all the argument is about is "what is the way we ought to live."[44]

Thesis II. In book I there is not the slightest allusion to the theory of transcendent Forms of books V–VII and X, nor yet to the detachable soul of book X.

Thesis III. In book I Socrates' disavowal of knowledge is represented as his "habitual" stance, well-known to people far from

---

43 "Weil er Alkibiades liebt, zur höchsten zwingenden Klarheit seiner elenktischen Fähigkeit steigert."
44 Socrates says the same thing, in the same words, in the *Gorgias* (500c).

the Socratic circle, like Thrasymachus (336B–337E).[45] Nothing of this in books II–X.

Thesis IV. In book I Socrates makes no allusion to the tripartite psyche to which Socrates moves in books II–IV. The first statement of the tripartite model is in book IV.

Thesis V. In book I Socrates gives no evidence of expertise in mathematics or of having the slightest interest in any of the mathematical sciences. Contrast the insistence on extensive knowledge of mathematics as philosophical propaedeutic in book VII.[46]

Thesis VII. The questions "What is a state?" "What is a perfectly good state?" "What is the institutional structure of its society?" await books II–V. There is no sign of them in book I, where the thesis that the ruler *qua* ruler rules not in his own interest, but in that of the ruled (342E), and that "if a city of good men were to exist" its rulers would rule reluctantly (347B–D), though argued for, are not pursued to construct, or even adumbrate, a theory of the ideal state (books IV–VII) and produce a ranking order of existing constitutions (book VIII).

Thesis IX. When the definition of the principal virtues of the perfectly good soul and good state is undertaken in book IV, piety is conspicuously absent from their roster. (Contrast, for example, *Pr.* 329cff., *G.* 507B–C.)

Thesis X. In book I Socrates' investigative procedure is clearly elenctic: he repeatedly insists on the observance of the "say what you believe" rule (346A, 349A, 350E). There is no allusion to this rule after book I. It is implicitly rejected from the start of book II, where Glaucon and Adeimantus present, without endorsing, an amplified statement of the purely instrumentalist conception of justice, and challenge Socrates to rebut it. Moreover in book I we get vigorous adversative argument: Thrasymachus is as tough an opponent and gives Socrates as stiff opposition as he ever gets in any of the earlier dialogues. In book II and continuously thereafter to the end of the *Republic* Socrates is given interlocutors who are "yes"-men, putting questions to him, soliciting his instruction, but undertaking no sustained defense of any thesis of their own. Adversative argument, strongly in evidence in book I, disappears thereafter.

This being the case, *R.* I will count as a sterling example of an Elenctic Dialogue, regardless of the time at which it was written. Though Leonard Brandwood[47] treats it for stylometric purposes as

45 Quoted in part as T1 in ch. 1.   46 Cf. T2, T3, T4 in ch. 4.
47 Cf. nn. 2 and 8 in ch. 2.

an integral part of the *Republic*, and thereby keeps the whole of the *Republic* as a work of Plato's middle period following {*Cra.*, *Phd.*, *Smp*}, there are, as he recognizes,[48] stylometric considerations to the contrary. On the strength of these, leading stylometrists Constantin Ritter[49] and von Arnim[50] had concluded that it should be treated as a separate dialogue, written in Plato's earliest period, and then used, at a later time, as the introductory book of the *Republic*.[51] This opinion has been followed by several scholars;[52] but it is by no means generally accepted. Several recent scholars have disregarded it, though without offering extended argument for their view and ignoring the stylistic arguments in its favor.[53]

For the purposes of my own investigation the question is of secondary importance, since the content of the dialogue leaves no doubt that it displays conspicuously the characteristics of Plato's earlier dialogues. But the hypothesis of its early composition may be favored on the strength of the preponderance of the stylistic evidence and also by this further consideration. The contrary hypothesis would put Plato in the position of beginning the greatest and longest of his dialogues by composing philosophical pastiche: in the arguments against Thrasymachus he would be *pretending* to discover moral truth by a method of investigation in which he had already lost faith, since the discarding of the elenchus as a method of philosophical investigation in the *Lysis*, the *Euthydemus*, and *Meno* 81Aff.[54] could only have been due to the conviction that it is useless for that purpose – a conviction which appears to surface in the closing lines of book 1 (353C1–3): "When I don't know what justice is, I shall hardly know *whether or not it is a virtue.*" Since the answer to the "What is it?" question has not yet been found, Socrates is here declaring that he does not know whether or not justice is a virtue. How so, when he had previously established by elenctic argument at 351A that it *is* "wisdom and virtue"? The simplest explanation of the discrepancy would be that when Plato comes to join book 1 to the new work he is about to start, he thinks it proper to provide even

48 1958: 403.
49 See 1910b: tables on pp. 236–7, listing ways in which *R*. 1 exhibits stylistic differences from those of the work considered as a whole.
50 1914: ch. 3 ("Thrasymachos über die Gerechtigkeit").   51 Cf. ch. 1, p. 33.
52 Friedländer even goes so far as to regard it as "practically certain" (1964: 5off. and the notes at 305ff. which give references to other scholars of the same persuasion).
53 Irwin, 1977a: 323ff., and Annas, 1981: 17ff. It is not clear that they have taken seriously enough the linguistic arguments adduced by Ritter (1888: 35ff.) and the further arguments by von Arnim (1914: 71ff.). Some of these are not strong. But their cumulative force is considerable.
54 Argument for this claim in Vlastos, 1983a: 57–8, and in ch. 4.

within this Book a confession that the results reached in it by the elenctic method are insecure – a confession which would be perfectly understandable if tacked on to a work produced at an earlier time when Socrates' faith in the efficacy of that method was still unshaken.

2.2　SOCRATIC PERSONALIA IN THE PLATONIC CORPUS[55]

Here are four things we would not have learned from Plato if only the Elenctic and Transitional Dialogues had survived:

(1)　His facial features are decidedly ugly by Greek standards of male beauty (*Tht.* 143E, 209C): flat-nosed (σιμός), his eyes protruding (ἐξώφθαλμος).

(2)　His social origins are lowly. His mother Phaenarete had been a midwife (*Tht.* 149A).

(3)　He has a habit of stopping suddenly wherever he is, standing stockstill wrapped in thought (*Smp.* 175B, 220C–D).

(4)　He sacrifices to Asclepius (*Phd.* 118A), prays to Pan (*Phdr.* 279B–C). Shortly before his death he puts some of Aesop's fables into verse with a prelude in Apollo's honour (*Phd.* 60D).

Why does none of this information come into the earlier dialogues? In the case of points (1), (2) and (3) the answer appears to be: because none of it strikes Plato as directly relevant to the philosophizing he shows Socrates pursuing in one or more of these works and he sees no point in dragging it in for the sake of its biographical interest. In the case of point (4) we can see a positive reason why he should omit it in the *Apology*. In glaring contrast to the defense Xenophon puts into Socrates' mouth,[56] citing the (alleged) conspicuous frequency of his sacrificing as the principal rebuttal of the accusation that he does not believe in the city's gods, in the Platonic *Apology* there is not a single reference to Socrates' sacrificing or praying to any of the gods of common belief; the sole evidence of Socratic piety Plato cites in the *Apology* is his philosophizing on the

55　Cf. ch. 2, p. 33.
56　*Mem.* 1.1.11: "That he did not believe in the city's gods, what proof could they have had of that? For he could be seen sacrificing often at home and on the city's public altars." *Apology of Socrates* 11: "What I marvel at most of all in Meletus is on what evidence he alleges that I do not believe in the gods in which the city believes. For all bystanders could see me at the common festivals sacrificing on the public altars, and so could Meletus himself if he wished."

streets of Athens, called "service"[57] to a god whom Socrates leaves anonymous, referring to him as "the god"[58] or "the god at Delphi,"[59] never by the proper name "Apollo" or by any of Apollo's cult-names (Phoebus, Pythius, etc.).

Conversely here are four personalia which do come into Group I dialogues because they bear directly on the particular aspect of Socrates' philosophizing which is expounded in their context:

(1)   His response to an oracle proves a turning-point in his life (*Ap.* 21C–23B).[60] Undertaking to refute the oracle that no one is wiser than himself, he keeps cross-examining people reputed for their wisdom, and spends many of his waking hours in the market-place, "examining himself and others" (*Ap.* 28E), thereby arousing much hostility (23A), but persisting nonetheless, for he regards this activity as his "service to the god" (23C, 38E).

(2)   He keeps out of politics (*Ap.* 31C–32A), believing that his own efforts to improve the souls of fellow-townsmen is "the true political art" (*G.* 521D).[61]

(3)   Though extremely disparaging of his wisdom, declaring he has none at all (*Ap.* 21D), he yet speaks confidently of his virtue, satisfied that he "has never wronged man or god in word or deed" (*G.* 522D).

(4)   He has harsh words for public conduct in Athens, lashing out at current lawlessness (*Ap.* 31D–32A), scorning its finest statesmen as flatterers (*G.* 517Aff.). But he says that he is deeply attached to Athens, preferring the city with its laws to any city in the world, Greek or barbarian (*Cr.* 52C–E).

It is a sobering thought that if Plato had portrayed his teacher only in Group II dialogues none of this information would have been conveyed. We would not have known that this man who moved so

---

57 λατρεία, ὑπηρεσία (23E, 38E).
58 He has been "in dire poverty" because of "his service to the god" (*Ap.* 23C); "the god" had commanded him to "live philosophizing"; he was "the god's gift to the city" (30E).
59 "I shall present as a witness the god at Delphi" (20E).
60 Just when did this event occur? We can be fairly confident of 423 as its *terminus post quem*: this is the date of the truce in the Archidamian war, making possible the resumption of travel between Athens and Delphi so that Chaerephon's trip to Delphi would have become possible; it was also the date of the production of the *Clouds*, where Socrates is still represented as a secretive figure teaching behind well-guarded gates in the "Thinkery." Its *terminus ante quem* might be dated, more tentatively, at 418, death of Laches, protagonist of the dialogue in which two boys, scions of old-fashioned aristocratic families with no intellectual interests or accomplishments, are said by the father of one of them to have been talking enthusiastically about Socrates among themselves, and Socrates is said to be "always spending his day" in gymnasia in the company of the young (*La.* 180C–E, quoted more fully in ch. 4, nn. 17 and 18).
61 Quoted more fully as T6 in additional note 1.1.

easily in the most elegant aristocratic circles had lived for a good third of his life[62] as an ἀγοραῖος, habitué of the market-place, missionary to the unwashed; nor yet that, though bitterly critical of Athens' leaders and indignant at the lawlessness of her public life, he thought of himself as her loving, obediently loyal, son. Since so much of this information comes from the *Apology* and from none of our other ancient sources,[63] it is well to remind ourselves that here (and only here in the whole of his corpus) Plato speaks as someone who, being present at the trial (34A, 38B), had direct access to the facts he relates; there is even less reason for doubting the substantial veracity of the speech Plato puts into Socrates' mouth[64] than that of the speeches Thucydides gives his characters in which, he says, he "put into the mouth of each of the speakers the sentiments proper to the occasion, expressed as I thought the speaker would be likely to express them,"[65] while endeavouring to come as close as possible to the general sense of what was said" (1.22): in Plato's case we are assured, as we are not in Thucydides,[66] that he writes as an eyewitness, and one whose personal ties to the speaker would have riveted his attention on every word of what was said.

---

62 Cf. p. 252, n. 60 above.

63 Xenophon's *Apology of Socrates* may be usefully compared: it washes out point (3), making Socrates present himself as a man of all-sufficing moral knowledge, whose wisdom is positively attested by the Delphic oracle (16), while in its Platonic counterpart the oracle says only that no one is wiser than Socrates and that Socrates' own, merely "human," wisdom is "worth little or nothing" in the eyes of the god (23A). As to point (1), Xenophon is wholly uninformative about the effect which the oracle had on Socrates' personal life, while Plato presents it as the event which had transformed Socrates into a street philosopher with a divine mandate to "philosophize, examining himself and others" (*Ap.* 28E; cf. 38A). Xenophon is almost equally uninformative on point (4): in none of his Socratic writings is there a parallel for the bitter denunciation of Athenian public life implied in the statement Plato puts into Socrates' mouth that "no man could survive if he undertakes, in opposition to the [Athenian] or any other multitude, to prevent many unjust and lawless acts in the city" (31E).

64 For a fuller argument for the "historicity" of Socrates' speech in the *Apology* see Brickhouse & Smith, 1989: 2–10. They would have strengthened it by citing as a parallel the speeches in Thucydides.

65 But *not* "in the language" in which the speaker would have been likely to express himself, as C. F. Smith's translation of Thucydides misleadingly renders this part of the text. Thucydides' speakers are allowed the writer's elegant antithetical style. No one would suggest that Cleon spoke Thucydidese or that Thucydides suggests he did. Gomme (1945: 144) makes the useful observation that Thucydides invariably introduces the speeches by saying that the speaker(s) said τοιάδε ("this sort of thing"), not τάδε ("these things"), which he uses only "when quoting verbally from a document."

66 Who could have heard only a few of the speeches he writes into his *History*; for several of them, he says, he had to rely "on those who from various sources brought me reports."

2.3   οὐσία[67]

Since εἶναι has both (1) an existential use, as in ἔστι (or, more commonly, ἔστι τι) δικαιοσύνη, "justice exists") and (2) a copulative one, as in σοφία ἐστι δικαιοσύνη "justice is wisdom," its participial noun οὐσία may nominalize the verb in either of the two uses. We may then translate the noun, according to context, "existence" in use (1), "essence" in the most important of its copulative uses, when the predicate expresses the essential or true, genuine, nature of the subject. "Essence" is clearly right in *Eu.* 11A, where it stands in polar contrast to πάθος and then again in *Cra.* 385E (= T9 in chapter 2), where it parallels φύσις. "Existence" (or "entity") would be appropriate in *Pr.* 349B, ἴδιος οὐσία καὶ πρᾶγμα, where οὐσία alternates with πρᾶγμα and is joined with it in hendiadys (I am correcting the uncritical translation "essence" in this passage in Vlastos, 1981: 225).

We must also allow for (3) a further use which may straddle the difference between (1) and (2) as "reality" may in English (the *O.E.D.* *s.v.* cites both "actually existent" and "genuine" [i.e. true to the essence] as possible uses of it). So for example at *Phd.* 78D1–2 [cited under T20 in ch. 2]: "That reality itself of whose essence we give account (αὐτὴ ἡ οὐσία ἧς λόγον δίδομεν τοῦ εἶναι) in asking and answering our questions." These questions which Socrates$_M$ and his friends are "asking and answering" here (and again at 75D) are clearly "What is the *F*?" questions, inquiring after the *essence* of the *F*; so the λόγος which is given in answer is a definiens D, stating that D is the εἶναι of the *F* (its τὸ τί ἦν εἶναι, as Aristotle would say); and what the *F* names is an existent. So the existential sense of the parent verb is also present when the *F* is described as οὐσία ἧς λόγον δίδομεν τοῦ εἶναι: the *F* is being regarded as *an essence which is an existent*. So "reality" is right for οὐσία at 78D and by the same token at 76D, ἃ θρυλοῦμεν ἀεί, καλόν τέ τι καὶ ἀγαθὸν καὶ πᾶσα ἡ τοιαύτη οὐσία, and also at 76E, τὴν οὐσίαν ἣν σὺ λέγεις; and in the phrase αὐτὸ ὃ ἔστι which "seals" the right answer to "What is the *F*?" (75D2) both essence and existence is conveyed. (There is no separate word for "existence" in Plato's Greek.)

Use (3) of ἐστί and its cognates, which straddles the essence/ existence contrast, enables us to understand how Plato invokes it in his "degrees [or grades] of reality" doctrine (see Vlastos, 1981: 49ff. and 65ff.), allowing for the intensive use of ὄντως in κλίνης ὄντως

---

67 Cf. n. 56 to ch. 2.

οὔσης (*R.* 597D) to mean exactly the same as π-αντελῶς ὄν (*R.* 577A), τελέως ὄν (*R.* 597A), εἰλικρινῶς ὄν (*R.* 477A7), making it possible for Plato to write without fatuous redundancy of the superlative reality of the forms as οὐσία ὄντως οὖσα, "really [= perfectly, completely, purely] real reality" (*Phdr.* 247C7). This fundamental feature of S_M's Forms allows the translation "are as real as anything could possibly be" for εἶναι ὡς οἷόν τε μάλιστα (cited at T13 in ch. 2). Alternative translations of this phrase invoke the dubious notion of "degrees of existence," as in Robin, 1956, "auquel le plus haut degré d'existence appartient," Bluck, 1955, "have full and complete existence," or resort to unclear English, as in Gallop, 1975, "*are* in the fullest possible sense," or shift to the formal mode, as in Hackforth, 1955, "most assuredly do exist" (which makes perfect sense but does not translate Plato's sentence which is firmly in the material mode: no counterpart for "assuredly" in it).

2.4   THE INTERDICT ON RELIANCE ON SENSORY DATA IN MATHEMATICS[68]

It might be thought that in this domain the interdict would be superfluous, for it was well understood by mathematicians that the sensible properties of geometrical figures have no evidential force, and Plato is well aware of this: he recognizes that when "they use visible figures and reason about them, they are not thinking about *them*, but about the things of which these are images: they are reasoning about the square itself and the diagonal itself, not the ones they draw" (*R.* VI, 510D). Even so, Plato's warning against the deceitfulness of sensory data would not be pointless. It would protect the mathematicians from Protagorean objections (like the denial that the tangent touches the circle at just one point)[69] which would have made an end of their science: without dimensionless points Greek geometry would collapse. Working mathematicians would no doubt laugh off Protagoras. But Plato gives them reasons for what would otherwise be no more than occupational dogmatism on their part. What is more, he would put them on their guard against *unconscious* reliance on the sensible properties of their figures, as e.g. when they assume that intersecting lines must have a point in common, misled by the fact that this is how lines look when they are drawn on papyrus or on sand. Thus a geometrician who took Plato's warning to heart might have been alerted to the fact that in the

68 Cf. ch. 2, p. 68.   69 Aristotle, *Metaph.* 998a3–4.

absence of a continuity-postulate the Euclidean axiom-set and its predecessors were incomplete.[70]

2.5 "SEPARATION"[71] IN PLATO[72]

I shall argue that in the Platonic corpus, and also in Aristotle's testimony about Plato, the same metaphysical claim may be expressed by either [P] or [Q]:[73]

[P] The Forms exist "themselves by themselves."
[Q] The Forms exist "separately."

(1) *Plato*

In the debate in the *Parmenides* Socrates puts his own thesis on the mat through the following question:

T1 *Prm.* 128E9–129A1: "Don't you believe that there exists itself by itself a certain Form of Similarity (εἶναι αὐτὸ καθ' αὐτὸ εἶδός τι ὁμοιότητος)?"

Plainly, this is [P]. When Parmenides enters the debate he begins by asking:

T2 *Prm.* 130B2–5: [a] "Have you yourself, as you say, distinguished (διήρησαι) in this way, on one hand, separately (χωρίς) certain Forms themselves,[74] on the other, separately (χωρίς) in turn, the things which participate in them? [b] And do you think that Similarity itself exists (τι...εἶναι) separately (χωρίς) from the similarity we have ourselves, and that so too do Unity and Plurality and all those things of which you heard just now from Zeno?"

A word about the translation at this point. Cornford renders T2[a], "Have you yourself drawn this distinction you speak of and

---

70 Cf. Heath, 1926: I 234ff. ("The Principle of Continuity").
71 Cf. n. 127 to ch. 2.
72 This is a slightly corrected version of a short paper which appeared, under the same title, in *Oxford Studies in Ancient Philosophy* (Vlastos, 1987a: 187–96).
73 Cf. Prior's (1985: 82) formulation of the theory Plato's critic attacks in the *Parmenides*: "that there are Forms [which] exist 'themselves in themselves' (i.e. separately from phenomena)." Agreeing with Prior, in additional note 2.5 I offer argument for the equivalence in the description of (Forms) as "existing by themselves" and as "existing separately" which he takes for granted.
74 At this point Parmenides is doing no more than restate, in abbreviated form, what Socrates had stated in the latter part of his opening discourse: "if one distinguishes separately the Forms themselves by themselves" (διαιρῆται χωρὶς αὐτὰ καθ' αὐτὰ τὰ εἴδη, 129D7–8). Parmenides now says: οὕτω διήρησαι, ὡς λέγεις, χωρὶς μὲν εἴδη αὐτά....

separated apart" etc. There is no Greek for "separated" in the text he is translating: Parmenides has not said διήρησαι καὶ ἐχώρισες. The verb χωρίζειν does not occur here nor anywhere else in the debate, nor is it ever applied to the Forms by Plato anywhere in his corpus. The difference between χωρίζειν and the verb Plato uses here, διαιρεῖν, is substantial. From the earliest occurrence of διαιρεῖν in Greek philosophical prose a purely logical use of the verb is normal. Heraclitus had described himself as διαιρέων πάντα κατὰ φύσιν, "distinguishing everything in accordance with its nature" (B 1). Could one imagine this apostle of cosmic unity writing the same sentence with χωρίζων substituted for διαιρέων? The use of διαιρεῖν for making distinctions without the least implication, or so much as insinuation, that the things distinguished are severed in nature is by no means confined to the philosophers. There are many examples of it in Herodotus.[75] And this is how Plato uses the word from his earliest[76] to his latest[77] works; it is the mainstay of his "method of division."[78] Not so χωρίζειν, whose primary sense is "to separate in space," "divide locally."[79] Though, as is well known, χωρίζειν can also be used at times in a purely logical sense, it generally stands for something far stronger, else Plato would not have used it to express the harshest of the dualisms in the credo of his middle period – that view of the soul, discussed above in chapter 2 (section II), which makes it an immigrant from another world, attached precariously to a piece of matter in this one, from which death shall "separate" it (χωρίσῃ, *R.* 609D7) to "exist separately" (χωρὶς εἶναι, *Phd.* 64C6–8; 67A1) until its next incarnation. Nor would Aristotle have picked χωρίζειν, χωριστόν to spearhead his attack on what he takes to be Plato's cardinal metaphysical indiscretion: the assignment of "separate," independent existence to instantiable Forms, which, in Aristotle's own considered view, can only exist "in" their instances.

Thus Cornford's translation would seriously mislead English readers on a point of vital importance in the debate: they would be left unaware of the fact that in part [a] of T2 Forms are being *distinguished* from their participants, while nothing is said at just this point to *separate* them from the latter. For this we have to go to part [b] of the text. And here the translation may spring another trap for

---

75 LSJ cites Hdt. 7.16.γ′ and 103 for διαιρέω = "to define expressly." For more examples see Powell, *Lexicon to Herodotus, s.v.*, sense 3.
76 *Pr.* 358A, "From Prodicus' verbal distinctions (διαίρεσιν τῶν ὀνομάτων) I abstain"; *Ch.* 163D4, "I have heard [of?] Prodicus making innumerable verbal distinctions (περὶ ὀνομάτων διαιροῦντος)."   77 *Lg.* 895E8, λόγῳ δίχα διαιρούμενον ἀριθμόν.
78 *Phdr.* 273E, κατ' εἴδη διαιρεῖσθαι τὰ ὄντα; *Sph.* 253D, κατὰ γένη διαιρεῖσθαι.
79 Its strong ties to χώρα, χῶρος are evident in derivatives like χωρίτης, χωρικός for "country person," "rustic."

the unwary. This is how T2[b] comes through in Allen's translation (1980b): "And do you think that likeness itself is something separate from the likeness that we have..." etc. The trouble here is of another sort. Strictly speaking there is no inaccuracy in rendering εἶναί τι χωρίς as "is something separate"; what is misrepresented is not the sense of the Greek words but the grammatical form of one of them; and this happens to be one of those cases where it is mandatory to preserve the grammatical form of Plato's Greek. For the precise Greek counterpart of "is separate" would be χωριστόν ἐστι; and Allen's translation would represent Plato as anticipating in the *Parmenides* the very phrase that was to figure so prominently in Aristotle's attack on him. In rejecting that translation of T2[b] (and parallel renderings of T4 and T5) we need not preclude the possibility that Plato might have wished to say that his Forms are χωριστά. In part (2) of this additional note I shall be suggesting that this should be regarded as not only possible, but probable. But this will call for a separate argument which would be grievously at fault if it presumed that χωριστόν is the word Plato had put into the mouth of his Parmenides in our present passage. Since it is clear that he does not, it behooves us to stick to the least tendentious rendering of εἶναί τι χωρίς, as "exists [or, still more literally, "is something"] separately."

I may now resume comment on T2[b]. When it is faithfully rendered it leaves no doubt that it is exactly [Q] to which Socrates is being asked to agree. When he does so he is presented with more examples of things he might believe exist "themselves by themselves":

T3 *Prm.* 130B7–9: "And of this sort of thing too – does a Form of Justice [exist][80] itself by itself and of Beauty and Goodness and of all things such as these in turn?"

Here we are back to [P]. But Parmenides' next question returns to [Q]:

T4 *Prm.* 130C1–2: "And a Form of man [exists] separately from us and our likes – a certain Form itself of Man or of Fire[81] or of Water?"

So does the one after that:

T5 *Prm.* 130C5–D2: "And what about these, Socrates, which might be thought ridiculous, like hair or mud or dirt or anything else that is

---

80 εἶναι is to be understood before αὐτὸ καθ' αὑτὸ at 130B8 (as a carry-over from 130B4) and then again before χωρὶς ἡμῶν at 130C1. It is allowed a place in the text at 130D1, τούτων ἑκάστου εἶναι χωρίς.   81 For Form of Fire see *Ti.* 51B8.

altogether worthless and trivial? Are you perplexed whether one should say that a Form of each of these exists separately, being something other than the things we handle?"

So we have [P] in T1, then again in T3, and then repeatedly thereafter in the debate (133A, 133C, 135A–B), from which Parmenides feels free to shift at pleasure, with Socrates' concurrence, to [Q] at T2[b], T4, T5. Can there be any reasonable doubt that [P] and [Q] are being used interchangeably to enunciate the same metaphysical claim which is staked out by Socrates at the start of the debate and is made the principal butt of Parmenides' critique of the theory of Forms?

Two possible grounds of doubt on this point might be suggested.

First, it might be supposed that the relation of Forms to their participants which is (implicitly) expressed in [Q] is symmetrical: If X exists separately [from Y], must not, conversely, Y exist separately [from X]? If this were true then, certainly, [Q] could not be logically equivalent to [P], which Plato uses to express the central affirmation of his theory of Forms throughout dialogues of his middle period[82] and also in the *Timaeus*:[83] for there can be no doubt that [P] is *not* meant to refer to a symmetrical relation between Forms and their participants. Thus in the central books of the *Republic* the Form is to its participants as is a model to its copies and as a physical object is to its shadows. And this relation is strongly antisymmetric: the copies "imitate" the model, but not the model the copy; the object causes its shadows, but the converse is not true. But is there good reason for the supposition that the relation to which [Q] (implicitly) refers *is* meant to be symmetrical? What evidence could be adduced on its behalf? Consider:

---

82 That Forms "exist themselves by themselves" is the backbone of the theory of Forms when presented at *Phd.* 100B5–6 (= T11 in ch. 2) as the "hypothesis" on which the final proof of the immortality of the soul will be hung. That the Form "exists itself by itself" had been previously built into the description of its immutability at 78D5–6 ("existing always itself by itself": T20 in ch. 2). Still earlier in the *Phaedo* we had been told that each Form is to be investigated ("tracked") "itself by itself" – 66A2 (= T18 *sub fin.* in ch. 2), and then again at 83B1–2 ("the soul must put its trust only in the reality which it comes, itself by itself, to understand, itself by itself"). In the description of the Form of beauty perceived in moments of climactic vision in the *Symposium* (T22 in ch. 2), the phrase is expanded to "itself by itself with itself." It is contracted to "by itself" at *Cra.* 386E3–4 and *R.* 476A11, having first entered an epistemological context in that form in Plato's corpus in the closing sentence of the *Meno*.

83 51C1 and D4–5, a passage of capital importance, where Plato raises afresh the question, "Are there really such things as Forms?" and answers it from scratch. He puts the "itself by itself" locution into the formulation of the question and also into that of the resoundingly affirmative answer.

T6 *Phd.* 64c5–8: "Isn't death just this: on one hand, that the body, rid of the soul, has come to exist separately, itself by itself; and, on the other, that the soul, rid of the body, exists separately from the body, itself by itself?" (Cf. also 67A1.)

Here it is clear that the relation in "X exists separately from Y" is *not* antisymmetric: it is reversible when X = the soul, Y = the body: the body *can* exist, albeit only for a short time, separately from the soul; the soul could exist for ever separately from a body.

But what does that prove for the point at issue? Does it show that the relation in "X exists separately from Y" is reversible for all values of X and Y? Clearly not: it shows only that it is reversible for some values of the variables; it does not show that it is reversible when X = Form, Y = its participants. That Plato thinks it irreversible in the latter case should be clear from the very analogies in the middle books of the *Republic* I cited above to show that the relation of Forms to their participants is antisymmetric. Taking "X exists separately from Y" to express the modal claim that X may exist when Y does not,[84] it should be obvious that while, say, trees may "exist separately" from their shadows (they are there day and night, hence regardless of whether or not they are casting shadows), their shadows cannot exist separately from them (no tree, no shadows); again, in Plato's creation story the eternal model had been in existence separately from created copies of it, while they could not have been in existence separately from it. So the objection fails: there is no reason to believe that Plato would think the relation in "X exists separately from Y" reversible for all values of X and Y, hence no reason to see here cause for doubt that [Q] at T2[b], T4, and T5 represents pukka Platonic doctrine. Only if one ignored the difference between [Q] and what is asserted in T2[a] – between asserting that Forms *exist separately* from their participants at T2[b], T4, T5, on one hand, and, on the other, *distinguishing separately* Forms and participants from each other at T2[a][85] – would one be seriously tempted to think[86] that the position to which Socrates agrees in

84 Following Allen (1980b) and Fine (1984): cf. below, additional note 2.7 "The meaning of χωρισμός."
85 In the latter the relation is clearly symmetrical: if I distinguish X from Y, I am distinguishing *ipso dicto* Y from X. It is not symmetrical *ipso dicto* in the former, and when one looks into the matter one will find ample reason to believe that it is not symmetrical at all.
86 So Allen: misled by his mistranslation of T2[a], he thinks that "Parmenides' first question assumes that, if Ideas are separate, separation is a symmetrical relation" (1980b: 100). Fine too claims (1984: 58) that "*choris* is ... used to indicate a symmetrical relation," citing *Prm.* 130B2–4 (= T2[a]) in support of the claim, having failed to notice that while distinguishing

T2[b], T4, T5 is out of whack with the ontology upheld by Plato throughout his middle period and even in the *Timaeus*.

The other objection would be that the *Parmenides* is aporetic.[87] Should this undoubted fact leave us in doubt that Socrates' concurrence with the equivalence of [P] to [Q] may be taken as firm, well-considered Platonic doctrine, rather than as a hasty, imprudent concession[88] wrested by a wily opponent from the immature, brash, unwary debater Plato makes Socrates for the nonce in this dialogue? So we might have cause to think, if that equivalence were something out of the blue, without strong antecedents in preceding dialogues of Plato's middle period. But it is nothing of the kind. If we look for antecedents we can find them as far back as the *Phaedo*, where the "itself by itself" existence of the Form is asserted repeatedly.[89] In this dialogue we are given the chance to understand what this phrase is supposed to mean, because here we see it used in the parallel, and perfectly clear, case of the "separate" soul in T6 above.

In this text the soul's relation to the body which Plato has in view is expressed by saying that at death it comes "to exist separately from the body," and then "[to exist] itself by itself" is brought in as a kind of tail to "exists separately," which could have easily sufficed without it to convey the message that death terminates the life-long mutual dependence of soul and body during the period of a soul's incarnation. By bringing in "itself by itself" in the way he does here (as an appositional appendage to "exists separately"), Plato gives his readers a perfect clue to what he means by "exists itself by itself" – which is far from self-explanatory and would have puzzled them if Plato had sprung it on them without supplying some such context as this. Here they should be able to see that to say of either body or soul that it "exists itself by itself" is the substantive claim that after death each exists "separately from" (independently of) the other for a spell (a brief one for the body, an unspecifiably long one for the soul). And the context resolves completely the semantic incompleteness in

Forms from their participants is indeed symmetrical, the separate existence of Forms and participants is not (cf. the preceding note).

87 This (true) claim should be kept entirely distinct from the (false) one that the *Prm.* records *rejection* of the ontology expounded in the dialogues of Plato's middle period. As I argued years ago (1954: 319–49), the objections Plato puts into the mouth of Parmenides are "a record of honest perplexity": Plato is now recognizing the gravity of difficulties he had taken lightly heretofore (if he had faced them at all). He is taking a second, very hard, look at the ontology of his middle period, which is not to say that he is ditching it: cf. n. 11 to ch. 3.

88 Allen 1980b: 98ff.) holds that it is a "wrong admission"; Fine (1984: 58–9) allows that it might be. They seem unmindful of the question which should haunt anyone who allows this possibility: Why should Plato make his great Parmenides direct his critique against a straw man?   89 Cf. n. 12 above.

"separately," which would otherwise have left them wondering: separately from *what*? What is said in the *Phaedo* shows that:

for X = body, "X exists *itself by itself*" = "X exists *separately from soul*";

for X = soul, "X exists *itself by itself*" = "X exists *separately from body*."

By the same token when it is Form which is said to exist *itself by itself* in the enunciation of the great "hypothesis" at *Phd.* 100B5–7 we may infer that what must be meant is something Plato might have expressed alternatively (as he does in the case of the soul's "itself-by-itself" existence) by saying that it exists *separately*; and if it were so expressed the answer to the question, "separately from *what*?" could only be, "from something which is to Form as is body to an incarnate soul"; and what could that be but the Form's embodiment in the world of time – its participants? So there is evidence as far back as the *Phaedo* that what Plato understands by the Form's "itself-by-itself existence" is what he could otherwise have expressed (and does express in the *Parmenides*) by "separate existence." Hence

for X = Form, "X exists *itself by itself*" = "X exists *separately from participants*."

(2) *Aristotle on "separation" in Plato*

In explicit or implicit reference to the Platonic Form Aristotle repeatedly uses appositional syntax to join "exists itself by itself" to "is separate" in the same way as we saw Plato in T6 above join appositionally "exists itself by itself" to "exists separately" in speaking of body and soul.

T7 *Nic. Eth.* 1096b31–4:   And similarly with regard to the Idea [of the Good in Plato], it is clear that if there did exist some Good which is separate (χωριστόν) itself by itself (αὐτὸ καθ' αὐτὸ), it would not be what human beings could do and possess.

T8 *Metaph.* 1060b11–13:   "This is the question before us: to see if something exists which is separate (χωριστόν) itself by itself (αὐτὸ καθ' αὐτό) and not belonging to any sensible thing.

In each of these texts Aristotle takes either of

"is separate"
"exists itself by itself"

to make the same substantive ontological claim which he would know had been made by Plato through either of

"exists separately"
"exists itself by itself"

about the soul in the *Phaedo* and also, though not by the same syntactical device, about the Forms in the *Parmenides*. Not surprisingly, Aristotle thinks of both "Form is separate" and "Form exists itself by itself" as entailed by the same premise, namely that Form is substance:

T9 [Arist.] *Peri Ideōn, ap.* Alexander, *in Aristotelis Metaphysica commentaria* 83.24–5: For them [the Platonists] the Ideas exist by themselves (καθ' αὐτὰς⁹⁰ ὑφιστάναι), if they are substances.

T10 Arist. *Metaph.* 1040b26–7: They are right to separate the Ideas, if they are substances.

In his illuminating study (1985b: 89ff. at 92), Donald Morrison points out that the word is not known to occur anywhere before Aristotle and suggests that "it is reasonable to suppose that Aristotle himself had coined it." The suggestion is certainly worth considering. But is it more likely than, or as likely as, the alternative possibility that Plato had previously used the word himself in oral discussion in the Academy? Having asserted repeatedly in the *Parmenides* that the Forms exist χωρίς,⁹¹ why should he not have found it natural to reach for the cognate verbal adjective when it would serve the needs of his discourse? If one starts off saying that something exists χωρίς, one might well wish in a later mention of it to refer to it as χωριστόν, and would be able to do so if the word was within reach of one's effective vocabulary, as χωριστόν surely was for Plato, for while (as Morrison [1985b: 91] points out) χωριστός never occurs in his corpus, both ἀχώριστος⁹² and χωρίζειν do, and it is safe to assume that one who controls the privative form of a verbal adjective as well as the parent verb, would also have access to the adjective without the privative prefix.⁹³

Anyhow there is independent evidence that reference to Forms as χωριστά was by no means confined to Aristotle in polemical references to Plato. As Cherniss has pointed out,⁹⁴ Aristotle ascribes "separately existing, non-sensible entities not only to Plato but to Speusippus and Xenocrates" as well; and Aristotle's interpretation

90 The contraction of the "itself by itself" phrase here could be due to Alexander's paraphrase or it might have been present in the original (Plato too occasionally clips off the first pronoun: cf. n. 12 *sub fin.* above).
91 With, or without, a dependent genitive. The latter usage comes closer to Aristotle's χωριστόν εἶναι, which does not require a dependent genitive, though it admits of one.
92 *R.* 524c1.
93 If you have heard me use both "flex" and "inflexible" would you have any doubt that I am in a position to use "flexible" also?
94 In the course of a powerful onslaught (1942: 206ff. at 208–9) on the view, still influential at the time, that Aristotle's imputation of χωρισμός to Plato had been rank misinterpretation.

is here supported directly by Xenocrates, who defined the Platonic Idea as "a paradigmatic cause of naturally constituted things,"[95] asserting that it was "separate and divine" (χωριστὴ καὶ θεῖα). If χωριστόν had been invented by the bright young man from Macedonia to pillory as a colossal blunder a doctrine common to Plato and his closest followers, it is hardly likely that they would have picked it up from their critic to put it at the centre of their own doctrinal self-description. In those circumstances it is far more likely that Aristotle had found the term in current use inside the Academy and had voiced his dissidence in insider's language.

2.6　FORMS IN THE *TIMAEUS*[96]

Owen's attempt to bring the *Timaeus* into Plato's middle dialogues, close to the *Republic*, and before the *Parmenides* (1953: 79–95) must be pronounced a failure: see Brandwood, 1958: 399–401 *et passim* and 1976: xvi–xvii); Prior, 1985: 168–90; Fine, 1988: 374–7. The right place for it is after the *Theaetetus* and before the *Sophist*. Here a natural philosopher, with a new-found interest in non-mathematical sciences (the constitution of metals, physiological psychology, medicine), displaces the Socrates of Plato's middle period, whose scientific interests (as shown in the curriculum of higher studies prescribed for the philosophers in the *Republic* [522Bff.]) had been confined to the mathematical sciences. The existence of Forms is now viewed as a question of burning importance which must be raised and answered *de novo* (*Ti.* 51B–C). When this happens, what S_M had put into his great "hypothesis" in the *Phaedo* (T11 in ch. 2) is reaffirmed resoundingly and in the same language as before: "there most certainly do exist (παντάπασιν εἶναι) Forms inaccessible to our senses, accessible to mind only (ἀναίσθητα ὑφ' ἡμῶν εἴδη, νοούμενα μόνον)" (51D). And a great point is made of the transcendence of the Forms: they "exist themselves by themselves" (εἶναι καθ' αὐτά ταῦτα, 51D3–4) or "in themselves" (ἔστιν τι πῦρ αὐτὸ ἐφ' ἑαυτοῦ, 51B7–8) and, unlike sensible phenomena, "do not enter into anything else anywhere" (οὔτε αὐτὸ εἰς ἄλλο ποι ιόν, 52A3) "or ever come to be in something else" (ἐν οὐδετέρῳ ποτὲ γενόμενον, 52C–D). Cf. Prior, 1985: 90.

2.7　THE MEANING OF χωρισμός

There is a lucid formulation of the import of this term in Fine, 1984: 31ff., at 35: "The separation (*chōrismos*) Aristotle typically has in

95 αἰτία παραδειγματικὴ τῶν κατὰ φύσιν συνεστώτων.　　　96 Cf. ch. 2, p. 75.

mind in connection with Forms is capacity for independent existence... To say the Form of *F* is separate is [for Aristotle] to say that it can exist without, independently of, *F*'s sensible particulars." The "separation" of the Form had been similarly understood as "existential independence" by Allen (1970: 132 *et passim*; so too, 1980b: "things are separate when they are capable of existing apart... Ideas are capable of existing apart from their [sensible] participants," 100–1, *et passim*). Fine makes it clearer that the claim in the "separate" existence of the Forms is modal: they *may* exist even if no instances of theirs do. Once this is clearly understood, the fact that Forms *can* be instantiated will be seen to be perfectly consistent with their being transcendent (or "separate") in their essential nature, which follows from the fact that they *would* exist, were they instantiated or not.

Failure to grasp this fundamental point led Ross to claim that Plato "was not entirely satisfied" with the view that his Forms were transcendent and "continues in later dialogues to some extent to use the language of immanence" (1951: 231 *et passim*). He takes expressions indicative of the instantiation of Forms in particulars (which, of course, Plato continues to use in the dialogues of his middle period no less than in his earlier ones) to be "language of immanence," failing to perceive that the eternal existence of the Forms would be absolutely unaffected by the contingent fact of their instantiation in the temporal world. And he takes "the failure of any particular to be a perfect exemplification of any universal" (231) to be crucially important to the "transcendence" of Platonic Forms, missing the point that even if a given Form *were* perfectly instantiated in some part or other of the sensible world, its own existential independence would still be absolutely unimpaired. The same failure is betrayed in his translating χωριστόν τι αὐτὸ καθ' αὐτό (*E.N.* 1096b33) "*is capable of* separate and independent existence" (the modal operator I have italicized has no counterpart in Plato's Greek and needs none), instead of simply "has separate and independent existence."

I too was a victim of the same confusion in earlier work; the analysis of "separation" in Plato and in Aristotle on which I proceeded in 1954: 319–49 is completely superseded by the present discussion. In particular, my discussion of the ontological implications of the "deficient" exemplification of Forms in the world was vitiated by my failure to grasp this truth. I am greatly indebted to Allen and Fine for their help in clearing up this confusion.

3.1 SOCRATIC ELENCHUS IN THE *THEAETETUS*?

What I understand by the Socratic elenchus I explained at considerable length in my 1983 paper on the topic; I explain it again, more briefly, in chapter 4. In its standard form it is a type of adversative argument in which Socrates refutes a thesis p, defended by the interlocutor as his personal belief, by eliciting from him additional premises, say {q, r}, whose conjunction entails the negation of p. The refutation is accomplished by "peirastic"[97] argument: the refutand p, proposed and defended by the interlocutor, is refuted out of his own mouth: p is shown to be inconsistent with propositions in his own belief-system.

Now consider what happens in the *Theaetetus*. The simple thesis which is put into Theaetetus' mouth and treated as the formal refutand is transformed by wonderfully inventive constructs which Socrates grafts on it. Thus in the case of (1), Theaetetus' thesis, "knowledge is perception (αἴσθησις)," Socrates proceeds to compound it with a strange metaphysical doctrine consisting of a view he fathers on Protagoras, calling it Protagoras' "secret doctrine," an amalgam of Protagorean subjective relativism enriched by a metaphysics of extreme Heraclitean fluxism (152D–154B). What Socrates then proceeds to refute is a doctrine which by no stretch of the imagination could have been fished out of Theaetetus' own belief system. The naive identification of knowledge with perception allowed him at the start is changed past recognition into a mini-metaphysical system which is only too patently Socrates' own invention: what he refutes in the course of the long-winded argument that follows is his own imaginative construct, with which he chooses to saddle his docile interlocutor. So also in the case of (2), that "knowledge is true belief" (187B) and (3) that "knowledge is true belief accompanied by a *logos*" (201D): the initial theses, of little interest in themselves, are made enormously interesting when Socrates breathes into them the metaphysical fantasies of the Aviary (196Dff.) and the Dream (201Dff.). This is as far as one could go in using the bare form of the elenchus to ventilate musings which Plato considers worth presenting and refuting. No one would wish to confuse these procedures with the peirastic arguments by which Socrates refutes interlocutors in the Elenctic Dialogues.

97 Cf. T14 and nn. 53 and 55, ch. 3.

3.2   EPAGOGIC ARGUMENTS[98]

Aristotle, *Met.* 1078b27–30: For two are the things one would justly assign to Socrates: epagogic arguments (ἐπακτικοὶ λόγοι) and universal definitions, both being concerned with the starting-point of knowledge.

The mistranslation of Aristotle's ἐπακτικοὶ λόγοι as "inductive arguments" is virtually ubiquitous in the scholarly literature.[99] But there has been no excuse for it since the publication of Richard Robinson's *Plato's Earlier Dialectic* in 1941.[100] In his chapter on "Epagoge" he explains the term as follows:

By epagoge I mean an argument from one proposition, or from a set of coordinate propositions, either [1] to another proposition superordinate to the premises as the more universal is superordinate to the less universal and the particular, or [2] to another proposition coordinate to the premises, or [3] first to a superordinate and thence to a coordinate proposition." (1953: 33)

And he points out that "there seems to be no clear case of the conception of epagoge as merely probable [inference] in the [Socratic] dialogues" (1953: 37).

Since I am not assaying a full treatment of the topic, let me stick to [1] where the distinctive genius of this kind of argument is already clear. A good example would be the argument in *Ion* 540B–D. To rebut the claim that the rhapsode has superior knowledge of matters which fall in the domain of crafts other than his own (539D–E), Socrates argues (540Bff.) as follows (I paraphrase and reformulate freely):

(1)   The pilot is the one who knows best what should be said to the crew of a storm-tossed ship.

(2)   The doctor is the one who knows best what should be said to the sick.

(3)   The cowherd is the one who knows best what should be done to calm down angry cattle.

---

98 Cf. ch. 3, p. 95.

99 Heinrich Maier, who had understood perfectly that of the two uses of epagoge in Aristotle, as *dialektische Begründungsform*, on one hand, as *wissenschaftliche Forschungsmethode*, on the other (he observes that "Socratic induction has nothing to do" with the latter) (1913: 376), had nonetheless lent his great authority to the perpetuation of the mistranslation. Gulley (1968: 13–22), who elucidates epagogic arguments, correctly enough, as reasoning by analogy, continues to speak of them as "inductive" and makes no effort to point out their essential difference from true induction.

100 My page-references here and throughout the book are to the second edition (Oxford, 1953).

(4)   The expert in wool is the one who knows best what should be said to women working wool.

(5)   The military expert is the one who knows best what the general should say to the troops.

Conclusion: If C is a craft then its master is the one who knows best matters falling within its subject-matter. (So if C is not the rhapsode's craft, then it is not he, but the master of C, who knows best matters which fall in the domain of C.)

In this argument the conclusion is obviously more general than are any of the premises. To that extent it is like an inductive argument, but with this vast difference that it is not *probable inference* from what is true of some cases to what is true of all. In inductive reasoning, having observed that X is true of certain members of class K, we hazard the inference that X will be true of all members of K, leaving logically open the possibility that the inference might be *falsified by experience*, holding the truth of the conclusion *subject to empirical confirmation*. Not so in the above epagoge. There we are not leaving logically open the possibility that there might be some craft C_a such that the master of some other craft C_b or a layman who is master of neither might have knowledge of matters falling in the domain of craft C_a which is superior to that of the master of craft C_a. Here the truth of the conclusion *is built into the meaning of its critical term* "master of a craft": anyone who claims to be a master of a given craft but does not possess relevant knowledge superior to that of a master of some other craft or of no craft at all would be *ipso dicto* disqualified as a fake.

So "induction" in the commonly understood sense of the word is a misnomer for argument of type [1] in Robinson's analysis above. So too in the case of [2] in his analysis: what we have here is straightforward argument by analogy: from some cases of C we argue by analogy to a further case of C. As for Robinson's [3], here we go by epagoge to the general statement about all cases of C and then infer by syllogism that this would be true of this or that case of C.

I must, therefore, reiterate what I said many years ago: in Socrates' epagogic arguments there is "reference to some instances [of a general statement] which *exhibit the meaning of the statement* by exemplifying it, rather than *prove* it; it is really only what logicians call 'intuitive induction'" (Vlastos, 1956: xxix, n. 18.) The reiteration is necessary when Socrates' epagogic arguments are cited as evidence that he seeks and gets "empirical support" for his theses,[101] which unhappily is not the case: his whole approach to ethics and, most particularly, his moral psychology would have been radically different if he had offered his great theses as subject to empirical confirmation.

4.1 EPISTEMIC VS. MORAL CERTAINTY[102]

Under "certain" the *Shorter Oxford English Dictionary* (3rd edn., 1955) recognizes a special sense in which the word is used in the expression "moral certainty,"[103] which it explains as "so sure that one is justified in acting upon the conviction." I wish to distinguish this clearly from what I would call "epistemic certainty" which, as I explained in my discussion of Socrates' profession of ignorance,[104] we possess concerning something p when, and only when, our evidence E for the truth of p *entails* p, i.e. that if E is true then, necessarily, p is true or, equivalently, it is impossible that p is false if E is true. In that discussion I emphasized that the knowledge on which we predicate our action in everyday life does not need to meet this ultra-strong condition – which is just as well, for if we had to wait until it could be met, we would never act. We would be in the position of the compulsive hand-washer who would not accept the fact that he had washed his hands with hisofex just a minute or two ago as evidence that they are now free from deleterious germs, so that he feels compelled to wash them again every time he considers the possibility that some germs might have settled on his hands since their last wash. The demand for epistemic certainty as the condition of action would be paralyzing.

When is it, then, that we attain evidence which, though falling well short of yielding epistemic certainty, is still strong enough to offer us the moral certainty needed for prudent action? The answer I would suggest is: when the cost of predicating action (or inaction) on the doubt would be prohibitive – when there is more to be gained by acting on that probability than on its denial. Let me suggest an example.

---

101 So Kraut, 1983: 60. He cites the argument in *R.* i, 349D–350A, that since a master-musician (or a doctor: these are the only cases offered) does not try to "outdo" other masters of his craft the same would be true in the case of all experts. But suppose we did some empirical looking-around and spotted some musicians (or doctors) doing that very thing. Would that rattle Socrates in the least? He would just retort that when so acting those experts were not acting *qua* experts. The facts we report would not be counted as negative instances disconfirming the generalization because they would not be allowed to count as instances in the first place.   102 Cf. ch. 4, p. 114.

103 I suspect this is a gallicism, adaptation of the expression "certitude morale" which I have seen often in French, rarely in English.   104 1985: 1–31, at 11–14.

Suppose I have accepted my friend N's invitation to dinner and
that at table I see that the vegetable dish is creamed mushrooms.
Here p = "Those mushrooms are good to eat." Having heard tales
of people who have died from poisonous ones the question crosses my
mind, "Do I know that p is true?" What is E, my evidence for p? It
is that N is known to be a sensible man with a highly reliable
character. This is good evidence for p, but falls far short of epistemic
certainty. People with a character as reliable as N's have been
known to make mistakes. It is not impossible that N should have
made one in this case. I think of ways of strengthening the
probability that E is true: I could cross-question N on the provenance
of those mushrooms. Did he buy them at a supermarket with a good
record for safety? And did he take further steps to ascertain that,
even so, this particular shipment to the supermarket was duly
certified for safety? Did he take a sample for examination to the
University's department of mycology? If I were to put N through
this kind of interrogation and get reassuring answers I would reduce
appreciably the risk of being poisoned by the mushrooms on N's
table. *But at what cost?* Unless N thought I was joking in plying him
with such a barrage of questions, he would be offended by the
implied aspersion on his good faith or good sense. If one accepts an
invitation to dinner one does so on the assumption that the host has
taken all reasonable precautions in securing safe supplies for his
cuisine. One's confidence in this assumption falls far short of
epistemic certainty. In theory there is still plenty of room for doubt
– but not for "reasonable doubt": though there is a risk that the
assumption might turn out to be false, the risk is so small that one is
better off accepting the invitation with that risk than declining. And
if one does accept, then moral considerations[105] – the interdict on
causing offense to someone who has done us a kindness – rule out
subjecting one's host to a cross-examination he would find offensive.
One eats the food that is served one, well aware that one incurs a risk
but with the moral certainty that the risk is worth taking.

   This I take to be the position in which Socrates finds himself in
living by the moral principles he has reached. People around him
believe in returning evil for evil and so act. Socrates does not. Is he
sure that he is right and they are wrong? Epistemic certainty he has
not: his evidence for that principle is elenctic: he has tested it in
many elenctic arguments and it has always come through those tests.

---

105 These need not involve anything more than the low-grade morality of prudence –
   maximizing morally unweighted utility.

That method is avowedly fallible. Even so, with all its hazards, it is the best truth-seeking, truth-testing procedure he knows. Any alternative open to him would be worse – would enhance, not reduce, the risk of moral error. If the elenchus is the best procedure available to him, he is morally justified in living by its results. As I had observed in my previous discussion of this question (1985: 14), living by the findings of fallible knowledge is built into the human condition. "Only a god could do without it. Only a crazy man would want to."

4.2 MATHEMATICAL TEXTS IN ELENCTIC DIALOGUES[106]

In the *Gorgias* Socrates distinguishes number-theory[107] from calculation[108] as follows:

T1 *G.* 451A–C: "If someone were to ask me about any of the arts I mentioned a moment ago, 'Socrates, what is the art of number-theory?' I would tell him... that it is an art which achieves its effect through speech. And if he continued, 'And what is that art about?' I would say that it is about the even and odd, regardless of how numerous each may be. And if he then asked, 'What is the art you call "calculation"?' I would say that it too achieves its effect through speech. And if he then asked me all over again, 'And what is *it* about?' I would say... 'In other respects it is the same as number-theory – both are about the same thing, the even and the odd – but they differ in this: calculation determines the quantity of odd and even, both relatively to themselves and in relation to each other.'"

In the *Hippias Minor* (366c) Socrates calls Hippias a master of *logistikē* because he can tell more quickly than anyone what is three times seven hundred. That this should be considered a fine accomplishment is understandable, for unlike grammar and "music," *logistikē* was not a school subject. Even so, in this highly developed commercial society some skill in computation would be within everyone's reach. *Arithmētikē*, on the other hand, unlike what is called "arithmetic" nowadays, is a theoretical pursuit. It engages in general investigations of number, proving theorems applying to any numbers, odd or even, such as those in Euclid IX, 21ff., which, it has been plausibly held[109] preserve fragments of archaic Pythagorean number-theory. Here are the first three:

106 Cf. ch. 4, n. 96.   107 ἀριθμητική, the science of number.
108 λογιστική, the art of computation, application of mathematical knowledge or skill to reach a determinate quantitative result. Cf. Socrates' request to the slave-boy: "How much is twice two? Calculate and tell me (λογισάμενος εἰπέ)," *M.* 82B.
109 Van der Waerden, 1954: 108ff., adopting a surmise by O. Becker.

T2 Euclid, *Elements* IX, Proposition 21: If even numbers, as many as we please, be added together, the sum is even.
Proposition 22: If odd numbers, as many as we please, be added together, and their multitude is even, the sum will be even.
Proposition 23: If odd numbers, as many as we please, be added together, and their multitude is odd, the sum will also be odd.

We may reasonably assume that in Socrates' life-time such elementary theorems would be widely known to educated Greeks. One would not need much mathematical background to understand that an even-numbered set of odd numbers, say {3, 5}, has an even sum, while an odd-numbered set of odd numbers, say {3, 5, 7}, has an odd sum, and to follow the number-theoretical proofs of these propositions: a look at Euclid IX.21ff. will show that they are simplicity itself. That Socrates would know that much mathematics and hence would be in a position to explain the difference between *logistikē* and *arithmētikē* in the terms he uses in T1, as also previously in *Ch.* 166A, can be taken for granted. No one would wish to suggest that he had been a mathematical illiterate.[110] We can safely assume that he had learned some mathematics before his concentration on ethical inquiry had become obsessive.[111] But it is one thing to have learned quite a lot of elementary geometry and number-theory, quite another to have the knowledge of advanced developments in those subjects which is displayed casually in that remark about irrationals in the *Hippias Major* (T22 in ch. 4), elaborately and ostentatiously in the *Meno* in the reference to the method of "investigating from a hypothesis" in geometry and in the accompanying geometrical construction (T19 in ch. 4). Even if Socrates had learned all the geometry there was to learn in his twenties and thirties, that knowledge would not begin to account for the mathematician he is made out to be in these passages unless he had come abreast of the new developments which occurred when he was in his middle years or later: the axiomatization of geometry began with Hippocrates of Chios in the last third of the fifth century,[112] when Socrates was in his fifties and sixties; the theory of

110 Compare the condition of college-educated adults nowadays who have learned high-school geometry and algebra and may have even had Freshman analytic geometry and calculus but had lost interest after that.
111 If Xenophon's remark (*Mem.* 4.7.3: cf. n. 96 in ch. 4) that Socrates was not himself unfamiliar with "the hard-to-understand proofs" in geometry has some basis in fact – as is entirely possible – it would fit perfectly the hypothesis that Socrates had studied mathematics in his youth, absorbing much of the mathematical knowledge available at the time, but had dropped those studies thereafter.
112 Those first moves of his (cf. ch. 4, n. 63) cannot have come long before the cascading developments in this area in the fourth century (ch. 4, n. 64).

incommensurability was developed early in the fourth century when he was already dead.[113]

In the *Euthyphro* we have positive evidence that in the Elenctic Dialogues Socrates does not have the same ready access to geometrical axiomatics which enables him to produce *ad hoc* the model definition of "figure"[114] in the *Meno*. To explain the part/whole relation of "piety" to "justice" Socrates invokes that of "even" to "number" and then proceeds to define "even" as follows:

T3 *Eu.* 12D: "If you were to ask me, 'Which part of number is the even, and what is that number?' I would say: 'It is that *number which is not scalene but isosceles.*'"

If the way "even" was being defined in contemporary geometry had been at Socrates' finger-tips, he would have surely offered Euthyphro a much simpler and better definition. This is the one in Euclid:

T4 Euclid, *Elements* VII, Definition 6: An even number is that which is divisible in two [equal] parts.[115]

In Greek mathematics, which recognizes only integers as numbers, this definition is flawless. And this is the very one to which Plato himself will resort after acquiring the mathematical knowledge he desiderates for all philosophers. The one he tosses out in the *Laws* anticipates Euclid's verbatim:

T5 Plato, *Lg.* 895E: "We may designate one and the same thing either by its name 'even', or by its definition, '*number divisible in two [equal] parts.*'"

The advantage of this definition over the one in T3 leaps to the eye: it is so much neater and more direct, rendering unnecessary resort to the undefined terms "scalene number," "isosceles number" for the purpose of defining "even number."[116] As portrayed in the *Euthyphro* Socrates is sadly deficient in the mathematical know-how his namesake proudly displays in the *Meno*.

113 The pioneering work in the exploration of irrationals by Theodorus, proving the irrationality of the roots of 3, 5, etc. up to 17 on a case-by-case basis (*Tht.* 147D–148B; cf. Burnyeat, 1978: 489ff. at 494–5), is naturally dated not long before the generalization of those proofs in a systematic theory of incommensurables by Theaetetus in the first third of the fourth century (he died young in 369 B.C.).   114 T14 in ch. 4.

115 I follow Heath (1926: 281 *et passim*) in assuming that the parenthetical augment is required to render the sense of δίχα διαιρούμενος in mathematical contexts.

116 Heath (1921: 292) charges the definition in T3 with a graver fault: "a defective statement unless the term 'scalene' is restricted to the case in which one part of the number is odd and the other even," thus implicitly using the definiendum in the definiens. We cannot positively convict the definition in T3 of such gross circularity, since we do not know how Socrates would have defined "scalene" if called upon to do so.

4.3   PLATO AND THEODORUS[117]

T1 Diogenes Laertius 3.6:   [a] As Hermodorus states, at the age of 28 Plato, with certain other Socratics, withdrew to Megara to Euclides.[118] [b] Next he departed for Cyrene to Theodorus the mathematician, and thence to Italy to the Pythagoreans Philolaus and Eurytus; and thence he went to Egypt to the prophets, where Euripides is said to have accompanied him...

Entirely credible is the story of Plato's journey to Megara after Socrates' death, in part [a] of this text, and also elsewhere in Diogenes Laertius (2.106), there too on the excellent authority of Hermodorus. But what confidence can we repose in the tale in part [b], which affords no clue as to its source? The gossipy story of a grand tour of the southern Mediterranean, which takes Plato to Cyrene,[119] Italy, and then Egypt, discredits itself by picking as Plato's companion on this journey none other than Euripides, who had died some 8 years before the tour could have begun. There is no mention of travel to Cyrene prior to the one in Sicily and Italy in the earlier report in Cicero (*De Rep.* 1.10.16; *De Fin.* 5.29.87), nor yet in the *Index Herculanensis* (ed. Mekkler), pp. 6–7.[120] But while Plato's travel to Cyrene to make contact there with Theodorus seems to rest on nothing better than doxographic gossip, there is no reason to doubt the report elsewhere in Diogenes which represents Plato as having received instruction from Theodorus:

T2 Diogenes Laertius 2.102:   There have been 20 persons named Theodorus... The second was the Cyrenaic, the geometrician whose auditor Plato became.

This could have occurred after Plato's first journey to Syracuse, on his return to Athens, where Theodorus' presence is well attested (*Tht.* 143Dff.; *Sph.* 216Aff.; *Pltc.* 257A–B).

How close was this relation to Theodorus? The nearest Plato comes to giving some indication of it comes in the following snatch of dialogue in the *Theaetetus*:

T3 *Tht.* 145C–D: Socrates to Theaetetus: "You are getting some instruction in geometry from Theodorus?" Theaetetus: "Yes." Socrates: "And also in astronomy and harmonics and computation?" Theaetetus: "I am eager to learn from him." Socrates: "I too, my boy – from him and

---

117 Cf. n. 98 in ch. 4.
118 Founder of the Megarian school; in the Platonic corpus: narrator in the *Theaetetus*: present at the death-scene in the *Phaedo* (59C).
119 Mentioned also by two other late sources, Apuleius (1.3) and Olympiodorus (*in Gorg.* 41.7), also without any clue as to *their* source.
120 Cf. Guthrie, 1975: 14–15; Riginos, 1976: 63–4.

from anyone else whom I believe to have some knowledge of such things (καὶ παρ' ἄλλων οὓς ἂν οἴομαί τι τούτων ἐπαΐειν). I do moderately well, in general. But I am puzzled about one small thing which I would like to investigate with you and these people."

Theodorus is represented as only one of those to whom "Socrates" (*alias* Plato) would be eager to turn for instruction in mathematics.[121] And as the dialogue proceeds we sense the absence of any close or intimate bond with Theodorus, who is portrayed as aloof from Plato's philosophical interests. When Socrates tries to draw him into the argument, he is rebuffed:

T4 *Tht.* 165A1–2: "At a rather early age I turned away from bare arguments to geometry (ἐκ τῶν ψιλῶν λόγων πρὸς τὴν γεωμετρίαν ἀπενεύσαμεν)."

Robin's gloss on ἐκ τῶν ψιλῶν λόγων here[122] "raisonnements tout formels, vides de substance," brings out the lack of interest in philosophical argument suggested by the reference to him in Plato's text. The attraction Plato could have felt for Archytas, who fused enthusiasm for mathematics with dedication to philosophy, he could hardly have felt for Theodorus.[123]

5.1 THE *HIPPIAS MINOR* — SOPHISTRY OR HONEST PERPLEXITY?[124]

Scholars who maintain that Socrates does not scruple to traffic in deception have a field-day when they come to the *Hippias Minor*. Thus Guthrie (1975: 195):

To read through this little dialogue without a growing sense of irritation at its manifest absurdities calls for a strong historical imagination. It is not easy to project oneself back into the ruthless infancy of dialectics and the agonistic atmosphere of a sophistic encounter, nor to understand the acceptance of obvious fallacies in the days before there had been any serious study of the rules of reasoning.[125]

A reply to this and similar accounts of Socrates' conduct in this

---

121 Knorr, 1975: 88–9), following earlier suggestions by H. Vogt and P. Tannery, hypothesizes a uniquely close relation to Theodorus, maintaining that the latter had been "Plato's master in mathematics"; he holds that it was from Theodorus that Plato had derived "his basic conception of the field of mathematics ... and a deep respect for matters of mathematical rigor." But T3 makes a pointed reference to the fact that there were other mathematicians to whom "Socrates" could also have turned for instruction in their area of expertise. There is no good reason to suppose that Plato had failed to take advantage of those other opportunities and learn as much, or more, from those others. Theodorus does not appear in the Eudemian history in Proclus among the mathematicians who were close to Plato.   122 In the note *ad loc.* in his translation (1956).

123 But neither am I proposing Archytas as Plato's preceptor in mathematics nor yet as his model in metaphysics. Cf. n. 64 in ch. 4.   124 Cf. ch. 5, pp. 132–3.

125 Cf. also the second citation from Friedländer (commenting on the *HMi.*) at the start of ch. 5: Socrates "knows how to deceive better than all the sophists."

dialogue must begin by noticing the common mistranslation of a word in Socrates' first and longest argument, which forms the dialogue's *pièce de résistance*, 365B–369B,[126] purporting to establish the following thesis:

S　The true man (ὁ ἀληθής) and the false man (ὁ ψευδής) are the same.

Often in paraphrase[127] and recently in a full translation of the dialogue[128] ψευδής has been translated "liar" in crucial argumentative contexts. If this rendering were right, then S becomes

S*　The truthful man and the liar are the same

i.e. a patent falsehood. If this had been the Socratic thesis, we would know right off that only by some kind of sophistry could Socrates presume to have established it. But the fact is that though ψευδής *can* mean "liar"[129] and does so in many contexts, it need not – it does not always do so.[130] Throughout the dialogue Socrates uses ψευδής to mean not someone whose *character* it is to speak falsehoods but only someone who has the *ability* to do so if he so chooses. Socrates stipulates, and Hippias consents, that this is how "false man" is to be defined in their debate:

TI 366B–C:　"False men (ψευδεῖς) are those who are clever and *capable of speaking falsely* (σοφοί τε καὶ δυνατοὶ ψεύδεσθαι) ... And capable is one who does what he wants when he wants."

Clearly then it would be wrong to paraphrase "false man" as "liar" in this dialogue. For it is not one who is *able* to speak falsely whom we call a "liar."[131] Truthful persons are also capable of doing the same, but no one would think of calling them "liars" on that account. Only if we intend an aspersion on their moral character, imputing to them readiness to lie whenever it suits their purpose, would we say that they are liars. This is what distinguishes liars from honest persons. Thus throughout this dialogue we have to reckon with the fact that ψευδής (and, by the same token, ἀληθής) may be used to refer exclusively to the ability to speak falsehood (or truth).

126 The refutand is stated at 365C3–4; its precise contradictory is derived in the argument which concludes at 369B.

127 So e.g. in A. E. Taylor, 1937: 35 (4th edn. of Taylor, 1929), and Guthrie, 1975: 192ff. The mistranslation even crops up in Roslyn Weiss's (1981: 287ff., at 289 *et passim*) valiant effort to vindicate Socrates' *bona fides* in this dialogue. An honorable exception to the frequent mistranslation is Sprague, 1962: 65; she consistently avoids rendering ψευδής as "liar."　　　　128 By Robin Waterfield, 1987.

129 For which, however, the proper word would be ψεύστης (in common use since Homer), which Socrates could have used if that were what he meant.

130 For ψευδής as applied to things or statements LSJ gives, "lying, false, untrue," as applied in persons, "lying, false." A false statement need not be a lying one, i.e. intended to be thought true. A person making false statements need not intend them to be thought true.

131 Cf. *O.E.D. s.v.* "liar": "teller (esp. habitual) of lies."

So we had best stick to the untendentious, literal rendering of the critical terms: "false man" for ψευδής, and "true man" for ἀληθής.[132]

When we do so we shall not find a single passage in this dialogue where Socrates obtains assent by dishonest means. It has been argued with great force by Roslyn Weiss (1981: 287ff.) that he establishes S at 366A–369B by valid elenctic argument, adhering consistently to the use of "true" man to refer exclusively to the man who has the ability to utter truth and, similarly, "false" man for the one who has the ability to utter falsehood. Should we then follow her in giving this argument a clean bill of health? To do so we would have to overlook the brazen departure from common usage which Socrates allows himself in his definition at T1.[133] If we heard someone called a "false man" what we would naturally understand is that the man is not what he pretends to be – that he is some kind of fake. It would never occur to us that he is "false" because he has the ability to speak falsely if he so chooses, which he would have even if he were scrupulously truthful. It would be the same in Greek. I know of no other case in contemporary or earlier Greek prose or verse where a man is called "false" merely because he is *capable* of speaking falsehoods if he so chooses. Anyhow, what is wrong with the definition is amply demonstrated by the conclusion established by its means: what would we think of a definition of "brave" from which it is supposed to follow, and does follow, that the brave man and the coward are the same?[134]

And there is a second feature of the passage to give us pause – a feature worth stressing because it is glossed over, at times even completely ignored, in major accounts of the argument, including the one by Weiss. This is that Socrates himself is sorely troubled by that conclusion. To be sure, when Hippias protests it Socrates' first response is to defend it. He is not content to point out that the sophist has only himself to blame for it; did he not agree to the definition at T1 whose logical consequence this is? And at first it looks as if this would be Socrates' only comment (369D–371E). But he changes course in the long speech at 372Aff., which starts with mockery of Hippias[135] but moves into a confession of uncertainty and vacillation

132 Following standard translations of the dialogue: Jowett's (1953), Léon Robin's (1956).
133 A highly tendentious one – a prime example of what used to be called a "persuasive definition," under the influence of Stevenson, 1944: 9.
134 Weiss says (1981: 290) that "the paradox vanishes" if we read the conclusion as "the man skilled at speaking truthfully and the man skilled at speaking falsely are the same man." But it is surely false that, in general, truthful people are *skilled* at speaking falsely. The ordinary truthful person has no such skill, and soon runs into trouble when he starts lying. Considerable talent and much practice would be required to become a skillful liar.
135 372A6–D3: as I pointed out in ch. 5, this is "irony laid on thick."

unparalleled in the elenctic dialogues. When it looks as though he will stand pat on the thesis that those who do wrong voluntarily (ἑκόντες) are better persons than those who do wrong involuntarily (372D3–7), he turns around and says that sometimes just the opposite seems true to him:

T2 *HMi.* 372D3–E2: "But there are times when quite the opposite also appears to me and I am all astray (πλανῶμαι) in this matter, evidently because I have no knowledge."

The view that those who do wrong voluntarily are better men than those who do so involuntarily he proceeds to blame on some "sort of paroxysm" which has now seized him (372E1–3).

Is there anything at all surprising about the fact that Socrates, who usually stands so firmly by the thesis he defends in elenctic argument, should feel that he may have gone "astray" in the present case, seeing himself as the victim of a "paroxysm" and, as he proceeds to confess, in need of "healing" (372E5)? Not if we take two things into account.

(1) In the present thesis he moves close to the center of that doctrine of his, that no one does wrong voluntarily, which, as I pointed out in section IV of chapter 5, is a misguided and confused doctrine into which he is trapped by a faulty move within his own theory of moral motivation; the theory requires him to hold that all men always desire good in all their voluntary actions; *but it does not warrant the corollary that men never desire to do evil* – which they surely do when they mistake evil for good.[136]

(2) A second indication that Socrates has good reason to have no truck with that thesis is that, as Hippias points out (371E9–372E5), it runs flatly against a principle of common morality and of law: there are both ethical and jurisprudential reasons for viewing wrongdoers more favorably if they are presumed to have acted involuntarily. Socrates himself acknowledges that principle in defending himself against Meletus in the *Apology* (25E–26A). But in his argument with Hippias he makes no effort to explain away the contradiction between that principle and his present thesis.

There is good reason then for taking Socrates at his word when he confesses in T2 above that he is floundering in perplexity, and then confesses it again, with even greater emphasis, at the conclusion of the dialogue. When Hippias rejects the thesis, Socrates joins him in saying that *so does he*:

T3 *HMi.* 376B–C: "Neither do I concede it to myself, Hippias, but this is how it appears from the argument. This is just what I was saying earlier

136 Cf. the last two paragraphs of section IV in ch. 5.

on: on this matter I go astray, up and down, and I am never of the same opinion..."

The Socrates portrayed in this dialogue is in a muddle: he has gone as far as discovering a sense in which a man who cheats and wrongs voluntarily is indeed *better* than one who does so involuntarily, but not far enough to pin down that sense and contrast it sharply with the one in which "better" is normally used when questions of right and wrong conduct are debated. And that residual failure vitiates the discovery, turns it from truth into flagrant error. Being the honest arguer we know him to be, Socrates does not try to conceal the failure from his interlocutor or from himself, and the dialogue ends in confessing it.

But why should Plato put his hero in that hole? Well, why not, if he had seen Socrates in it and had not himself hit on just the right move required to pull him out of it? For there is no reason to think that in this matter Plato's own moral insight went farther than that of his teacher – no reason to believe that when Plato wrote this dialogue he had himself spotted the root of the trouble. What he would need for this purpose would be to identify the difference between the sense of "better" which is so conspicuous in this dialogue, the morally neutral sense of superior executive *power* or *skill*, on one hand, and that centrally and uniquely moral sense of superior *character* or *disposition*, recognizing that possession of the former is by no means a sufficient condition of possession of the latter. This was to await Aristotle's clearer vision, which empowered him to discern how wrong it would be to define moral virtue as a power or craft, for power or craft could be used for either good or evil: the physician's skill in healing is also power to damage his patients' health and even to finish them off were he to choose to misuse it. Aristotle enriched the vocabulary of moral analysis by introducing the word ἕξις to designate the state of character which chooses to exercise power for the right ends and resolutely declines to exercise it for the wrong ends. Irwin has stated in masterly fashion this Aristotelian insight; I can do no better than quote from his formulation of it:

A craftsman may have or lack the further excellence which uses his skill correctly; but a wise man needs no further excellence (*aretē*) since wisdom includes the right use (*N.E.* 1140b21–2) and the wiser man is not, like the better craftsman, more capable of acting badly, since wisdom is a virtue, a state and not a capacity (1149b22–4). (1977a:77).[137]

---

137 Irwin remarks that Aristotle's answer is not open to Socrates "because it will wreck the craft analogy" (*loc. cit.*). So it would, if Socrates had thought that the relation of virtue

In the *Hippias Minor* Plato chooses to present Socrates in a confused and troubled state of mind. Failing to discern that moral virtue would be underdescribed as a power or a craft, since if it were only this it could be used for either good or evil ends, he finds himself betrayed into concluding, however hesitantly,[138] that he who uses such power voluntarily for evil ends must be the better man. When we see where and why his analysis is at fault and that the faulty conclusion to which it leads him elicits no conviction in his adversary, or even in himself, we shall be more understanding of his predicament, less prone to stigmatize as deceitful discourse what is, all too plainly, self-confessed perplexity.

6.1   SOCRATES' *DAIMONION*[139]

At its first mention in Plato's *Apology* (31C) Socrates refers to it as "something godlike and divine" (θεῖόν τι καὶ δαιμόνιον), but elsewhere frequently as simply τὸ δαιμόνιον. In its latter use δαιμόνιον is "elliptically substantival" (Riddell, 1867: 102), an adjective flanked by a semantic hole where a substantive has to be understood; as Burnet reminds us in his note on *Eu.* 3B5, "there is no such noun-substantive as δαιμόνιον in classical Greek" and the regular use of the word in that way "makes its first appearance in the Septuagint, where it is pretty clearly a diminutive of δαίμων rather than the neuter of δαιμόνιος."[140] So in Plato we should always read the word as a contraction for the phrase we see filled out in *R.* 496C, "the divine sign" (τὸ δαιμόνιον σημεῖον) and again in *Eud.* 272E, "the customary divine sign" (τὸ εἰωθὸς σημεῖον τὸ δαιμόνιον = τὸ εἰωθὸς δαιμόνιον σημεῖον: cf. *Phdr.* 242B3).[141] As Zeller noted (1885: 82, n. 5), in Plato the substantival use of τὸ δαιμόνιον to refer to a divinity is restricted to his accusers; it is they who understand

---

to craft were identity instead of mere analogy. If A is analogized to B, it will be meant to hold (forcefully and illuminatingly, if it is a good analogy) in some, but by no means in all, respects. The crucial difference for Socrates is that no ordinary craft is sufficient to ensure happiness (the pilot can save his passenger's lives, but does not presume to ensure that the lives he saves will be worth living: *G.* 511D–512B), which is precisely what Socrates holds that virtue does ensure (so e.g. at *G.* 507B7–C7 [quoted as T22 in ch. 8]).

138 The qualification at 376B4–6, "Hence he who does wrong and shameful and unjust things voluntarily, O Hippias, *if there be such a man*, is none other than the good man," has often been noted.   139 Cf. ch. 6, p. 167.

140 He also reminds us that Socrates' *daimonion* "is never called a δαίμων, though the idea of the δαίμων as a guardian spirit was quite familiar" (*loc. cit.*).

141 There is no textual foundation for the assumption (Edmunds, 1985: 211 *et passim*) that in Plato τὸ δαιμόνιον is a contraction for "the divine *thing*."

ἄλλα δαιμόνια καινά to mean the new deities which they allege Socrates introduced to take the place of the city's gods. No less significant is Socrates' alternative use of expressions in which δαιμόνιον does not occur at all, replaced by phrases in which the operative word is "sign": "the god's sign" (τὸ τοῦ θεοῦ σημεῖον, *Ap.* 40B1; "the customary sign" (τὸ εἰωθὸς σημεῖον, *Ap.* 40C3); or just "the sign" (τὸ σημεῖον, *Ap.* 41D6). It comes to Socrates in the form of a "voice": "this is what I have had since childhood: a voice comes to me, and when it comes it always turns me away from what I am about to do, never towards it" (*Ap.* 31D; tr. after Allen).

Xenophon's usage does not make this nearly as clear. Here the word *is* used as a quasi-substantive. Marchant is not clearly wrong in translating τὸ δαιμόνιον σημαίνειν at *Mem.* 1.1.4, "the deity gave a sign." The difference from Plato is not so marked as to *require* that translation. We could still read his phrase as "the divine [sign] signified"; but if we did the resulting redundancy would suggest that Marchant's reading of the Greek phrase is more likely to be the right one. In any case, a material difference from Plato is that in Xenophon the *daimonion* does a lot more work and of a different kind from any it ever does in Plato. In Xenophon its promptings to Socrates are not restricted to dissuasion; they also give positive injunctions and, what is still more striking, the *daimonion* affords Socrates an intelligence service he can use to benefit third parties as well: "for many of his companions he advised beforehand (προηγόρευε) to do this, not to do that, in accordance with the forewarnings of the deity (τοῦ δαιμονίου προσημαίνοντος); those who heeded the advice prospered, those who did not would regret it" (*loc. cit.*).

This use of the *daimonion* as an occult prognosticator, never encountered in Plato, occurs repeatedly in Xenophon both in the *Memorabilia* (1.1.4–5, cited in part above) and in the *Apology of Socrates* 13, where it is put on a par with prognostications by diviners and is again put to work for the benefit of Socrates' friends ("I have announced to many of my friends the advice [about future events] the god has given me and it has never turned out false").[142] We see the *daimonion* functioning in this way again in the pseudo-Platonic *Theages*, and there its treatment as a divine being in its own right becomes explicit. Young Theages speaks of it as a full-fledged

---

142 For the difference in Xenophon's treatment of the *daimonion* by contrast with Plato's see Maier, 1913: 456–7: "In Plato the *daimonion* does not yet have the magical character which Xenophon has given."

divinity which they should "propitiate[143] by prayers and sacrifices and by any other means the diviners may prescribe." The youth's father endorses the suggestion, and Socrates goes along: "if it seems that we should do so, let us do it" (131A). The mentality of the writer of this curious work is indicated by the fact that a young man is supposed to make moral progress simply by being in the same house with Socrates and "much greater if [he] sat at Socrates' side and most of all when sitting right next to Socrates, touching him" (130E).

Once we set aside the *Theages* (except as a monument to the level of credulity to which some of Socrates' superstitious admirers could sink after his death), our choice of sources of information about the *daimonion* falls between Plato and Xenophon. And if we assume that in this case, no less than in that of the others that have been noticed previously in chapter 3 and will be noticed again in the present chapter[144] and in additional note 7.1, the former's testimony should be preferred as that of the more reliable witness, then the first thing we should do in our effort to get to the bottom of this very puzzling feature of Socrates' conduct is to follow out the implications of his unique susceptibility to certain peculiar mental states which he construes as signs from the god. Does he see in these signs *revelation* in the proper sense of the word, i.e. "knowledge disclosed to man by divine or supernatural agency"?[145] To do so he would have had to think of the god as providing him with not only (a) the sign, whose presentational content is immediately clear, but also (b) *the sign's correct interpretation*, which is not immediately clear, and may be highly problematic. That Socrates assumes that (a) is true is clear enough in our texts. That he also believes that (b) is true is not: *there is not a single Platonic text in which Socrates says or implies that the god causes him not only to hear "the voice" but also to discern the right interpretation of its message.*[146] As I pointed out above (pp. 167–8), in the parallel

---

143 παραμυθεῖσθαι. The notion that a divine being would need to be (or could be) "propitiated" by special cult-services prescribed by diviners would give away the spuriousness of the *Theages* all by itself, even if there were no other grounds on which it would be suspect.   144 Additional notes 6.3, 6.5.

145 Here again, as in n. 65 in ch. 6, I am quoting the *O.E.D.*'s definition of the word.

146 Had this crucial difference between (a) and (b) been duly noticed by Brickhouse & Smith they might have been saved from their view that "there are some moral truths to which [Socrates] has direct and certain access" through the *daimonion* (1989: 241 *et passim*). The error is a long-standing one. Thus Zeller (1885: 86) maintains that "Socrates was conscious within of divine revelations" and proceeds to explain this consciousness as "the general form which a vivid, but unexplored sense of the propriety of particular actions assumed for the personal consciousness of Socrates" (*ibid.* 95), dodging the question of the epistemic import which these states of consciousnes would have had for someone who did truly think of them as "divine *revelations*."

case of the prophetic dream Socrates explicitly recognizes that the interpretation he puts on the surface-content of a supernatural sign at a given time may be in need of revision at a subsequent time, thereby acknowledging the possibility that at the earlier time he may have put the wrong interpretation on its message. There is no reason to suppose it would be different in the case of the *daimonion*. What the voice brings him is a message. For the true interpretation of that message he must rely entirely on his own, highly fallible, human resources.

If we review the passages in Plato whose context is informative enough to enable us to tell what goes on in Socrates' mind when he speaks of receiving a monition from the *daimonion*, we shall find that they fall into two classes:

(A)   Socrates has independent grounds for accepting what the voice tells him to do or to believe – grounds which would have sufficed to persuade him of the correctness of that action or belief even in the absence of that signal.

(B)   Socrates has a "hunch" – a strong intuitive impression – that a certain belief or action is correct without being able to articulate his grounds for it at the moment.

Here are the passages that fall under (A):

(A)   1. *Ap.* 31C–32A. The *daimonion* has been opposing his participation in politics. He says he "believes that it does very well in opposing me" (παγκάλως γέ μοι δοκεῖ ἐναντιοῦσθαι) for if he had got into politics long ago he "would have perished long ago and done no good to [them] or to himself." His perception that participation in politics would be unlikely to benefit the Athenians, while being virtually certain to bring about his own destruction is, clearly, a rational ground for keeping out of politics, regardless of what, if anything, he heard from the *daimonion* on that score.

(A)   2. *Ap.* 40A–C. The silence of the *daimonion* – the fact that it did not oppose the line of defense he took at his trial – is, he says, "a great indication (μέγα τεκμήριον)[147] for him" that no evil will befall

---

147 "Indication" for τεκμήριον in Allen, "intimation" originally in Jowett. The word is frequently rendered "proof" in translations of the passage (so most recently in Brickhouse & Smith, 1989: 237ff.). But the Greek counterpart for "proof" would be ἀπόδειξις. No interpretation of this text which understands Socrates to be getting "proof" of something or other from the silence of the *daimonion* could be justified by appeal to the use of τεκμήριον in this passage.

him as a result of the death to which he has been sentenced. But that death is no evil he establishes on rational grounds which are entirely independent of input by the *daimonion*. He does so at 29A, where the *daimonion* has not yet been brought into his speech, and then again, more elaborately, at 40C–41C, a passage he introduces by saying "and let us understand (ἐννοήσωμεν) the matter in this way." If the divine monition had not come, Socrates would still have had the rationally grounded belief that death is no evil.

(A)   3. *Ap.* 28E, taken together with 33C. The *daimonion* is not named in either passage. In the former he says that "the god has commanded me, *as I assumed and believed*, that I ought to live philosophizing, examining myself and others," without specifying the means by which the command was conveyed to him. In the latter he says that "to do this, *as I maintain*,[148] was commanded me by the god through both divinations and oracles and by every other means by which divine dispensation has ever commanded a human being to do anything" – this is sweeping enough to allow us to infer that "the command" was supported *ex silentio* by the *daimonion* though not articulated by its "voice" (which would contradict the subsequent statement that "the voice always deters, never enjoins"). That Socrates has rational grounds for philosophizing should go without saying. From these he would infer that the god being what he is (wishing the best that could be achieved by human means for the Athenians), and Socrates being what he is (uniquely endowed with the capacity to bring home to his fellows the supreme importance of the pursuit of moral perfection), philosophizing is what would constitute the best service he could render the god.

Here are the passages that fall under (B):

(B)   1. *Tht.* 151C. When one-time associates of his who have drifted away from him return and beg to be readmitted to his company "the *daimonion* which comes to me forbids it in the case of some, allows it in that of others, and they are the ones that make progress." Here Socrates stops from doing something "without being able (at the time) to explain to himself the motive of reason and feeling which checked him" (Campbell, 1861: *ad loc.*). He is acting, as we all do often enough in life, on a "hunch" – on grounds we cannot articulate explicitly at the moment, but which seem nonetheless convincing enough to justify action.

148 The words I have italicized here and in the preceding quotation emphasize the personal
   nature of the interpretation he is putting on the supernatural signs to which he refers.

(B)   2. *Eud.* 272E. He was alone in the palaestra, sitting, and was about to get up, when "the customary divine sign" checked him, so he sat down. He acted on just a "hunch" that he had best sit a little longer, and so he did.

(B)   3. *Phdr.* 242B–C. "As I was about to cross the stream the customary divine sign came to me – it holds me back from doing what I am about to do on each occasion [on which it comes] – and I seemed to hear a voice, forbidding me to leave the spot until I had made atonement for some offense to the god." Here Socrates has good reasons for making atonement for that offense. He proceeds to state them: he had spoken irreverently about love in his first speech. But at the moment to which he refers those reasons had not yet been clearly articulated in his mind, and they had been even less clearly articulated earlier on, while delivering that first speech, when "something divinatory" (242C7) "disturbed him." Divination and the *daimonion* are cited in explanation of his reluctance to leave before making amends to god for his impious first speech about love – reluctance which had been insistent, but became articulate only in retrospect.

From these passages, which give us content enough to enable us to tell what is going on in Socrates' mind when a visitation of the *daimonion* occurs, we can satisfy ourselves that none of them implies or even suggests that he would have been willing to accept a prompting from that source *if it had offered counsel obnoxious to his moral reason*. To be sure, if Socrates *knew* that X is a command from the infinitely wise god this would trump any rational scruples he might have had about it. But that is precisely what he does *not* know. All he has is subjective states of mind, putatively caused by the god, whose import remains to be determined by himself. Think, for example, of a command like that which Abraham gets in Genesis 22: "Take thou thy son, thine only son, Isaac, whom thou lovest. Get thee into the land of Moriah and offer him as a burnt offering." While Abraham could have taken, and did take, the surface content of the sign he got from God as its real meaning, Socrates could not. Both Abraham and Socrates believe that God is good and wills only good for those who serve him. And this would give both Abraham and Socrates a reason for doubting that God could be commanding something so horrendously iniquitous as killing an innocent child. But for Abraham faith trumps reason and he is praised for this by Kierkegaard as a "knight of faith." Not so in the case of Socrates, who lives with a commitment to argumentative reason (TI in chapter 6) for which there is no parallel in Abraham or any other Old Testament figure. The god Socrates serves has only the attributes which Socrates' elenctic reason would approve. If the *daimonion* were ever to give a message which contradicts the character Socratic reason establishes for the gods the message would thereby condemn itself as a vagary of his own fancy instead of a true command from his god.

Nonetheless the impression persists in the mind of some readers of the *Apology* that Socrates does allow his "sign" to trump a decision he has reached on rational grounds. The impression is articulated as a formal thesis by my friends, Thomas Brickhouse and Nicholas Smith (1989), in their book *Socrates on Trial* and then again in their letter to *TLS* of January 26 – February 1, 1990. To support their thesis that Socrates does allow it they refer to *Apology* 31D–E. But does that passage really provide evidence for their thesis? It certainly would if what is said there were, as they claim in their letter, that Socrates had "already decided to engage in [political] activity" and the "sign" supervened to oppose the decision. They had made the same claim previously in their book: the *daimonion* opposed him "each time he has resolved to undertake political activity" (1989: 168); "it opposed him each time he has tried" to go into politics (169).

But is this said in the text? Does Socrates say he had *decided* to go into politics, had *resolved* to do so, and had *tried* to do so? No. Not a word there to indicate that he had done any of these things. All he says is that the *daimonion* "opposes my engaging in politics" (31D5), and that he sees good reason for its doing so (31D6– E2). When the text is closely read all we learn from it is that his "sign" opposes his going into politics, and that so does his reason. "Sign" and reason are in accord. There is no trumping.

How is it then that Brickhouse and Smith take that text as evidence to the contrary? The answer is made disarmingly plain in their letter to *TLS*: "the *daimonion* could not have 'turned [Socrates] away' from political activity unless he had already decided to engage in such activity." Surely this is false. Consider: I am offered a job that would double my pay but might prove disastrous in other ways. I spend a sleepless night turning over the offer, sugar-plums of bigger pay dancing in my head. I rise *almost* ready to write the letter of acceptance. If I were favored with a divine sign solicitous of my welfare wouldn't that be a good time for it to speak its "Don't", instead of waiting until after I "had already decided" to accept?

Socrates must have often been in like need of his sign's advice. Living in a city that practices participatory democracy and enjoins the ethos epitomized by Pericles in Thucydides (2.40.2), "the man who takes no part in politics we regard not as one who meddles with nothing but who is good for nothing," Socrates, an ultra-conscientious man, seeing dreadful goings-on close to him, must often have had twinges of self-questioning, often wondered if he was right to persist with mulish obstinacy in his principled abstention from politics, and in specially trying circumstances – say, on the morning when the question of exterminating Melos would be coming up for debate in the Assembly – had all but reached the point of doing what his conscience had vetoed heretofore. But did he ever go as far as *deciding* and *resolving* to do it? Would he have *tried it*, if his "sign" had not intervened? This is what we do not know and shall never know if we stick to the evidence and continue doing history instead of switching to historical romance.

6.2   *ION* 533D–536A[149]

This is a remarkable passage, unique among Plato's earlier compositions in its exuberance of poetic imagery: the poet is a "magnet"; he is a "winged" creature; he is a "bee" carrying away sweetness from honied fountains (untranslatable pun on μέλι, μέλη, μέλιτται, μελιρρύτων, μελοποιῶν, 534A–B); he is like the "bacchantes drawing milk and honey from streams" (534A). In explaining the poet to us, Plato lets Socrates speak like a poet for the nonce. But he does not make Socrates abandon his customary elenctic role on that account. What is different here in Socrates' practice of elenchus is his propounding *in extenso* a challenging theory *before* proceeding to vindicate it argumentatively. This reversal of the usual order in no way diminishes the vigor of his elenctic argument when he does come around to it. *Pace* Verdenius (1943: 233ff. at 235, "il ne saurait démontrer cette conviction"), Socrates uses elenctic argument forcefully (536Dff.) to refute Ion's claim that *he* "does not praise Homer in a state of possession and madness (κατεχόμενος καὶ μαινόμενος)." And *pace* the remark of Wilamowitz (1948: 100) that in this dialogue Socrates does more "dozieren" than questioning, once Socrates gets past the exposition of the "possession" theory (533D–535A and 535E–536D), Socrates is as assiduous and deft a questioner and arguer in the *Ion* as in any of Plato's Socratic dialogues.

With this passage we should read *Ap.* 22B–C(= T10 in ch. 6) – a

149 See ch. 6, p. 168.

precious parallel, for without it we would be left wondering if the theory of poetic inspiration expounded in the *Ion* is pure Platonic invention, without any foundation in authentic Socratic thought, as has been often assumed in the scholarly literature: so e.g. Guthrie (1975: 209) who, like so many others, blandly ignores the replication in the *Apology* of what is said by Socrates in the *Ion* (cf. ἐνθουσιάζοντες ὥσπερ οἱ θεομάντεις καὶ οἱ χρησμῳδοί, *Ap.* 22C, paralleling the bracketing of the inspired poets with the seers and oracle-givers in *Ion* 533E–534C). Worse yet, he conflates the theory of divine possession in the *Ion* with its counterpart in the *Phaedrus*, shutting his eyes to the fact that in the *Ion* (and the *Apology*) the "madness" of ἐνθουσιασμός is viewed as mental aberration, lapse of rationality (a psychic state in which the person is out of mind, ἔκφρων, 534B, bereft of νοῦς, 534C–D), while in the *Phaedrus* Plato annuls Socrates' epistemic denigration of ἐνθουσιασμός by grafting on it the Platonic theory of "recollection," thereby finding in divine possession *the highest grade of knowledge open to man*, though mistaken by the vulgar for craziness (249C–D).

6.3   THE ORACLE STORY IN PLATO AND IN XENOPHON[150]

This is how it runs in Plato:

Plato, *Ap.* 20E–21A: "You surely know Chaerephon... Once upon a time he came to Delphi and requested an oracle on this – I say, gentlemen, don't make a disturbance – he asked if there is anyone wiser than myself. And the Pythia responded (ἀνεῖλεν) that no one is. Chaerephon is now dead. But his brother is here and will testify about it."

And here is Xenophon's version of the tale:

Xen. *Ap. of Socrates* 14: "When Chaerephon once inquired about me at Delphi in the presence of many, Apollo responded (ἀνεῖλεν) that no man was more liberal, more just, or more wise than myself. On hearing this the jurors, naturally enough, made a still greater disturbance."

In Xenophon we are not told what the question was – only that laudatory epithets spilled out. In Plato we are told that it was, precisely, "Is anyone wiser than Socrates?" and that the answer was, precisely, "No." Which of the two shall we believe? The forensic credibility of their two stories is decidedly different. That of

---

150 Cf. n. 73 in ch. 6.

Xenophon could hardly be weaker: all that the court is offered is the defendant's say-so. In Plato a well qualified witness is in court to attest the story. Moreover, in Plato's version Chaerephon's question is answerable by "Yes" or "No"; so the inquiry could have been processed by cleromancy which, as Pierre Amandry has shown (1950: 53 and 245), is known to have been practiced at Delphi during the fourth century and may well have been practiced much earlier.[151] A vessel containing two beans sits before the priestess. She picks one at random. She answers "Yes" if it is white, "No" if it is black. If this had been the method used in the present case a nasty problem would dissolve: how was it that a stay-at-home Athenian philosopher, who had published nothing, had acquired such extraordinary fame that Delphi risked its reputation on the verdict that no one was wiser than he? If cleromancy had been the method used, there would have been no need for Socrates to have acquired great fame, or any fame. All the Pythia would have needed to do would be to pick up a bean.

A further reason for preferring Plato's to Xenophon's version of the story is that in the former the Pythia's response would be given privately to the inquirer in writing (Amandry, 1950: 150) while in the latter it is said that it was given publicly ("in the presence of many"), and if this were true it is hard to believe that the event had failed to become public long before Socrates' trial, while the impression we get from both Plato and Xenophon is that the Pythia's response was being made public for the first time.[152] If cleromancy had been used, Chaerephon could have kept it to himself and divulged it only to Socrates.

6.4 XENOPHON ON SACRIFICE[153]

The staple of Greek religion had always been petitionary prayer predicated on the ritual honours the petitioner had paid the supplicated god or gods. So Apollo's priest prays to him in the *Iliad* (1.40–1).

---

151 His view has been disputed (Fontenrose, 1978: 220–2), but on a ground – that in extant historical oracles there are no negative replies – which is hardly conclusive. The widespread use of the term ἀναιρεῖν ("to take up," LSJ *s.v.*, sense III) for the Pythia's responses suggests that divination by lot may have been the original mode of oracular response.

152 In neither Xenophon nor Plato is there any allusion to the oracle prior to its introduction in connection with the trial. And if such an oracle had been public property Socrates' prosecution for impiety would be more difficult to explain: however interpreted, the fact that Delphi had paid this tribute to his wisdom would have been for many Athenians powerful certification of his piety.　　153 Cf. n. 94 in ch. 6.

       If ever I burned to thee fat thighs of bulls and rams,
       Fulfill thou this prayer of mine.

And so do countless others in real or imagined Greek devotions.

    In Xenophon Socrates' piety is not so crass. He counsels that we should only ask the gods "to give good things," trusting them to send whatever they, in their greater wisdom, deem best for us (*Mem.* 1.3.2). He teaches that there is no advantage in lavish offerings, for the gods are as pleased by modest ones (*ibid.* 1.3.2). But even so the *do ut des* rationale of divine worship remains in place:

Mem. 4.3.17: "It is by falling no whit short of one's power to honor the gods that one may hope confidently for the greatest goods. From whom could a prudent man expect more than from those who have the power to confer the greatest benefits?"

This is at the core of Socrates' conception of piety in Xenophon:[154]

Mem. 4.3.4: "He who knows the lawful usages (νόμιμα) concerning the gods would honor the gods lawfully?... And he who honors lawfully honors as he should?... Should we not then define the pious man as the one who knows aright the lawful usages concerning the gods?"

These "lawful usages" concerning the gods are the prescriptions of sacral law which regulate the sacrifices due the gods:

Mem. 4.3.16: "You see that when the god at Delphi is asked, 'How am I to please the gods?' he replies: 'By the lawful usage (νόμῳ) of the state.'"

This is just the conception of piety encapsulated in the last of the definitions proposed by Euthyphro at T14 in chapter 6 and ridiculed by Socrates for reducing piety to "an art of commercial exchanges between gods and men" (*Eu.* 14E6). Thus the *Memorabilia* imputes to Socrates the conception of piety which he refutes in Plato's *Euthyphro*.

    Have we any means of telling which of these conflicting testimonies has the greater historical credibility? We have. If Socrates, practicing the cult-centered piety Xenophon imputes to him, had been "most visible of men" (*Mem.* 1.2.64) in cult-service to the gods of the state, it would be impossible to understand how he could have been prosecuted for *impiety* and, if prosecuted, how a jury made up of ordinary Athenians, for whom the cult-centered conception of piety would be *de rigueur*, could have convicted him on that charge, for he would have been able to cite, as he in fact does in Xenophon[155]

---

154 And of Xenophon's own too. See e.g. Marchant, 1971: 1143.
155 *Mem.* 1.1.1; *Ap. of Socrates* 11 and 24.

(never in Plato), the very kind of exculpatory evidence an Athenian jury would have found most convincing.

6.5 XENOPHON VS. PLATO ON SOCRATES' SPEECH OF DEFENSE

Their respective representations of the speech are at loggerheads on two points of critical importance (abbreviating, I shall be referring to Plato's representation of Socrates as "Socrates$_P$", to Xenophon's as "Socrates$_X$").

1. Socrates$_P$ makes a serious effort to convince the court of his innocence, well aware, he says (*Ap.* 18E–19A), that this "would be difficult" but "would be best for you and for me."[156] The speech of Socrates$_X$ is, on the contrary, deliberately provocative, aiming to enhance the chances of conviction because this, he believes, would be a welcome escape from the ills of impending old age (*Mem.* 4.8.6–8; *Ap. of Socrates* 1 *et passim*).

2. When the "guilty" verdict has been reached, and court procedure calls for the offer of a counter-penalty, Socrates$_P$'s first gambit is to say that to get what he deserves he should be given no penalty but a high civic honor, the very highest Athens can bestow: public maintenance at the Prytaneum. But then he changes course and does propose a counter-penalty after all: one mina from his own funds or thirty by subscription from his friends. Xenophon$_X$, on the other hand, "when bidden to offer a counter-penalty, offered none himself and would not let his friends do so, saying that this would be an admission of guilt" (*Ap. of Socrates* 23).[157]

Which of the two should be believed? On (1) it is clear that if Socrates$_X$, believing himself, as he does, to be completely innocent of all the charges (*Mem.* 4.8.9–12; *Ap. of Socrates* 10–13), had chosen to provoke the court by the "haughty tone"[158] of his speech to vote for his conviction, he would have willfully connived at a grave miscarriage of justice: the condemnation for impiety and for corrupting the youth of a man who throughout his life had given conspicuous evidence of his piety (*Mem.* 1.1.2; *Ap. of Socrates* 11) and

---

156 Cf. Brickhouse & Smith, 1989: 60–1.
157 The veracity of Xenophon's testimony on this point is rightly rejected by Brickhouse & Smith (1989): 215.   158 μεγαληγορία, literally "big talk."

of devoting himself to the moral improvement of his fellows, young and old. On this ground alone, if there were no other, we would have to reject Xenophon's testimony, for such action would be grossly inconsistent with Socrates' rocklike integrity of character attested by Xenophon, no less than Plato: how could we believe that Socrates had never wronged anyone (*Mem.* 4.8.10) *and* that he had egged on the hundreds of Athenians who sat on his case to commit an act of flagrant injustice?

Moreover, by his own admission (*Ap. of Socrates* 1), Xenophon is in a minority of one in taking this view of Socrates' speech: he remarks that while "all others" who had written about it[159] had taken note of its μεγαληγορία, none had anticipated Xenophon's explanation of it, i.e. none had stated that Socrates' defense had been willfully provocative, motivated by the wish to secure "suicide by judicial verdict."[160] So we have compelling reasons for accepting Plato's alternative account of this matter: his testimony is corroborated by that of several others while Xenophon's is not; and Plato's testimony on this point is consistent with his and Xenophon's testimony concerning Socrates' moral character, while Xenophon's is not.

Should we then suppose that Xenophon is prevaricating? The evidence does not compel us to do so. His view of Socrates as an overwhelmingly persuasive speaker[161] would have made it very difficult for him to believe that on this single occasion, when Socrates had the strongest possible case,[162] Socrates had failed miserably. He would find it far easier to believe that the adverse verdict had been willfully provoked by Socrates.

159 He does not name them. Their writings would include Plato's *Apology* (which, as A. E. Taylor [1956: 120, n. 1] argues, must have been known to Xenophon); the one by Lysias (mentioned in a scholion on *Ap.* 18B by Arethas); probably also an *Apology* by Theodectes (see testimonium v and accompanying references in Deman, 1942: 35–6), and, in any case, the *Accusation* by Polycrates which Xenophon rebuts at length in the opening chapters of the *Memorabilia*.

160 Allen's (1980: 35) apt description of Xenophon's construction of the motive for the μεγαληγορία in Socrates' defense.

161 *Mem.* 4.6.15: "Whenever he argued he gained a greater measure of assent from his hearers than anyone I have ever known." Cf. also *Mem.* 1.2.14. Plato's picture of him is decidedly different. Against determined opponents Socrates always wins the argument, but seldom, if ever, wins over his opponent. Polus, compelled in argument to agree that doing injustice is always worse for the agent than for his victim, remains as unpersuaded of the truth of the Socratic thesis as he had been at the start; he still thinks the thesis "absurd" (ἄτοπα, *G.* 480E). Unpersuaded too are Callicles in the *G.*, Protagoras in the *Prt.*, Hippias in the *HMi.*, Ion in the *Ion.*

162 On Xenophon's view Socrates was in a position to present (and did present: *Mem.* 1.1.1; *Ap. of Socrates* 11) just the sort of evidence of his piety which Athenian jurors would have found most appealing.

On (2) the (independent) case for believing Plato against Xenophon would also be a strong one. Plato was present at the trial, while Xenophon had been far away in Anatolia at the time and long after; he is relying on what he heard about it, many years later, from Hermogenes, of whose veracity we know nothing. The effrontery of Socrates$_p$'s claim that public maintenance at the Prytaneum, instead of punishment, is what he deserved would have created a furor which Plato would, while Xenophon could not, have witnessed at the trial and thereafter. Moreover in Plato's version of the story not only he himself but several friends of his, each of whom would be well-known in Athens, were personally involved in the counter-offer. It is very hard to believe that so circumstantial a report of facts known to those friends and to their numerous acquaintance, as also to the hundreds of other Athenians who had been present at the trial was the outright fiction it would have had to be if the Xenophontic story were true. It is much easier to believe that Xenophon in retrospect, writing many years later, when public memories of the event had faded, manipulated the facts for apologetic reasons.

6.6 WHY WAS SOCRATES CONDEMNED?

Would mere adherence to unorthodox belief constitute culpable guilt under the Athenian law of impiety? The question has often been debated and answers on both sides of the dispute keep appearing.[163] So far the affirmative seems to have had the best of the debate. In fact there seems to be hardly any case at all for the negative given the salience of belief in Socrates' formal indictment: the first two of the three charges ("disbelieving in the gods of the state and introducing new divinities") are clearly matters of belief, the first one entirely so; and in the *Euthyphro* the content of the third seems to be reduced to that of the first two. Asked what it is that his accusers claim he does to corrupt the youth, Socrates replies:

T1 *Eu.* 2B1–4: "They say I am a god-maker: for making new gods and disbelieving in the old ones [Meletus] has brought this indictment against me."

However, the picture changes if we take into account two of

---

163 Most recently: for the affirmative, Brickhouse & Smith (1989: 3 1ff.) and David Cohen (1980: 695–701); for the negative, Allen (1980a: 15–18).

Socrates' remarks in the *Euthyphro* to which little attention has been paid so far in the debate.[164]

T2 *Eu.* 37–D2: "In my opinion, the Athenians don't much mind anyone they think clever, so long as he does not teach his wisdom. But if they think he makes others like himself, they are incensed."

He then proceeds to contrast himself with Euthyphro, who spouts idiosyncratic religious notions in the Assembly, but makes no sustained effort to disseminate them among his fellow-Athenians: "He gives of himself sparingly and does not wish to teach his wisdom," while he, Socrates, is untiring in sharing his with every Tom, Dick and Harry:

T3 *Eu.* 3D6–9: "But I fear my own generosity is such that they think me willing to pour myself out in speech to anyone – not only without pay but glad to even pay anyone who will listen." (Translation mainly after Allen),

Thus, as Socrates understands the matter, what has provoked the "anger" of the traditionalists is not just the fact that he happens to hold wrong beliefs about the gods, but that he is so assiduous in pushing them on the streets of Athens.

But would their "anger" at this behavior of his have a bearing on the legal question of whether or not spreading those views of his made him legally guilty of the crime of impiety? It would indeed. For as David Cohen has pointed out, since the Athenian legal system laid down no formal definition of the crime of impiety (or, for that matter, of most other crimes), its legally effective definition would be simply the one "inherent in the collective consciousness of the community as manifested through the 500 or more judges who happened to be sitting on a particular day to hear a particular case" (1980: 698). This is a fact about the Athenian judicial system to which all parties to the dispute agree. Allen does so emphatically: "the elements of impiety were what a simple majority of dicasts on a given day thought was impious."[165] So what Socrates is telling us in T2 above is that the mere fact of his having had unconventional beliefs would be of no great concern to the Athenians (and if it was not, those of them empaneled to sit on his case could hardly vote to impose on him those extreme penalties prescribed by the law of impiety) while matters would be entirely different if they thought of him as propagating those beliefs ("making others like himself"): *this* would "incense them."

164 No perception of the bearing of *Eu.* 3c6–D9 on Socrates' indictment and condemnation in the copious comments of Burnet *ad loc.* No listing of this text in the *index locorum* in Allen, 1980a, nor yet in Brickhouse & Smith, 1989, who are exceptionally thorough in their scrutiny of Platonic texts bearing on the condemnation of Socrates. 165 1980a: 28.

But would it "incense" them in a way which has judicial force, making them feel that he is guilty of the dread crime of impiety? This seems to be the drift of what he says in T2, T3 above. The following hypothesis is suggested by these remarks: it is not for the mere holding of heterodox religious opinions that one would be judged guilty of impiety by dicasts sitting on one's case, but for what one did about those opinions; only if one proceeded to proselytize (to "make others like himself"), would he be found guilty. If we scan our sources for collateral evidence *pro* and *con* we shall find nothing whatever that tells against the hypothesis; what there is of it agrees with it in every case, and to that extent confirms it.

In Xenophon's *Memorabilia* (1.4.2), to begin with, we hear of one of Socrates' close associates, Aristodemus,[166] who "was known to make no sacrifices to the gods nor prayers to them nor use divination, but ridiculed those who did." Aristodemus is not an atheist, but thinks the deity "too great to be in need of my tendance" (1.4.10). Even so, that he could not only deliberately opt out of participation in the ritual, but brag about it with impunity, scoffing at those who did comply with the prescribed observances, speaks eloquently for the wide margin of deviant religious belief and practice that was tolerated in Athens. Though his conduct is clearly impious, Aristodemus has no fear of prosecution under the law, for if he did he would have kept his delinquencies to himself; he would certainly not have acknowledged them provocatively, ridiculing observers of the ritual. His case would be inexplicable unless there was some special circumstance which made him feel that he had nothing to fear. Our hypothesis tells us what this circumstance could be: while he thinks the cult observances ridiculous and says so freely upon occasion, there is no indication in Xenophon's narrative that he makes active efforts to "teach" his impious views; he laughs at those who do not share them, but makes no effort to convert them.

Consider further Plutarch's report of the decree of Diopeithes:[167]

T4 Plutarch, *Pericles* 32.1: About this time [near the start of the Peloponnesian War]...Diopeithes brought in a decree providing for the impeachment of those who did not believe in the gods or taught doctrines about the heavens, directing suspicion at Pericles by means of Anaxagoras.

166 Cf. Plato, *Smp.* 173B–174A; the dialogue purports to derive from Aristodemus' eyewitness account of the original events.
167 The historical accuracy of this report has been disputed, but no cogent ground has yet been cited, in my view, for its denial. The one given by David Cohen (1980: 699) – that we have no corroboration of it in near-contemporary sources – is insufficient: Plutarch was exceedingly well-read in the fifth- and fourth-century literature; it is not likely that he would cite the decree in such circumstantial form without some support in his sources.

Anaxagoras, the obvious butt of this first attempt to bring impious belief explicitly under the ban of the law was not a private investigator of the heavens, sojourning in Athens on a personal visit to Pericles and other friends. He was the author of books which reached a wide public: three decades later, at the time of Socrates' trial, they were still being sold at popular prices in Athens. There can be little doubt that it was for this – for the influence of his teachings, so pernicious, in the eyes of traditionalists – that his presence in Athens would provoke this unprecedented legislation.

And as for Socrates himself, despite his protestations that he "had never been anyone's teacher" (*Ap.* 33A5–6),[168] his public persona was most certainly perceived as that of a teacher of the young. When the Thirty introduced repressive legislation aimed directly at him it was only through his teaching that they tried to shut him up:

T5 Xenophon, *Mem.* 1.2.31: When Critias was one of the Thirty and was drafting laws along with Charicles...he inserted a clause which made it illegal to teach the art of speech.[169]

"Teaching the art of speech," however inept as a description of Socrates' elenctic encounters with youthful interlocutors, would capitalize on the popular impression, fostered by Aristophanes in the *Clouds*, that he was a "teacher" of the young; the formula would be elastic enough to cover whatever activities were involved in his relation to younger associates. Though no reference to his teaching is made in the formal indictment at his trial, we know that his efficacy as a teacher figured prominently in the public recollection of his condemnation. Addressing a popular court 50 years after the event Aischines singles it out as *the* cause of the verdict.

T6 Aeschines, *Contra Timarchum* 173: Men of Athens, you executed Socrates the sophist because he was shown to have been the educator of Critias, one of the Thirty who subverted the democracy.[170]

Rank-and-file Athenians would have no idea of what went on between Socrates and high-born younger friends of his, like Critias and Alcibiades, in the supposed process of "education" which was alleged to have corrupted them. But neither would they have any difficulty in generalizing from the personal experience many of them had had with Socrates in chance encounters with him on the street or in the marketplace. Knowing his uncanny power to make

---

168 Cf. Xenophon, *Mem.* 1.2.3–8.
169 Cf. Xenophon, *Mem.* 4.4.3: "they forbade him to converse with the young."
170 Alcibiades' name was coupled with that of Critias in other versions of the accusation: Xenophon, *Mem.* 1.2.12–16.

mincemeat of traditional opinions of theirs which he "examined," they would infer that the honest beliefs about the gods these young men had retained from their earlier education would stand no chance of withstanding the force of Socrates' dialectic.

From these data, meager though they are, we can infer with considerable confidence that if Socrates had been content to pursue his philosophizing in private conversations with fellow-seekers after truth, he need have had no fear that his unorthodox religious views would have got him into trouble with the law. Since he wrote no books, the opinions he debated with his friends would not have made him vulnerable to prosecution. What did, was the aggressiveness of his public mission – the fact that he felt constrained to philosophize on the streets of Athens, "examining himself and others,"[171] deploying his corrosive dialectic "on everyone of you I happen to meet," "everyone of you I run into, young and old, alien or citizen."[172]

7.1   PLATO VS. XENOPHON ON SOCRATES' REJECTION OF RETALIATION

In chapter 3, I confronted one of the main divergences between Plato's and Xenophon's testimony: Socrates' profession of ignorance, made so emphatically and recurrently in Plato, is never heard in Xenophon. As I remarked at the time the latter's silence on a theme which figures so prominently in the former has the force of implicit denial. In chapter 7 we run into an even sharper clash. Xenophon's Socrates endorses fulsomely the traditional good-to-friends, evil-to-enemies sentiment[173] which Plato's rejects so sharply that he makes its rejection the touchstone of whether or not one is prepared to side with him against "the many."[174] Whose testimony should we accept? When faced with the conflict on Socratic ignorance we had other witnesses to break the deadlock. Aristotle, Aeschines Socraticus, Colotes, Cicero, Aelius Aristides support Plato to a man. Xenophon is the odd man out. In the present case there are no other witnesses. No one beside Plato says or implies that Socrates believes that the just man will not return evil for evil. Why take Plato's word against Xenophon's?

---

171 *Ap.* 28E and 38A (previously quoted in ch. 4, n. 13). As I have emphasized in ch. 4, "examining" *others* is the life-blood of the elenchus. When he shifts to "examining" only himself, as in the *Lysis*, the elenchus is already dead.
172 *Ap.* 29D, 30A (quoted in ch. 4, n. 14).   173 See n. 52, in ch. 7.
174 Cf. T13 in ch. 8.

We may fall back on the general grounds on which Plato's testimony has the greater credibility: he had come to know Socrates intimately over a period of years before his master's death and then had spent many years deepening and clarifying that knowledge by writing philosophy as a Socratic. Xenophon's acquaintance with Socrates is of unknown duration and probably no better than casual. And in Plato we have a witness who could be counted on to understand the philosopher in Socrates as only a philosopher could, while the best we could expect from Xenophon is what we could learn about Socrates from a gifted litterateur. Suppose we had two accounts of Bertrand Russell's philosophy, one from G. E. Moore, the other from H. G. Wells. Would we hesitate for a moment between the two?

But there is still one more thing to consider which may help us decide. In that single text quoted as T25 in chapter 3 we saw Xenophon put into the mouth of Hippias a sentiment which sits poorly with the account of Socrates throughout the *Memorabilia* as a tirelessly didactic thinker, hardly ever at a loss for the answer to any of the questions he asks or is asked, trotting out in a single chapter (3.6) nine potted definitions of ethical and political terms[175] for just four of which Socrates had searched in vein in as many dialogues in Plato, while in T25 Hippias in Xenophon, much like Thrasymachus in Plato, protests Socrates' "questioning and refuting everyone, while never willing to render an account yourself to anyone or state your own opinion about anything."[176] There is nothing in any of Xenophon's Socratic writings to undercut as sharply the representation of Socrates in the *Memorabilia* as falling in blandly with the conventional ethos of helping friends and harming enemies. But if we go to the *Cyropaedia* we can find, in its book III, something which gives us good reason to question if Xenophon is really unaware of Socrates' rejection of this ethos. This comes in a charmingly related episode in the *Cyropaedia*. I shall recount it briefly.

Such terms of peace as Thucydides' Athenians had been challenged to propose after the Spartan reverse at Sphacteria[177] – terms generous enough to evoke a "return of virtue" – Xenophon's Cyrus does offer with panache to a defeated enemy in book III of the *Cyropaedia*. The king of Armenia had treacherously breached his treaty obligations to his Persian overlord, defaulting on a payment of the stipulated tribute, fortifying a stronghold on the sly, and

---

175 Of piety (4.6.2–4), justice (4.6.6), beauty (4.6.9), courage (4.6.10), kingship and tyranny, aristocracy, plutocracy, democracy (4.6.12).
176 Cf. n. 95 in ch. 3.   177 Cf. the discussion of T14 in ch. 7.

attempting to spirit his queen out of the danger-zone and much treasure with her. When Cyrus gets wind of this he acts with lightning speed: his forces surround the Armenian king's and capture the queen, her retinue, and the treasure. With the enemy now completely in his power Cyrus ponders how he should deal with the king's treachery. Tigranes, the latter's eldest son, had been a hunting-mate of Cyrus. He now asks if he may give advice. Cyrus says he is "most eager" to hear it because Tigranes had had as tutor a much-admired "sophist" (3.1.14). This is what Tigranes counsels (the advice coming directly from himself, but undoubtedly reflecting the teaching of the "sophist"): let Cyrus give the captured rebel terms whose generosity will not only "bring him to his senses" – the shock of his debacle has already done that – but evoke such gratitude as to turn him into a devoted friend for ever after.

But who is the mysterious "sophist"? Up to this point, he could have been anyone who had read that passage in Thucydides (T14 in chapter 7) and pondered its lesson. But something stranger is yet to come. Tigranes discloses that his father had ordered the execution of the "sophist," fearing he had "corrupted" the prince by supplanting the father in the youth's affections. Here is the rest of his report to Cyrus:

Cyrop. 3.1.38: "When he was about to be put to death the sophist called out to me, 'Tigranes, don't hate your father for killing me: he didn't do it from ill-will but from ignorance. For everything men do from ignorance I consider involuntary.'"

In no surviving Greek text is the origin of the Socratic paradox that all wrongdoing is due to ignorance credited directly to anyone but Socrates.[178] If no more than this doctrine had been put into the mouth of the "sophist," this would itself have given us good reason for associating the mysterious figure with Socrates. But this is just the half of it. What the Armenian king feared above all was the loss of his son's affection. The "sophist," knowing this, does his best to prevent the loss. Instead of railing at the king for the cruel murder of an innocent man, who moreover had been his own guest as his son's tutor, the "sophist" tries to make Tigranes understand and

---

178 Plato puts it into Socrates' mouth in *Ap.* 25E–26A, *Pr.* 345E, and *G.* 509E (quoted as T20 in ch. 5). It is never ascribed to Socrates by Xenophon, *pace* Zeller, 1885: 143, who so alleges because he thinks it *follows* from the doctrines in *Mem.* 3.9.4; 4.6.6 and 11. That it does follow is doubtful; but even if it did, it is clear from Zeller's quotations *ad loc.* that only in Plato is it ascribed directly to Socrates (and, less directly, in Aristotle, *Magna Moralia* 1187a5–13: cf. comment on this and associated texts by Deman, 1942: 107–11), never in Xenophon.

forgive the crime, retaining, in spite of it, affection for his erring
father.

On the identity of the "sophist" we get no further clue in the
Cyropaedia. But just from this fleeting off-stage appearance of his we
can tell that two doctrines – that all evil action is involuntary, and
that one should never return evil for evil – which Plato treats as
uniquely Socratic, never credited to Socrates in Xenophon's Socratic
writings, Xenophon nonetheless knows well enough to dramatize
them poignantly in his edifying fiction. Can we doubt he also knows
their Socratic provenance?

8.1   HEDONISM *FAUTE DE MIEUX*[179]

Agreeing with Zeyl (1980: 250–69), I firmly detach Socrates in the
Protagoras from the hedonistic premise ("H" for short) on which he
hangs his argument for the impossibility of *akrasia* in that dialogue
(*Pr.* 351B–360E). Is then that argument sophistical? By no means.
There is no sophistry in arguing to some such effect as this:
"Protagoras, when you were first asked point-blank if you accept H
you demurred (351C–D7); but then it turned out by your own
admission (358B3–6) that you do accept it after all. Let me then
show you that if H is what you do believe in your heart of hearts,
then I can claim you as a fellow-believer in the impossibility of
akrasia, surprising and unwelcome though you might find this."

Years ago (1956: xl, n. 50) I had thought it "most unlikely" that
Socrates would have so used H: for this, I had said then, "would
have encouraged the listener *to believe a falsehood*." But this was long
before I had caught on to the import of Socratic irony and had not
yet pondered the fidelity with which Socrates lives out his conception
of himself as an elenctic teacher. If you are Xenophon and assume
that Socrates thinks as all *bien pensants* do about piety or about
benefiting friends and harming enemies, Socrates will feel no
obligation to apply therapy to your myopia: he lets you be. And if
you are Alcibiades in his *belle époque* and read into Socrates'
innocently flirtatious *double entendres* what most people would in
Athens, again he lets you be. If Xenophon or Alcibiades are to find
out that they are wrong, they must find out their error for
themselves. That Alcibiades did and Xenophon didn't seems to have
caused Socrates no loss of sleep. Why then should he have worried
over the fact that Protagoras or any of those other folk who heard
that debate were "encouraged to believe" that Socrates had a soft

179 Cf. n. 24 in ch. 8.

spot in his heart for hedonism or even, perhaps, that he was a hedonist himself? Is it even clear that, if they did so believe, Socrates would have thought it a disaster? Not clear at all, considering that Aristippus, arch-hedonist, founder of the doctrine, was a member of Socrates' own inner circle. I take Socrates' view to be that if one has not yet come in sight of the Sovereignty of Virtue, hedonism *faute de mieux* would still be better than living in a muddle: it would provide one with a low-grade morality of utility which, bad as it is, could at least save one from the self-destructive ways of the likes of Critias and Alcibiades.

Here pleasure would serve as the measure of the relative value of non-moral goods *in abstraction from moral ones*, thus providing a limited use of the "measuring art" of *Pr.* 356E–357A. As I have pointed out elsewhere,[180] all of the examples in the debate with the men of "the multitude" in the *Pr.* involve exclusively non-moral goods (health, wealth, national power, 353C–354B). The hedonistic equation, "good = pleasant," is effected by suppressing all moral considerations (no reference to καλόν, δίκαιον, etc. in the whole of 354E–357E), thus ignoring for the purposes of the argument the necessary bond between goodness and moral virtue. Socrates might well allow that in those cases in which that bond offers no guidance for choice (because we are confronting alternatives which are equally consistent with virtue) the issue between practicable alternatives is legitimately decidable on the basis of hedonic values. (Later in the debate with Protagoras moral virtue is grafted on pleasure by *ad hoc* agreement[181] and the graft is used at 359E – ironically, I think – to show Protagoras that he must regard all honorable actions as pleasant and therefore regard the brave man's preference for wounds or death to life-saving flight as hedonistically justifiable [contrast *G.* 498A5–498E8].)

In elucidating *Pr.* 354A–357E we should be on our guard against the lofty connotations of "salvation" triggered by so translating (unavoidably, no doubt) ἔσωσεν ("saved") at 356E1 and σωτηρία ("salvation") at 357A6–7. As a caution against such spurious evocations we might compare the sea-captain who "saves" his passengers, the general who "saves" cities, the doctor who "saves" patients (*G.* 512B–D), leading Socrates to remark, "see if what is noble and good is something different from saving [one's life] and having it saved" (512D6–8); and we might recall that Sophocles

---

180 Vlastos, 1969: 71–88, a paper much in need of revision at other points.
181 "Are not all actions honorable when taken with a view to leading a painless life?" Protagoras agrees (358B3–6).

makes Odysseus invoke "salvation" to justify the low trick on Philoctetes. Neoptolemus: "Don't you think that it is base to lie?" Odysseus: "Not if the lie brings salvation" (*Philoct.* 108–9).

8.2 EUDAEMONISM IN THE *CRITO*?[182]

In view of the fact that the eudaemonist principle is not stated in the *Cr.*, nor in the *Ap.* (neither of these dialogues makes any reference to εὐδαιμονία as the ground of commitment to the Sovereignty of Virtue), objection may be taken to my use of it to elucidate the reasoning in the *Crito*. I would reply that there is no need to suppose that Plato feels constrained to articulate in any given dialogue all of the major assumptions which govern the reasoning in that dialogue – least of all in the *Cr.*, which is conspicuously elliptical in its exposition of Socratic teaching, using the device of off-stage agreements (notably at 49A6, "have we not frequently agreed in times past...") to simplify the argument, licensing Plato to leave unmentioned premises which are incontestably common ground as between Socrates and Crito. (When a proposition is part of the uncontroversial consensus Plato may feel free to leave it unmentioned *throughout* the Socratic dialogues: so, certainly, the assumption to which I call attention [n. 14 in chapter 8], *sc.* that what is of ultimate concern for any given person is, essentially, that person's own happiness – a proposition which strikes the modern reader as contestable in the extreme.) In any case, we do get in the *Crito* (T15 in chapter 8) a statement equivalent to the Axiom, given the interchangeable use of "happiness" and "good" (n. 20 in chapter 8).

8.3 THE GRAVEST FLAW IN THE INSTRUMENTALIST INTERPRETATION[183]

To avoid the *prima-facie* implication of the identity of happiness to virtue in T15 (chapter 8) Socrates would have had to believe that the bond between virtue and happiness is purely instrumental, i.e. that the two are entirely distinct and are only causally connected. (I follow the definition of "instrumental means" in Irwin, 1977a: 300, n. 53.) But if this were his view the all-important question, "What then *is* happiness?" would draw a blank: the composition of happiness, which every Greek moral theory undertakes to specify – as pleasure in position (1) above (pp. 204–8), as virtue in position (3),

---

182 Cf. ch. 8, pp. 209–10.   183 Cf. ch. 8, pp. 204–5.

as virtue and intelligence along with a variety of subordinate goods in position (2) – would be left mysteriously indeterminate. This, I now feel, is the gravest flaw in the instrumentalist interpretation of Socrates' moral theory in Irwin, 1977a: chapter 3, from whose detailed analyses of Socratic arguments I have learned so much. In Socrates' moral theory, as expounded in that book, any good we care to mention (virtue, health, or whatever) has value only as an instrumental means – *to what*? To a happiness, allegedly the object of all men's desire, which is left completely contentless (Irwin allows it content – pleasure – only in 1977a: chapter 4, where Socrates is made an out-and-out hedonist).

In the Introduction I contested that interpretation on other grounds. Here I may point out that the whole interpretation is predicated on the assumption that if Socrates holds (as he unquestionably does) that virtue is desirable for the sake of happiness, he cannot hold that it is *also* desirable for its own sake. Irwin sees very clearly how mistaken were the Oxford moralists who imputed that assumption to Plato and to Aristotle; but he believes that there is textual evidence for imputing it to Socrates just the same. As I argue in additional notes 8.4 and 8.5, there is no such evidence: when the texts on which he relies are fairly read, his instrumentalist interpretation of the Socratic theory will be seen to be textually groundless.

8.4   ON *GORGIAS* 468B–C[184]

In his Commentary on the *Gorgias* (1979: 141) Irwin rightly protests Socrates' statement:

T1 468B9–C1: "those things which we do for the sake of something *we do not want them* but that for whose sake we do them."

It is perfectly proper to retort that if we consent to medical treatment we most certainly do want it. But does Socrates really mean to affirm the contrary? Does he mean to tell us that after we have gone to great trouble to get hold of a famous doctor, and paid him our good money for his treatment, we do not want that treatment? Wouldn't he be flying in the face of the most ordinary common sense if this were what he meant to say? Pressing the words Socrates has used in T1, Irwin proceeds to generalize their import, inferring that Socrates is endorsing the thesis that *we can never want anything both for its own sake and for the sake of something else.*

184 Cf. n. 84 in ch. 5.

But let us read just beyond the above quoted statement to what Socrates says (468c2–5) right after, in elucidation of it:

T2 468c2–5:   "Therefore (ἄρα) to slaughter anyone or banish him from the city or confiscate his property *we do not wish just like that* (ἁπλῶς οὕτως) but if these things are beneficial *we do wish them.*"

As I pointed out above in chapter 5, n. 77, in comment on this text, that curious expression βουλόμεθα ἁπλῶς οὕτως, aptly translated by Irwin "desire just like that," can only refer to desiring an intermediate *qua* intermediate – desiring it without reference to the good expected from it; and this, according to Socrates would be *impossible*: whatever we do desire, he believes,[185] is desired only in so far as it is good; and since intermediates are, by definition, neither good nor bad, to desire an intermediate "just like that" would be an unperformable psychological act. To make excellent sense of the preceding statement we need only take Socrates to mean also at T1 that we do not want the things he is talking about here, intermediates, "just like that" – a qualification which he neglected to make then, recouping the loss in T2, the very next thing he goes on to say: "we do want them," he says – we do want each and all of those things he classifies as intermediates, beginning with medical treatment – "if they are beneficial." Reading the "just like that" qualification into T1, we make excellent sense of it, instead of the arrant nonsense it would otherwise be. This being the case, the principle of charity requires us to so read it.

To recommend this charitable reading of T1 is not to suggest that it be given a clean bill of health. Taken by itself it would indeed be perverse. That Plato, a very exact stylist, should have allowed it in his text betrays an area of unclarity in his thinking – the very one, as I suggested in chapter 5, in my discussion of T17, which traps his Socrates into saying later on in the dialogue that he and Polus had agreed "that no one commits injustice desiring it, but that all who commit it do so involuntarily" (*G.* 509E [= T20 in chapter 5), the peg on which the doctrine that no one errs voluntarily (οὐδεὶς ἑκὼν ἁμαρτάνει) will be hung. But it is one thing to convict Socrates of dangerously unclear speaking and thinking in T1, quite another to infer that he clearly intends there to affirm an absurd proposition, ignoring the fact that in T2, the statement he then proceeds to make immediately after T1 and in elucidation of it, shows that he means something entirely different which is completely free of that absurd implication.

185 And has just asserted (468b7–8), in this immediate context, and will reiterate in it (468c5–7).

8.5 αὐτὰ καθ' αὐτὰ ἀγαθά[186]

In *Eud.* 281D–E (T28 in chapter 8 above) a new phrase enters Socrates' moral vocabulary: used here for the first time in the Platonic corpus, it describes the moral virtues (wisdom explicitly and implicitly, by synecdoche, all the other virtues which are inter-entailing with it) αὐτὰ καθ' αὐτὰ ἀγαθά. I take the literal translation to be "good just by themselves" or, equivalently "by themselves alone." I take καθ' αὐτά to mean "by themselves" (so Méridier, 1956, and Robin, 1956: "par eux-mêmes"), and αὐτά to be used in the sense of αὐτός = *solus*; for examples see Riddell, 1867: 134; and cf. Burnet's note (1911) on αὐτό in the phrase δίκαιον αὐτό at *Phd.* 65D4–5: "in this technical sense αὐτό is a development of αὐτός, 'alone.'"

That this is the sense of αὐτὰ καθ' αὐτά in T28 can be derived, in any case, directly from the context: the denial that the non-moral goods are αὐτὰ καθ' αὐτὰ ἀγαθά brings to a head the thesis (profusely illustrated by examples) that "without wisdom there is no benefit in any possession" (281B5–6). So too in the doublet of T28 in the *M.* (87E–88D), where argument for the thesis that nothing is good χωριζόμενον ἐπιστήμης (87D5) culminates in the assertion that πάντα τὰ κατὰ τὴν ψυχὴν αὐτὰ μὲν καθ' αὐτὰ οὔ τε ὠφέλιμα οὔτε βλαβερά ἐστιν, but become beneficial or detrimental προσγενομένης φρονήσεως ἢ ἀφροσύνης.

This tells against "goods in themselves" for αὐτὰ καθ' αὐτά in T28 (so in the Jowett translation and in Irwin's paraphrases of the passage in 1977a: 32): it builds into the translation the questionable claim that in speaking of non-moral goods as not good αὐτὰ καθ' αὐτά Socrates is asserting that their value is merely instrumental (which there is no reason to believe: he has said nothing which implies that health, wealth, and their likes have purely instrumental value), and would be inconsistent with what he says in T25 (chapter 8), at *G.* 467E, where he ranks health and wealth with wisdom *in contrast* to the "intermediates" which are clearly the things which have only instrumental value. Still more questionable is the rendering of the Greek phrase by "goods, *considered in themselves*," as e.g. in von Arnim's paraphrase of the passage (1914: 126), "an sich betrachtet keine Güter sind": how could Socrates be saying that health and wealth, taken by themselves, are not good but "neither good nor evil" (von Arnim, *loc. cit.*) without welshing on what he has

---

186 Cf. ch. 8, pp. 227–8.

said at T25, where he contrasts them with the "intermediates,"
which are "neither good nor evil" (*G.* 467E6–7, 468c6)?

A glance back at the use of the αὐτὸ καθ' αὐτό existence of the
Platonic Form may be useful at this point. The same phrase is used
for homologous purposes. In *Eud.* 281D–E Plato uses the phrase to
express the eudaemonic independence of the Socratic virtues; shortly
after he would use it to express the existential independence of the
Platonic Forms.

8.6   ON *LY.* 219B–220B[187]

The place of moral goods in contradistinction to non-moral goods,
on one hand, or intermediates, on the other, is not considered in this
passage. But this is no reason for supposing that they have been tacitly
degraded to the status of instrumental goods. When Socrates warns
at 219D2–4 against being deceived by "all those other things which,
we said, were dear for its sake [*sc.* that of the *prōton philon*], images of
it, as it were" (219D2–4), it is tempting to take him to be warning
that *anything* may so deceive us (hence that moral goods, no less than
non-moral ones and intermediates, may). We should resist the
temptation, reflecting how absurd it would be for *Socrates* to say that
moral virtue (which "is" wisdom) should deceive us and recognizing
that (*pace* Irwin, 1977a: 85) nothing in 219D2–4 requires this, for
moral goods did not figure in that antecedent passage (219C1–D2) to
which "we said" at 219D3 refers: only items in categories III and IV
were mentioned, medicine and health; and it would be unwarranted
to generalize from items in category III to items in category II (from
non-moral goods to moral ones) – as much so as it would be to
generalize from intermediates to goods in T25 (chapter 8).

The same temptation must be resisted at 220A7–B5: "those things
which we say are dear to us for the sake of something else seem to be
dear only in a manner of speaking, while really dear is that very
thing in which all those affections terminate." If that last clause were
allowed unrestricted generality (so Irwin, 19771: 85), it would carry
the same implication as before, i.e. that moral goods, no less than
other things, are not themselves "really dear." But nothing was said
at 219D–220A6 (from which the quoted statement is inferred: this is
the force of γάρ at 220A7) to commit Socrates to holding that not
only items in categories III and IV – the only ones figuring in the
examples in 219D–220A6 from which he is generalizing, all of them
either intermediates (the wine serving as antidote to the poison; the

vessel carrying the wine) or non-moral goods (the gold and silver with which the wine is bought) – but also items in category II as well, moral goods (of which no mention whatever had been made in 219D–220A6) are "dear only in a manner of speaking."

If we heed this caution we shall not follow Irwin, who infers[188] from the present passage in the *Lysis* that Socrates holds that if we choose something for the sake of something else we cannot *also* choose it for its own sake, and that if something contributes to another good it cannot be a good in itself. This faulty reading of *Ly.* 219C1–5 and 219D2–220B5 is the major textual support he offers for the instrumentalist interpretation of Socrates' moral theory.[189]

188 1977a: 85.
189 He also claims (in his Commentary on the *Gorgias* [1979: 141]) some support from *G.* 468B–C (discussed in additional note 8.4); but he says that "wanting something both as a means and as an end is more clearly ruled out in *Ly.* 220A–B."

BIBLIOGRAPHY

Ackrill, John (1973). *Aristotle's Ethics*, London
(1974). "Aristotle on *Eudaimonia*," *Proceedings of the British Academy* 60: 339–60
(1980). *Aristotle the Philosopher*, Oxford
Adam, J. (1902). *The Republic of Plato*, vol. I of 1st edn., Cambridge
(1963). *The Republic of Plato*, vol. II of 2nd edn., with introduction by D. A. Rees, Cambridge
Adam, J., and Adam, A. M. (1905). *Platonis Protagoras*, with introduction, notes, and appendices, 2nd edn., Cambridge
Allen, R. E. (1970). *Plato's "Euthyphro" and the Earlier Theory of Forms*, London
(1980a). *Socrates and Legal Obligation* (Plato's *Apology of Socrates* and *Crito*, translated with essays and notes), Minneapolis
(1980b). *Plato's "Parmenides"* (translation and commentary), Minneapolis
(1984). *The Dialogues of Plato* (translation with analysis), vol. I, New Haven
Amandry, Pierre (1950). *La Mantique Apolinienne*, Paris
Andrews, A. (1962). "The Mytilene Debate: Thuc. 3.36–49," *Phoenix* 16: 62–85
Annas, Julia (1981). *Introduction to Plato's Republic*, Oxford
(1982). "Plato's Myths of Judgment, "*Phronesis* 27: 119–43
Anscombe, Elizabeth (1958). *Intention*, Oxford
Arrowsmith, William (1962). *The "Clouds" of Aristophanes*, translated with introduction and notes, Ann Arbor
Ast (D. Fredericus Astius) (1835). *Lexicon Platonicum*, 1st edn., Munich; 2nd edn., Berlin, 1908
Barabas, Marina (1986). "The Strangeness of Socrates," *Philosophical Investigations* 9: 89–110
Barnes, Jonathan (1982). *The Presocratic Philosophers*, rev. edn., London
(ed.) (1984). *Complete Works of Aristotle: The Revised Oxford Translation*, 2 vols., Princeton
Barrett, W. S. (1964). *Euripides' "Hippolytus,"* Oxford

Beckman, James (1979). *The Religious Dimension of Socrates' Thought*, Waterloo, Ontario

Beversluis, John (1987). "Does Socrates Commit the Socratic Fallacy?" *Amer. Philos. Quarterly* 24: 211ff.

Bloom, A. (1968). *The Republic of Plato*, translated with notes and an interpretive essay, New York

Bluck, R. S. (1955). *Plato's "Phaedo,"* translation with introduction and notes, London

(1961). *Plato's Meno*, Cambridge

Blundell, Mary Whitlock (1989). *Helping Friends and Harming Enemies: A Study in Sophocles and Greek Ethics*, Cambridge

Bonitz, H. (1870). *Index Aristotelicus*, Berlin

Booth, Wayne C. (1974). *The Rhetoric of Irony*, Chicago

Bowen, A. C. (1982). "The Foundations of Early Pythagorean Harmonic Science," *Ancient Philosophy* 2: 79ff.

Brandwood, L. (1958). "The Dating of Plato's works by the Stylistic Method," unpublished dissertation, London

(1976). *Word Index to Plato*, Leeds

Brickhouse, Thomas C., and Smith, Nicholas D. (1983). "The Origin of Socrates' Mission," *Journal of the History of Ideas* 4: 657–66

(1984). "The Paradox of Socratic Ignorance in Plato's *Apology*," *Hist. of Philos. Quarterly* 1: 125–31

(1987). "Socrates on Goods, Virtue and Happiness," *Oxford Studies in Ancient Philosophy* 5: 1–27

(1989). *Socrates on Trial*, Oxford

Bruns, Ivo (1896). *Das literarische Porträt bei den Griechen*, Berlin

Burkert, W. (1962) *Weisheit und Wissenschaft: Studien zu Pythagoras, Philolaos und Platon*, Nuremberg

(1985). *Greek Religion*, trans. J. Raffan, Cambridge, Mass.

Burnet, John (1900). *Aristotle: Ethics*, London

(1911). *Plato's "Phaedo,"* text with notes, Oxford

(1914). *Greek Philosophy, Thales to Plato*, London

(1916). *The Socratic Doctrine of the Soul*, Proc. British Academy, vol. 7, London

(1924). *Plato's "Euthyphro," "Apology of Socrates" and "Crito,"* Oxford

Burnyeat, Myles (1976). "Protagoras and Self-Refutation in Later Greek Philosophy," *Philos, Review* 85: 44–69

(1977a). "Socratic Midwifery, Platonic Inspiration," *Bulletin of the Institute of Class. Studies* (University of London) 24: 7–15

(1977b). "Examples in Epistemology," *Philosophy* 52: 381–98

(1978). "The Philosophical Sense of Theaetetus' Mathematics," *Isis* 87: 489ff.

(1986). "Good Repute," *London Review of Books*, November 5

(1987). "Wittgenstein and Augustine *De Magistro*," *Proc. Aristotelian Society*, Suppl. 61, 1ff.

Bury, R. G. (1932). *The Symposium of Plato*, with introduction, critical notes and commentary, 2nd edn., Cambridge

Caizzi, Fernanda (1964). "Antistene," *Studi Urbinati* 38: 48–99

Campbell, Lewis (1857). *The Sophistes and Politicus of Plato*, revised Greek text with introductions and notes, Oxford

  (1861). *The Theaetetus of Plato*, Oxford

Campbell, Lewis (with Jowett, Benjamin) (1984). *Plato's "Republic,"* edited with notes and essays, in 3 vols., vol. II: *Essays*, Oxford

Canto, Monique (1987). *Plato, Gorgias*, translation with introduction and notes, Paris

Carrière-Hergavault, Marie-Paule (1973). "Esclaves et affranchis chez les orateurs," *Annales Littéraires de l'Université de Besançon, Actes du Colloque 1971* (Sur l'esclavage), Paris

Carter, L. B. (1986). *The Quiet Athenian*, Oxford

Cherniss, H. (1942). *Aristotle's Criticism of Plato and the Early Academy*, vol. I, Baltimore

  (1947). "Some Wartime Publications Concerning Plato," *AJP* 68: 113ff.

  (1951). "Plato as a Mathematician," *Rev. of Met.* 5: 393ff.

  (1955). "Aristotle, *Metaphysics* 987a32–b7," *AJP* 76: 184–6

  (1957a). "The Relation of the *Timaeus* to Plato's Later Dialogues," *AJP* 76: 225–67

  ed. (1976). Plutarch, *Moralia*, vol. 13, with introduction, translation and notes, Cambridge, Mass.

Cohen, David (1980). "The prosecution of Impiety in Athenian Law," *Zeitschrift der Savigny-Stiftung für Rechtsgeschichte* 118: 695–701

  (1987). "Law, Society, and Homosexuality in Classical Athens," *Past and Present* 17

Cohen, S. Marc (1971). "Socrates on the Definition of Piety," in Vlastos, 1971

Connor, W. Robert (1984). *Thucydides*, Princeton

Cooper, John (1973). "The *Magna Moralia* and Aristotle's Moral Philosophy," *AJP* 94: 327–49

  (1975). *Reason and Human Good in Aristotle*, Cambridge, Mass.

  (1977). "The Psychology of Justice in Plato," *Amer. Philos. Quarterly* 14

Cope, E. M. (1867). *Introduction to Aristotle's Rhetoric*, London

Cornford, Francis M. (1932). *Before and After Socrates*, Oxford

  (1935). *Plato's Theory of Knowledge*, London

  (1937). *Plato's Cosmology*, London

  (1939). *Plato and Parmenides*, London

  (1945). *The "Republic" of Plato*, New York

  (1950). *"The Unwritten Philosophy" and Other Essays*, Cambridge

  (1952). *Principium Sapientiae*, Cambridge

Croiset, A., and Bodin, L. (1955). *Gorgias and Meno* in *Platon, Œuvres complètes*, vol. III, part 2, text and translation, Paris

Crombie, A. C. (1962). *An Examination of Plato's Doctrines*, vol. I, *Plato on Man and Society*, London

(1963) *An Examination of Plato's Doctrines*, vol. II, *Plato on Knowledge and Reality*, London

Cross, R. C., and Woozley, A. D. (1964). *Plato's "Republic": A Philosophical Commentary*, London

Davidson, Donald (1985)."Plato's Philosopher," *London Review of Books*, August 1: 15–16 (reprinted in *Plato's "Philebus*," New York, 1990)

(1986). "A Coherence Theory of Truth and Knowledge" in Ernest LePore, ed., *Truth and Interpretation: Perspectives on the Philosophy of Donald Davidson*, 307–19, Oxford

Deichgräber, Karl (1952). *Der listsinnende Trug des Gottes*, Göttingen

Delatte, A. (1934). *Les Conceptions de l'enthousiasme chez les philosophes présocratiques*, Paris

Delatte, A. (1934). *Les Conceptions de l'enthousiasme chez les philosophes présocratiques*, Paris

Deman, Th. (1942). *Le Témoignage d'Aristote sur Socrate*, Paris

De Romilly, J. (1963). *Thucydides and Athenian Imperialism*, Engl. translation by Ph. Thody, Oxford

De Strycker, E. (1937). "Une énigme mathématique dans *l'Hippias Majeur*," *Mélanges Emile Boisacq*, vol. I, 317–26

(1941). *Antiquité classique*, 25–36

(1950). "Les Témoignages historiques sur Socrate," *Mélanges H. Grégoire. Annuaire de l'Institut de Philologie et d'Histoire Orientales et Slaves* 10: 199–230

Devereux, Daniel (1977). "Courage and Wisdom in Plato's *Laches*," *Journal Hist. of Philos.* 15: 129–42

Diels, H., and Kranz, W. (1952). *Die Fragmente der Vorsokratiker*, 6th edn., 3 vols., Berlin (abbr. to "DK")

Diès, Auguste (1956). *Platon "Parmenide": texte établi et traduit*, 3rd edn., Paris

Dijksterhuis, E. J. (1961). *The Mechanization of the World Picture*, Engl. translation by C. Dikshoorn, Oxford

Dittmar, Heinrich (1912). "Aischines von Sphettos," *Philologische Untersuchungen* 21

Dodds, E. R. (1951). *The Greeks and the Irrational*, Berkeley

(1959). *Plato's "Gorgias*," Oxford

Döring, Klaus (1988). "Der Sokratesschüler Aristipp und die Kyrenaiker," *Mainz Akad. von Wissenschaft und Literatur, Abhandlunger der Geistes und Sozialwiss. Klasse* 1

Dover, K. R. (1968). *Aristophanes, "Clouds*," Oxford

(1974). *Greek Popular Morality*, Oxford

(1978). *Greek Homosexuality*, Cambridge, Mass.

(1983). "The Portrayal of Moral Evaluation in Greek Poetry," *JHS* 103: 35–48

Dybikowski, John (1975) "Was Socrates as Rational as Professor Vlastos?" *Yale Review* 64
    (1981). "Is Aristotelian *Eudaimonia* Happiness?" *Dialogue* 20: 185–200
Edelstein, Emma (1935). *Xenophontisches und platonisches Bild des Sokrates*, Berlin
Edmunds, Lowell (1985). "Aristophanes' Socrates," *Proc. of the Boston Area Colloquium in Ancient Philosophy*, vol. 1.
Ehlers, Barbara (1966). "Eine vorplatonische Deutung des sokratischen Eros: der Dialog Aspasia des Sokratikers Aischines," *Zetemata* 41
Einarson, B., and De Lacy, P. (1967). *Plutarch's Moralia*, vol. 14, text, translation, introductions and notes, London
Erbse, Hartmut (1961). "Die Architektonik im Aufbau von Xenophon's *Memorabilien*," *Hermes* 89: 257–87
Feinberg, Joel (1970). "The Expressive Function of Punishment" in *Doing and Deserving*, Princeton
Ferejohn, Michael (1984). "Socratic Thought-Experiments and the Unity of Virtue Paradox," *Phronesis* 29: 105–22
Ferguson, John (1964). "On the date of Socrates' Conversion," *Eranos*
Fine, Gail (1984). "Separation," *Oxford Studies in Ancient Philosophy* 2: 31–87
    (1988). "Owen's Progress": review of Owen's *Collected Papers in Greek Philosophy*, ed. by M. Nussbaum, in *Philos, Review* 97: 373–99
Flashar, H. (1958). *Der Dialog "Ion" als Zeugnis platonischer Philosophie*, Berlin
Fontenrose, Joseph (1978). *The Delphic Oracle*, Berkeley
Foucault, M. (1985). *The History of Sexuality*, vol. ii: *The Use of Pleasure*, translation by R. Hurley, New York
Fowler, H. N. (1926). *Plato: Cratylus, Parmenides, Greater Hippias, Lesser Hippias*, translation with notes, London
Fränkel, Hermann (1946). "Man's 'Ephemoros' Nature according to Pindar and Others" in *Trans. Amer. Association* 77: 131–45
Frankena, W. (1963). *Ethics*, Englewood Cliffs, N.J.
Friedländer, Paul (1958). *Plato*, translation by H. Meyerhoff, vol. 1: *An Introduction*, London (2nd edn., 1969)
    (1964) vol. ii: *The Dialogues, First Period*
    (1969) vol. iii: *The Dialogues, Second and Third Period*
Fritz, K. von (1971). *Grundprobleme der Geschichte der antiken Wissenschaft*, Berlin
Gallop, David (1975). *Plato, "Phaedo,"* translated with notes, Oxford
Giannantoni, Gabriele (1983). *Socraticorum Reliquiae*, Texts (vols. 1 and ii), Notes (vol. iii), Bibliopolis
Gigon, Olof (1959). *Grundprobleme der antiken Philosophie*, Berne
Glucker, John (1978). *Antiochus and the Late Academy, Hypomnemata* 56: 1–510, Göttingen

Gomme, A. W. (1945). *A Historical Commentary on Thucydides*, vol. ɪ, Oxford

Gosling, J., and Taylor, C. C. W. (1982). *The Greeks on Pleasure*, Oxford

Gould, Thomas (1963). *Platonic Love*, London

Greenwood, L. H. G. (1909). *Aristotle's "Nicomachean Ethics," Book VI*, with essay, notes and translation, Cambridge

Groden, Suzy (1970). Translation of Plato's *Symposium* in J. A. Brentlinger, ed., *The Symposium of Plato*, Amherst, Mass.

Grote, G. (1865). *Plato and Other Companions of Socrates*, vols. ɪ–ɪɪɪ, London

Grube, George (1935). *Plato's Thought*, 1st edn., London (repr. London, 1981)

    (1974). *The Republic of Plato*, translation, Indianapolis

    (1986). *The Trial and Death of Socrates: "Euthyphro," "Apology," "Crito," Death Scene from the "Phaedo,"* translated with introduction, 2nd edn., Indianapolis

Gulley, Norman (1968). *The Philosophy of Socrates*, London

Guthrie, W. K. C. (1969). *History of Greek Philosophy*, vol. ɪɪɪ: *The Fifth-Century Enlightenment*, Cambridge

    (1975). *History of Greek Philosophy*, vol. ɪᴠ: *Plato, the Man and His Dialogues: The Earlier Period*, Cambridge

Hackforth, R. (1933). *The Composition of Plato's "Apology,"* Cambridge

    (1952). *Plato's "Phaedrus,"* translated with introduction and notes, Cambridge

    (1955). *Plato's "Phaedo,"* translated with introduction and commentary, Cambridge

Hamilton, W. (1951). *Plato, "Symposium,"* translated with introduction, Baltimore

    (1960). *Plato, "Gorgias,"* translated with introduction, Baltimore

Hardie, W. F. R. (1936). *A Study in Plato*, Oxford

Havelock, Eric (1934). "The Evidence for the Teaching of Socrates," *TAPhA* 22: 282–95 (repr. in Andreas Patzer, 1987, *Der historische Sokrates*, 249–59, Darmstadt)

    (1963). *Preface to Plato*, Cambridge, Mass.

    (1976). *Origins of Western Literacy* in Monograph Series of the Ontario Institute for Studies in Education 14, Toronto

Heath, T. L. (1921). *A History of Greek Mathematics*, vol. ɪ, Oxford

    (1926). *The Thirteen Books of Euclid's Elements*, 3 vols., 2nd edn., Oxford

Helmbold, W. (1952). *Plato's "Gorgias,"* translated with introduction, New York

Higgins, W. E. (1977). *Xenophon the Athenian*, Albany, N.Y.

Huffman, Carl (1985). "The Authenticity of Archytas Fr. 1," *CQ* 35: 344ff.

Hume, David (1957). *Enquiry Concerning the Principles of Morals*, with introduction by C. W. Hendel, New York

Irwin, T. H. (1973). "Theories of Virtue and Knowledge in Plato's Early and Middle Dialogues," dissertation, Princeton

(1974). Review of Leo Strauss, "Xenophon's Socrates," *Philos. Rev.* 83: 409–13

(1977a). *Plato's Moral Theory: The Early and Middle Dialogues*, Oxford

(1977b). "Plato's Heracleiteanism, "*Philos. Quarterly* 27: 1–13

(1979). *Plato's "Gorgias,"* translated commentary, Oxford

(1985). *Aristotle: " The Nicomachean Ethics,"* translated with explanatory notes, Indianapolis

(1986). "Socrates the Epicurean," *Univ. of Illinois Class. Studies*, 85–112

(1988) *Aristotle's First Principles*, Oxford

Jaeger, W. (1947). *The Theology of the Early Greek Philosophers*, Oxford

Joël, Karl (1921). *Geschichte der antiken Philosophie*, vol 1, Tübingen

Jowett, B. (1953). *The Dialogues of Plato translated into English with Analyses and Introductions*, 4 vols., 4th edn., Oxford

Kahn, Charles (1979). *The Art and Thought of Heraclitus*, Cambridge

(1981). "Did Plato Write Socratic Dialogues?" *CQ* 31: 305ff.

(1983). "Drama and Dialectic in Plato's *Gorgias, "Oxford Studies in Classical Philosophy* 1: 75–122

Karasmanis, Vassilis (1987). "The Hypothetical Method in Plato's Middle Dialogues," unpublished dissertation, Oxford

Kidd, I. G. (1967). "Socrates" in *Encyclopedia of Philosophy*, New York

Kierkegaard, Soeren (1965). *The Concept of Irony*, translated by Lee Capel, Bloomington, Ind.

Kleve, Knute (1981). "Scurra Atticus: The Epicurean View of Socrates" in G. R. Caratelli, ed., *Suzetesis, Studi Offerti a Marcello Gigante*, vol 1, 228–88, Naples

Klosko, George (1983). "Criteria of Fallacy and Sophistry for Use in the Analysis of Platonic Dialogues," *CQ* 33: 363–74

Kneale, William and Mary (1962). *The Development of Logic*, Oxford

Knorr, W. B. (1975). *The Evolution of the Euclidean Elements*, Dordrecht

Kraut, Richard (1979). "Two Conceptions of Happiness," *Philos. Review* 88: 167–97

(1983). "Comments on Vlastos' *The Socratic Elenchus,"* Oxford Studies in Classical Philosophy: 59–70

(1984). *Socrates and the State*, Princeton

Leavis, F. R. (1984). "Memories of Wittgenstein," in R. Rees, ed., *Recollections of Wittgenstein*, Oxford

Lefkowitz, Mary (1989a). "Impiety and Atheism," *CQ* 39

(1989b). "Comments on Vlastos' 'Socratic Piety,'" *Proc. of Boston Area Colloquium in Ancient Philosophy* 5

Lesher, James (1987). "Socrates' Disavowal of Knowledge," *Journal of the History of Philosophy* 15: 275–88

Lesky, Albin (1967). *Greek Tragedy*, translated by H. A. Frankfort, 2nd edn., London

Lindsay, A. D. (1935). *The Republic of Plato*, Everyman's Library, London

Lloyd, G. E. R. (1979). *Magic, Reason and Experience*, Cambridge
   (1983a). *Science, Folklore and Ideology*, Cambridge
   (1983b). "Plato on Mathematics and Nature, Myth and Science," *Humanities* 18: 11–30
   (1987a). "The Alleged Fallacy of Hippocrates of Chios," *Apeiron* 22: 103–28
   (1987b). *The Revolutionary of Wisdom*, Berkeley
Long, A. A. (1986). "Diogenes Laertius, Life of Arcesilaus," *Elenchos* 7: 431–49
   (1988). "Socrates in Hellenistic Philosophy," *CQ* 38: 150–71
Lowrie, Walter (1936). *Kierkegaard*, Princeton
MacDowell, Douglas M. (1963). "Arete and Generosity," *Mnemosyne* 16: 127ff.
   (1978). *The Law in Classical Athens*, Ithaca
Mackenzie, M. M. (1981). *Plato on Punishment*, Berkeley
Macleod, C. W. (1978). "Reason and Necessity," *JHS* 98: 64–78
Maier, Heinrich (1913). *Sokrates*, Tübingen
Marchant, E. C. (1971). "Xenophon" in *Oxford Classical Dictionary*, Oxford
McDowell, John (1973). *Plato, " Theaetetus,"* translation with philosophical commentary, Oxford
McPherran, Mark L. (1985). "Socratic Piety in the *Euthyphro*," *Journal of the History of Philosophy* 23: 283–309
McTighe, Kevin (1984). "Socrates on Desire for the Good and the Involuntariness of Wrongdoing," *Phronesis* 29: 193–236
Méridier, L. (1956). "Plato's *Euthydemus*" in *Platon, Œuvres complètes*, vol. v, part 1, Paris
Momigliano, Arnaldo (1971). *The Development of Greek Biography*, Cambridge, Mass.
Montuori, Mario (1981a). *Socrates, Physiology of a Myth*, translated by J. M. P. Langdale and M. Langdale in *London Studies in Classical Philology*, vol. vi, Amsterdam
   (1981b). *De Socrate Juste Damnato: The Rise of the Socratic Problem in the Eighteenth Century* in *London Studies in Classical Philology*, vol. vii, Amsterdam
Morrison, Donald (1985a). "Separation in Aristotle's *Metaphysics*," *Oxford Studies in Classical Philosophy* 3: 125–58
   (1985b). "*Choristos* in Aristotle," *Harvard Studies in Classical Philology* 39: 89ff.
   (1987). "On Professor Vlastos' Xenophon," *Ancient Philosophy* 7: 9–22
Morrow, G. R. (1962). *Plato's Epistles*, translation with critical essays and notes, revised edn, Indianapolis
   (1970). *Proclus' Commentary of the First Book of Euclid's Elements*, translation with introduction and notes, Princeton
Mourelatos, A. D. P. (1981). "Astronomy and Kinematics in Plato's

Project of Rational Explanation," *Studies in Hist. and Philos. of Science* 12: 1ff.

Muecke, D. C. (1969). *The Compass of Irony*, London

Murphy, N. R. (1951). *The Interpretation of Plato's Republic*, Oxford

Nehamas, Alexander (1985). "Meno's Paradox and Socrates as a Teacher," *Oxford Studies in Ancient Philosophy* 3: 1–30

(1986). "Socratic Intellectualism," *Proc. of Boston Area Colloquium in Ancient Philosophy* 2: 274–85

Nozick, Robert (1981). *Philosophical Explanations*, Cambridge, Mass.

Nussbaum, Martha (1976–7). "Consequences and Character in Sophocles' *Philoctetes*," *Philosophy and Literature* 3: 25–53

(1980). "Aristophanes and Socrates on Learning Practical Wisdom," *Vale Classical Studies* 26: 43–97

(1986). *The Fragility of Goodness*, Cambridge

O'Brien, M. J. (1967). *The Socratic Paradoxes and the Greek Mind*, Chapel Hill

Oldenquist, A. (1985). "An Explanation of Retribution," *Journal of Philosophy* 82: 464–78

Owen, G. E. L. (1953). "The Place of the *Timaeus* in Plato's Dialogues," *CQ* 3: 79–95

Patzer, Andreas, ed. (1987). *Der historische Sokrates*, Darmstadt

Polansky, R. B. (1985). "Professor Vlastos' Analysis of Socratic Elenchus," *Oxford Studies in Ancient Philosophy* 3: 247–60

Prichard, H. A. (1928). *Duty and Interest*, Oxford

(1949). *Moral Obligation*, Oxford

Prior, W. J. (1985). *Unity and Development in Plato's Metaphysics*, La Salle, Ill.

Ribbeck, O. (1876). "Über den Begriff des *Eiron*," *Rheinisches Museum* 31: 381ff.

Riddell, J. (1867). *The "Apology" of Plato*, with digest of Platonic idioms, Oxford

Riginos, Alice Swift (1976). *Platonica: The Anecdotes Concerning the Life and Writings of Plato*, Columbia Studies in the Classical Tradition, vol. 3, Leiden

Ritter, Constantin (1888). *Untersuchungen über Platon*, Stuttgart

(1910a). *Platon*, vol. I, Munich

(1910b). *Neue Untersuchungen über Platon*, Munich

(1923). *Platon*, vol. II, Munich

Robin, Léon (1910). "Les 'Mémorables' de Xenophon et notre con-naissance de la philosophie de Socrate," *L'Année Philosophique* 21: 1–47

(1928). *La Pensée grecque et les origines de l'esprit scientifique*, rev. edn., Paris

(1935). *Platon*, Paris

(1956). *Platon: Œuvres complètes*, translated with notes, Paris

Robinson, Richard (1941). *Plato's Earlier Dialectic*, 1st edn., Ithaca, N.Y.

(1953). *Plato's Earlier Dialectic*, 2nd edn., Oxford

Ross, W. D. (1910–32). "Aristotle's *Nicomachean Ethics*," translated in

W. D. Ross and J. A. Smith, eds., *The Works of Aristotle translated into English*, vol. IX, Oxford

(1923). *Aristotle*, London

(1924). *Aristotle's "Metaphysics,"* revised text, with introduction and commentary, vol. I, Oxford

(1933). "The Problem of Socrates," *Proc. of Classical Association* 30: 7–24 (repr. in Andreas Patzer, 1987)

(1951). *Plato's Theory of Ideas*, Oxford

Russell, Bertrand (1933). *Principles of Mathematics*, 2nd edn., Cambridge

(1945). *History of Western Philosophy*, New York

Santas, Gerasimos (1964). "The Socratic Paradox," *Philos. Rev.* 73: 147–64

(1979). *Socrates*, London

Shorey, P. (1930). *Plato, Republic*, vol. I, translated with introduction, London

(1933). *What Plato Said*, Chicago

Sidgwick, Henry (1907). *Methods of Ethics*, 7th edn., London

Solmsen, Friedrich (1983). "Plato and the Concept of the Soul *(Psyche)*: Some Historical Perspectives," *Journal of the History of Ideas* 44: 355–67

Sprague, Rosamond K. (1962). *Plato's Use of Fallacy: A Study of the "Euthydemus" and Some Other Dialogues*, London

Stanford, W. B. (1963). *Sophocles: Ajax*, London

Stenzel, J. (1927). "Sokrates (Philosoph)," article in Pauly–Wissowa, *Real Encylopädie der klassischen Altertumswissenschaft*, 811–90

(1940). *Plato's Method of Dialectic*, translated and edited by D. J. Allan, Oxford

Stephen, James FitzJames (1883). *History of the Criminal Law in England*, vols. I and II, London

Stevenson, C. L. (1944). *Ethics and Language*, New Haven

Stewart, J. A. (1892). *Notes on the "Nicomachean Ethics" of Aristotle*, 2 vols., Oxford

Stokes, Michael (1986). *Plato's Socratic Conversations: Drama and Dialectic in Three Dialogues*, Baltimore

(1987). "Socratic Ignorance in Plato's *Apology*" (unpublished)

Stone, I. F. (1988). *The Trial of Socrates*, Boston

Tarrant, Dorothy (1928). *The "Hippias Major" Attributed to Plato*, with introduction and commentary, Cambridge

Taylor, A. E. (1924). "Aeschines of Sphettus," *Philosophical Studies*, London

(1928). *A Commentary on the "Timaeus,"* Oxford

(1929). *Plato, the Man and his Work*, 3rd edn., London (4th edn., 1937)

(1956). *Socrates*, New York (first published in England in 1933)

Taylor, C. C. W. (1976). *Plato, "Protagoras,"* translated with notes, Oxford

(1982). "The End of the *Euthyphro*," *Phronesis* 27: 109–18

Theiler, W. (1925). *Zur Geschichte der teleologischen Naturbetrachtung bis auf Aristoteles*, Zurich

Thesleff, Holger (1982). *Studies in Platonic Chronology*, Commentationes Humanarum Litterarum 70, Helsinki

Thompson, E. S. (1901). *Plato's " Meno,"* text and commentary, London

Thomson, George (1938). *Aeschylus: " The Oresteia,"* vol. 1, text and translation, Cambridge

Tsouna, Voula (1988). *Les Philosophes cyrenaiques et leur théorie de la connaissance*, dissertation (unpublished), Nanterre

Van der Waerden, B. L. (1954). *Science Awakening*, translated by A. Dresden with additions by the author, Groningen

Verdenius, W. J. (1943). "L'*Ion* de Platon," *Mnemosyne* 11: 233–62

Versenyi, L. (1963). *Socratic Humanism*, New Haven

  (1982). *Holiness and Justice: An Interpretation of Plato's " Euthyphro,"* New York

Vlastos, G. (1945–6). "Ethics and Physics in Democritus," *Philos. Review* 54: 578–92 and 55: 53–64

  (1952). "Theology and Philosophy in Early Greek Thought," *Philosophical Quarterly* 2: 97–123

  (1954). "The Third Man Argument in the *Parmenides*," *Philos. Review* 63: 319–49

  (1956). *Plato's " Protagoras,"* ed. with introduction, translation by Benjamin Jowett, revised by Martin Ostwald, New York

  (1958). "The Paradox of Socrates," *Queen's Quarterly*, Winter (reprinted in Vlastos, 1971)

  (1962). "Justice and Equality" in *Social Justice*, ed. R. Brandt, New York, 31–72 (reprinted in J. Waldron, ed. [1964]. *Theories of Rights*, Oxford)

  (1965). "Anamnesis in the *Meno*," *Dialogue* 4: 143–67

  (1967). "Was Polus Refuted?," *AJP* 88: 454–60

  (1969). "Socrates on Acrasia," *Phoenix*, suppl. vol. 23: 71–88

  (1971). *The Philosophy of Socrates: A Collection of Critical Essays*, Garden City, New York

  (1974). "Socrates on Political Obedience and Disobedience," *Yale Review* 63: 517–34

  (1975). *Plato's Universe*, Oxford

  (1978a). Review of T. Irwin (1977a) in *The Times Literary Supplement*, February 24

  (1978b). Review of H. Cherniss, *Selected Papers*, ed. by L. Taran, in *AJP* 99: 937–43

  (1980). "Socrates' Contribution to the Greek Sense of Justice," *Archaiognosia* 1: 301–24

  (1981). *Platonic Studies*, 2nd edn., Princeton

  (1983a). "The Socratic Elenchus," *Oxford Studies in Ancient Philosophy* 1: 27–58

  (1983b). "The Historical Socrates and Athenian Democracy," *Political Theory* 11: 495–515

(1984a). Review of R. Kraut (1984) in *The Times Literary Supplement*, August 24

(1984b). "Happiness and Virtue in Socrates' Moral Theory," *Proceedings of the Cambridge Philological Society*, N.S. 30: 181–213; also in *Topoi* 4: 3–32

(1985). "Socrates' Disavowal of Knowledge," *Philosophical Quarterly* 35: 1–31

(1987a). "'Separation' in Plato," *Oxford Studies in Ancient Philosophy* 5: 187–96

(1987b). "Socratic Irony," *CQ* 37: 79–96

(1988a). "Elenchus and Mathematics," *AJP* 109: 362–96

(1988b). "Socrates," *Proceedings of the British Academy*, vol. 74, 89–111

(1989). Review of Brickhouse and Smith (1989) in *The Times Literary Supplement*, December 15–21

Von Arnim, Hans (1914). *Platons Jugenddialoge und die Entstehungszeit des "Phaidros,"* Leipzig

Waterfield, Robin (1987). *Plato, "Hippias Minor,"* translation with introduction in Trevor Saunders, ed., *Plato: Early Socratic Dialogues*, New York

Watling, E. F. (1953). *Sophocles: "Electra" and Other Plays*, Baltimore

Weiss, Roslyn (1981). "*Ho Agathos* as *ho Dunatos*," *CQ* 31: 287–304

(1985). "Ignorance, Involuntariness and Innocence," *Phronesis* 30: 314–22

(1987). "The Right Exchange: *Phaedo* 69A–D," *Ancient Philosophy* 7: 57–66

Wilamowitz, Ulrich von (1948). *Platon: Sein Leben und seine Werke*, 3rd edn. by Bruno Snell, Berlin

Woodhead, W. D. (1953). *Plato, Gorgias*, translated in *Socratic Dialogues*, Edinburgh

Woodruff, Paul (1982). *Plato, "Hippias Major,"* translation with commentary and essay, Indianapolis and Cambridge

(1987). "Expert Knowledge in the *Apology* and *Laches*: What a General Needs to Know," *Proc. of Boston Area Colloquium in Ancient Philosophy* 3: 79–115

Zeller, E. (1885). *Socrates and the Socratic Schools*, translated by O. J. Reichel, London

Zeyl, Donald (1980). "Socrates and Hedonism," *Phronesis* 25: 250–69

(1982). "Socratic Virtue and Happiness," *AGPh* 64: 225–38

INDEX OF PASSAGES CITED

INDEX OF NAMES IN PLATO AND
XENOPHON

INDEX OF MODERN SCHOLARS

INDEX OF GREEK WORDS